The Culture of
Sex in Ancient China

Paul Rakita Goldin

University of Hawai'i Press
Honolulu

Library of Congress Cataloging-in-Publication Data

Goldin, Paul Rakita

The culture of sex in ancient China / Paul Rakita Goldin.

p.   cm.

English and Chinese.

Includes bibliographical references and index.

ISBN 0-8248-2405-9 (cloth : alk. paper)—ISBN 0-8248-2482-2 (pbk. : alk. paper)

1. Sex—China—History—To 1500.   2. Sex and history—China.   3. Sex in literature.   4. Chinese literature—To 221 B.C.—History and criticism.   5. Chinese literature—221 B.C.–960 A.D.—History and criticism.   6. China—Civilization— To 221 B.C.   7. China—Civilization—221 B.C.–960 A.D.   I. Title.

HQ18.C6 G63   2002

306.7'0931—dc21   2001027687

University of Hawai'i Press books are printed on acid-free
paper and meet the guidelines for permanence and durability
of the Council on Library Resources.

Book design by Kenneth Miyamoto
Printed by The Maple-Vail Book Manufacturing Group

*The Culture of Sex
in Ancient China*

Contents

Acknowledgments

Portions of this book were originally read as public lectures. Chapter 2 was presented as "The View of Women in Early Confucianism" at the annual conference of the Eastern Division of the American Philosophical Association, Washington, D.C., December 29, 1998; at Stanford University, February 8, 1999; and at the University of California, Los Angeles, February 9, 1999. Chapter 3 was presented as "Sex, Politics, and Ritualization in the Early Chinese Empire" at the University of Pennsylvania, September 28, 1999. I would like to thank the audiences at these lectures for critical discussions that aided me in making final revisions for the book. An abbreviated version of chapter 1 appeared as "Imagery of Copulation in Early Chinese Poetry," in *Chinese Literature: Essays, Articles, Reviews* 21 (1999), 35–66; and an earlier version of chapter 2 appeared as "The View of Women in Early Confucianism," in *The Sage and the Second Sex: Confucianism, Ethics, and Gender,* ed. Chenyang Li (Chicago: Open Court, 2000), 133–161.

The idea for this study came to me in the course of several sustained conversations with my colleague, Matthew H. Sommer, a specialist on sex law in late imperial China. I have also benefited from discussions with other scholars: Constance Cook, Scott Cook, Bernard Faure, Amy Gadsden, Eric Henry, Eric Hutton, Jiang Xinyan, Li Chenyang, Tina Lu, Victor H. Mair, Gilbert L. Mattos, Andrew Meyer, William H. Nienhauser, Jr., David W. Pankenier, Moss Roberts, Haun Saussy, David Schaberg, Nancy S. Steinhardt, Bryan W. Van Norden, Robin Wang. The Center for East Asian Studies of the University of

Pennsylvania provided a grant to prepare an undergraduate course entitled "Sex and Society in Ancient China," for which I gathered much of the material incorporated in this book. Many thanks also to Patricia Crosby and the staff at the University of Hawai'i Press, as well as Rosemary Wetherold and the G&S editors, for the care with which they have handled the production of this book.

君子之道二，吾未能一焉。所求乎父母以事子，未能也。所求乎
賢妻以先施之，未能也。

Introduction
The Aims of This Book

This is a study of intellectual conceptions of sex and sexuality in China from roughly 500 B.C. to A.D. 400. Ancient Chinese writers discussed sex openly and seriously as one of the most important topics of human speculation. This sophisticated and long-standing tradition has been almost entirely neglected by historians for a number of reasons that will be considered presently. The consequence is that studies of writings dealing with sex are sorely needed to redress our ignorance of a subject that was central to the ancient Chinese tradition. The sources for this book are primarily philosophical, literary, and religious texts. This work is not intended as a history of sexuality or sexual behavior (and the material on which it is based sheds very little light on people's sexual practices). Historians have begun to question whether any such history can—or should—be written;[1] and in any case, for ancient China, the extant sources are not sufficiently informative for that purpose. The sources do reveal, however, that Chinese authors wrote earnestly about sexual activity and expected their readers to consider the subject thoughtfully. Sexual intercourse constituted a fundamental source of imagery and terminology that informed the classical Chinese conception of social and political relationships.

The book is divided into three chapters and an epilogue that progress in roughly chronological order. Chapter 1 surveys the major preimperial sources that employ the image of copulation as a metaphor for various human relations, such as those between a worshipper and his or her deity, or between a ruler and his subjects.

1

These sources include some of the most revered and influential texts in the Chinese tradition, such as the *Shih-ching* 詩經 (*Canon of Odes*), the *Tso-chuan* 左傳 (an orthodox commentary to the *Springs and Autumns*), and the *Ch'u-tz'u* 楚辭 (*Lyrics of Ch'u*). The study focuses on such central works in order to highlight the significance and utility of the metaphor of copulation in the ancient Chinese literary world. I intend to show, first, that there is far more sexual symbolism in ancient Chinese literature than is often recognized and, second, that there are crucial dimensions of the classical texts that can be appreciated only with a greater sensitivity to both the presence and the literary functions of these images. It is especially important for readers to be aware of these issues because some of the most powerful uses of sexual imagery lie at the very core of the literary tradition and profoundly influenced succeeding generations.

The next chapter focuses on the Confucian view of women. What mental capacities did early Confucians recognize in women? This is a critical question because Confucians viewed the mind (and its corresponding moral responsibilities) as the fundamental distinction between humans and animals. The early Confucian tradition conceived of women as moral equals of men—despite the charges of sexism and misogyny that have been voiced in modern times. Views of women from other philosophical camps are also considered. According to one popular paradigm, females are soft and pregnable whereas males are hard and impregnable, and the two sexes must be assigned duties commensurate with this basic difference. *Methods of War* 兵法, by Sun Pin 孫臏 (fl. 354–341 B.C.), for example, divides all fortresses into "male" and "female," depending on how easily they can be penetrated by an attacker.[2] Such texts as the *Lao-tzu* 老子 (*Tao-te ching* 道德經) expand on this concept by elevating the "female" and her welcoming softness. The "female" conquers by submitting, for, like water, she is formless and can adapt to any situation, whereas the rigid "male" cannot mold himself to the shape of the Way. However, it should be noted that the *Lao-tzu* (like other texts that made use of these categories) was referring not to men and women but to ideal "male" and "female" aspects present in all human beings.

The focus of the third chapter is the new imperial ideology of the Ch'in and Han dynasties. In accordance with the conceptions reflected in the metaphors of copulation described in chapter 1, sexuality was now conceived as the most telling indication of one's political intentions. Consequently, unregulated or illicit sexual activity was associated with, or construed as symptomatic of, unregulated or illicit political activity. The four centuries of the Han dynasty witnessed an increasing emphasis on the regulation of sexual relations and the concomitant ritualization of relations between male and female. Chinese scholars have long pointed out that many of the famed liaisons of preimperial times would have violated the rituals that were set down in the Han. (The original point of such observations was to show that these rituals, which subsequent generations took to be documents from highest antiquity, were really imposed products of a later age.) This tendency shows the imperial ideology at work, gradually tightening the reins on permissible sexual activity in order to contain lawlessness in political life.

Finally, the epilogue surveys the aristocratic rejection of this ideology after the fall of the Han, at a time when real political power came to lie in the hands of wealthy hereditary families, who continually resisted the claims of sovereignty made by the impotent emperors of a succession of short-lived dynasties.

An ancillary intention of this study is to provide for theorists and comparativists an account of the ancient Chinese case. One of the most basic ideas in the history of sexuality is constructionism, which holds that our own notions of sexuality and identity are a function of our culture and society—our discourse, as it is sometimes called.[3] The point is often made by invoking what we call sexual orientation; a sexual human being is typically considered today to be heterosexual, homosexual, or bisexual. In ancient Greece, however, such distinctions are famously absent, as historians have demonstrated repeatedly. Simply put, the only relevant distinction was between the penetrator and the penetrated.[4] So the consequence of constructionism must be that we cannot understand sexuality apart from its cultural environment, and we would gain far more insight into our own sexualities if we compared as many different sexual discourses as possible. However, the fact remains that the modern case has been compared almost exclusively with that of ancient Greece. So far, most recent work in the sexuality of cultures other than that of ancient Greece has taken the form of discrete lecture-length articles bound together in collaborative volumes, and not in synthetic, book-length histories.

The history of "Chinese studies" as a field helps to explain why the subject matter of this book, crucial though it may be, has been ignored for so long. The first Western scholars of China tended to fall into one of two categories: missionaries or Orientalists. The missionary tradition extends all the way back to Jesuits like Matteo Ricci (1552–1610), whose avowed intention was to bring the Christian faith to all parts of the globe, but who soon discovered that they would be vastly more persuasive if they could claim to know something about the cultures in which they established their missions.[5] Other missionaries—such as James Legge (1815–1897)[6] and Séraphin Couvreur (1835–1919)—contributed greatly to the understanding of China in the West, but they were primarily interested in those aspects of Chinese civilization that would help them become more effective proselytizers: Confucianism and the Chinese classics; religion; literature; history; and so forth. Understandably, they were not much interested in books about sex. Their legacy has silently influenced posterity in this respect as in so many others. Because much of the later work was designed to further the scholarship of missionaries like Legge, it was perhaps inevitable that sex would be overlooked as a legitimate subject of inquiry.

The other great branch of early Sinologues was the Orientalists, or scholars who perceived "the Orient" essentially as a monolithic, coherent entity. Their work was often intended to show the ubiquitous similarity of various cultural forms, whether in India, China, Mesopotamia, or Persia. Perhaps the greatest example of the Orientalist approach was that of Arthur Waley (1889–1966), whose English translation of the canonical *Odes* is accompanied by numerous footnotes pointing out that such-and-such a practice is found today among Koreans, Annamese, Jews, and so on.[7] For the Orientalist, these comparisons are compelling because they are thought to demonstrate the basic unity of cultures throughout the Orient.[8] For our purposes, the general problem with Orientalism is that it is primarily concerned with China not as China but only as part of a putative "Orient." Orientalists were never interested in studying the Chinese discourse as a unique case in the history of world civilizations; to them, it merely represented an "Oriental" case that could be fruitfully compared to that of other "Oriental" cultures. (The specter of imperialism is inescapable here. "The Orient" never made any sense as a geographical unit except as one that was available to Europe in

the eighteenth, nineteenth, and early twentieth centuries for exploitation and colonization.)[9] Moreover, the Orientalists were professional
academics and were encumbered by the same prudishness that has
infected the entire academy until only recently.[10] Like the missionaries, but for different reasons, they were not inclined to publish
scholarly works dealing with sexuality as an intellectual problem.

Times have changed, and it is much more feasible now to engage
in the kind of study proposed here. There have, in fact, been many
recent studies of sex in modern and early modern China in the context of various disciplines, such as law, literature, and history.[11] But
there still are almost no works that consider the ancient period.
The most notable exception is R. H. van Gulik's *Sexual Life in Ancient
China*,[12] first published in 1961 and still the only secondary source
available for much of its subject matter. However, van Gulik's work
needs to be superseded in many respects. His decision to render all
potentially indelicate passages into Latin is outmoded and indicative
of his ambivalent attitude toward his own subject of inquiry. In addition, his citation errors are too frequent, even though his erudition
is equally admired by his supporters and his critics. But the main problem is more serious: the book relies on an obsolete methodology.

Van Gulik has been both praised[13] and criticized[14] for his contention that ancient Chinese "sexual habits were healthy and normal"
and that "pathologia sexualis" was not largely represented. As van
Gulik himself declares, one of the main purposes of his *Sexual Life in
Ancient China* was to refute the idea that ancient Chinese sex practices were abnormal or depraved.[15] Herein he is hamstrung by his
Victorianism. It is clear from his book that he is thinking mostly of
sadism and masochism, categories that he evidently inherits directly
from the great Austrian psychologist Richard von Krafft-Ebing (1840–
1902).[16] The whole notion of sexual perversion (or pathologia sexualis) is a well-documented product of nineteenth-century Europe,
when psychiatrists as professionals arrogated to themselves the task
of defining "healthy" and "perverted" sexual impulses.[17] Reading
perversion or the lack or perversion back into the ancient Chinese
arena is analogous to projecting our conceptions of homosexuality
and heterosexuality back onto ancient Greece: it is fundamentally
anachronistic. So the limitations of van Gulik's work on China, and
in particular his concern with the idea of perversion, are the result
of his failure to set aside the paradigms of his own time and place.

Van Gulik is also famous for his admiring comments on the ancient Chinese and their enlightened concern for the sexual pleasure of women.[18] He has thereby misled untold numbers of casual readers. The noted contemporary critic and psychoanalyst Julia Kristeva,[19] for example, engaged in a lengthy meditation on the Chinese conception of female *jouissance* (she was apparently working from a French translation of van Gulik's book, in which the term *"jouissance"* must have been used to denote orgasm) in terms that sound so Freudian and mystical as to obscure any remaining affinity with the original Chinese context. The reality is much less pretty and has to do with early Chinese medical theories.

All human beings were thought to be made up of *ch'i* 氣, literally "vapor," or undifferentiated matter, which appears in the world in two complementary aspects, *yin* 陰 and *yang* 陽. Furthermore, human beings were thought to contain *ching* 精, or "refined essence," which is *ch'i* in its most concentrated form and which is emitted from the body at the moment of orgasm. For men, the *ching* was conceived as the semen, or *ch'i* in its ultimate *yang* state; for women, the *ching* was conceived as vaginal secretions, or *ch'i* in its ultimate *yin* state. Furthermore, it was believed that all human beings needed a healthy balance of *yin-ch'i* and *yang-ch'i*, and one of the best ways to obtain the aspect of *ch'i* that one lacked naturally was by having sexual intercourse with a member of the opposite sex and absorbing his or her *ching* in the process. It was especially beneficial if one could stop up one's own *ching*, so as not to lose any of one's own precious essence, while taking in that of one's partner. This is the source of the basic idea that a man should refrain from ejaculating excessively and should either injaculate or repress his ejaculation entirely.[20] But for the sex act to have any medical value, the male had to make sure that the female reached orgasm and emitted her *yin-ch'i*. This is why so many sex manuals—which were written exclusively for men—go to great lengths to counsel the reader on the art of pleasing women sexually. In theory, of course, a woman could do the same thing to a man by repressing her own orgasm and encouraging his, and a number of later texts refer to that possibility explicitly.[21] But the concern for female sexual pleasure that van Gulik observed ultimately derives from those works, intended for male audiences, which explain how to tap the life essence of unsuspecting females. Certain other manuals stress the importance of pleasing a woman so as to keep her by one's side as a willing victim in a state of constant sexual readiness.[22]

The motivation was hardly an egalitarian concern for the woman's pleasure.[23]

This model may help to explain, incidentally, why there are so few notices in ancient Chinese literature of homoeroticism, whether between men or women.[24] In the calculus of *ch'i* exchange, sexual intercourse between members of the same sex was absolutely irrelevant, because the losses and gains of each party effectively canceled each other out. There are some references to sexual encounters between women in the same harem[25] (one of many indications that the extant texts belong to the world of the social elite), but these women, of course, are never portrayed as homosexual or even bisexual. Women were simply containers of *yin-ch'i*, and it was immaterial how they exchanged their *ch'i* with each other, as long as they remained healthy sources of energy for the males who kept them. As we shall see, there were other, less reifying images of women as well; nevertheless, it was inconceivable for anyone to consider sexual relations between women as an issue with social ramifications or as a sign that different women might have different sexual orientations.

We must not forget that these issues were not commonly recognized by historians until well after van Gulik's day. It would hardly have been possible for van Gulik to take into account historiographical problems that we ourselves have only recently come to appreciate. However, now that the historical study of human sexuality has reached a requisite level of sophistication, it is possible to begin the daunting task of reexamining Chinese conceptions of sexual relations.

1

Imagery of Copulation

Some of the oldest and most problematic love poems in the Chinese tradition are those contained in the anthology called *Canon of Odes* (*Shih-ching* 詩經), one of the most venerable collections in the Confucian corpus. It has been observed for centuries that this text contains many poems that describe in straightforward language the pleasures and emotions associated with carnal love. The following is a typical example.

維鵜在梁	There is a pelican on the bridge.
不濡其咮	It does not wet its beak.
彼其之子	That boy there
不遂其媾	does not consummate his coition.
薈兮蔚兮	Oh, dense! Oh, lush!
南山朝隮	The morning rainbow on South Mountain.
婉兮孌兮	Oh, pretty! Oh, lovely!
季女斯飢	This young girl is starving.[1]

(*Mao* 151: "Hou-jen" 候人)[2]

The poetic significance of the pelican is derived from the fact that it eats fish—for the capture of fish is an image that frequently accompanies union between male and female in the *Odes*.[3] In this poem, however, the pelican does not wet its beak; that is to say, it does not enter the water to catch fish. The boy, true to the image, does not consummate his courtship of the young girl, leaving her to "starve."

8

It is evident also that the girl's hunger is intended figuratively: naturally, we understand that she is starving for the boy's love, not literally for food. As one would expect, hunger is a frequent image for sexual appetite.[4] Thus when we encounter in one poem a discussion of the various species of fish available for one to eat, we should be prepared to take the image as a metaphor for copulation—that is, of joining one human being with another.

豈其食魚	When you eat a fish,
必河之魴	must it be a bream from the river?
豈其取妻	When you take a wife,
必齊之姜	must she be a Chiang of Ch'i?

豈其食魚	When you eat a fish,
必河之鯉	must it be a carp from the river?
豈其取妻	When you take a wife,
必宋之子	must she be a Tzu of Sung?

(*Mao* 138: "Heng-men" 衡門)

Traditional commentators point out that Chiang and Tzu are the surnames of the rulers of Ch'i and Sung, respectively.[5] The point here seems to be that there are other fish in the river. Just as one must be willing to eat fishes other than bream and carp—the finest that one can catch—one ought not limit one's choice of wife solely to women of important ducal houses.

"Crafty youths" frequently make ardent girls suffer.

彼狡童兮	Oh, that crafty youth!
不與我言兮	Oh, he does not talk to me.
維子之故	It is your fault.
使我不能餐兮	Oh, you make me unable to eat.

彼狡童兮	Oh, that crafty youth!
不與我食兮	Oh, he does not eat with me.
維子之故	It is your fault.
使我不能息兮	Oh, you make me unable to rest.

(*Mao* 86: "Chiao-t'ung" 狡童)

This poem expands on the image of eating on two levels. The Chinese text distinguishes between two types of eating: *ts'an* 餐 in the first stanza, *shih* 食 in the second. The line "Oh, you make me unable to eat" conveys a double message. On the one hand, it can easily be read, in light of the previous poems, as the girl's complaint that the boy is depriving her of sexual gratification. But on a different level, her heartache really does make it impossible for her to eat (*ts'an*). Food would be a poor substitute for—and at the same time a reminder of—the pleasure that she is now missing.

"The Crafty Youth" is also interesting for its traditional interpretation, which invokes a political significance to the poem that a casual reader could hardly have surmised. The oldest critical utterance is simply that "'The Crafty Youth' criticizes indifference" 狡童 刺忽也.[6] The orthodox Mao commentary, however, takes this statement as a reference to Lord Chao of Cheng 鄭昭公 (r. 700 B.C.), whose personal name was Hu 忽 (Indifferent). This lord was raised to the throne of Cheng by a minister named Chung of Chai 祭仲—only to be forced to flee later that same year when the state of Sung 宋 captured Chung and compelled him to crown someone else.[7] How could even an ancient reader possibly be expected to recognize such an allusion? Moreover, whose "indifference" is being criticized? One might have assumed that the poem intends to chastise the crafty youth for being indifferent to the poor girl's plight. However, the analogy suggested by the Mao commentary implies that Lord Chao is represented by the jilted girl and consequently that he brought on his own fate by allowing a mere minister to anoint feudal lords. But saying that Lord Chao is culpable for his own indifference is analogous to blaming the girl for her own sorrow—and there is no indication in the poem that she is at fault. These problems are not tractable. The orthodox commentaries do not work out all the ramifications of this peculiar reading, which is, in any case, presented too sketchily to be fully understandable.[8]

Such complicated and unapparent interpretations have led several twentieth-century critics to ridicule the entire commentarial tradition to the *Odes*. Herbert A. Giles, for example, complains,

> Early commentators, incapable of seeing the simple natural beauties of the poems, which have furnished endless household words and a large stock of phraseology to the language of the present day, ... set to work to read into country-side ditties deep moral and political significations. Every single one of the immortal Three Hundred has thus been forced to yield some hidden meaning and point an appropriate moral.[9]

This process has been labeled by another modern reader as "exegetical debris," fit only to be cleared away.[10]

Why did generations upon generations of commentators insist that the *Odes*, however bawdy, contained important symbolic and moral meaning? Specifically, why do they commonly explain the images of manifestly sexual unions in such poems as "The Crafty Youth" as metaphors for the relation between a ruler and one or more of his subjects? For many, it may have been impossible to ignore the weighty opinion of Confucius (551–479 B.C.).

子曰：詩三百，一言以蔽之，曰：思無邪。[11]

The Master said: The *Odes* are three hundred, but they are appraised[12] in one phrase: "There is no improper thinking."[13]

As is well known, Confucius considered the *Odes* to be one of the most important texts for students to master because of the moral lessons to be gained from it.[14] Consequently, traditional commentators did not feel that one had understood a poem in the *Odes* until one could elucidate its moral significance—and for poems like "The Crafty Youth," fulfilling that mission requires a liberal dose of creative reading. But Confucius' statement contains a dimension that has not been fully appreciated by readers ancient and modern alike. The phrase that Confucius takes here to mean "There is no improper thinking" appears in one of the *Odes*, and commentators since Hsiang An-shih 項安世 (d. 1208) have argued that the Master has misconstrued the original text.

思無邪   Ah, without mishap
思馬斯徂   may these horses replicate.[15]

(*Mao* 297, "Chiung" 駉)

Confucius seems to have misunderstood—deliberately or not—the function of the character *ssu* 思. In the poem, *ssu* is merely an interjection, or at best an initial particle intended to evoke a certain mood. But Confucius takes it in its full verbal sense, "to think."[16] Commentators dissatisfied with Confucius and his didactic approach to literature hasten to point out that, in distorting the original, he set the tone for centuries of readers who would not reject any reading, however tortured, as long as it illustrated an appropriate moral.

The extended senses of the verb *ssu* include pining for a lover and yearning for carnal pleasures. One of the most famous examples comes from the epithalamium that opens the entire collection, namely "The *Kuan*-ing Ospreys" (*kuan* is the sound of ospreys' characteristic call).

關關雎鳩	*"Kuan, kuan"* [cry] the ospreys
在河之洲	on the isle in the river.
窈窕淑女	The reclusive, modest girl
君子好逑	is a good mate for the noble man.
參差荇菜	Long and short is the duckweed
左右流之	To the left and to the right we look for it.
窈窕淑女	The reclusive, modest girl—
寤寐求之	waking and sleeping he seeks her.
求之不得	He seeks her and does not obtain her.
寤寐思服	Waking and sleeping he pines and yearns for her.
悠哉悠哉	Oh, anxious! Oh, anxious!
輾轉反側	He tosses and twists and turns onto his side.
參差荇菜	Long and short is the duckweed.
左右采之	To the left and to the right we gather it.
窈窕淑女	The reclusive, modest girl—
琴瑟友之	among lutes and citherns, he shows her his friendship.
參差荇菜	Long and short is the duckweed.
左右芼之	To the left and to the right we pick it.
窈窕淑女	The reclusive, modest girl—
鐘鼓樂之	as a bell to a drum, he delights in her.

(*Mao* 1: "Kuan-chü" 關雎)

The distraught lover is certainly thinking, but there is an unmistakably lustful element in his thoughts. Some commentators, such as Ma Jui-ch'en 馬瑞辰 (1782–1853),[17] even take the phrase *wu-mei* 寤寐 (here "waking and sleeping") to mean "dreaming and sleeping"; that is to say, he fantasizes about the fine girl in his bed at night. And how can we forget what the horses are doing in the poem that Confucius alludes to: "Ah, without mishap / may these horses replicate." The point of the phrase is to express the desire that the fine horses procreate successfully.

Confucius certainly must have been aware of the poem that he was quoting, and it is clear that he was familiar with "The *Kuan*-ing Ospreys" as well.

子曰：關雎樂而不淫，哀而不傷。[18]

The Master said: In "The *Kuan*-ing Ospreys," there is joy without licentiousness, grief without injury.[19]

Suppose we assume that Confucius knew what he was doing. He knew that "There is no improper thinking" originally came from a poem about horses copulating; and he knew that in construing the character *ssu* as a verb, he was inviting the reader to think of the aroused lover from "The *Kuan*-ing Ospreys." Confucius' point is that the symbolism of the *Odes* embodies meaning beyond its literal significance. In making this argument, Confucius consciously misreads the line, for he intends to show that this more elevated level of discourse is attainable only by breaking out of a literal frame of mind. One *must* "misread" the *Odes*.[20]

This exegetical spirit was congenial to classical readers. They were well aware, for example, that the metaphor of copulation was often employed in liturgies sung by priests and priestesses in rituals intended to attract ancestral spirits. One poem in the collection is written in such a style.

呦呦鹿鳴	"*Yu, yu*," the deer cries.
食野之苹	It eats the artemisia in the wild.
我有嘉賓	I have a lucky guest.[21]
鼓瑟吹笙	Sound the cithern; blow the pipes.
吹笙鼓簧	Blow the pipes; sound the reeds.
承筐是將	This receiving basket—take it.
人之好我	The man who likes me
示我周行	will show me the practices of Chou.

(*Mao* 161: "Lu-ming" 鹿鳴)

The deer grazing on the artemisia is what traditional literary criticism refers to as an "arousal" (*hsing* 興), a natural image arousing the emotions and introducing the theme that is to follow.[22] As we have seen, the image of eating portends sexual activity in these poems, and sure enough, within four lines, the speaker makes her desires clear. The "receiving basket" is a well-attested euphemism for the female reproductive organs.[23] She is entreating the "lucky guest" to show her how they do it in Chou.

The lucky guest, moreover, is probably preternatural. To be sure, the poem is comprehensible as an unexceptional celebration of love between man and woman. But classical readers would have recognized instantly that the word for "guest" (*pin* 賓) is also the name of an important rite wherein a ruler or ritual celebrant "hosts" a god

or spirit, offering him food. In this sense, *pin* means "hosting."
The word recurs constantly with this meaning both in oracle-bone
inscriptions and in later texts.[24] In "The Deer Cries," the woman
hosts her guest not only by providing food and music, like any good
hostess, but also by presenting her "receiving basket," where the
spirit might descend and sojourn.[25]

Hierogamous unions like those implied in "The Deer Cries" are
described in greater detail in the so-called *Lyrics of Ch'u* (*Ch'u-tz'u*
楚辭), a later collection named after the great warlike state that
dominated the south of the ancient Chinese world.[26] One poem
is dedicated to "The Eastern August Magnificent One" 東皇太一, a
sidereal deity.[27]

吉日兮辰良	Auspicious is the day, the hour good.[28]
穆將愉兮上皇	Respectfully we will please the Supreme August One.
撫長劍兮玉珥	Fondle the long sword, the jade hilt-ring.
璆鏘鳴兮琳瑯	The girdle gems chime and call out, *lin-lang*.
瑤席兮玉瑱	The *yao*-gem mats are laden with jade.
盍將把兮瓊芳	Why not take and hold the fragrance of the *ch'iung*-branch?
蕙肴蒸兮蘭藉	The melilotus and meat are presented on an orchid mat.
奠桂酒兮椒漿	We offer cassia wine and pepper spirits.
揚枹兮拊鼓	Raise the drumstick and beat the drum.
疏緩節兮安歌	In broad and easy measures, a peaceful song.
陳竽瑟兮浩倡	They arrange in order the reed-organs and citherns, the ocean of musicians.
靈偃蹇兮姣服	The enchantress dances, with gorgeous robes.
芳菲菲兮滿堂	The fragrance wafts in the air and fills the hall.
五音紛兮繁會	The Five Tones are mixed; luxuriously they combine.
君欣欣兮樂康	The lord is rejoicing, happy and content.[29]

This invocation[30] employs many of the same images as "The Deer
Cries." After arousing the divinity with organs and citherns, the
priestess then offers her body. *Ling* 靈, "the enchantress," is a common term for a shamaness who pleases a spirit by copulating with
him.[31] Moreover, *chiao-fu* 姣服, the phrase that commentators generally take to mean "gorgeous robes," can readily mean, "lewdly she
longs for it." *Fu*, we remember, appears in "The *Kuan*-ing Ospreys"
as one of the verbs describing the lover's nocturnal agitation. The

next two lines continue the image. *Fang* 芳, "the fragrance," as we shall see, is a recurring epithet of a lord or god, and *fan-hui* 繁會, "luxuriously they combine," can refer either to the Five Tones of the same line—or to the enchantress and her spirit-lover in the middle of the hall.

Another hierogamous union appears in an ancient myth.

禹治鴻水，通轘宛山，化為熊，謂塗山氏曰：欲餉，聞鼓聲乃來。
禹跳石，誤中鼓。塗山氏往，見禹方作熊，慚而去，至嵩高山下化為
石，方生啟。[32]

When Yü set the floodwaters in order, opening a passage to Mount Huan-yüan, he turned into a bear. He said to a woman of T'u-shan, "When I desire to feed, you will hear the sound of my drum and come." Yü tripped on a stone, and mistakenly hit the drum. The woman of T'u-shan approached; when she saw that Yü had just "done the bear," she was embarrassed and left. She arrived at Mount Sung-kao and turned into a stone. Then she gave birth to Ch'i.

Yü is the great culture-hero who tamed the floods and designed the rivers for the water to flow in. The T'u-shan woman is usually taken to be his wife, but she might also have been a priestess or sha-maness who worshipped him in the manner of the "enchantress." This aspect of the myth is made clear when Yü announces that he will soon desire to "feed" 餉.[33] His strange act of turning into bear lends this passage most of its significance; it is usually adduced by scholars as evidence of shamanic practices in ancient China. After all, the animal-dance, which is intended to harness the superhuman powers of animals such as bears, is a notable feature of shamanism. It is in the form of a bear, moreover, that Yü impregnates his mate. She is embarrassed 慚 and soon gives birth to their son, Ch'i.

The myth of Yü's bear-dance and the invocation to "The Eastern August Magnificent One" are important in that they illustrate unambiguously how the language of sex could be employed in a sustained metaphor only a few centuries after the compilation of the *Canon of Odes*. In other words, if we are to accept the testimony of these sources, then we must recognize that the commentators to the *Odes* were not entirely unjustified in reading metaphorically the images of copulation present in poems like "The Deer Cries" and "The Crafty Youth." A reader attuned to the significance of the feast for the "lucky guest" can discern many more instances of hierogamy in the *Odes* even where traditional commentators do not.

彤弓弨兮	Oh, the red-lacquered bows are unbent.
受言藏之	We receive and store them.
我有嘉賓	I have a lucky guest.
中心貺之	The core of my heart I bestow on him.
鐘鼓既設	The bells and drums are already set up.
一朝饗之	All morning I feast him.

彤弓弨兮	Oh, the red-lacquered bows are unbent.
受言載之	We receive and carry them.
我有嘉賓	I have a lucky guest.
中心喜之	The core of my heart delights in him.
鐘鼓既設	The bells and drums are already set up.
一朝右之	All morning I honor him.

彤弓弨兮	Oh, the red-lacquered bows are unbent.
受言櫜之	We receive and set them in their cases.
我有嘉賓	I have a lucky guest.
中心好之	The core of my heart loves him.
鐘鼓既設	The bells and drums are already set up.
一朝醻之	All morning I toast him.

(*Mao* 175: "T'ung-kung" 彤弓)[34]

Other poems make it even clearer that the "lucky guest" is a deceased ancestor.[35] Several pieces describe, for example, how the "impersonator" (*shih* 尸; literally "corpse") becomes possessed by the spirits during a ceremony intended to appease them.[36] One such hymn adds,

執爨踖踖	They grasp the furnace with grave steps.
為俎孔碩	They prepare the trays, very large:
或燔或炙	some have roast meat, some have broiled.
君婦莫莫	The wives of the lords are reverent.
為豆孔庶	They prepare the dishes, very many,
為賓為客	for the guest, for the visitor.

At the end of the ceremony, the "impersonator" rises and the spirits, satiated, depart.

禮儀既備	The ritual ceremony is already completed;
鐘鼓既戒	The bells and drums have already given their warning.
孝孫徂位	The filial grandsons proceed to their station.
工祝致告	The officiating priest[37] brings down the announcement:
神具醉止	"The spirits have all drunk and ceased."

皇尸載起	The august impersonator rises.
鼓鐘送尸	The drums and bells send the impersonator off.
神保聿歸	The spirit-guardians[38] suddenly go back.

(*Mao* 209: "Ch'u-tz'u" 楚茨)

And similarly,

疆場翼翼	The boundaries and fields are uniform.
黎稷彧彧	The mass of millet is abundant.
曾孫之穡	The harvest of the great-grandson
以為酒食	is used to make wine and food.
畀我尸賓	Confer on me, impersonated guest,
壽考萬年	a long life of myriad years.

(*Mao* 210: "Hsin Nan-shan" 信南山)

The speaker here is addressing an ancestral spirit—perhaps, if we take the "great-grandson" literally, he is addressing his deceased great-grandfather—who is being "impersonated" by a medium. In exchange for wine and food, the supplicant hopes to be granted long life.

These poems force us to reconsider the entire collection. The sexual imagery in "The *Kuan*-ing Ospreys," for example, can now easily be seen as a metaphor for the yearning of a worshipper for his goddess. For we remember that the bells and drums, which are virtually ubiquitous in the invocational literature, appear in the final stanza of that poem as well.

參差荇采	Long and short is the duckweed.
左右芼之	To the left and the right we pick it.
窈窕淑女	The reclusive, modest girl—
鐘鼓樂之	as a bell to a drum, he delights in her.

(*Mao* 1)

In this light, it makes sense that the girl is "reclusive" 窈窕; the ardent male is separated from his goddess, who remains aloof.[39] With bell and drum, the forlorn supplicant, like the "enchantress" of the *Lyrics of Ch'u*, hopes to entice his beloved to mate with him on earth. The bell and drum are so frequently coupled in the literature that their function here may be to suggest metaphorically the harmonious union of the girl and her admirer: "As a bell to a drum, he delights in her."

However, while commentators regularly take the lover's yearning here as a metaphor for something less licentious, I do not know
of any that read "The *Kuan*-ing Ospreys" as the invocation of a goddess. In typical fashion, the traditional interpretations attribute some
political or historic significance to the poem. Not all commentators
agree on the specifics, but most read the love song allegorically, as an
indication of a ruler's relations with his wives and hence as a telling
indicator of the prevailing mores.[40]

There are several poems in the collection that elucidate this symbolic dimension to the metaphor of copulation. Many of the same
accoutrements of the hierogamic union between priestess and god-
head appear also in poems where the figure of the divinity is clearly
replaced by that of a ruler.

山有樞	On the mountain there are thorn-elms.
隰有榆	In the marshes there are elms.
子有衣裳	You have a robe and skirt.
弗曳弗婁	You do not drag them, do not wear them.
子有車馬	You have carriage and horse.
弗馳弗驅	You do not gallop them, do not spur them.
宛其死矣	It is as though you are dead!
他人是愉	Another will enjoy them.

山有栲	On the mountain there are *k'ao*-trees.
隰有杻	In the marshes there are *niu*-trees.
子有廷內	You have courts and halls.
弗洒弗埽	You do not sprinkle them, do not sweep them.
子有鐘鼓	You have bells and drums.
弗鼓弗考	You do not strike them, do not beat them.
宛其死矣	It is as though you are dead!
他人是保	Another will take care of them.

山有漆	On the mountain there are lacquer trees.
隰有栗	In the marshes there are chestnut trees.
子有酒食	You have wine and food.
何不日鼓瑟	Why do you not play your cithern daily?
且以喜樂	You should be happy and pleased.
且以永日	You should make your days endless.
宛其死矣	It is as though you are dead!
他人入室	Another will enter your chamber.

(*Mao* 115: "Shan yu ou" 山有樞)

This ruler or lordling is courted with all the trappings that the priestess uses to seduce the god: wine and food, citherns, bells and drums. (The sexual connotations of the carriage and horse, furthermore, will become evident later.) Similarly, in the phrase "happy and pleased" 喜樂 we see two familiar terms used to describe the joy of mating. But if all the laden imagery were not enough, the final line makes the sexual dimension explicit: "Another will enter your chamber," that is, make you a cuckold. If you do not enjoy the favors that are bestowed upon you, someone else will.

The oldest extant interpretation of this poem focuses on its political ramifications. "'On the Mountain There Are Thorn-Elms' criticizes Lord Chao of Chin [r. 744–738 B.C.]" 山有樞刺晉昭公.[41] Supposedly, that lord had all the materials of good government at his disposal, but because he did not "cultivate the Way" 脩道, he ended in ruin. In his failure to sprinkle and sweep his courtyards, we are given to understand that he neglected to keep his state in order. Whether or not we accept the specific allusion to Lord Chao of Chin, we see that in the case of this poem, despite the derision of scholars like Giles, an interpretation along political lines fits well. The indolent addressee of the poem displays traits that are readily associated with a king or ruler.

One of the most famous poems in the collection addresses the themes of copulation and rulership in a sophisticated idiom that engages the reader's critical acumen.

交交黃鳥	Back and forth [fly] the yellow birds.[42]
止于棘	They settle on the jujube tree (*krək).[43]
誰從穆公	Who follows Lord Mu?
子車奄息	Tzu-chü Yen-hsi (*sək).
維此奄息	This Yen-hsi
百夫之特	is the finest in a hundred.
臨其穴	He approaches the pit.
惴惴其慄	In fear, in fear he trembles.
彼倉者天	That azure Heaven
殲我良人	annihilates my good man.
如何贖兮	Oh, how can he be redeemed?
人百其身	A hundred men for him alone.
交交黃鳥	Back and forth [fly] the yellow birds.
止于桑	They settle on the mulberry tree (*saang).
誰從穆公	Who follows Lord Mu?
子車仲行	Tzu-chü Chung-hang (*gaang).
……	…

交交黃鳥	Back and forth [fly] the yellow birds.
止于楚	They settle on the thorn tree (*tshra:).
誰從穆公	Who follows Lord Mu?
子車鍼虎	Tzu-chü Ch'ien-hu (*xaa:).

(*Mao* 131: "Huang-niao" 黃鳥)

"Lord Mu" is Lord Mu of Ch'in 秦 (r. 659–621), and the three men named Tzu-chü are nobles whom the Lord has commanded to be buried with him. The event is narrated in the *Tso-chuan* 左傳 (a literary chronicle from approximately 300 B.C.).[44]

秦伯任好卒，以子車氏之三子奄息、仲行、鍼虎為殉，皆秦之良也。
國人哀之，為之賦黃鳥。[45]

Jen-hao, Earl of Ch'in [i.e., Lord Mu], died. Three sons of the Tzu-chü family—Yen-hsi, Chung-hang, and Ch'ien-hu—were buried alive. They were all the best in Ch'in. The citizens[46] grieved for them, and recited[47] "The Yellow Birds."[48]

The historical background explains the significance of the epithet *t'e* 特 for Tzu-chü Yen-hsi ("the finest in a hundred"): *t'e* also means the male of a domesticated species, a fine victim for a sacrifice. But the key to the entire poem lies in the image of the yellow birds. Every time they land on a different tree, another scion of the household dies. Indeed, their movements take on the import of prognostications; the name of each tree that they rest on rhymes with that of the hero about to be sacrificed.[49] Chung-hang, for example, knows that his time has come when the yellow birds settle on the mulberry (*saang).

The "yellow bird" is a name for the oriole that appears in the context of the *Odes* as a specific symbol for separation between man and wife.[50] One poem juxtaposes the beautiful orioles to the plight of a widow with seven young children.

凱風自南	The gentle wind from the south
吹彼棘心	blows on the heart of that jujube tree.
棘心夭夭	The jujube tree is verdant.
母氏劬勞	The mother pains and toils.
凱風自南	The gentle wind from the south
吹彼棘薪	blows on the wood of that jujube tree.
母氏聖善	The mother is sage and good.
我無令人	We do not have a compassionate man.

爰有寒泉	There is a cold spring
在浚之下	beneath [the city of] Chün.
有子七人	There are seven sons.
母氏勞苦	The mother toils in misery.

睍睆黃鳥	Dazzling are the yellow birds,
載好其音	lovely their tones.
有子七人	There are seven sons.
莫慰母心	They do not soothe the mother's heart.

(Mao 32: "K'ai-feng" 凱風)

But the most telling images appear in another poem called "The Yellow Birds."

黃鳥黃鳥	Yellow birds, yellow birds,
無集于穀	do not gather on the corn.
無啄我粟	Do not peck at my grain.
此邦之人	The people in this country
不我肯穀	are not willing to nourish me.
言旋言歸	I will return; I will go back,
復我邦族	back to my country and kin.

黃鳥黃鳥	Yellow birds, yellow birds,
無集于桑	do not gather on the mulberry.
無啄我粱	Do not peck at my liang-millet.
此邦之人	The people in this country
不可與明	I cannot ally with.
言旋言歸	I will return; I will go back,
復我諸兄	back to my several brothers.

黃鳥黃鳥	Yellow birds, yellow birds,
無集于栩	do not gather in the oak.
無啄我黎	Do not peck at my li-millet.
此邦之人	The people in this country
不可與處	I cannot dwell with.
言旋言歸	I will return; I will go back,
復我諸父	back to my several ancestors.

(Mao 187: "Huang-niao")

The speaker is a widow or an abandoned woman; the only manner in which she could have left her "country and kin" in the first place is by having married a man from another district. The people of the alien region refuse to support her, and she must go back to her homeland. The yellow birds gathering on the trees are an image of loss and desolation.

We understand, then, the import of the orioles alighting on the trees in the first "Yellow Birds" poem. It is a trope of arousal intended to evoke the appropriate mood. Moreover, the yellow birds make the reader think of the widowed women in "The Gentle Breeze" and the second "Yellow Birds," and we immediately realize that the party who will feel the greatest loss for the Tzu-chü brothers is not the "citizens" 國人 but the men's own wives, who are unnaturally separated from them.

The full message emerges in the phrase "back and forth" 交交. *Chiao* can mean "back and forth," or "crosswise," but specifically in the sense of "crossing," or "meeting." The significance of the image cannot have been lost on ancient readers. When birds fly in such a way that they keep crossing each other's path, they are mating. It is no coincidence that *chiao* is also the most basic term for sexual intercourse. The intentionally ambiguous phrase *chiao-chiao huang-niao* means not only "Crosswise, crosswise fly the yellow birds" but also "They copulate, they copulate, the yellow birds." The poem is about two competing relations: that between the brothers and their lord on the one hand, and that between the brothers and their wives on the other. Lord Mu forces his vassals to be true to him to the end, severing whatever connection they had with their own wives and family.

Poems like "The Yellow Birds" forge a profound link between the image of sexual intercourse and the relation between a ruler and his subjects,[51] shedding greater light on the hermeneutic tradition that could read a simple poem like "The Crafty Youth" as an indictment of a petty lord whom most readers probably had never heard of. Perhaps that poem really was intended as an allusion to Lord Chao of Cheng; perhaps not. What is important is that the ancient critics recognized a dimension of the *Odes* that many modern readers overlook: imagistic poems with a veneer of simplicity can pack several layers of meaning for a sophisticated audience.

Consider the traditional interpretation of another poem, "The Nine-Meshed Net."

九罭之魚	The fish in the nine-meshed net
鱒魴	are rudd and bream.
我覯之子	I see this young man
袞衣繡裳	in regal robes and embroidered skirt.

鴻飛遵渚	The wild geese fly along the sandbar.
公歸無所	When the Duke goes back, there will be no place [for us].
於女信處	I will stay with you one more time.

鴻飛遵陸	The wild geese fly along the hill.
公歸不復	The Duke is going back and will not return.
於女信宿	I will lodge with you one more time.

是以有袞衣兮	Oh, here we had the regal robes.
無以我公歸兮	Oh, do not go back with our Duke.
無使我心悲兮	Oh, do not make my heart grieve.

(*Mao* 159: "Chiu-yü" 九罭)

Evidently, the poem depicts the end of a love affair between a girl and a man in the service of "the Duke." Unfortunately, the Duke is about to go back, and that change will be the end of their relation: "There will be no place [for us]." The opening arousal is appropriate; the fish caught in the net, as we have seen, constitute a versatile symbol for the sex act. It has been pointed out, furthermore, that the wild geese, like the yellow birds, consistently signify conjugal separation, both in the *Odes* and in the ancient divination literature.[52] They figure as the natural arousal for a sorrowful song of parting.

The traditional interpretation, which even some of the most receptive modern readers cannot accept,[53] is that "The Nine-Meshed Net" is a hymn of praise to the Duke of Chou, who served as Regent to the infant King Ch'eng 成王 (r. 1042/1035–1006) in the years 1042–1036 B.C.[54] It was allegedly written by the "Grand Masters of Chou" 周大夫 when the Duke of Chou was about to return home after having subdued a rebellion led by his brothers in the east.[55] The female speaker represents the people of the east, who have benefited from his enlightened rule; now they yearn to "lodge" with him one last time. We might be reluctant to let the specific reference stand—after all, other bronze-age documents paint a portrait of the Duke of Chou that is not entirely flattering[56]—but for the most part, there is nothing far-fetched about an allegorical reading. We have seen repeatedly how the *Odes* employ sexual imagery to metaphoric effect. If the image of the enchantress' receiving basket can convey her cultivation of an ancestral spirit, and if the copulating birds can serve as an emblem for the relation between the Tzu-chü brothers and Lord

Mu of Ch'in, then little should stand in the way of understanding the girl cohabiting with a young man in regal robes as a figure for the people serving their beloved lord. The ancient authorities do not bother with the manifest sexual dimensions of the poem precisely because these are the elements of the poem that require no commentary.

The metaphorical understanding of sexual intercourse—that is, as a representation of the relationship between a ruler and his subjects, or between a divinity and his human worshippers—rests on the communal conception of the sex act itself. The analogy of the male as ruler and the female as subject, for example, has its roots in the social roles played by males and females in ancient China. This point is developed in the closing stanzas of another poem.

乃生男子	A male child is born.
載寢之床	He is made to sleep on a bed.
載衣之裳	He is made to wear a skirt.
載弄之璋	He is made to play with a scepter.
其泣喤喤	His crying is loud.
朱芾斯皇	His red knee-covers are august.
室家君王	He is the hall and household's lord and king.
乃生女子	A female child is born.
載寢之地	She is made to sleep on the floor.
載衣之裼	She is made to wear a wrap-cloth.
載弄之瓦	She is made to play with pottery.
無非無儀	She has no wrong and right.
唯酒食是議	Only wine and food are for her to talk about.
無父母詒罹	May she not send her father and mother any troubles.

(*Mao* 189: "Ssu-kan" 斯干)

Each line in one stanza parallels the corresponding line in the other stanza. For example, while the baby boy plays with a scepter, a clear symbol of might and rulership, the baby girl is given pottery in order to acquaint her with the chores that await her in the future.[57] And whereas the boy's knee covers are "august" 皇, the same term used in the *Lyrics of Ch'u* for the "Magnificent One," the girl tends to the wine and food that she will present to her several rulers: husband, king, and god.[58]

The last lines in each stanza highlight another crucial dynamic in the metaphor of copulation. The line "May she not send her father and mother any troubles" calls to mind various poems in which the girl urges her lover to proceed quietly, lest their love-play waken her parents and cause her shame.

野有死麕	In the field there is a dead roe.
白茅包之	With white grass we wrap it.
有女懷春	There is a girl who longs for spring.
吉士誘之	A fine fellow seduces her.
林有樸樕	In the forest there is the *p'u-su* tree.
野有死鹿	In the field there is a dead deer.
白茅純束	With white grass we bind it.
有女如玉	There is a girl like jade.
舒而脱脱兮	Oh, undress me slowly.[59]
無感我帨兮	Oh, do not upset my kerchief.[60]
無使尨也吠	Do not make the shaggy dog bark.

(*Mao* 23: "Yeh yu ssu chün" 野有死麕)

One of the most famous and enigmatic poems to make use of the theme is "The Banks of the Ju," a river in the east.

遵彼汝墳	Along those banks of the Ju,
伐其條枚	I cut the long branches.
未見君子	I have not seen my lord.
惄如調飢	My pangs are like the morning hunger.
遵彼汝墳	Along those banks of the Ju,
伐其條肄	I cut the long twigs.
既見君子	I have seen my lord.
不我遐棄	He has not abandoned me.
魴魚赬尾	The bream has a reddened tail.
王室如燬	The royal hall is as if ablaze.
雖則如燬	Although it is as if ablaze,
父母孔邇	My parents are very near.

(*Mao* 10: "Ju-fen" 汝墳)

It has recently been suggested that the "royal hall" (*wang-shih* 王室) should be read "jade hall" (*yü-shih* 玉室), a likely euphemism for the vagina.[61] To be sure, the blazing hall is a sign of the girl's excitement. The various arousals in the poem, furthermore, are true to the scene. The bream with the rubescent tail, coupled with the narrator's morning hunger, set the tone for sexual tension.

But we must also recall here the twin stanzas describing the birth of boys and girls. The point of the conclusion to "The Banks of the Ju," like that of "In the Field There Is a Dead Roe," is that the girl cannot risk being caught with her lover by her father and mother— that would send her parents troubles. Moreover, the phrase "royal hall" echoes the parallel line for boys: "He is the hall and household's lord and king" 室家君王. The hall, some commentators argue, is the hall of worship for the family's ancestors.[62] This is why the boy is so valuable; he is entitled to cultivate the ancestors and ensure harmonious relations with them. In "The Banks of the Ju," the lovers choose the ancestral hall as their meeting place precisely because it is occupied only on extraordinary occasions. The image of the blazing hall contains a subtle but unmistakable connotation of illicit sexual congress. On the one hand, the hall is supposed to be the locus of ancestor worship, which, as we have seen, is conventionally portrayed in terms of a sexual relation. In this poem, however, rather than having sublimated or ritual intercourse with their ancestors, the boy and girl have sexual intercourse *with each other*, knowing full well that they must keep their liaison secret. Who knows what may happen if the "father and mother" should hear their passion? Perhaps we even ought to read *fu-mu* 父母 as "fathers and mothers," for the innumerable ancestral spirits present in the hall.

The striking image of the illicit affair in the family shrine illuminates exactly what was considered dangerous about extramarital sexual relations: they confuse the issue of patrimony. Nowhere is this issue more graphically apparent than in the chaotic story of Lord Hsüan of Wei 衛宣公 (r. 718–700 B.C.), as related in the *Tso-chuan*.

初，衛宣公烝於夷姜，生急子，屬諸右公子。為之娶於齊，而美，公取之。生壽及朔。屬壽於左公子。夷姜縊。宣姜與公子朔構急子。公使諸齊。使盜待諸莘，將殺之。壽子告之，使行。不可，曰：棄父之命，惡用子矣？有無父之國則可也。及行，飲以酒。壽子載其旌以先，盜殺之。急子至，曰：我之求也，此何罪？請殺我乎！又殺之。[63]

Before [coming to the throne],[64] Lord Hsüan of Wei had illicit relations with Chiang of I [his father's concubine]. She gave birth to Chitzu; [Lord Hsüan] entrusted him to the Right Noble Son. He found him a wife from Ch'i, but since she was beautiful, Lord [Hsüan] took her [for himself]. She gave birth to Shou and Shuo. [Lord Hsüan] entrusted Shou to the Left Noble Son. Chiang of I hanged herself. Hsüan's other wife and the Noble Son Shuo slandered Chi-tzu. Lord [Hsüan] sent him to Ch'i, and sent thugs to wait for him at Hsin, where they would kill him. Shou-tzu informed [Chi-tzu], and told him to flee. [Chi-tzu] was unwilling, saying, "If I reject my father's command, what use am I as a son? If there is a state without a father, then it would be acceptable." When it came time to go, [Shou-tzu] intoxicated [Chi-tzu] with wine. Shou-tzu carried his banner ahead of him, and the thugs killed him. When Chi-tzu arrived, he said, "It is I that you seek; what was his crime? I beg you to kill me!" So they killed him too.[65]

Modern readers are often shocked when it comes time for Chi-tzu to offer his own life, but we must remember that had he taken advantage of the situation to flee, it would have proven wholly incongruous with his earlier determination not to avoid his death. The point is that Chi-tzu refuses to "reject [his] father's command" 棄父之命, an ideal of filial piety that his own father failed deplorably to live up to. Lord Hsüan fornicated with the wives of his father and his son, and it could only have been foreordained that the offspring of these abominable unions met with their tragic end. However, the real calamity, from the point of view of classical readers, is not that Chi-tzu and Shou-tzu are both slain, but that the succession of the state of Wei has been thrown into confusion because of Lord Hsüan's philandering. Who will tend the ancestral hall? One son is a murderer; the other two are dead.[66]

Another famous case of adultery among rulers and their wives is said in the *Tso-chuan* to have induced the countryfolk to compose ballads like those found in the Odes.

衛侯為夫人南子召宋朝。會于洮，大子蒯聵獻盂於齊，過宋野。野人歌之曰：既定爾婁豬，盍歸吾艾豭？[67]

The Marquis of Wei [i.e., Lord Ling 靈公 of Wei, r. 534–493 B.C.] invited Sung Ch'ao for his lady, Nan-tzu. They met at T'ao. The Heir-Apparent [of Wei], K'uai-k'uei, was offering [the city of] Yü to Ch'i, and passed through the fields of Sung. The people in the fields were singing about it, saying, "You have already settled your sow in heat. Why not send back our fine boar?"

Nan-tzu was a daughter of the ruling house of Sung who was notorious for her incestuous relationship with Sung Ch'ao, her brother.[68]

Here Nan-tzu's lawful husband, Lord Ling of Wei, not only condones her lewdness but actually encourages it by inviting her brother to copulate with her in T'ao. In case the image of the sow and boar were not clear enough, the commentator Tu Yü 杜預 (A.D. 222–284) remarks: "A *lou-chu* ['sow in heat'] is a pig that is seeking offspring. It is used as an analogy for Nan-tzu. The 'fine boar' is an analogy for Sung Ch'ao" 婁豬，求子豬，以喻南子。艾豭喻宋朝.

Here too, the consequence of adultery is that the ancestral line is thrown into disorder. In surrendering his wife to another, Lord Ling ultimately paves the way for the loss of his own son.

大子羞之，謂戲陽速曰：從我而朝少君，少君見我，我顧，乃殺之。
速曰：諾。乃朝夫人。夫人見大子。大子三顧，速不進。夫人見其
色，啼而走，曰：蒯聵將殺余。公執其手以登臺。大子奔宋。[69]

The Heir-Apparent was ashamed at [the farmers' song], and he said to Hsi-yang Su, "Follow me to visit Her Majesty. When Her Majesty has an audience with me, I will turn and look at you. Then kill her." Su said, "Yes." So he visited the Lady. The Lady had an audience with the Heir-Apparent. The Heir-Apparent turned three times, but Su did not advance. The Lady saw his expression, and screamed as she ran away, saying, "K'uai-k'uei is going to kill me." Lord [Ling] grasped her hand so that she might climb up to a terrace. The Heir-Apparent absconded to Sung.[70]

Lord Ling then had no choice but to appoint a secondary son as Heir-Apparent, but when Ling died three years later, the new Heir-Apparent refused to ascend the throne. Nan-tzu was finally forced to accept the son of her would-be assassin as the next Lord of Wei. Peace was not restored to the realm until 476 B.C.—a full twenty years after Nan-tzu's ill-fated coupling with her brother.[71]

Adultery and its awful consequences for the next generation are a favorite theme of the *Tso-chuan*.

郤犨來聘，求婦於聲伯。聲伯奪施氏婦以與之。婦人曰：鳥獸猶不
失儷，子將若何？曰：吾不能死亡。婦人遂行。生二子於郤氏。郤氏
亡，晉人歸之施氏。施氏逆諸河，沈其二子。婦人怒曰：己不能庇其
伉儷而亡之，又不能字人之孤而殺之，將何以終？遂誓施氏。[72]

Hsi Ch'ou [of Chin] came on an embassy [to Lu], and sought a wife from Sheng-po. Sheng-po took away Mr. Shih's wife in order to give her to [Hsi Ch'ou]. The wife said, "Even birds and beasts do not lose their mates. What will you do?" [Shih] said, "I cannot die or be banished" [i.e., he fears the consequences of disobeying]. So his wife left.

She bore two sons to Hsi. When Hsi died, the men of Chin sent her back to Shih. Shih met her at the Yellow River, and drowned her two sons. His wife was angry, saying, "You yourself could not shelter your mate, but caused her to go away. Moreover, you cannot succor a man's orphans, but kill them. What will be your end?" Then she swore [separation] from Shih.[73]

The stories of Mr. Shih and Lord Ling of Wei—and of their wives—may differ radically from the point of view of individual culpability, but they both have the same result for the children. It is as though unlawful sexual relations *cannot* produce offspring that will survive. Indeed, this is the opinion of a figure as renowned as Tzu-ch'an 子產 (otherwise known as Kung-sun Ch'iao 公孫僑), the chief minister of the state of Cheng from 543 until his death in 522 B.C.[74]

僑又聞之，內官不及同姓，其生不殖。美先盡矣，則相生疾，君子是以惡之。故志曰：買妾不知其姓，則卜之。違此二者，古之所慎也。男女辨姓，禮之大司也。[75]

Moreover, I have heard that there should not be [women] of the same surname [as their husband] in the inner quarters. Their offspring will not prosper. The beauty [of those who commit incest] will first be exhausted; then they will breed disease in each other. Therefore the gentleman hates [incest]. A former record says, "In buying a consort, if you do not know her surname, divine it."[76] The ancients were careful about offenses against these two principles [i.e., as Tzu-ch'an has made clear earlier, observation of the incest taboo and excessive nocturnal activity]. That male and female be of different surnames is a great concern of ritual.[77]

Tzu-ch'an is speaking here specifically of incest rather than of adultery, but the figure of Nan-tzu shows how the two transgressions are but different manifestations of the same basic violation. Marriages that offend against the ancestral hall, whether incestuous or adulterous—or both—beget death and disease. That is precisely why the ritual codes address the issues of marriage and the purchase of consorts; the sex act is inherently a ritual act. We may even apply Tzu-ch'an's principle to "The Yellow Birds." Lord Mu's relations with the Tzu-chü brothers, we remember, are portrayed in images of sexual union. Having the men buried alive with him is improper and, above all, excessive. It is tantamount, if we extend the metaphor, to necrophilia. An abomination of that magnitude must bring on all the disasters that Tzu-ch'an warns us of—and these, as we have seen, are embodied in the complex figure of the yellow birds.

Women and men knew the larger consequences of adultery and incest, because the connection between marriage and the husband's ancestral hall were well established. One young woman interpreted a dream about another family's temple as an omen that she must wed one of their sons.

泉丘人有女，夢以其帷幕孟氏之廟，遂奔僖子，其僚從之。[78]

A man of Ch'üan-ch'iu had a daughter who dreamt that she used her curtains as a screen for the temple of the Meng family. Thereupon she eloped with [Meng] Hsi-tzu; her companion followed her.[79]

In the larger context of the *Tso-chuan*, the girl of Ch'üan-ch'iu plays but a minuscule role. She is never named, and we do not hear from her again. But the episode illustrates well the ancients' awareness of marriage and its significance for the ritual integrity of the clan.[80] These stories further the association, first made in the *Odes*, between the "hall and household" and the baby boy. In a sense, the girl is not a full member of the group, because she is destined to serve in someone else's ancestral hall.

This conception of sexuality explains why the improper cultivation of spirits is called *yin-ssu* 淫祀, or "licentious worship." The phrase became especially well known in imperial times as the term used by Taoist patriarchs to denote heterodox divinity cults.[81] One of the oldest articulations of the idea occurs in the *Tso-chuan*.

晉侯改共大子。秋，狐突適下國，遇大子。大子使登，僕，而告之曰：夷吾無禮，余得請於帝矣，將以晉畀秦，秦將祀余。對曰：臣聞之：神不歆非類，民不祀非族。君祀無乃殄乎？[82]

The Marquis of Chin moved [the body of] Heir-Apparent Kung [to a new grave]. In the autumn, Hu T'u was going to the lesser capital, when he happened upon [the ghost of] the Heir-Apparent. The Heir-Apparent made him ascend [his carriage] and act as his charioteer. He said to him, "I-wu [the ruler of Chin] has no propriety. I have made a request of Ti: I will bestow Chin unto Ch'in, and Ch'in will cultivate me." [Hu T'u] responded, "I have heard, 'Spirits do not consume what is not of their kind; people do not cultivate what is not of their lineage.' Will the sacrifices to you not be wasted?"[83]

Heir-Apparent Kung is Shen-sheng 申生 (d. 656 B.C.). The operative belief behind his request is that spirits need human beings to feed them with sacrifices. As one commentary points out, the "lesser capital" is the city of Ch'ü-wo 曲沃, the former capital of Chin, where the ancestral shrines are located and preserved.[84] If anyone is going to "happen upon" 遇 a ghost, therefore, it will be in the vicinity of the lesser capital. Shen-sheng is enraged that his body has been disinterred and transferred somewhere else, and he wishes to punish the offender—I-wu, his half-brother—by handing the state over to his greatest rival. Hu T'u, his former charioteer, warns him that his plan will not succeed, because there will be no one to sacrifice to him if Chin is destroyed.[85]

This understanding of sacrifice informs another famous story in the *Tso-chuan.*

> 鄭人相驚以伯有，曰：伯有至矣！則皆走，不知所往。鑄刑書之歲二月，或夢伯有介而行，曰：壬子，余將殺帶也。明年壬寅，余又將殺段也。及壬子，駟帶卒，國人益懼。齊燕平之月，壬寅，公孫段卒，國人愈懼。其明月，子產立公孫洩及良止以撫之，乃止。子大叔問其故。子產曰：鬼有所歸，乃不為厲，吾為之歸也。[86]

The people of Cheng alarmed each other about [the ghost of] Po-yu [i.e., Liang Hsiao 良霄, d. 543 B.C.], saying, "Po-yu is coming!" Then they would all run around, not knowing where they were going. In the second month of the year in which the legal codes were cast [i.e., 536 B.C.], someone dreamt that Po-yu was walking in armor, saying, "On *jen-tzu* day, I will kill [Ssu] Tai [Po-yu's killer]. On *jen-yin* day of next year, I will also kill [Kung-sun] Tuan." When *jen-tzu* day arrived, Ssu Tai died, and the citizens increased their fears. In the month of peace with Ch'i and Yen [i.e., 535 B.C.], on *jen-yin*, Kung-sun Tuan died, and the citizens were even more frightened. The next month, Tzu-ch'an elevated Kung-sun Hsieh and Liang Chih [Po-yu's son] in order to placate [the ghost]. Then things ceased. Tzu-t'ai-shu asked the reason. Tzu-ch'an said, "When ghosts have a place to return to, they do not become a menace. I afforded him a returning-place."[87]

The "place to return to" 所歸, of course, is an ancestral hall filled with sacrifices. Liang Chih had to be appointed officially as a successor to his father for Po-yu's spirit to be satisfied. As Tzu-ch'an goes on to explain, the ghost was justified. Like the ghost of Shen-sheng, that of Po-yu had been wronged; he was starving, and the people of Cheng should not have neglected him.[88] It is not clear why it took eight years—and two deaths—for Tzu-ch'an finally to solve the problem.[89]

In any case, the essential point was that sacrifices to Po-yu's spirit could be successful only if they were carried out by his legitimate descendant, Liang Chih. Otherwise, they would be what Hu T'u calls "wasted" 殄, or, in the parlance of ritual texts, "licentious." The

Record of Rites (*Li-chi* 禮記) states, "Sacrificing to a [spirit] to whom one ought not sacrifice is called 'licentious worship.' There is no fortune in licentious worship" 非其所祭而祭之，名曰淫祀。淫祀無福。[90] *Yin* 淫, "licentious," is the same word that Confucius used in his characterization of "The *Kuan*-ing Ospreys": "There is joy without licentiousness." The basic meaning of the character is "downpour," but it is commonly used in place of its homophone, *yin* 婬, meaning "excessive sexual activity," or "promiscuity."[91] It is an explicit and shocking word, and it may be a little surprising that the *Record of Rites* uses it so freely to describe a ritual transgression.

The sexual sense of *yin* is exemplified in the salacious story of Lady Hsia 夏姬, the daughter of Lord Mu of Cheng and widow of Yü-shu 御叔, a grand master of the state of Ch'en 陳.[92]

> 陳靈公與孔寧、儀行父通於夏姬，皆衷其衵服，以戲于朝。洩冶曰：公卿宣淫，民無效焉，且聞不令。君其納之！公曰：吾能改矣。公告二子。二子請殺之，公弗禁，遂殺洩冶。[93]

> Lord Ling of Ch'en [r. 613–599 B.C.], K'ung Ning, and I Hang-fu had congress with Lady Hsia. They all used her intimate clothes[94] for their undergarments, and jested about it at court. Hsieh Yeh said, "The Lord and his chamberlains are proclaiming their licentiousness; will this not have an effect on the people? Moreover, the rumor [of this affair] will not be good. Lord, will you not put [her bedclothes] away!"[95] Lord [Ling] said, "I will reform myself." Lord [Ling] informed the two gentlemen. The two gentlemen requested permission to kill him, and Lord [Ling] did not forbid it. Thus they killed Hsieh Yeh.[96]

This indecent affair soon became even more outrageous and finally roused the anger of Lady Hsia's son.

> 陳靈公與孔寧、儀行父飲酒於夏氏。公謂行父曰：徵舒似女。對曰：亦似君。徵舒病之。公出，自其廄射而殺之。二子奔楚。[97]

> Lord Ling of Ch'en was drinking wine at the Hsia household with K'ung Ning and I Hang-fu. Lord [Ling] addressed Hang-fu, saying, "[Hsia] Cheng-shu [Lady Hsia's son] resembles you." He responded, "He also resembles you, my lord." Cheng-shu was distressed at this. When Lord [Ling] left, he shot him from his stable and killed him. The two gentlemen fled to Ch'u.[98]

Evidently Lord Ling and I Hang-fu were jesting over who might be the natural father of Lady Hsia's son.[99]

King Chuang of Ch'u 楚莊王 (r. 613–591 B.C.), meanwhile, seizes upon the opportunity as a pretext to attack Ch'en.

冬，楚子為陳夏氏亂故，伐陳。謂陳人無動！將討於少西氏。遂入陳，殺夏徵舒，轘諸栗門。因縣陳。[100]

In the winter [of the next year], the Viscount of Ch'u used the disorder caused by the Hsia house in Ch'en as a reason to attack Ch'en. He addressed the people of Ch'en: "Do not move! I will punish the Shao-hsi household [i.e., the house of Hsia]." Then he entered Ch'en and killed Hsia Cheng-shu, tearing him apart with chariots at the Chestnut Gate. Following this, he made Ch'en a district [of his kingdom].[101]

A minister subsequently convinces the Viscount to restore Ch'en, because annexing its territory would make a mockery of his original justification, which was that he was merely punishing a regicide.[102] The Viscount agrees but later wishes to take Lady Hsia into his harem. Once again, he is dissuaded, for there could be no reason why he would want the woman who was the cause of all this turmoil except for sexual gratification. After all, Lady Hsia could hardly have a worse reputation. She had been intimate with the late Marquis of Ch'en and his two favorites. She was the reason for her son's death, as well as that of the Marquis (and she is even accused elsewhere of having caused the death of more than one husband, too).[103] To harbor such a wanton woman can only be *yin.*

楚之討陳夏氏也，莊王欲納夏姬。申公巫臣曰：不可。君召諸侯，以討罪也，今納夏姬，貪其色也。貪色為淫。淫為大罰。[104]

When Ch'u punished the Hsia household of Ch'en, King Chuang wished to take Lady Hsia. Wu-ch'en, Duke of Shen, said, "You cannot. When you called out the various rulers [i.e., to attack Ch'en], my lord, it was to punish a crime. Now if you take Lady Hsia, it is because you covet her sex. Coveting sex is licentious, and licentiousness is a great malfeasance."[105]

These are the powerfully erotic connotations of the word *yin.* When ancient readers came across the term "licentious worship," therefore, they would have recalled cases like that of Lady Hsia and her indiscriminate fornications. Worshipping alien gods is akin to whoring. Just as copulating with the wrong woman is decried as a violation of the ancestral hall, so sacrificing to the wrong god is understood as spiritual adultery.[106]

The literary use of copulation as a metaphor for the relation between lord and vassal, already apparent in the *Odes* in such pieces as "The Yellow Birds," comes to form the dominant theme in the longest poem of the *Lyrics of Ch'u*, "Encountering Sorrow" ("Li-sao" 離騷). The work is attributed to Ch'ü Yüan 屈原, a loyal officer of King Huai of Ch'u 楚懷王 (r. 328–299 B.C.) who is said to have fallen into disfavor as a result of slander.[107] "Encountering Sorrow" is framed as an autobiography from the time of the speaker's birth down to an "envoi" (*luan* 亂) that he apparently intones just before drowning himself in a river. Whether the author really was Ch'ü Yüan, and whether a figure by that name ever really existed, are questions that remain at present unanswerable.[108]

The speaker's downfall begins soon after the opening of the poem. He remonstrates too often with his lord.

日月忽其不淹兮	The days and months passed quickly, not tarrying.
春與秋其代兮	Springs and autumns succeeded each other.
惟草木之零落兮	I considered the wilting and falling of the grasses and leaves,
恐美人之遲暮	and I feared the slow dusking of my Beautiful One.
不撫壯而棄穢兮	He does not cherish what is fertile and discard weeds.
何不改此度[109]	Why will you not amend this habit?
……	…
荃不察余之中情兮[110]	But the Fragrance did not examine my innermost feelings.
反信讒而齌怒[111]	Instead, he trusted slanderers and began to simmer with rage.[112]
……	…
眾女嫉余之蛾眉兮	The thronging ladies were jealous of my moth-eyebrows.
謠諑謂余以善淫	They spread a rumor saying that I was licentious with my favors.

At this point, the commentator Wang I 王逸 (fl. ca. A.D. 120) remarks that the women are a metaphor for ministers.

言眾女嫉妒蛾眉美好之人，譖而毀之。謂之美而淫，不可信也。猶眾臣嫉妒忠正，言己淫邪，不可任也。[113]

This is to say that the thronging women are jealous of the beautiful and good person with the moth-eyebrows, so they destroy her by slandering her. They say that she is beautiful but licentious and cannot be trusted. They are like thronging ministers envious of [one who is] loyal and upright; this is to say that they themselves are licentious and perverse and cannot be employed.

The imagery is so unambiguous that few readers are inclined to disagree with this interpretation. Wang I might also have pointed out that the poet is treating his lord like a god. We remember the "fragrance," the motif by which the poem "The Eastern August Magnificent One" expresses the hierogamic union between the enchantress and the spirit that she has attracted. Here, in "Encountering Sorrow," the fragrance is an appellation of the ruler who has lost faith in his minister. The poet is speaking as though he were a shamaness whose deity has ceased to favor her.[114]

The poem continues, describing the relationship between lord and minister by using language and images pertaining to the union of male and female. The speaker flies through the air, courting goddesses and noble daughters but failing each time. Having lost his mate, his Beautiful One, he tries over and over to find another consort. The genders are interchangeable. The vassal may be cast either as the male suitor or as the female concubine. The lord may likewise be portrayed either as coveted female or as capricious male.

折瓊枝以繼佩	I break off a *ch'iung*-branch in order to attach it to my girdle.
及榮華之未落兮	Before the luxuriant flowers have fallen,
相下女之可詒	I will see a girl below whom I can give it to.
吾令豐隆椉雲兮	I order Feng-lung to ride a cloud,
求虑妃之所在	and find the location of Fu-fei.[115]
解佩纕以結言兮	Loosening my girdle-band as my word of betrothal,
吾令蹇脩以為理	I order Chien-hsiu to be the go-between.
紛總總其離合兮	Numerous and confused are the separations and unions.[116]
緯繣其難遷	Obstinate and rebellious, she is difficult to move.
夕歸次於窮石兮	In the evenings she returns to sojourn at Ch'iung-shih.
朝濯髮乎洧盤	In the mornings she washes her hair in Wei-p'an stream.
保厥美以驕傲兮	She guards her beauty with arrogance.
日康娛以淫遊	She amuses herself every day with licentious wanderings.
雖信美而無禮兮	Though indeed beautiful, she has no propriety.
來違棄而改求[117]	Let us leave her and find someone else.

At first the poet hopes for a new love affair with the goddess Fu-fei, but as soon as he learns that she is precisely what his former rivals have accused *him* of being—a beautiful woman, but wanton and untrustworthy—he becomes disenchanted and rejects her.

After more failures, a diviner finally offers some words of encouragement.

命靈氛為余占之	I command Ling-fen to divine for me.
曰兩美其必合兮	He said, "It must be that two beauties will unite!
孰信脩而慕之	Whoever is trustworthy and cultivated, one admires.
思九州之博大兮	Think how expansive and great are the Nine Continents.
豈唯是其有女	Is it only here that there are women?"
曰勉遠逝而無狐疑兮	He said, "Endeavor to pass far away and do not be dubious like a fox.
孰求美而釋女[118]	Whoever seeks beauty will pick you."

Ironically, in the phrase "pass far away" 遠逝, the diviner Ling-fen has made a prediction that the speaker does not yet understand. *Shih* 逝, "to pass," "to perish," is a common word for death. The god Wu-Hsien 巫咸 subsequently verifies Ling-fen's prognostication, and the speaker is encouraged to make a vast journey through the outer reaches of the universe. But disaster strikes at the last instant.

陟陞皇之赫戲兮	I rise and ascend the gloriously bright empyrean.
忽臨睨夫舊鄉	Suddenly, I come within view of my own home.
僕夫悲余馬懷兮	The coistrel is grieved; my horses long for it.
蜷局顧而不行	They turn to look back and will not go on.
亂曰	Envoi:
已矣哉	That is all!
國無人莫我知兮	There is no one in the state, none who know me.
又何懷乎故都	And why should I long for my former city?
既莫足與為美政兮	Since there is no one adequate to make a beautiful government with,
吾將從彭咸之所居[119]	I will follow P'eng and Hsien to their abode.[120]

P'eng and Hsien are spirits or divinities whose abode is the otherworld. The brilliant envoi serves to tie the whole poem together on two levels. At the last moment, the poet fulfills the prophecy of Ling-fen, "passing far away" 遠逝 into death. And by killing himself, he actually finds his mate after all, hurling himself into the abode of the gods. They are the only ones adequate to his devotion.

Moreover, the envoi explains unmistakably that the many appearances of "beauty" 美 in the poem are intended to have moral and political overtones.[121] The speaker's own beauty lies in the fact that he alone is capable of effecting "beautiful government" 美政. The Beautiful One, the appellation by which he first refers to his lord, reveals himself in the end to be inadequate on moral grounds and undeserving of the poet's loyalty. Similarly, Fu-fei, though undeniably beautiful ("Though indeed beautiful..." 雖信美), also turns out to be an inappropriate match because of her promiscuous "wanderings" 遊. There are two levels of beauty, just as there are two levels of copulation. The poem may refer to the beauty of the body or the spiritual beauty of "loyalty and uprightness" 忠正. In the same way, it may portray copulation in a carnal sense, or in the metaphorical sense of joining ruler and subject. Even in the notion of wandering, the poet forges a similar dualism. His own wandering is the consequence of his lifelong quest to find a proper mate, ending finally in his suicide and union with the spirit world. The debased wandering of Fu-fei, however, is merely an opportunity for her to flaunt her divine hair and fulfill her earthly desires.[122]

This theme of beauty in its competing literal and allegorical senses is also apparent in a characteristic passage from the "inner chapters" (*nei-p'ien* 內篇) of the *Chuang-tzu* 莊子, the philosophical work named after the thinker Chuang Chou 莊周 (fl. fourth century B.C.).[123]

魯哀公問於仲尼曰：衞有惡人焉，曰哀駘它。丈夫與之處者，思而不能去也。婦人見之，請於父母曰與為人妻寧為夫子妾者，十數而未止也。未嘗有聞其唱者也，常和人而已矣。無君人之位以濟乎人之死，無眾祿以望人之腹。又以惡駭天下，和而不唱，知不出乎四域，且而雌雄合乎前，是必有異乎人者也。寡人召而觀之，果以惡駭天下。與寡人處，不至以月數，而寡人有意乎其為人也；不至乎期年，而寡人信之。國無宰，寡人傳國焉。悶然而後應，汜若而[124]辭。寡人醜乎，卒授之國。無幾何也，去寡人而行，寡人卹焉若有亡也，若無與樂是國也。是何人者也？[125]

Lord Ai of Lu (r. 494–468 B.C.) asked Confucius, saying, "In Wei there is an ugly man named Ai-t'ai T'o. When men live with him, they cherish him and cannot leave him. When women see him, they beg their parents, saying, 'Rather than become another man's wife, I would prefer to be that man's concubine.' There were more than ten women like that, and they did not cease. There was no one who ever heard him take the lead;[126] he would always simply be in harmony with other people. He had no lordly position with which to save people from death; he did not have amassed riches with which to satiate people's stomachs.[127] He also terrified the world with his ugliness. He always went along and never took the lead. His knowledge did not extend to the four directions. And yet male and female combined before him. He must have been different from other people. We summoned him and observed him. Indeed, he terrified the world with his ugliness. When he lived with Us, within the space of one month We took an interest in his personality. Within the period of one year, We trusted him. The state had no prime minister, so We handed over the state to him. After a while he responded, indistinctly, as though declining. We were disgraced! In the end We gave him the state, but before long, he left Us and went. We were grieved by this, as though We had had a loss, as though there were no one with whom We could enjoy the state. What kind of a man was this?"[128]

Confucius then explains. Ai-t'ai T'o is someone whose inner power (*te* 德) is not apparent from his external form. However, it is one's inner power that attracts others, not one's physical beauty. If the inner power remains amorphous and flexible, the rest of the world will take note of it. "Inner power is the cultivation of completed harmony. If one's inner power is not formed, things cannot depart from one" 德者，成和之脩也。德不形者，物不能離也.[129] Unformed inner power takes the same shape as the unformed *tao.*

The figure of Ai-t'ai T'o could only have come from the *Chuang-tzu.* He embodies ideals, such as rejecting official life and "not taking the lead" 不唱, that are typical of that text more than any other.[130] Nevertheless, it is clear how this story expands on themes that are familiar from "Encountering Sorrow." Ai-t'ai T'o is unbelievably ugly, and yet the women in Wei wish for nothing more than to be available for his sexual convenience. This is because his "inner power," like the "beauty" of the virtuous minister in the *Lyrics of Ch'u,* proves more attractive than the physical beauty of less talented rivals. The Lord of Lu is even persuaded to hand over his state to Ai-t'ai T'o, and when the lord is abandoned by his new minister, he seems to feel as though his consort has perished.

In light of this story and "Encountering Sorrow," with their highly charged themes of beauty and copulation, other poems in the *Lyrics of Ch'u* must also be read with an awareness of their multiple meanings. Consider "The Lesser Administrator of Fate" 少司命, an erotic poem that avoids explicit political references until the very end.

秋蘭兮麋蕪	The autumn orchid and the *mi-wu*
羅生兮堂下	grow in a carpet at the bottom of the hall.
綠葉兮素枝	The green leaves and white branches
芳菲菲兮襲予	have a fragrance that wafts and invades me.
〔夫人自有兮美子	["The people naturally have beautiful children.
蓀何以兮愁苦〕	Iris, why are you sad and bitter?"][131]
秋蘭兮青青	The autumn orchids are blue,
綠葉兮紫莖	with green leaves and purple stems.
滿堂兮美人	The hall is filled with beauties.
忽獨與余兮目成	Unexpectedly, his eyes fall entirely on me.
入不言兮出不辭	He enters me without a word and exits without a farewell.
乘回風兮載雲旗	He rides back on the wind, his banners supported by the clouds.
悲莫悲兮生別離	No sorrow is more sorrowful than that of parting for the living.
樂莫樂兮新相知	No joy is more joyous than having someone new with whom to know each other.[132]
荷衣兮蕙帶	With a lotus robe and a melilotus belt
儵而來兮忽而逝	Quickly he comes and suddenly he departs.
夕宿兮帝郊	In the evening he will lodge in the precincts of Ti.
君誰須兮雲之際	"Lord, whom do you await at the edge of the clouds?
與女遊兮九河	I will wander with you to the Nine Rivers.
衝風至兮水揚波	The rushing wind arrives and the water raises waves.
與女沐兮咸池	I will bathe with you in Hsien's pool.
晞女髮兮陽之阿	I will dry your hair on the bank of the sun."
望美人兮未來	I gaze at the Beautiful One, but he has not come.
臨風恍兮浩歌	Near the wild wind, I pour out my song.
孔蓋兮翠旍	With a peacock's canopy and a kingfisher's pennant,
登九天兮撫慧星	He ascends the Nine Heavens and strokes the Broom Star.
竦長劍兮擁幼艾	Drawing up his long sword, he brings together young and old.
蓀獨宜兮為民正[133]	"Only you, Iris, are fit to be the ruler of the people."

On the one hand, given the obvious affinities of this poem to "The Eastern August Magnificent One," one can readily take it as an ode to a god or spirit. The phrase *fang fei-fei* 芳菲菲, "the fragrance wafts," appears in both poems, as does the "long sword" 長劍—and, above all, the idea of copulating with the sweet-smelling lord. However, the final line recalls "Encountering Sorrow" in particular and reminds us that the Fragrant One can also be understood as a ruler of men. He is called Iris 蓀 in "The Lesser Administrator of Fate," and Fragrant One 荃 in "Encountering Sorrow," but the image is largely the same.[134] The final phrase, "ruler of the people" 民正, moreover, affirms the worldly and political dimensions of the poem. If we envision the poet of "Encountering Sorrow" reciting the lines of "The Lesser Administrator of Fate," then we can easily imagine him delighting in the privileges that his lord showers on him, portraying them as the sexual favors that Iris bestows on his enchanted lover. It is only to be expected then, that the poet describes Iris in language fit for a god. For the premier metaphor in both liturgical poems like "The Eastern August Magnificent One" and political-satirical poems like "Encountering Sorrow" is that of copulation with a superior being.

In this respect, "Encountering Sorrow" and "The Lesser Administrator of Fate" are typical of their cultural context. By the third and fourth centuries B.C., it had become commonplace to liken the ruler's ministers to his women, as is evident from writings of various genres.[135] The "Wen-yen" 文言 commentary to the *Canon of Changes* (*I-ching* 易經), for example, draws the following analogy under the hexagram *k'un* 坤 (six broken lines, or pure *yin* 陰).

陰雖有美，含之以從王事，弗敢成也。地道也，妻道也，臣道也。[136]

Although *yin* possesses beauty, it contains [its beauty] in order to follow in the affairs of the king. It does not dare complete [its beauty on its own]. It is the Way of Earth, the Way of the wife, the Way of the minister.

This attitude is now familiar. The Way of the minister is the Way of the wife because both minister and wife are feminine roles complementing the masculine ruler. Similarly, the political philosopher Shen Pu-hai 申不害 (fl. 354–340 B.C.)[137] points out that the sagacious ruler must treat his wives and ministers with the same degree of circumspection.

夫一婦擅夫眾婦皆亂，一臣專君群臣皆蔽。故妒妻不難破家也，亂臣
不難破國也。是以明君使其臣並進輻湊，莫得專君。[138]

When one wife acts on her own responsibility with regard to her husband, the throng of wives all become disorderly. When one minister
monopolizes the lord, the flock of ministers all become deceptive.
Thus a jealous wife can break a family without difficulty; a disorderly
minister can break the state without difficulty. Therefore the enlightened lord makes his ministers advance together like wheel spokes to
a hub; none of them are able to monopolize the ruler.

The later essayist Han Fei 韓非 (d. 233 B.C.) is so comfortable with
this manner of thinking that he does not even distinguish between
the ruler's women and his ministers. They are all "tigers," lurking in
the crevices and awaiting the right moment to rise up against him.

不固其門，虎乃將存。不慎其事，不掩其情，賊乃將生。弒其主，代
其所，人莫不與，故謂之虎。處其主之側，為姦臣，聞其主之忒，故
謂之賊。散其黨，收其餘，閉其門，奪其輔，國乃無虎。大不可量，
深不可測，同合刑名，審驗法式，擅為者誅，國乃無賊。[139]

If you do not secure your gates, tigers will come into being. If you are
not careful about your affairs and do not suppress your emotions, bandits will arise. They slay their rulers, taking their place, with none of
them failing to participate; thus they are called tigers. They dwell by
their ruler's side; they are treacherous[140] ministers, hearing of their
ruler's errors;[141] thus they are called bandits. Disperse their cliques;
gather the rest [onto your side]; shut their gates; and snatch away
their support. Then there will be no tigers in the state. Make your
greatness immeasurable, your depth unfathomable; make "forms and
names" match;[142] investigate and test standards; execute those who act
on their own. Then there will be no bandits in the state.[143]

But as Han Fei writes elsewhere, it is not only treacherous ministers
who are bandits.

且萬乘之主，千乘之君，后妃、夫人、適子為太子者，或有欲其君
之蚤死者。何以知其然？夫妻者，非有骨肉之恩也，愛則親，不愛則
疏。語曰：其母好者其子抱。然則其為之反也，其母惡者其子釋。丈
夫年五十而好色未解也，婦人年三十而美色衰矣。以衰美之婦人事好
色之丈夫，則身見[144]疏賤，而子疑不為後，此后妃、夫人之所以冀其
君之死者也。唯母為后而子為主，則令無不行，禁無不止，男女之樂
不減於先君，而擅萬乘不疑，此鴆毒扼昧之所以用也。[145]

Moreover, whether he is the ruler of [a state with] myriad chariots, or
the lord of [a fiefdom] with a thousand chariots, among his consorts,

wives, and the son whom he has deemed appropriate to be his heir apparent, there will be some who wish for the early death of their lord. How do we know that this is so? Wives do not have the affection of bone and flesh [i.e., they are not related to their husbands by blood]. If he loves them, they are intimate with him; if he does not love them, they are distant. There is a saying: "If the mother is favored, the son is embraced." But its opposite is that if the mother is despised, the son is set loose. When the husband is fifty years old, his fondness for sex has not dissolved; when the wife is thirty years old, her beauty and sex have decayed. If a wife of decaying beauty serves a husband who is fond of sex, then she will be distant and base [in his eyes], and her son will not be likely to be [his father's] successor. This is why consorts and wives hope for their lord's death. If only the mother is made Queen Dowager and her son the next ruler, then none of her commands are not carried out, nothing that she prohibits not caused to cease. Her sexual joy will not be less than with her former lord, and she can manipulate [a state of] myriad chariots without suspicion. These are the uses of poisonings and assassinations.[146]

Han Fei follows the lead of Shen Pu-hai and the authors of the *Lyrics of Ch'u* but extends their imagery to the extreme. In this passage, he has reduced all political questions to a simple calculus of sex. Whichever consort is favored sexually will prosper and see her son anointed as heir, whereupon her opportunity for "sexual joy" 男女之樂 is only increased. "Beauty" 美 is, once again, the most important characteristic for ambitious parties at court, but by "beauty," Han Fei means the beauty of the flesh. The woman who is the most beautiful copulates the most; the woman who copulates the most is the most powerful. There is no room for morality or virtue in Han Fei's worldview, because rulers are more interested in enjoying their women than in questions of ethics and good government. His opinion of palace women is abysmal—they are all merely whores—but, implicitly, his appraisal of the rulers is even worse. They are the lecherous sons of lascivious mothers, who, once on the throne, merely perpetuate the cycle of sexual intrigue by devoting their days and nights to carousing with the next generation of consorts.

This connection between sexual activity and political power came to inform the conception of sexuality that prevailed during the early imperial period. This topic will be the focus of chapter 3. For now, let us observe that the common word for any kind of action by an emperor with regard to one of his inferiors is the same as the word used to describe sexual intercourse with a woman. The word is *yü* 御,

"to drive," as in "to drive a chariot."[147] In its sexual sense, *yü* appears even in ritual texts. The *Record of Rites*, for example, tells us that "even if a concubine is aging, if she is not yet fully fifty years old, one must drive her once every five days" 妾雖老，年未滿五十，必與五日之御.[148] Similarly, that same text notes elsewhere that the ancient kings kept eighty-one *yü-ch'i* 御妻 in their seraglios.[149] *Yü-ch'i* is the lowest rank in the palace hierarchy, and though it is usually understood in the sense of "serving lady" (or the like), literally the title means "drive-wife," that is, a woman available for copulation.[150] But the term *yü* is also frequently encountered in the sense of "imperial," as in *yü-fu* 御服, "imperial robes," or *yü-chu* 御注, "imperial commentary." The connection is explained by Ts'ai Yung 蔡邕 (A.D. 132–192).

> 天子所進曰御。御者，進也。凡衣服加於身，飲食入於口，妃接於寢，皆曰御。[151]

> What the Son of Heaven causes to advance is called *yü*. *Yü* means "to be advanced." Whatever clothing he adds to his body, or drink and food he brings into his mouth, or consorts and concubines he receives in his bedchamber, are all called *yü*.

Every sexual act is thus in some sense a political act, just as every political act is in some sense a sexual act. This is not to say that the people of classical China necessarily thought of the emperor's bed-chamber every time they referred to the imperial chariot or vest-ments. But it is revealing that the word for driving horses is borrowed without further ado to express both the emperor's control of his people and a man's coition with a woman.

Finally, the rich imagery of the *Lyrics of Ch'u* highlight one other cru-cial aspect of the metaphor of copulation in ancient China. Another famous poem in that anthology, "Wandering into the Distance" ("Yüan-yu" 遠遊), takes up much of the same imagery as "Encoun-tering Sorrow" but without the heavy political overtones. "Wander-ing into the Distance" focuses instead on the aesthetic of ascension and astral flight.

悲時俗之迫阨兮	Grieved by the distresses and difficulties of the times and mores,
願輕舉而遠遊	I wish to rise lightly and wander into the distance.
質菲薄而無因兮	But my abilities are exiguous and meager, and I have nothing to rely on.

焉詑乘而上浮[152]	How could I employ a carriage and float up?
… …	…
奇傅說之詑辰星	I marvel at how Fu Yüeh became a star in a constellation.
羨韓眾之得一	I admire Han Chung for having attained the One.[153]
形穆穆以浸遠兮	Their bodies began to fade as they became immersed in the distance.
離人群而遁逸	They left the throng of humanity and became hidden and lost.
因氣變而遂曾舉兮	They complied with the transformations of matter and then rose up high,
忽神奔而鬼怪	with the sudden fleeing of a spirit and the strangeness of a ghost.
時髣髴以遙見兮	At times they are seen vaguely and distantly.[154]
精皎皎以往來[155]	Their essence is brilliant as they come and go.

The poem then continues in a manner reminiscent of "Encountering Sorrow." The speaker is distressed at the passage of time. He engages in certain practices intended to forestall death and meets a shaman or diviner, who gives him words of encouragement. Thereupon he begins his celestial journey.

聞至貴而遂徂兮	I hear this supremely precious [advice] and then go ahead.
忽乎吾將行	Oh, suddenly I begin to go.
仍羽人於丹丘兮	I come upon feathered people at Cinnabar Hill.
留不死之舊鄉[156]	I stay in the old home of immortality.

As he passes from place to place, visiting gods and fantastic sites, more and more beings join his train.

風伯為余先驅兮	The Earl of Wind charges before us in the van,
氛埃辟而清涼	removing the vapor and dust to make it clear and cool.
鳳凰翼其承旂兮	Phoenixes form our flank, bearing banners.
遇蓐收乎西皇[157]	We happen upon Ju-shou in the Western Empyrean.

The speaker and his escort continue to ascend, passing out of the realm of geography into the world of Heaven—and then beyond Heaven too, into the primordial place describable only in the vaguest of abstractions.

經營四荒兮	We pass through the Four Wildernesses.
周流六漠	We flow around the Six Deserts.
上至列缺兮	We arrive up to the Crack of Lightning.[158]
降望大壑	We gaze down at the Great Gully.
下崢嶸而無地兮	Below, it is majestic, and there is no Earth.
上寥廓而無天	Above, it is vast, and there is no Heaven.
視儵忽而無見兮	I look, but quickly there is nothing to be seen.
惝怳而無聞	In the agitated flurry, there is nothing to be heard.
超無為以至清兮	We transcend Non-Action and arrive at Clarity.
與泰初而為鄰[159]	I am a neighbor of the Magnificent Beginning.

And with the "Magnificent Beginning" 泰初, the poem ends. The speaker has attained the immortality that he has been seeking from the very beginning.

It has been pointed out that "Wandering into the Distance" shares certain basic features with shamanic incantations that have been preserved in ethnographic literature.[160] The idea of ascending the heavens with the aid of friendly beasts, so striking in "Wandering into the Distance," is by all accounts a fundamental characteristic of shamanism.[161] Moreover, the portrayal of the ascension as occurring in stages is a richly attested shamanic motif. In "Wandering into the Distance," the speaker rises from level to level, ever higher, recounting the sights and sounds that he experiences along the way. Similarly, an Altaic shaman, after a successful entreaty to the Celestial Bird, cries out,

I have ascended one step.
　　Aikhai! Aikhai!
I have reached one celestial region.
　　Šagarbata!
I have climbed up to the summit of the *tapty!*
　　Šagarbata!
I have raised myself up to the full moon!
　　Šagarbata!

Then he recites the following as he rises up another level.

I have crossed the second stage;
I have ascended the second step.
... the third ... [etc.][162]

This comparison between "Wandering into the Distance" and the oration of an Altaic shaman is not intended to suggest that the authors of *Lyrics of Ch'u* were necessarily shamans. On the contrary, it is important to remember that the speaker of "Wandering into the Distance" ends his poem in the misty regions of the outer universe, without ever having had any intention of returning from his voyage to earth. Real shamans, on the other hand, must always come back to their communities after completing their spirit journeys, because they serve as the crucial link between the terrestrial and the celestial spheres.[163] The *Lyrics of Ch'u* merely apply shamanic motifs to literary effect.

The shamanic dimensions in these poems help explain why sexual activity is recommended in many ancient texts as an exercise conducive to one's health. For the speaker of "Wandering into the Distance," rising up to Heaven like a shaman is the sign that one has become a *hsien* 仙, or someone who has attained immortality. Similarly, a recently excavated sex manual called *Joining Yin and Yang* (*Ho yin-yang* 合陰陽) depicts the act of coition in the form of a "wandering" across the geography of the human body, progressing in stages from arousal, through foreplay, to orgasm and cosmic harmony.

凡將合陰陽之方。
握手，出捥陽。
肘房。
抵掖旁。
上灶綱。
抵領鄉。
揗承匡。
覆周環。
下缺盆。
過醴津。
陵勃海。
上常山。
入玄門。
御交筋。
上欲精神。
乃能久視而與天地存。[164]

The recipe for whenever you will be conjoining Yin and Yang:
Grip the hands, and emerge at the Yang side of the wrists;
Stroke the elbow chambers;
Press the side of the underarms;
Ascend the stove trivet;
Press the neck zone;
Stroke the receiving canister;
Cover the encircling ring;

Descend the broken basin;
Cross the sweet-liquor ford;
Skim the Spurting Sea;
Ascend Constancy Mountain;
Enter the dark gate;
Ride the coital muscle;
Suck the essence and spirit upward.
Then you can have enduring vision and exist in unison with heaven
    and earth.[165]

Florid phrases like the "Spurting Sea" 勃海 and "Constancy
Mountain" 常山 are technical names for parts of the female body.
Some are better understood than others; as we have seen, the "receiving canister" 承匡 (or "receiving basket") is a name for the vagina
that appears even in the *Odes*.[166] The reader of this manual (which is
evidently intended solely for men) is told that he can "exist in unison
with heaven and earth" precisely because he has sucked "the essence
and spirit upward." Sex with women constitutes a form of nourish-
ment for men because they can draw in the woman's *yin* essence
while driving the "coital muscle" 交筋. In that respect, copulation
serves as a form of food, once again echoing a theme prevalent in
the *Odes*. Moreover, the understanding of coitus as a form of carnal
wandering—from places like the "stove trivet" to the "encircling ring"
—recalls the hierogamy of poems like "The Lesser Administrator of
Fate." "Lord," says the speaker in that piece, "whom do you await at
the edge of the clouds? / I will wander with you to the Nine Rivers."
By wandering with her lord or god, the enchantress draws him near
and copulates with him, just as the practitioner of *Joining Yin and
Yang* wanders across the body of his mate, visiting the sites along the
way to the "receiving basket." The female body is thus conceived as a
universe of its own, a place where one can wander like a shaman tra-
versing the sky.

This conception of sex is the Yangist answer to figures like Han
Fei.[167] Both parties see sex as an avenue to power, but for those with
no interest in politics, power means neither dominating the court
nor seeing one's son installed as Heir-Apparent, but bodily health
and, if possible, immortality. Health and immortality, furthermore,
entail rising up to Heaven like a shaman or a *hsien* unfettered by the
impediments of mundane life. For those who followed the prescriptions of *Joining Yin and Yang*, copulation was godly; for when one is
copulating, one is emulating the immortals.

2

Women and Sex Roles

It has become something of a scholarly commonplace to criticize traditional Chinese thought—and especially traditional Confucian thought—for its repressive and deprecating stereotypes of women.[1] Indeed, there appears to be no shortage of textual justification for this point of view. We have already seen the different descriptions in the *Odes* of the treatment of infant boys and girls: the boys cry lustily as they play with their toy scepters, whereas the girls instead receive little pieces of clay in order to establish their subordinate status.[2] Similarly, other poems in the *Odes* depict vividly the chaos that must ensue when women have too much influence over political affairs. Consider the oft-cited example of "I See on High" ("Chan-yang" 瞻卬).[3]

人有土田	People had land and fields
女反有之	but you possess them.
人有民人[4]	People had followers
女覆奪之	but you seize them.
此宜無罪	This one is properly without guilt
女反收之	but you arrest him.
彼宜有罪	That one is properly with guilt
女覆說之	but you set him loose.
哲夫成城	A clever man completes a city;
哲婦傾城	a clever woman overturns a city.
懿厥哲婦	Alas, that clever woman!
為梟為鴟	She is a *hsiao*-bird;[5] she is an owl.
婦有長舌	Women have long tongues.
維厲之階	They are the foundation of cruelty.

亂匪降自天	Disorder does not descend from Heaven.
生自婦人	It is born of woman.
匪教匪誨	There is no one to instruct or admonish [the king]
時維婦寺	because those who attend him are always women.[6]

鞫人忮忒	They exhaust others; they are jealous and fickle.
譖始竟背	At first they slander; in the end they turn their backs [on authority].
豈曰不極	Will you say it is not so extreme?
伊胡為慝	Oh, how they are wicked!
如賈三倍	They are like merchants who make a threefold profit.
君子是識	The noble man knows this.
婦無公事	There is no public service for women.
休其蠶織	They stay with their silkworms and weaving.

(*Mao* 264: "Chan-yang")

These stanzas are evidently addressed to a ruler whose domain is in complete disorder. The innocent are arrested, the guilty set free, and the people deprived of their land and livelihood. As we go on to read, all the problems stem from the fact that the ruler surrounds himself with women. The word *ju* 女 in the first stanza can be interpreted in at least two ways. One the one hand, it can easily mean "you" (in the sense of *ju* 汝)—that is, the addressee who dispossesses the people. However, there is no reason the character cannot also be read *nü*, "woman." For ultimately it is the women who, having left their proper place behind the loom, begin to meddle with affairs of state and steal the wealth of the people. The ambiguity of the character 女 may even represent a subtle accusation that the real rulers of the land are the king's destructive women.

What women is the poem referring to? It is never clear whether the designation is singular or plural, one woman or many. There is a brief reference to a certain "clever woman" 哲婦 who brings down a clever man's work, but then the poem lapses into contexts in which the female sex is clearly intended generally: "Women have long tongues" 婦有長舌; "There is no public service for women" 婦無公事; and so on.

Later commentators have attempted to take this poem as the work of one Earl of Fan 凡伯, criticizing his lord, the King Yu of Chou 周幽王 (r. 781–771 B.C.), and the king's concubine, Pao Ssu 褒姒 (or Ssu of Pao).[7] Pao Ssu was a petulant girl of supposedly miraculous birth who manipulated the benighted King Yu, finally persuading him to set aside his rightful queen and designate her own son as heir apparent. But this fateful stratagem proved shortsighted, for Pao Ssu was imprisoned when the Marquis of Shen 申侯, the queen's father, killed King Yu and set in his place the queen's son, who is known to history as King P'ing 平王 (r. 770–720 B.C.). Many of the later traditions surrounding Pao Ssu are manifestly romanticized. We are told, for example, that there was a system of alarm beacons that the king would use to summon his vassals to battle; King Yu would repeatedly light these beacons in vain because it amused Pao Ssu to see the feudal lords rushing to the rescue but finding no enemy. Unfortunately, the King tried this trick so often that, by the time of the climactic battle with the Marquis of Shen, none of the king's allies heeded the alarm beacons, and so he was overpowered quickly.[8] This story is, in other words, the ancient Chinese counterpart of our "Little Boy Who Cried 'Wolf!'"

In spite of these suspicious details, however, there may have been some kernel of truth to the story, which must originally have been the tale of a fierce succession dispute. The Marquis of Shen wished to see his grandson crowned as King of Chou; the king himself had other ideas. But with the increasing weakness of the Chou throne in the eighth century, it turned out that the Marquis of Shen had enough military might to realize his ambition. The affair served as a harbinger of times to come. From this point on, real administrative power in Chou China would lie with feudal lords in the mold of the Marquis of Shen.[9] So if the Earl of Fan really did write "I See on High," we can appreciate the momentous concerns of the poem. King Yu was endangering the political order by doting on that "clever woman" who wished only to "overturn a city" 傾城. According to the author, it is dangerous for the ruler to surround himself with female attendants because women are not naturally suited to affairs of government. They are "jealous and fickle" 忮忒 and are properly left at home to tend to sericulture.

The Earl of Fan's point would be not that all women are inherently wicked—only those who, like Pao Ssu, scheme to alter the line of succession and thereby bring on catastrophes that they cannot have thought through. And of course King Yu himself is ultimately to blame for everything; for it is he who has failed to keep his women in their appropriate place. I believe an interpretation along these lines is warranted for several reasons. Most important, other passages in the *Odes* and other canonical works do not represent women as uniformly wicked and conspiratorial. On the contrary, as we shall see, the nature of men and women and their proper sex roles is acknowledged in these texts to be one of the most difficult problems in philosophy.

Moreover, Pao Ssu is mentioned by name elsewhere in the *Odes*, so we know that her legacy was indeed prominent in the authors' minds.

心之憂矣	The sorrow of my heart
如或結之	is as though someone tied it.
今茲之正	This ruler now—
胡然厲矣	how can he be so cruel?
燎之方揚	The flames, as they rise—
寧或滅之	will someone extinguish them?
赫赫宗周	The majestic capital of Chou—
襃姒威之	Pao Ssu destroyed it.

(*Mao* 192: "Cheng-yüeh" 正月)

Several rhetorical features of this stanza invite the reader to compare it to "I See on High." Most noticeably, the reference at the end to "the majestic capital of Chou" 赫赫宗周 recalls the "city" 城 that the clever man completed and the clever woman overturned. Furthermore, the ruler here is described as *li* 厲, "cruel," evoking the line, "They are/She is the foundation of cruelty" 維厲之階 in "I See on High." Finally, it is not farfetched to observe the structural similarity of the rhetorical question, *hu-jan li i* 胡然厲矣, "How can he be so cruel?" and the exclamation *i hu-wei t'e* 伊胡為慝, "Oh, how they are wicked!" which appears in "I See on High." So we cannot simply dismiss the assertion of the commentators that "I See on High" refers specifically to King Yu and his concubine. It is a very plausible reading in the context of the *Odes*. And they were certainly right, in any case, that "I See on High" has to do with destructive women who are granted undue influence over royal affairs and does not necessarily promote the idea that all women are wicked and destructive by nature.

Furthermore, the poem appears in a section of the *Odes* that includes a number of poems contrasting the prosperous and blessed reigns of virtuous rulers with the harsh and blighted reigns of rulers who neglect their Mandate 命. A common figure in the poems is the ruler who does not tend to the "king's business" 王業 but indulges himself in women and drink.

無競維人	Does he not exert himself, he who is humane?[10]
四方其訓之	Are the four quarters not instructed by him?
有覺德行	Sensing his virtuous conduct,
四國順之	the four regions obey him.
訏謨定命	With grandiloquent counsel he confirms his Mandate.
遠猶辰告	With farsighted plans and timely announcements
敬慎威儀	he is reverently cautious about his awesome deportment.
維民之則 、	He is a pattern for the people.
其在于今	The one of today
興迷亂于政	is aroused and seduced by disorder in government.
顛覆厥德	He overturns his own power.
荒湛于酒	He abandons and dissipates himself in wine.
女雖湛樂從	You devote yourself only to dissipated pleasures.
弗念厥紹	You do not ponder your lineage.
罔敷求先王	Why do you not apply yourself to seeking the [Way of the] former kings
克共明刑	so that you could hold fast to their enlightened law?

(*Mao* 256: "I" 抑)

These two stanzas illustrate the difference between a ruler who cultivates his "power" (*te* 德) and one who "overturns" 顛覆 it. The "power" is the quality that a ruler obtains through his pious obedience to Heaven and tireless efforts to effect virtuous government on earth.[11] "The one of today" 其在于今, whom later commentators identify as King Li of Chou 周厲王 (r. 857/853–842/828),[12] turns his back on the ancient practice of his ancestors ("You do not ponder your lineage" 弗念厥紹) and spends all his energy in dissolute pleasures. The poem delineates two paths that a ruler can follow. He can dedicate himself to "enlightened law" 明刑 and thereby cause his subjects in all quarters of the realm to submit of their own will, thus confirming his Mandate. This path, however, is the more difficult of the two; the ruler must be prepared to "exert himself" 競. Or the ruler can simply waste his days in debauchery, like King Yu with his concubine. Words like "seduced" 迷 and "pleasures" 樂 merely hint at the sexual nature of the king's excesses. Unlike "I See on High," the present poem does not mention the destructive women directly. For the proper object of blame is unquestionably the ruler himself.

These poems from the *Odes* highlight some of the problems in assessing references to women in classical Chinese texts. The bipolar discourse of virtuous government versus immoderate licentiousness is so basic to the political consciousness of the literature that the mere mention of women at the royal level is often intended to evoke a king who has failed to consider his priorities. But it would be a mistake to take the manifold, and indeed stereotyped, images of "long-tongued" women as an authorial attitude that can be extended to cover all women. After all, the *Odes* contain at least as many references to virtuous women whose moral perfection contributes to the flourishing of the age. A favorite heroine is the mother of King Wen 文王, the founder of the Chou dynasty.

摯仲氏任	Jen, the second princess of Chih,[13]
自彼殷商	from that Yin-Shang,
來嫁于周	came to marry in Chou.
曰嬪于京	Oh, she became his wife in the capital.
乃及王季	And she, with King Chi,
維德之行	acted only with virtue.[14]
大任有身	T'ai Jen became pregnant
生此文王	and bore this King Wen.

維此文王	This King Wen
小心翼翼	was circumspect and reverent.
昭事上帝	Brilliantly he served [the god] Ti Above.
聿懷多福	Thereupon he caused many blessings to arrive.
厥德不回	His power was never refractory.
以受方國	Thus he received the surrounding states.

(*Mao* 236: "Ta Ming" 大明)

T'ai Jen was the second princess of Chih, a state within the realm of the Yin or Shang overlord. She married King Chi of Chou and gave him a son, the future King Wen. The phrase *nai chi wang Chi* 乃及王季, "and she, with King Chi," emphasizes that her own virtuous conduct contributed to the brilliant success of her husband and son. Similarly, another poem in the sequence praises King Wen's mother for her relationship to her mother-in-law and daughter-in-law.

思齊大任	Ah, reverent was T'ai Jen,
文王之母	the mother of King Wen!
思媚周姜	Ah, loving was she to Chiang of Chou,
京室之婦	the woman of the royal chamber!

大姒嗣徽音   T'ai Ssu inherited her excellent reputation.
則百斯男   Thus her sons were numerous.

(*Mao* 240: "Ssu chai" 思齊)

Chiang of Chou is T'ai Chiang, the mother of King Chi. Thus the poem lauds T'ai Jen for treating her mother-in-law with respect, which has always been a principal duty of a wife in traditional China. T'ai Ssu was King Wen's wife; she is also praised in the collection for her womanly virtues.[15] In the word *tse* 則 ("thus"), the poem takes pains to point out that T'ai Ssu was able to bear her many sons and continue the Chou line precisely because she followed in the exalted footsteps of her own mother-in-law. Thus T'ai Jen played a pivotal role in the history of the Chou lineage: she honored her mother-in-law, as was appropriate, and then influenced her daughter-in-law to carry on the noble tradition of the Chou wives. These poems assert that the women of Chou played a critical role alongside their husbands in the establishment of the dynasty. T'ai Jen and T'ai Ssu are hardly "long-tongued" vixens like Pao Ssu who conspire to disrupt the royal line. They are the exact opposite: chaste and industrious women who lay the foundations for the splendid accomplishments of their husbands and descendants.[16]

To be sure, such poems seem to allow for female virtue within very narrow boundaries. Women earn recognition only when they excel at their allotted sex roles of wife and mother. Female paragons such as T'ai Jen and T'ai Ssu are singled out precisely because they prove helpful to their husbands and sons. Nowhere in the *Odes* do we find women praised for artistic or intellectual accomplishments, and even their moral attainments are never explained in any detail. Of T'ai Jen we know only that she shared in her husband's virtue, honored her mother-in-law, and impressed her daughter-in-law with her conduct. Of T'ai Ssu we know even less: she learned from her mother-in-law's example and bore many talented sons. It is with this background in mind that scholars often impugn Confucian education for concentrating solely on training females to "meet the demands of motherhood and household management."[17]

Even this assessment, however, does not tell the entire story. It is important to remember that the fulfillment of one's social role represents one of the most estimable human accomplishments in the context of Confucian philosophy. This is no less true of men than it is of women.[18] Confucius himself, for example, is said in the *Application of Equilibrium* (*Chung-yung* 中庸) to have declared:

君子之道四，丘未能一焉。所求乎子以事父，未能也。所求乎臣以事君，未能也。所求乎弟以事兄，未能也。所求乎朋友以先施之，未能也。[19]

There are four [elements of] the Way of the noble man of which I have not been able to accomplish one. I have not been able to serve my father as I require of my son. I have not been able to serve my lord as I require of my servant. I have not been able to serve my elder brother as I require of my younger brother. I have not been able to undertake first for my friends what I require of them.[20]

Since the *Application of Equilibrium* is a relatively late work, these cannot be taken as the genuine words of Confucius, but the duty to behave toward others as one would want them to behave toward oneself represents one of the cornerstones of the Confucian tradition. This is precisely what Confucius meant by *shu* 恕 (reciprocity) in the *Analects*.[21] So by acting like model wives and mothers, women such as T'ai Jen and T'ai Ssu actually discharged their ethical duties more successfully than Confucius himself, who considered himself imperfect as son, brother, subject, and friend. Let us keep in mind also that Confucius considers the moral obligations of those of lower social status more difficult than those of their superiors. It is in his behavior as son, subject, and younger brother—and not as father, lord, and elder brother—that Confucius finds reason to chastise himself. How much more difficult would he have found the job of wife and daughter-in-law, at the very bottom of the domestic hierarchy? Knowing his own failings despite his relatively privileged position, Confucius can only have admired T'ai Jen and T'ai Ssu's virtue all the more; therefore we must take care not to underestimate the magnitude of these heroines' achievements in the minds of classical readers.

And it is indisputable that Confucius placed women at the very bottom of the domestic hierarchy, as in the following infamous comment.

子曰：唯女子與小人為難養也，近之則不孫，遠之則怨。[22]

The Master said: Only women and petty men are difficult to nourish. If you are familiar with them, they become insubordinate; if you are distant from them, they complain.[23]

Like "I See on High," this quote from Confucius is frequently cited in the recent literature as the quintessential expression of the Master's sexism.[24] He compares women to "petty men" 小人, or the antithesis of the Confucian moral ideal of the "noble man" (*chün-tzu* 君子). The charge that they are "difficult to nourish" 難養 is more severe than is commonly recognized. It does not mean simply that women and petty men are difficult to handle. "Nourishing" frequently has a philosophical or pedagogical component in Confucian parlance (as when Mencius speaks of "nourishing the mind" 養心, for example);[25] so Confucius may in fact be questioning women's ability to grow in an intellectual sense. The consequences of this passage are considerable. Self-cultivation is the foundation of Confucian ethics, and if Confucius means to say that women are physiologically unable to learn and improve themselves, then he has effectively excluded them from the Confucian project. If Confucius believes that women cannot participate in moral discourse, it is unclear how he distinguishes them from animals. From the point of view of the later thinker Mencius, "petty men" is what we call all those who fail to cultivate their minds, thereby obscuring the slight difference that exists between humans and animals.[26] Where women belong in this scheme is problematic.[27]

Commentators have sometimes tried to soften the impact of Confucius' utterance in a number of ways. One of the oldest methods seems to have been to read the phrase *nü-tzu yü hsiao-jen* 女子與小人 as nothing more than a reference to male and female servants.[28] But there are many other expressions that Confucius might have used had he so intended his saying; it is difficult to ignore the usual connotations of *hsiao-jen* as men who are morally, and not socially, inferior. Another recent attempt to "rehabilitate" the quote takes 女 in 女子 as an alternate form of *ju* 汝, "you" (we encountered this usage above, in the context of "I See on High"); thus "Only your children and petty men are difficult to nourish."[29] The obvious problem with this reading—aside from the fact that this is not how Confucius' statement was ever understood—is that it is a complete mystery whose "children" Confucius would be talking about. Finally, chapter 17 of the *Analects*, where this statement occurs, is part of a section at the end of the book that scholars have long suspected might be spurious. One suggestion places the chapter around 270 B.C., or more than two centuries after Confucius' death.[30] So Confucius might never have said such problematic things about women after all.

Two points about this passage are not often observed. First, Confucius says that women are *difficult* to nourish, not that they *cannot* be nourished, and the Confucian mode of self-cultivation is not exactly easy for men, either. Later thinkers, such as Hsün-tzu, would go on to emphasize just how difficult it is for anyone to become a "noble man."[31] Furthermore, Confucius made other, more important statements about women. Elsewhere in the *Analects*, he points out that an exceptional woman can be just as talented as an exceptional man:[32]

舜有臣五人而天下治。武王曰：予有亂臣十人。孔子曰：才難，不其然乎？唐虞之際，於斯為盛。有婦人焉，九人而已。[33]

Shun had five ministers and the world was ordered. King Wu [of Chou, r. 1049/1045–1043 B.C.][34] said: I have ten ministers who make order. Confucius said: Is it not so that talent is rare? The era after[35] T'ang and Yü [i.e., the sages Yao 堯 and Shun] flourished to this extent. There was a woman among them, so there were no more than nine men.[36]

The early commentator Huang K'an 皇侃 (A.D. 488–545) fastened onto the significance of this passage. He understands the "woman among them" as Wen-mu 文母, "The Refined Mother" (probably T'ai Ssu),[37] and says,

又明言有婦人者，明周代之盛，匪唯丈夫之才，抑婦人之能匡弼於政化也。[38]

Moreover, when he clearly says, "there was a woman," this is to make clear that the flourishing of the Chou was not due only to the men's talent; the abilities of the women also assisted in the transformation of their government.

Whether or not Huang K'an is right that "woman" refers specifically to T'ai Ssu, his general conclusion, which is in line with the admiring view of T'ai Ssu that we have seen in the *Odes*, cannot be far removed from Confucius' intended lesson. The main thrust of the passage is that talent is exceedingly rare and potent. The offhanded comment that one of King Wu's ministers was a woman is made to show that there were not even ten capable men serving the dynasty at the time, and yet it was an era of unparalleled moral excellence. But Confucius' argument rests on an idea that is even more revolutionary, namely, the unspoken assumption that a woman could take her place alongside the most capable men in the world.

This extraordinary woman, moreover, is singled out not for her virtuous behavior as wife or mother but as one who contributed to the flourishing of an entire era. If indeed Confucius was thinking of T'ai Ssu, it is doubtless the case that he would have considered her virtuous behavior as wife and mother to have been an essential part of that contribution. But it is a form of virtuous behavior that is taken seriously for its power to effect moral government. A model wife and mother is not simply a woman who silently obeys her husband and gently nurtures her son, but one who participates in bringing about the kind of universal moral transformation that the Confucian tradition upholds as the ultimate purpose of humanity.

Thus Confucius may have considered women "difficult to nourish," but he emphatically did not believe that they were incapable of moral self-cultivation. On the contrary, he placed the most cultivated women, rare though they were, on a level no lower than that of the most cultivated men. These points come out especially clearly in the following saying, also attributed to Confucius:

女知莫若婦，男知莫若夫。公父氏之婦智也夫！欲明其子之令德。[39]

A girl's knowledge is not like that of a woman; a boy's knowledge is not like that of a man. The wisdom of the woman of the Kung-fu clan is like that of a man![40] She desired to make clear her son's estimable virtue.

This passage is from the *Discourses of the States* (*Kuo-yü* 國語), a collection closely related to the *Tso-chuan* and dating from approximately 300 B.C.[41] Given the source, we might be reluctant to treat this as a genuine statement from the mouth of the Master, but it is still representative of the Confucian tradition in its earliest stages, and the idea that it articulates is not inconsistent with what we have heard from Confucius in the *Analects*. The "woman of the Kung-fu clan" 公父氏之婦 is Lady Ching 敬姜, who was the mother of Kung-fu Ch'u 公父歜 (better known as Kung-fu Wen-po 文伯), a high official in the state of Lu 魯. She is praised by Confucius or one of his disciples in the *Discourses of the States* on no fewer than six occasions.[42] In this passage, Confucius has heard the instruction that she has given her son's concubines after his death. She has told them not to weep or grieve demonstratively for her son but to "follow the rites and be silent" 從禮而靜, lest it be said of him that he was fond of household pleasures.[43]

Perhaps Lady Ching and Confucius both made too much of this affair—they may strike us as excessively concerned with appearances—but the episode is valuable for our purposes because of the light that it sheds on early Confucian views of women. In the prefatory comment "a girl's knowledge is not like that of a woman" 女知莫若婦, Confucius implies that a girl can grow intellectually as she matures. The statement confirms again that women are not barred by the tradition from the lifelong journey of self-cultivation. Furthermore, Confucius asserts that the wisdom of Kung-fu Wen-po's mother is like that of a man, showing once again that he thinks women can be as wise as men. Granted, it is only an exceptional woman who earns such praise; but it is no less true that Confucius is characteristically interested only in exceptional people, never the run-of-the-mill. He does not mince words when criticizing men whom he considers mediocre and unconscientious.[44]

Lady Ching's concerns about her son's reputation highlight another crucial theme in early discussions of women.

> 吾聞之：好內，女死之；好外，士死之。今吾子夭死，吾惡其以好內聞也。[45]

> I have heard: If a man loves the inner, women die for him. If he loves the outer, men die for him.[46] Now my son has died young; I would hate for others to hear of him on account of his love of the inner.

This distinction between "the inner" (*nei* 內) and "the outer" (*wai* 外) informed much of the traditional Chinese discourse concerning the difference between women and men.[47] In this particular passage, it seems clear enough what Kung-fu Wen-po's mother means: "the inner" refers to the women in his household, "the outer" to the business of governmental administration that her son undertook outside his home. But the precise contours of this dichotomy are difficult to reconstruct. In effect, the terms *nei* and *wai* come to refer to women and men, respectively, but the reasoning behind these associations is complex and indeed varies from text to text as well as from period to period.[48]

In this sense, *nei* seems to have originally denoted the interior area of a domicile, where the women of the household had their apartments. Consequently, it often means "harem." Thus, for example, the "Minor Official of the Interior" 內小臣 is listed in the *Rites of Chou* (*Chou-li* 周禮) as the one who "handles the commands of the royal queens" 掌王后之命.[49] Similarly, *i-nei* 易內, "to exchange interiors," appears as a euphemism for wife swapping among elite men.

> 齊慶封好田而耆酒，與慶舍政，則以其內實遷于盧蒲嫳氏，易內而飲酒。[50]

Ch'ing Feng[51] of Ch'i loved hunting and was fond of drink. He gave over the government to [his son] Ch'ing She,[52] and then moved with his harem and valuables to Lu-p'u Pi's house. They exchanged interiors and drank wine.[53]

Given these connotations, we can empathize with Mother Kung-fu's wish that her son not be remembered for his "love of the interior." Ch'ing Feng was just the kind of wastrel from whose image she was trying to distance her family name.[54]

As a term that referred to women in their role as consorts to men, *nei* came to be used generally for anything and everything that was considered appropriate for women, especially in contrast to *wai*, which was considered appropriate for men. Thus "Males do not speak of *nei*; females do not speak of *wai*" 男不言內，女不言外.[55] But this distribution of the terms according to gender is precisely where the ambiguities arise, because not everyone agreed as to what is appropriate—or inappropriate—for women. Most later writers routinely took *wai* to refer to politics, as, for example, when the Han official Yang Chen 楊震 (d. A.D. 124) presented to the emperor several august precedents establishing that "women ought not participate in government affairs" 言婦人不得與於政事也.[56] This understanding of the difference between *nei* and *wai* appears to conform to that of Kung-fu Wen-po's mother, who wants her son's memory to be honored for his political accomplishments. Any other reputation would not befit his manhood.

These nuances of *nei* and *wai* suggest that for a man to be "fond of the inner" does not simply constitute a moral failing; it is fundamentally *unmanly*. *Nei* is the province of women, and a man who spends too much time in the interior apartments is a man who is devoted to womanly pursuits.[57] The potential consequences of this view are manifold. Most immediately, there is the inescapable implication that excessive sexual desire—like that of Ch'ing Feng, who went everywhere with his harem and abdicated his responsibilities as a politician—is somehow essential to women and effeminate in men.[58] That is to say, it is unseemly in either sex, but it is more basic to women's nature, because they are creatures of the "interior." For we find precisely this opinion expressed without reservation in certain passages in the classics that approach outright misogyny.

The *Tso-chuan*, for example, records an event dated to 636 B.C. King Hsiang of Chou 周襄王 (r. 651–619 B.C.), grateful to a nation

known as the Ti 狄 for military assistance, proposed to take one of
their women as his queen. His minister objected.

富辰諫曰：不可。臣聞之曰：報者倦矣，施者未厭。狄固貪惏，王又
啟之。女德無極，婦怨無終，狄必為患。[59]

Fu Ch'en remonstrated, saying: You cannot. I have heard: "When
the one who rewards has become weary, the one who [is rewarded for
his] actions is still not satisfied." The Ti are covetous and greedy, yet
Your Majesty begins [to appease them]. Female *te* is without limit; the
complaints of women are without end. The Ti will surely become a
vexation.[60]

In this "remonstrance," Fu Ch'en avails himself of three convenient tropes: rewarding a subordinate can be dangerous for an overlord; the Ti are covetous and greedy; and women are creatures of
limitless sexual desire—for this is what he means by "female *te*" 女德,
as we shall see presently. This speech is not a shining example of
ancient Chinese rhetoric. By the first argument, a ruler should never
reward anyone, because the vague warning that one who is rewarded
will never be satisfied can be applied to any circumstance whatsoever.
Similarly, in denigrating the Ti for their greed and covetousness, Fu
Ch'en is merely expressing a vulgar form of cultural bigotry; in fact,
the Chou king's Chinese vassals were hardly less eager to expand
their wealth at their lord's expense.

And the final plank in his argument is the least effective of all.
What is the relevance of his conviction that women's desires are
limitless and their complaints ceaseless? Does Fu Ch'en mean to
suggest that the king should not marry at all for that reason? Fu
Ch'en's use of this theme may belie the fact that he has not even convinced himself; for if he truly believes that all women are nothing
more than vexatious containers of unbridled sexual energy, he
should have reconciled himself long ago to the necessary evil of
marrying women for the sake of procreation. There is no forensic
reason to bring up the issue now; he could just as well complain
about any other disappointing but immutable fact of life. Perhaps he
means to suggest that Ti women are even more licentious than normal women, but he does not make the point explicitly. It is more
likely that he is simply repeating a readily available stereotype that he
hopes will dissuade the King, if only momentarily, from entertaining
thoughts of marriage.

What is "female *te*"? The phrase is used revealingly in a diagnosis performed by one Physician Ho 醫和. Lord P'ing of Chin 晉平公 (r. 557–532 B.C.) is suffering from a certain malady, which the learned doctor identifies immediately as *ku* 蠱, or the disease that arises when one "keeps males at a distance and brings females close" 遠男而近女. The disease is incurable. When later asked to elaborate, the doctor remarks that the only way to mitigate the ravages of *ku* is to surround oneself with "male *te*" and "diminish female *te* at night" 宵靜女德. In practical terms, this means surrounding oneself with male advisors and not sleeping so frequently with women.[61] So we might translate "female *te*" as "female potency," the innate sexual power of females that can enfeeble a man if he copulates with them excessively.[62]

This view of women as sexually insatiable beings became widespread in later periods of Chinese history.[63] We have already seen Han Fei's discussion of palace women, which is based on the presupposition that they are interested in nothing other than satisfying their lust. The logical conclusion of this trend came in the eleventh century, when Ou-yang Hsiu 歐陽修 (1007–1070) declared that "females are nothing more than sex" 女，色而已.[64] But such passages are purely chauvinistic, because the more reflective thinkers of the ancient period admitted frankly that sexual desire was a basic problem in men as well.

For example, "female potency" is sometimes used even by women to refer to sexual pleasure.

> 重耳曰：人生安樂，孰知其他！必死於此，不能去。齊女曰：子一國公子，窮而來此，數士者以子為命。子不疾反國，報勞臣，而懷女德，竊為子羞之。[65]

> Ch'ung-erh [i.e., the future Lord Wen of Chin 晉文公, r. 635–627 B.C.] said: Human life is peaceful and pleasant; what else is there to know? I am resolved to die here [i.e., in exile in Ch'i]; I cannot go. The girl of Ch'i [i.e., his wife, the daughter of Lord Huan of Ch'i 齊桓公, r. 685–643 B.C.] said: You are the Noble Son of a state. When you came here in straitened circumstances, your numerous warriors took you as their destiny. You do not hasten to return to your state and reward your toiling vassals, but cherish female potency. I am ashamed on your account.

In this little lecture, the future Lord Wen is upbraided by his sagacious wife for neglecting the serious, manly business of claiming his rightful place as ruler of Chin, and enjoying instead the "peace and

pleasure" 安樂 of his wife's sex. But it is Ch'ung-erh, and not his
wife, who is to blame for frittering away his life. When the girl of Ch'i
refers to "female potency," then, she means not voracious sexual
appetite on her part but her natural sexual allure, which her husband has been enjoying in excess. She is "ashamed" 羞 on his account precisely because she does not wish to be known unjustly as a
sexually destructive woman who sapped her husband's vital energy
and prevented him from establishing his name. Her husband has
been harming his reputation all by himself.

This very anecdote may have been the background to a famous
saying of Confucius that appears twice in the *Analects*.

子曰：吾未見好德如好色者也。[66]

The Master said: I have yet to see anyone who loves virtue as much as
sex.[67]

Here Confucius is decisively using the term *te* in the ethical sense
that we have seen anticipated in the *Odes*, as the moral power that
one attains through virtuous conduct. Simply put, the problem is
one of conflicting *te*. Everyone is naturally enticed by the pleasures of
sexual potency but all must learn to rein in these desires and strive
for the moral potency that is the hallmark of a cultivated person.

This theme of transcending one's sexual appetite in order to lead
a moral life is basic to early Confucianism. Consider, for example,
this question posed by Mencius.

踰東家牆而摟其處子則得妻，不摟則不得妻，則將摟之乎 ?[68]

If you could get a wife by passing over the wall of the house to your
east and dragging off [your neighbor's] virgin child, but could not get
a wife if you did not drag her off, would you drag her off?[69]

The question is never answered. Mencius' interlocutor is supposed
to answer forthwith that he would rather forgo the pleasures of a wife
than drag off his neighbor's virgin daughter. The context is a discussion of ritual (*li* 禮). Mencius intends to make the point that we must
learn to subdue our orectic nature lest we come to violate the rituals
in the process of satisfying ourselves.[70] The idea and manner of fram-
ing the issue are thoroughly Confucian. Not long after Mencius,
Hsün-tzu would build famously on the principle of using rituals to
curtail our desires and would make it one of the cornerstones of his
ethical philosophy.[71]

It is understandable, then, that some early Confucians considered the separation of the sexes to be the germ of all morality. Consider the orthodox commentary to "The *Kuan*-ing Ospreys."

后妃説樂君子之德，無不和諧，又不淫其色。慎固幽深，若關雎之有別焉，然後可以風化天下。夫婦有別則父子親，父子親則君臣敬，君臣敬則朝廷正，朝廷正則王化成。[72]

The royal consort takes delight in her lord's virtue. There is nothing in which she does not accord with him, and she is not licentious about her sex. Her caution is firm and her seclusion deep, like the *kuan*-ing ospreys that have separation among themselves. Then she can transform the world. When husband and wife have separation, father and son are intimate; when father and son are intimate, lord and vassal are respectful; when lord and vassal are respectful, the court is upright; when the court is upright, the royal transformation is complete.[73]

The above interpretation starts from the belief that male and female ospreys naturally congregate in different places. This is what is meant by the ospreys' separation. A cautious and secluded queen imitates the ospreys in observing the separation of male and female and thereby lays the foundations for the completion of the "royal transformation" 王化, or establishment of perfect morality throughout the world. The lengthy argument by *sorites*, leading from the separation of husband and wife all the way to the achievement of utopia on earth, is understandable only in the context of the Confucian belief that human morality entails the suppression of our animalistic desires, of which lust is simply taken to be the cardinal example.[74] Once we have learned to regulate our sex drives, the process of self-transformation has already begun.[75]

Once again, the morally persuasive power of the virtuous female is singled out in this program for special praise. The basis of this attitude, therefore, lies not in any demeaning view of women, despite what is commonly alleged. But the difficulty of this view is that it does not conceive of any form of morally acceptable sexual activity other than for the express purpose of producing offspring. All nonprocreative sex is corrupting and enervating. The highest gift that a man can receive from Heaven is a girl who might give him sons. This we read explicitly in the *Odes*.[76] But the sexual pleasures of sexual love, as we have seen, are continually feared rather than explored.[77]

Given such forthright admissions of the possibility of moral weakness in men, why do some texts insist on portraying women as sexual miscreants? I suspect that many of the fulminations against women represent carelessly articulated animadversions that are really aimed at dissolute men. We have seen in "I See on High," for example, that the underlying issue was probably not a universally conceived evil in women, nor even the destructive power of Pao Ssu, but the irresponsibility of King Yu himself for allowing the situation to deteriorate as it did. Consider also the following.

齊人歸女樂，季桓子受之，三日不朝。孔子行。[78]

The people of Ch'i sent some female musicians. Chi Huan-tzu [i.e., Chi-sun Ssu 季孫斯, d. 492 B.C.] received them, and for three days court was not held. Confucius left.[79]

Obviously, Confucius did not leave his native state of Lu because there were female musicians in the land; he would be sure to find female musicians wherever he chose to go. Confucius left because the ruling parties in Lu suspended court for three days for no better reason than to gratify their desires. They chose pleasure and idleness over statecraft and deliberation—or *nei* over *wai.*

Aside from the danger that the commonplace distinction between *nei* and *wai* could evoke unreflective generalizations about men and women, there is the additional problem that the terms are not used consistently.

We remember Kung-fu Wen-po's mother, who urged her son's concubines not to make a grand show of mourning for his death, lest he go down in history as a man who was more devoted to the feminine pleasures of domestic life than the masculine pursuit of service to the state. Elsewhere, she expands on the notions of *nei* and *wai* along similar lines.

公父文伯之母如季氏，康子在其朝，與之言，弗應，從之及寢門，弗應而入。康子辭於朝而入見，曰：肥也不得聞命，無乃罪乎？曰：子弗聞乎？天子及諸侯合民事於外朝，合神事於內朝；自卿以下，合官職於外朝，合家事於內朝；寢門之內，婦人治其業焉。上下同之。夫外朝，子將業君之官職焉；內朝，子將庀季氏之政焉，皆非吾所敢言也。[80]

Kung-fu Wen-po's mother went to the Chi clan. K'ang-tzu [i.e., her great-nephew Chi-sun Fei 季孫肥, d. 468 B.C.] was in the courtyard. He spoke to her; she did not respond to him. He followed her to the door of her bedroom; she did not respond to him, and entered. K'ang-tzu left the courtyard and entered [her apartment] to see her, saying: "I have not heard your command; have I offended you?" She said: "You have not heard it? The Son of Heaven and the feudal lords tend to the affairs of the people in the outer court; they tend to the affairs of the spirits in the inner court. From the chamberlains down, they tend to official duties in the outer court; they tend to affairs of the household in the inner court. Within the doors of her bedroom is where a woman conducts her business. This is the same for superiors and inferiors. The outer court is where you should take the lord's official duties as your business; the inner court is where you should regulate the governance of the Chi clan. These are all matters on which I dare not speak."

Chi K'ang-tzu was an important official in the state of Lu who is mentioned on a number of occasions in the *Analects*.[81] In this passage, his actions betray his ignorance of the difference between the "inner court" 內朝 and the "outer court" 外朝. The former is the locus of the house and hearth, the latter that of the ruler's deliberations on matters of state. Lady Ching's handling of the incident seems to suggest that Chi K'ang-tzu was out of place by barging into a woman's bedroom, because this is the inner area of the house where women "conduct their business" 治其業.[82] She also seems to imply that it was wrong of him to expect advice from her; because her place belongs properly to the inner court, she dares not speak of matters that do not pertain to her.

Her lecture, however, raises more questions than it answers. First, her conclusion implies that Chi K'ang-tzu should be in charge of both the inner court and the outer court. The duties belong to different categories, but as the head of his clan and a premier official at court, he is expected to regulate both courts. Therefore, when Lady Ching says that "these are all matters on which I dare not speak" 皆非吾所敢言也, she cannot mean that she dares not speak on *wai* because she belongs to the world of *nei* as a woman; she must mean that she dares not speak on either *nei* or *wai*, because her great-nephew is her superior in both realms. But this does not make much sense either. The fact that her great-nephew is her superior is no reason why she might not still advise him. Indeed, we find her elsewhere continually advising Chi K'ang-tzu, and not solely on affairs pertaining to the inner court.

季康子問於公父文伯之母,曰:主亦有以語肥也。對曰:吾能老而已,何以語子。康子曰:雖然,肥願有聞於主。對曰:吾聞之先姑曰:君子能勞,後世有繼。[83]

Chi K'ang-tzu asked Kung-fu Wen-po's mother, saying: "Do you have something else to say to me?" She replied: "I have been able to become old and nothing more; what would I have to say to you?" K'ang-tzu said: "Though that is the case, I wish to hear from you." She replied: "I have heard my former mother-in-law say: 'If a noble man is able to toil, his posterity will continue.'"

On another occasion, she instructs her son in subjects that can only be considered *wai*:

是故天子大采朝日，與三公、九卿祖識地德；日中考政，與百官之政事，師尹維旅、牧、相宣序民事；少采夕月，與大史、司載糾虔天刑；日入監九御，使潔奉禘、郊之粢盛，而後既安。[84]

Therefore the Son of Heaven salutes the sun in the morning in his five-colored robes. With the Three Dukes and Nine Chamberlains, he studies and knows the potency of Earth. At midday he considers the government and participates in the governmental affairs of the many officials. The Grand Masters direct the troops, regional representatives, and ministers; they set in order all the affairs of the people. [The Son of Heaven] sacrifices to the moon in the evening in his three-colored robes. With the Grand Scribe and Director of Records, he investigates and reveres the laws of Heaven. When the sun has set, he oversees the Nine Concubines; he commands them to clean and present the millet vessels for the *ti* and *chiao* sacrifices. Only then does he rest.[85]

How do we reconcile Lady Ching's earlier unwillingness to advise Chi K'ang-tzu with these other passages, in which she not only proves eager to instruct, but also apparently transcends the boundaries between *nei* and *wai* by discoursing at length on the Son of Heaven's administrative and religious duties? I do not believe there are any answers that account for the widely varied usage that we have encountered. For it is never clear in any early text how the authors conceive of the difference between *nei* and *wai*, and consequently what they consider to be appropriate subjects for women to discuss. There is no shortage of references to women who give wise political counsel or who influence the government of the world through their behavior.

In the course of a philosophical discussion in the *Mencius*, for example, we read,

華周、杞梁之妻善哭其夫而變國俗，有諸內必形諸外。[86]

The wives of Hua Chou and Ch'i Liang were good at weeping for their husbands and changed the customs of the state. What one possesses on the inside, one must formulate on the outside.[87]

The extant records include several accounts of the story alluded to here. Hua Chou (or Hua Hsüan 華旋) and Ch'i Liang (or Ch'i Chih 杞殖) were soldiers in the army of Ch'i who refused to accept a bribe from the Viscount of Chü 莒子 and were killed by his forces as a consequence of their loyalty. According to the *Tso-chuan*, Marquis Chuang of Ch'i 齊莊侯 (r. 553–548 B.C.)[88] then met the wife of Ch'i Liang in the suburbs and sent someone to offer his condolences; she protested that the marquis should have sent his condolences to her in her house.[89] The commentaries explain that it is improper to offer condolences outside for anyone other than commoners and the lowest ministers.[90] Ch'i Liang's widow apparently believed that her deceased husband deserved more formal rituals of commemoration from his thoughtless ruler. In the statement that the wives of Hua Chou and Ch'i Liang "changed the customs of the state" 變國俗, we are evidently given to understand that the Marquis of Ch'i learned a lesson about valuing loyal soldiers more highly.[91]

Weeping for one's late husband, as we know from the instructions of Kung-fu Wen-po's mother, is a characteristically *nei* form of behavior. We remember that Lady Ching warned her son's concubines not to mourn excessively after his death, lest their grief reflect poorly on Wen-po's reputation as a statesman. In this story, however, the mourning of Ch'i Liang's widow is not taken as a sign that her husband was excessively fond of domestic pleasures. On the contrary, this is a story of a woman whose skillful and pointed demonstrations of *nei* behavior succeed in transforming the *wai* world over which she is not expected to have any influence. For this accomplishment, she is recorded as a moral heroine and a subtle instructress for the age. But readers of texts that incorporate the stories of Kung-fu Wen-po's mother and Ch'i Liang's wife are likely to find the messages conflicting.[92] Is a widow supposed to cry for her dead husband or not? There are no universally valid answers. Part of the solution comes in the statement that "what one possesses on the inside, one must formulate on the outside" 有諸內必形諸外. If, in crying, a widow might impart a moral lesson to an observer, then there is nothing wrong with making her *nei* sentiments known to the world outside. On the other hand, if a concubine seems to convey nothing more than that she will miss her master's sexual favors, then it is unseemly for her to make a spectacle. This difficult idea, in bridging the distinction between *nei* and *wai*, opens the way for women to the outside world. If people's inner sentiments are necessarily reflected in their outer demeanor, then everyone who has an inner life, whether male or female, must be a participant in the space of *wai.*

Other passages show that women can have an effect on *wai* by transcending the conventional requirements of *nei* behavior. Consider the wife of Hsi Fu-chi 僖負羈.

> 及曹，曹共公聞其駢脅，欲觀其裸，浴，薄而觀之。僖負羈之妻曰：
> 吾觀晉公子之從者，皆足以相國。若以相，夫子必反其國。反其國，
> 必得志於諸侯。得志於諸侯，而誅無禮，曹其首也。[93]

When [Ch'ung-erh, who was famous for his outlandish ribs] arrived at Ts'ao, Lord Kung of Ts'ao [r. 652–618 B.C.] asked about his linked ribs and wanted to see his nakedness. While [Ch'ung-erh] was bathing, [Lord Kung] observed him through the curtain. The wife of Hsi Fu-chi said: "When I observe the followers of the Noble Son of Chin [i.e., Ch'ung-erh], they are all adequate to being the prime minister of a state. If he is advised by them, he will certainly return to his state. When he returns to his state, he will certainly fulfill his ambition with the feudal lords. When he fulfills his ambition with the feudal lords, he will punish those who are without ritual. Ts'ao will be at the head of the list."[94]

This wife's behavior does not conform to *nei* in any respect whatsoever. She speaks entirely on the basis of her observations and knowledge of the political world, which are evidently extensive. And unlike that of many wise women in these stories (such as Ch'ung-erh's wife from Ch'i, discussed above), the rare knowledge of Hsi Fu-chi's wife does not derive from the fact that she is a mother or wife of one of the men in question. The Lord of Ts'ao is her lord, Ch'ung-erh a stranger in her country. Yet this woman proves herself well versed in protocols of ritual, as well as an incisive judge of human talent. Her prognostication in this passage, as we might expect, is verified years later, when Ch'ung-erh, now having taken his rightful place as Lord of Chin, decides to attack Ts'ao as part of a larger campaign against Ch'u.[95] As far as the action is concerned, it is irrelevant that this character is female. Indeed, she is placed in a role hardly different from that of an exemplary male sage, minister, or general.[96]

Why, then, do the sources paint such an inconsistent picture of *nei* and *wai,* of appropriate areas of concern for males and females? What end is served by this paradigmatic dualism when it is clear from so many passages that the distinctions are blurry at best and often thoroughly irrelevant? The early Confucian tradition never resolved these potential contradictions, precisely because its view of women was too sophisticated for it to make very much use of the simple rubrics of "inner" and "outer." Confucian thinkers insisted on the moral autonomy of all human beings regardless of sex, and when this commitment forced them to break down the traditional categories of *nei* and *wai*, they were not reluctant to do so. Therefore, it is not surprising that they were criticized bitterly in their own time for the extraordinary respect with which they regarded women.[97]

There are at least three reasons why Confucianism has been repeatedly assailed as "sexist,"[98] even though the sources we have surveyed typically allow for women to participate meaningfully in the Confucian project, and they reserve places in the pantheon of moral paragons for heroines as well as heroes. First, the tradition does not argue for the social equality of women—it argues only for their moral equality. It is taken as a matter of course, for example, that women should follow their husbands.[99] But ancient China was not a civilization that identified social equality as a special value. Men, too, were allotted hierarchical social roles that they were required to fulfill whether it pleased them or not, all the way up to the ruler, who, in theory at least, could not escape his obligations to Heaven and the spirits. It is therefore misleading to say, as has one eminent scholar, that "from Confucius down, Confucianists have always considered women inferior."[100] This is certainly not the case if we mean "inferior" in an aretaic sense. As we have seen, Confucians did not consider virtuous women inferior to immoral men, just as they did not consider an upright minister inferior to a wicked overlord.

The second reason why Confucianism is frequently accused of sexism has to do with later manifestations of sexism and misogyny perpetrated in the name of the tradition. It is in imperial times that we see the proliferation of those sanctimonious manuals that outline "appropriate" behavior for women—serve wine and food in silence, obey thy husband and mother-in-law unquestioningly, and so on—without attributing to women the same moral and intellectual capacities that we find them exhibiting in the original Confucian canon. Examples of this arid genre suffer from the twofold inadequacy that they trivialize the value and abilities of women as well as the rich discussions of women found in the Confucian classics. As we shall see in chapter 3, it was possible for women themselves to compose such works.[101]

Finally, and most important, texts from the Confucian tradition (such as "I See on High") are sometimes compared simplistically with certain vaguely uplifting passages from the *Lao-tzu* 老子 that marvel at the "Mysterious Female."

谷神不死，是謂玄牝，玄牝之門，是謂天地之根。綿綿若存，用之不勤。[102]

The Spirit of the Valley never dies; it is called "Mysterious Female." The Gate of the Mysterious Female is the root of Heaven and Earth. Gossamer, it seems to exist; it is not exhausted by use.[103]

And similarly,

大國者下流，天下之交，天下之牝。牝常以靜勝牡，以靜為下。[104]

A great state is a low-lying flow. It is the Confluence of the World, the Female of the World. The Female constantly overcomes the Male through quietude. She lies low in her quietude.[105]

These passages exemplify the characteristic image of the soft, yielding Female, which the *Lao-tzu* contrasts with the image of the rigid and competitive Male. The *Lao-tzu* focuses here on the Female's traditional position of inferiority and surprises the reader by identifying this very inferiority as the foundation for the Female's success. It has been rightly pointed out that the Spirit of the Valley 谷神 and the low-lying Female 牝 are probably intended as a calculated attack on Confucian rhetoric, which typically describes the process of self-cultivation as a journey higher and higher.[106]

However, it is important to temper these paeans to the Female with a few observations. The main point here is that the sage must recognize the value of the Female as well as that of the Male, not that the Female is inherently superior to the Male. The text stresses the Female only because it is more likely to be ignored than the Male. Thus we read,

知其雄，守其雌，為天下谿。為天下谿，常德不離，復歸於嬰兒。[107]

Know the Male; maintain the Female; become the ravine of the world. When you are the ravine of the world, constant power will not desert you; you will return to being an infant.[108]

It is only by knowing the Male and maintaining the Female that one can reach the pure state of being "the ravine of the world" 天下谿. The deepest secret is not how to be Female rather than Male—but how to be both.[109]

Similarly, we must take care not to misread these appreciative references to the Female as an indication that the author of the *Lao-tzu* especially appreciated women.[110] The Female and the Male are illustrative motifs designed to shed light on the complementary aspects of the universe. They need not refer to actual females or males. The text itself was probably aimed exclusively at men, or more precisely, at the ruler of men. This explains why the passages dealing with the Female and her "quietude" 靜 are intertwined with a sustained political discourse. "A great state is a low-lying flow" 大國者下流: a lord can transform his domain into a great state if he learns how to embody the characteristics of the Male and Female as the circumstances warrant.

Later political writers of the so-called "Huang-Lao" 黃老 school adopted wholesale the *Lao-tzu*'s rhetoric of Female and Male, but it is always evident in their work that the intended audience is a male ruler and that the salubrious Female element is to be understood as nothing more than a convenient abstraction. The essay on the "Female and Male Modes" 雌雄節, for example, consistently favors the Female.

> 皇后屯歷吉凶之常，以辨雌雄之節，乃分禍福之鄉。憲傲驕倨，是謂雄節；□□恭儉，是謂雌節……凡人好用雄節，是謂妨生。大人則毀，小人則亡……凡人好用[雌節]，是謂承祿。富者則昌，貧者則穀。[111]

> The Emperor collected and calculated the constancy of auspiciousness and inauspiciousness, in order to distinguish the Female and Male Modes. He divided the provinces of misfortune and fortune. To be stubborn, proud, haughty, and arrogant—this is called the Male Mode; to be [*lacuna*] reverent and frugal—this is called the Female Mode.... Whenever people are fond of using the Male Mode, this is called obstructing life. A great person will be destroyed; a small person will be doomed.... Whenever people are fond of using the Female Mode, this is called receiving favor. A rich person will prosper; a poor person will be nourished.[112]

Nevertheless, these same texts make clear that "using the Female Mode" does not by any means entail sharing power with women.

> 主兩則失其明，男女爭威，國有亂兵，此謂亡國……主兩，男女分威，命曰大迷。國中有師；在強國破，在中國亡，在小國滅。[113]

> When there are two rulers, [the state] loses its brilliance. Male and female contend for power and there are disorderly troops in the state;

this is called a doomed state.... When there are two rulers, male and female divide power; this is called a great seduction. Within the state there are armies. A strong state will be broken; a middling state will be doomed; a small state will be destroyed.[114]

"When there are two rulers" 主兩 refers to a situation that is vividly described by Han Fei.

后妻淫亂，主母畜穢，外內混通，男女無別，是謂兩主。[115]

> The queen and other wives are disorderly in their licentiousness. The ruler's mother accumulates uncleanliness. *Nei* and *wai* are confused and interconnected. Males and females are not separated. This is called having two rulers.[116]

Despite all the imagery of the Female Mode and the Spirit of the Valley, therefore, we must not be misled into thinking that the writers who popularized this idiom were feminists or had views of women that were any more charitable than those of the Confucians. In fact, the opposite is more likely. This last passage, by describing a situation of political chaos as one in which the women in the palace give full vent to their carnal desires, points us toward another crucial issue in ancient discussions of sexuality: order and disorder of a political nature are frequently associated with order and disorder of a sexual nature. We shall return to this topic in chapter 3.

The entire spectrum of views of women examined in this chapter share one important conviction: that the natural differences between males and females constitute one of the most difficult problems in all philosophy and, more specifically, that moral and political excellence are attainable only after the relations of the sexes have been properly ordered. Confucius and his followers believed that the Chou rulers brought about an ideal society, and it is no coincidence that the discussions of Chou greatness continually stress the virtue of founders' wives and mothers. Like the chaste queen in the Confucian interpretation of "The *Kuan*-ing Ospreys," these women contributed to their husbands' success by separating male and female, thereby eliminating licentiousness; and this single achievement laid the foundations for everything else, all the way down to the "royal transformation." No Confucian ever gives a practicable definition of *nei* and *wai*—of the inner and the outer spaces of human interaction —that can account for the various uses to which these terms are put. In the end, this is because *nei* and *wai* are acknowledged as the two most elemental, and therefore problematic, concepts that one can master. One who knows how to organize *nei* and *wai* has already taken the first and most difficult step toward sagehood.

The political thinkers who took their inspiration from the *Lao-tzu* did not formulate the problem in the same way but still agreed that mastering the Female and the Male was a precondition for effecting a well-ordered government. Their model ruler had to learn how to appreciate the Female and the Male as ideal types and also how to rule *human* females and males. Like the Confucians, these writers also placed great store in the value of "separating male and female," or assigning appropriate tasks to males and females. But the frequency with which writers of *all* persuasions invoked the phrase, and the rarity with which they explained it clearly, betrays the extent to which they struggled for a solution to the basic problem. There was a natural consensus that males and females are different, and an equally natural interest in articulating the essence and consequences of the difference. At that point, there ceased to be any consensus.

3

Sex, Politics, and Ritualization in the Early Empire

The career of the historian Ssu-ma Ch'ien 司馬遷 (145?–86? B.C.) took a fateful turn in 99 B.C. His contemporary Li Ling 李陵 (d. 74 B.C.) was a general who had had great success in fighting the Hsiung-nu 匈奴, a nomadic empire on the steppes that had been plaguing China's northwestern frontier for more than a century. After having penetrated deep into Central Asia, Li Ling was unexpectedly defeated by the enemy, whereupon he surrendered to the "barbarian" nomads—the supreme disgrace for a Chinese general.[1] When Emperor Wu 武帝 (r. 140–187 B.C.) asked Ssu-ma Ch'ien for his opinion of this affair, the historian praised Li Ling by pointing out that the defeated general had been outnumbered by the enemy and had fought bravely; he added that Li Ling was not entirely to blame, because his "relief troops never arrived" 救兵不至. This comment was incautious, because the emperor understood Ssu-ma's lecture as a veiled attack on Li Ling's superior, Li Kuang-li 李廣利 (d. 90 B.C.), who happened to be a brother of one of the emperor's consorts.[2] The historian was promptly thrown into prison and convicted of "libel against the Emperor" (wu-shang 誣上), a capital crime. At this point, he expected to die. For reasons that have never been adequately explained, the penalty was subsequently commuted to castration, and Ssu-ma Ch'ien lived on for more than a decade as a eunuch, during which time he completed his magisterial history of ancient China, known to posterity as the *Records of the Historian* (*Shih-chi* 史記).[3]

This is one of the most famous stories in the entire Chinese tradition. Generations of readers have lauded Ssu-ma Ch'ien for his forthrightness before the emperor and for the courage with which he bore his unjust punishment, persevering to complete his masterpiece. The story is often interpreted as proof that Ssu-ma Ch'ien was willing to sacrifice his life for the truth—he saw that everyone at court was criticizing Li Ling unfairly and insisted on setting matters straight. This image of Ssu-ma Ch'ien reinforces his position as the model court historian, for that official has been expected since ancient times to value his obligation to pass on a reliable record more highly than his own personal well-being.[4]

It is rarely asked, however, why Ssu-ma Ch'ien was castrated. The few relevant legal texts that are extant all imply strongly that castration (in contrast to execution) was a very rare punishment in Ssu-ma Ch'ien's time. Moreover, it is far from clear how the punishment fits Ssu-ma Ch'ien's alleged crime—and Han legal theorists consciously followed Hsün-tzu 荀子 (i.e., Hsün K'uang 荀況, ca. 310–ca. 210 B.C.) in asserting that punishments should always fit the crime.[5] "Libel against the Emperor" 誣上 was considered to be a very serious political crime for which the natural punishment—like that for treachery in the West—was execution.[6] Castration, on the other hand, was traditionally reserved specifically for sex crimes. The *Great Commentary to the Exalted Documents* (*Shang-shu ta-chuan* 尚書大傳, attributed to Fu Sheng 伏勝, fl. third–second centuries B.C.), for example, states that castration (*kung* 宮) is the punishment for "those men and women who have intercourse without morality" 男女不以義交者.[7] One of the oldest explanations of *kung* comes in the *Comprehensive Discussions in the White Tiger Hall* (*Po-hu t'ung* 白虎通),[8] which explain that *kung* is the punishment for *yin* 淫, i.e., "licentiousness" or "promiscuity."

> 女子淫，執置宮中，不得出也。丈夫淫，割去其勢也。[9]

> When a woman is licentious, she is to be seized and held inside a room, and not allowed to leave. When a man is licentious, his genitals are to be cut off.[10]

Not even the emperor himself ever accused Ssu-ma Ch'ien of fornication or licentiousness, so how could a punishment of castration be justified? According to one popular answer that goes back at least to Ma Tuan-lin 馬端臨 (1254–1325), castration was routinely substituted for the death penalty when the court was willing to show mercy, because, by all accounts, castration was seen as the worst punishment short of execution.[11] Contemporary documents, however, suggest that the normal substitute in such cases was for the convict to be shaved and collared, and sentenced to a term of hard labor.[12] It is hard to escape the thought that Ssu-ma Ch'ien was punished as though he had committed a sex crime—that the court must have perceived his crime, in other words, to have had some underlying sexual dimension.

Part of the solution to this puzzle can be found in the story of Empress Dowager Lü 呂太后 (d. 180 B.C.)—the wife of Liu Pang 劉邦 (247–195 B.C.), the founder of the Han dynasty—and her son, Emperor Hsiao-hui 孝惠帝 (r. 194–188 B.C.). Empress Dowager Lü was the bitter rival of Lady Ch'i 戚姬, a concubine whom her husband had taken soon after having embarked on his meteoric rise from commoner to Emperor of China. Each consort had a son who was a potential successor to the throne. Empress Dowager Lü had a "humane and weak" 仁弱 boy who was to become the future Emperor Hui; Lady Ch'i, a boy named Ju-i 如意 whom the emperor considered to be more like himself. Liu Pang wished to designate Ju-i his heir apparent, but several influential officials interceded and persuaded him to keep that dignity in the hands of Empress Dowager Lü's gentle son.

When Liu Pang died in 195 B.C., Empress Dowager Lü got her wish and saw her son crowned emperor. Her resentment of Lady Ch'i was so great, however, that she had her rival imprisoned and her rival's son poisoned, even though neither still posed a threat to her plans. Then she took care of Lady Ch'i once and for all.

> 太后遂斷戚夫人手足，去眼，煇耳，飲瘖藥，使居廁中，命曰人彘。居數日，迺召孝惠帝觀人彘。孝惠見，問，迺知其戚夫人，迺大哭，因病，歲餘不能起。使人請太后曰：此非人所為。臣為太后子，終不能治天下。孝惠以此日飲為淫樂，不聽政，故有病也。[13]

The Empress Dowager then cut off Lady Ch'i's hands and feet, removed her eyes, burned her ears, gave her a potion to make her mute, and caused her to live in a pigsty,[14] calling her Human Swine. When she had lived there for several days, she summoned Hsiao-hui to observe the Human Swine. Hsiao-hui saw her, and asked; then he was given to know that this was Lady Ch'i. Then he cried greatly, whereupon he became sick; for more than a year, he could not get up. He sent someone to plead with his mother, saying: "This is not the action of a human being. I am the Empress Dowager's son, but to the end I will not be able to rule the world." From this point on, Hsiao-hui drank daily and indulged in licentious pleasures. He paid no attention to government; that is why he was sickly.[15]

The poor Emperor's reaction to seeing his father's consort brutally mistreated was so severe that he was unable to continue ruling. He withdrew from court and left all political affairs to his inhuman mother. (We remember that he was first introduced to us as "humane and weak" 仁弱.) How, then, did he spend his days if he would not "rule the world" 治天下? He "drank daily and indulged in licentious pleasures" 日飲為淫樂. He was affirming that excessive sexual activity is the opposite of maintaining order and government.[16]

The idea is not entirely new to us. We remember, for example, the connection between sexual activity and political machination forged by Han Fei in his essay on the sybaritic palace women (chapter 1). The woman who copulated the most, that thinker argued, naturally gained the most power and therefore constituted the most serious threat to the ruler's absolute authority. After the unification of China and the founding of the empire under the First Emperor of Ch'in 秦始皇帝 (r. 221–210 B.C.), it became even more critical for the ruler to take into account Han Fei's manner of thinking, for now every subject in the empire was a potential usurper. With so much more to lose than any ruler before him, the First Emperor took the momentous step of having a code of proper sexual conduct inscribed in stone atop the famous Mount Kuei-chi 會稽.[17] The text begins with a description of the world before unification:

六王專倍	The six kings concentrated on rebellion.
貪戾傲猛	They were rapacious, violent, haughty, and fierce.
率眾自強	They led their hosts, thinking themselves mighty.
暴虐恣行	Cruel and oppressive, they acted on their own authority.
負力而驕	They relied on their strength and were arrogant.
數動甲兵	Repeatedly they mobilized their troops.
陰通閒使	They made clandestine contact and sent emissaries among each other.
以事合從	They formed a Vertical Alliance against us.[18]
行為辟方	They carried out brutish plans.
內飾詐謀	Within the state, they prettified their conspiracies.
外來侵邊	Outside the state, they came and encroached upon our borders.

The First Emperor then explains that, for all their deceitful tactics, his competitors still could not avoid succumbing to his virtuous might. He has rid the land of those cruel brigands—and more important still, he has unified the world and ushered in an era of unprecedented peace and purity.

遂起禍殃	Ultimately they brought disaster [on themselves].
義威誅之	With the might of morality I chastised them.
殄熄暴悖	I annihilated the cruel and unruly.
亂賊滅亡	The disorderly brigands were destroyed.
聖德廣密	My sage virtue is broad and thorough.
六合之中	Within the six directions
被澤無疆	I cover a fertile region that is without limits.
皇帝并宇	I, the Emperor, have united the cosmos.
兼聽萬事	I hear myriad affairs together.
遠近畢清	Near and far, I have made everything pure.
運理群物	I revolve, setting in order the throng of things.
考驗事實	I investigate and verify the reality of affairs.
各載其名	Everything bears its proper name.
貴賤並通	I am connected to noble and base.
善否陳前	Good and bad are arranged before me.
靡有隱情	There are no hidden matters.

At this point, the First Emperor takes up the issue of sexual relations between his subjects, insisting that he will tolerate no immorality in this regard, either.

飾省宣義	Those who conceal their transgressions[19] while proclaiming their own morality
有子而嫁	are [widows] who have a son and still remarry.
倍死不貞	They rebel against the dead and are not chaste.
防隔內外	I separate and divide the inner and outer [i.e., males' and females' quarters].
禁止淫溢	I prohibit and stop licentiousness and dissipation.
男女絜誠	Men and women will be pure and faithful.
夫為寄豭	If a husband becomes a sojourning boar [i.e., an adulterer],[20]
殺之無罪	one can kill him with impunity.
男秉義程	This is the path to making men maintain morality.
妻為逃嫁	If a wife absconds and marries [someone else],
子不得母	her sons will not be allowed to consider her as their mother.[21]
咸化廉清[22]	Everyone will be made modest and pure.[23]

The logic behind this bombastic inscription is consistent and clear. Everything follows from the basic axiom that unity and harmony are the prime ideals of the empire. The most telling crime committed by the six vanquished kings is that they "acted on their own authority" 恣行. Obviously, in a unified empire that revolves around an all-powerful ruler, acting on one's own authority cannot be tolerated. Six different kings will have six different agendas, six different moral philosophies, six different worldviews. The consequence can be only "chaos" 亂, or the opposite of "unity" 并. The private interests of the six kings are incompatible with a universal morality, and so the ideal of harmony demands their pacification.

In the last section of the inscription, the First Emperor discloses his belief that his subjects' most consequential moral and political acts are their sexual acts. He makes no specific prescriptions beyond the vague warning that they "maintain morality" 秉義 and be "modest and pure" 廉清. In accordance with the same principle of unity, the First Emperor condemns clandestine sexual relations among the populace. Husbands and wives must be faithful to each other, for the integrity of the glorious new era depends on the sexual morality of the emperor's subjects. It is important to note that in this regard the First Emperor's sexual code is not sexist; men and women must both be chaste.[24] The only difference is that widowed mothers have an explicit obligation to remain faithful to their deceased husbands, while the emperor makes no similar demand of widowers, whether childless or not. As we shall see, later formulations of ideal sexual relations would be far less equitable in the requirements that they placed on men and women.[25]

The inscription on Mount Kuei-chi also helps to elucidate Ssu-ma Ch'ien's seemingly inappropriate punishment. By praising a disgraced general and disputing the official assessment of an embarrassing defeat, the candid historian was doing exactly what the First Emperor had called "acting on one's own authority" 恣行 and hence rebelling. Unwittingly or not, Ssu-ma Ch'ien was threatening the unassailable "unity" of the empire by putting forward an alternative explanation of historical events. From the point of view of the emperor, such divisive talk might have the same consequences as sexual licentiousness— and for that crime, Ssu-ma Ch'ien got exactly what he deserved, in accordance with such codes as the *Great Commentary to the Exalted Documents*. His licentiousness was intellectual rather than carnal.

Example after example from his great book shows that Ssu-ma Ch'ien himself accepted the basic equivalence of sexual misconduct and political rebellion.[26] In other words, if Ssu-ma Ch'ien *had* jeopardized the security of the empire, he could not have argued that castration was unjust in his case, because, as we shall see, he was also committed to the same manner of thinking by which his punishment is comprehensible in the first place. This is why he never once protests his punishment; his only possible defense is that his words are true, even if the present generation is unwilling or incapable of recognizing them as such.

今雖欲自彫瑑，曼辭以自解，無益，於俗不信，祇取辱耳。要之死日，然後是非乃定。[27]

Now, even if I wanted to carve [a name] for myself, excusing myself with elegant phrases, I would have no reward. I would not be believed by the vulgar, and would only be seeking further disgrace. What is important is that right and wrong be settled after the day of death.[28]

So Ssu-ma Ch'ien is content to take the patient route and let us decide through his work who the real villains were. He takes us all the way back to the founding of the empire and endeavors to show that the very figures responsible for having "united the cosmos" 并宇 had a record of sexual conduct that was far from unblemished—just as the "united cosmos" itself lacked both unity and purity.

Some of the most revealing material is found in his biography of Lü Pu-wei 呂不韋 (d. 235 B.C.), a merchant who lived in the economic center of Han-tan 邯鄲, the capital of the state of Chao 趙 in central China. There he met by chance with Tzu-ch'u 子楚, a young son of the Heir Apparent of Ch'in who had been sent to Chao as a hostage. Tzu-ch'u's father had a favorite wife named Lady Hua-yang 華陽夫人, who was herself childless. The crafty merchant Lü Pu-wei calculated that it would be worth his while to cultivate this lady's friendship with manifold gifts; ultimately he convinced her to ask her mighty husband to designate young Tzu-ch'u as his principal heir.

The plan worked seamlessly, and although it cost Mr. Lü a prodigious amount of money, he eventually found himself as the benefactor of the principal heir of the Heir Apparent of Ch'in, the most powerful kingdom in the world.[29] This is when he struck the one obstacle in his course that would eventually lead to his downfall.

呂不韋取邯鄲諸姬絕好善舞者與居，知有身。子楚從不韋飲，見而説
之，因起為壽，請之。呂不韋怒，念業已破家為子楚，欲以釣奇，乃
遂獻其姬。姬自匿有身，至大期時，生子政。子楚遂立姬為夫人。[30]

Lü Pu-wei had taken from among the various ladies of Han-tan one
who was surpassingly lovely and skilled at dancing. He lived with her
and came to know that she was with child. Tzu-ch'u visited Pu-wei to
drink with him; he saw her and was pleased by her. Then he arose and
made a toast to Lü's long life, and requested her. Lü Pu-wei was furi-
ous, but he remembered that in this enterprise, wishing to fish up
something marvelous, he had already ruined his family on behalf
of Tzu-ch'u. So he presented his lady to [Tzu-ch'u]. The lady concealed the fact that she was with child. When her term was up,[31] she
gave birth to the boy Cheng. Tzu-ch'u then established the lady as his
consort.[32]

The child was born in 259 B.C. In 250 B.C., Tzu-ch'u finally ascended the throne, ruling as King Chuang-hsiang 莊襄王 until his
death in 248 B.C.—whereupon he was succeeded by Cheng, the boy
he thought was his son. The lad went on to become the First Emperor
of Ch'in, and Lü Pu-wei, his natural father, reaped the rewards of his
investment by being installed as the prime minister of the state.

But the story does not end here. The First Emperor's mother—Lü
Pu-wei's former consort—was simply too licentious.

始皇帝益壯，太后淫不止。呂不韋恐覺禍及己，乃私求大陰人嫪毐以
為舍人，時縱倡樂，使毐以其陰關桐輪而行，令太后聞之，以啗太
后。太后聞，果欲私得之。呂不韋乃進嫪毐，詐令人以腐罪告之。不
韋又陰謂太后曰：可事詐腐，則得給事中。太后乃陰厚賜主腐者吏，
詐論之，拔其鬚眉為宦者，遂得侍太后。太后私與通，絕愛之。有
身，太后恐人知之，詐卜當避時，徙宮居雍。嫪毐常從，賞賜甚厚，
事皆決於嫪毐。[33]

The First Emperor[34] was growing into manhood, but the Queen
Dowager's licentiousness was ceaseless. Lü Pu-wei feared that if this
became known, misfortune would reach him. So he privately found
a man with a large penis named Lao Ai and made him his retainer.
At times he would indulge in song and music, making Lao Ai walk
around with his penis stuck through a wheel of t'ung-wood.[35] He had
the Queen Dowager hear of this, in order to entice her. When the
Queen Dowager heard, as expected, she wanted to have him in private. Lü Pu-wei then presented Lao Ai and conspired to have someone accuse him of a crime for which he should be castrated. Pu-wei
then addressed the Queen Dowager secretly, saying: "If you permit

this trumped-up castration, then you can have him in your apartment." The Queen Dowager then secretly gave rich gifts to the official in charge of castrations, instructing him to pluck out [Lao Ai's] beard up to the eyebrows,[36] making him a "eunuch" so that he could serve the Queen Dowager. The Queen Dowager had congress with him in private and loved him very much. She became pregnant by him, and fearing that someone would come to know of it, she produced a sham divination saying that she should avoid [an inauspicious] period; she moved her palace and lived in Yung. Lao Ai often visited her; she rewarded him with very rich gifts, and all the affairs [in the house] were decided by Lao Ai.[37]

But they were all found out.

始皇九年，有告嫪毐實非宦者，常與太后私亂，生子二人，皆匿之。與太后謀曰：王既葬，以子為後。於是秦王下吏治，具得情實，事連相國呂不韋。九月，夷嫪毐三族，殺太后所生兩子，而遂遷太后於雍。諸嫪毐舍人皆沒其家而遷之蜀。[38]

In the ninth year of the First Emperor [i.e., 238 B.C.], someone reported that Lao Ai was not really a eunuch; that he often privately fomented chaos with the Queen Dowager; that she had given birth to two sons; and that they had concealed everything. He had conspired with the Queen Dowager, saying: "Once the king is dead, we will make one of these sons his successor." Therefore the King of Ch'in handed this [matter] down to his officials to investigate; they grasped the truth of the situation, and the affair was linked to the Prime Minister, Lü Pu-wei. In the ninth month, [the king] exterminated Lao Ai's clan to the third degree of relation, killed the two boys that the Queen Dowager had borne, and banished the Queen Dowager to Yung. All of Lao Ai's henchmen had their families' wealth confiscated and were banished to Shu.[39]

Ultimately Lü Pu-wei, too—in spite of the great service that he had rendered the king and his family—was asked to commit suicide.

This story appealed to Confucians, for they considered the First Emperor to have been one of the arch-enemies of civilization, and they could point to this scurrilous tale as proof that he was a bastard with no legitimate right to rule. That his mother is depicted as a perfect strumpet only added to their glee.[40] Pan Ku 班固 (A.D. 32–92), for example, a historian about whom we shall have more to say presently, referred to the First Emperor unceremoniously as Lü Cheng, after his natural father, Lü Pu-wei.[41] Scholars have long argued, however, that the tale is doubtful and may even have been interpolated by someone other than Ssu-ma Ch'ien.[42] After all, the First Emperor's own *Shih-chi* biography says nothing of his disputed parentage and asserts that his surname was Chao 趙.[43]

There is another reason to doubt the veracity of the account—one that is rarely pointed out: the name of the man with the prodigious penis, Lao Ai, is hardly believable.[44] *Lao* 嫪 means "lustful"; it might have been a surname in ancient times, but as far as I know, it is not so used in another context.[45] *Ai* 毐, furthermore, was defined in classical times as "when a person misbehaves" 人無行也;[46] it is probably a graphic component in the word for "poison" (*tu* 毒).[47] The name "Lao Ai," in other words, means "lustful misdeed." Who would bear the name "Ai"?[48] The character begs to be taken allegorically. In a Western morality play, this villain with his wondrous priapism might have been called Carnal Concupiscence. Moreover, the name was synonymous for centuries with copulation and male genitalia. Within seventy years of Lü Pu-wei's demise, the famous statesman Chia I 賈誼 (201–169 B.C.) asserted, "The mother of the First Emperor of Ch'in fornicated with Lao Ai; he was executed, so the world reviled fornicators by calling them 'Lao Ai'" 秦始皇母與嫪毐淫，坐誅，故世罵淫曰嫪毐.[49] Similarly, there is evidence that in later colloquial language, wags would call anything big a "Lao Ai" (by an obvious process of antonomasia).[50] He was imagined by Lü Pu-wei, by Ssu-ma Ch'ien, and by all posterity as a personified phallus.

His most striking attribute is called *ta-yin* 大陰 in the text, and it is significant that this phrase can mean both "great sex-organ" and "great conspiracy." Indeed, Ssu-ma Ch'ien hints at this essential identity by repeatedly using the term *yin* in both senses.[51] We are first introduced to Lü Pu-wei's new servant as *ta-yin jen Lao Ai* 大陰人嫪毐, which, at first glance, is readily understood as "Lao Ai, a man with a great penis." On rereading the story, however, we can see how easily this might be taken to mean, "Lao Ai, a great conspirator." Later, when Lü Pu-wei tells his former lover of the sham castration that he has arranged, we read that he *yin-wei* 陰謂, or "conspiratorially addressed her"—which thus carries the additional meaning, "addressed her with respect to a penis." The very next sentence says that the Dowager *yin hou-ssu* 陰厚賜 ("clandestinely gave rich gifts") to the Officer of Castration, which, given the context, implies that she was not ashamed to offer her sex to him as well. "Rich gifts" is precisely the term used soon afterward to describe her lavish treatment of Lao Ai.

Considering, then, that Ssu-ma Ch'ien, the supposed author of the story, really was castrated—and that it was for behavior that, as in the case of Lao Ai, subverted the foundations of the empire—we should recognize that the suggestive symbolism is entirely intentional. Lao Ai's abnormal genitals, in addition to his very name, function as an image for his outrageous sexual conduct; and his sexual transgressions, in turn, are inseparable from his seditious activities. By conspiring to replace the legitimate heir with one of his two bastard sons, Lao Ai represents a basic threat to the transmission of the imperial bloodline and hence the purity of the "united cosmos." Licentiousness is shown here to be dangerous for the same reason as in the *Tso Commentary* and *Canon of Odes*: it confuses the issue of patrimony. The only difference is that, under the new empire, the stakes are incomparably greater. When the emperor's subjects fornicate with each other, no one knows who is whose father, and this luridly instructive story demonstrates that even the emperor himself may be illegitimate and thoroughly unworthy of "setting in order the throng of things" 運理群物. Whether or not we believe the story of Lü Pu-wei, we can agree that the challenges to any palace ruler that it reflects are by no means insubstantial. The First Emperor himself could imagine only too readily the social and political consequences of rampant licentiousness. That is precisely why he tried so hard to regulate the sexual mores in his empire.[52]

The same emperor who had Ssu-ma Ch'ien castrated is notable for having accused many of his own relatives of horrific sex crimes. The wave of indictments began in 128 B.C., when the affair of Liu Ting-kuo 劉定國, Prince of Yen 燕王 (r. 151–128 B.C.), came to light. The prince had apparently fornicated with his father's concubine, producing a son. He also took his younger brother's wife as his own concubine and fornicated with three of her daughters. One of his subjects, fearing for his life, reported his lord's actions to the throne, but the prince had him arrested and killed, in order to keep him quiet. The brothers of the deceased then sent another epistle to the throne, detailing Liu Ting-kuo's actions. The emperor launched an investigation. Once the facts were known, the ministers recommended execution, and Liu Ting-kuo committed suicide.[53]

The relevant texts take pains to make clear that the Prince of Yen was convicted for his abominable sexual acts, and not for having murdered an inconvenient subordinate. "Ting-kuo has acted like a beast; he has thrown human relationships into disorder and opposed the Way of Heaven. He ought to be executed" 定國禽獸行，亂人倫，逆天道，當誅. "He has thrown human relationships into disorder" must refer to his incestuous orgies and not to his brutal methods of silencing opposition.[54]

The following year, Chu-fu Yen 主父偃 (d. 127 B.C.) accused Liu Tz'u-ch'ang 劉次昌, Prince of Ch'i (r. 131–127 B.C.), of similar transgressions. Chu-fu Yen was a rags-to-riches councilor who had attained much fame through his part in bringing down Liu Ting-kuo. This official sent a messenger to inform the Prince of Ch'i that he knew all about His Lordship's incestuous liaison with his elder sister. The prince thought he would never be able to escape conviction and committed suicide so as not to be compared with the late Prince of Yen.[55] That same year, yet a third imperial kinsman, Liu P'eng-tsu 劉彭祖, originally Prince of Kuang-ch'uan 廣川 and subsequently Prince of Chao 趙 (r. 155–193 B.C.), feared that he would meet the same fate as his cousins the Princes of Yen and Ch'i. So he accused Chu-fu Yen of various "conspiracies" 陰事 of his own. Chu-fu and his entire clan were executed before the year was out.[56]

Modern readers are likely to be puzzled by these events. Why was Liu P'eng-tsu, a cousin of the emperor, so afraid of the upstart Chu-fu Yen that he had to have him framed? Why did the authorities calling for Liu Ting-kuo's execution focus on his incestuous relationships, neglecting to mention the crime that we today would consider far more serious, namely murder? And, above all, why were so many of the emperor's cousins accused of sexual perversions? The actions of Liu P'eng-tsu, who was never indicted, imply that he too had some kind of sexual deviance to hide—and we know from the sources that indeed he did.[57]

The answers to these questions have to do with the political history of the Han dynasty. When Liu Pang founded the dynasty, he installed many of his kinsmen as feudal vassals, following the prominent model of the legendary Sage-Kings Wen and Wu of Chou. Such feudal arrangements, as historians have made clear, are typically the result of power bargains. They occur when a conqueror, though naturally unwilling to share his newfound might, finds himself unable to administer his new empire by himself—whereas his kinsmen and capable followers have acquired considerable power of their own. An agreement is reached whereby the lord cedes certain lands (fiefs) to his vassals, granting them limited autonomy in exchange for vows of loyalty and service. Over the course of subsequent generations, the situation degenerates into a primal tug-of-war. The lord tries to limit as much as possible his vassals' rights over their fiefs—or, if he is in a position to do so, he aims to eliminate them entirely—while the vassals try to exact ever-greater concessions from their lord. Understandably, the vassals' right to pass their fief on to the next generation is often a major bone of contention.[58]

Emperor Wu's father, Emperor Ching 景帝 (r. 156–141 B.C.), had taken significant steps in his lifetime to undermine the power of the feudal landholders. Emperor Wu continued this trend by reducing the size of several principalities, often confiscating fiefs outright on the slightest pretext.[59] He initially favored Chu-fu Yen precisely because of the latter's policy of *divide et impera*:

偃說上曰：古者諸侯不過百里，強弱之形易制。今諸侯或連城數十，地方千里，緩則驕奢為淫亂，急則阻其強而合從以逆京師。今以法割削之，則逆節萌起，前日鼌錯是也。今諸侯子弟或十數，而適嗣代立，餘雖骨肉，無尺寸地封，則仁孝之道不宣。願陛下令諸侯得推恩分子弟，以地侯之。彼人人喜得所願，上以德施，實分其國，不削而稍弱矣。[60]

[Chu-fu] Yen persuaded the Emperor, saying: "In ancient times, the land of the feudal lords did not exceed one hundred *li*, and it was easy to control their strength. Now some of the feudal lords have connected several tens of cities, so that their territory [covers] a thousand *li*. If they are neglected, they will become haughty and extravagant, and may easily become licentious and disorderly. If they are treated strictly, they will rely on their strength and ally with one another in order to oppose the capital. If you slice or pare their territory by passing laws, this will give rise to germs of opposition against such regulations, as in the case of Ch'ao Ts'o [d. 154 B.C.] of former days.[61] Now some of the feudal lords have ten or more sons and younger brothers, but only one legitimate heir succeeds to the title. The others, though they are of the same flesh and bone, do not have a single foot of territory. Thus the Way of humanity and filiality is not promulgated. I urge Your Majesty to order the feudal lords to extend your grace to their sons and younger brothers by enfeoffing them with land. They will all rejoice, having attained what they desire—while the Emperor, through a virtuous undertaking, will really be dividing their realms. Without your doing violence to them, they will decline and weaken.[62]

In other words, the emperor's clansmen represent precisely the same threat as the old Six Kings in the First Emperor's inscription at

Kuei-chi. They are "licentious and disorderly" 淫亂; they form private alliances and defy the power of the center. The Prince of Chao knew what was as stake: Chu-fu Yen was assaulting his fief, his dignity, and his livelihood and had to be stopped immediately. Chu-fu and the emperor were not content simply to let their shrewd policies gradually take effect. Rather, they tried to hasten the inevitable outcome by accusing princes right and left of sexual misdeeds. So it was immaterial whether Prince So-and-so actually copulated with his sister or his father's widow. The point was that by accusing them of heinous sex crimes, Chu-fu Yen was really branding them as political rebels in the mold of Lao Ai. And the princes knew full well that they had no defense against such charges, for their very existence was licentious in the political sense; as landed princes with territorial power, they threatened the integrity of the centralized empire. Their only options were to commit suicide or to fight back by accusing their accuser of licentious acts more dangerous than their own.

The life of Liu Chien 劉建, Prince of Chiang-tu 江都 (r. 127–121 B.C.), illustrates further the interrelated themes of sexual misconduct and political rebellion.

> 淮南、衡山謀反時，建頗聞其謀。自以為國近淮南，恐一日發，為所并，既陰作兵器，而時佩其父所賜將軍印，載天子旗以出。易王死未葬，建有所説易王寵美人淖姬，夜使人迎與姦服舍中。及淮南事發，治黨與頗及江都王建。建恐，因使人多持金錢，事絕其獄⋯⋯建又盡與其姊弟姦。事既聞，漢公卿請捕治建。天子不忍，使大臣既訊王。王服所犯，遂自殺。[63]

When [the Princes of] Huai-nan and Heng-shan were planning rebellion,[64] [Liu] Chien heard much about it. He considered that his fief was close to Huai-nan, and feared that if [the rebellion] were to erupt one day, he would be involved. So he secretly manufactured weapons, and sometimes would wear on his belt the general's seal that his father had been granted; he would set out carrying the Emperor's banner. When Prince I [i.e., Chien's father, r. 153–128 B.C.] had died but was not yet buried, Chien sent an emissary at night to fetch Lady Nao, his father's favorite harem-girl who delighted him as well. He fornicated with her in the mourning lodge. When the affair of Huai-nan erupted [i.e., 122 B.C.], the investigation into partisans and accomplices pointed toward Chien, Prince of Chiang-tu. Chien was afraid, and sent an emissary bearing much gold and money in an attempt to avoid imprisonment.... Chien also fornicated with all his sisters. Once the matter was heard, the officials of Han requested that Chien be arrested and tried. The Emperor could not bear this, and sent a great minister to interrogate the Prince. The Prince confessed his crimes, whereupon he committed suicide.[65]

Here is a case of a man who is undone by his own anxiety and stupidity. If he genuinely fears being implicated in a rebellion, the worst thing he can do is stockpile weapons and ride around with a flag reserved for the Son of Heaven. His attempt to bribe his way out of trouble only confirms his guilt. He can hardly fit more closely the profile of a guilty party.

It is remarkable how the account of Liu Chien's sexual transgressions is completely intermeshed with that of his very shortsighted acts of treason. The comment that he committed incest with all his sisters is inserted almost parenthetically. Like most of his disgraced cousins, this prince fornicated with his stepmother as well; the added remark that he fornicated with her in the "mourning lodge" 服舍 reminds us of the poem "The Banks of the Ju" and its searing image of the illicit liaison in the ancestral hall (see chapter 1 in this book). This one act embodies well Liu Chien's folly. Copulating with his widowed stepmother would not have been so egregious—after all, countless other members of his class were doing it; it was a gesture signifying that a son had succeeded his father[66]—but only Liu Chien took the further step of revolting everyone by doing the deed in the precinct reserved for expressions of filial grief.

Once the figure of Liu Chien was confirmed as the model of a scheming and licentious feudal lord, later writers could elaborate on his crimes however they wished. His biography in the *History of the Han*, for example, includes many racy details of his debauchery not related by Ssu-ma Ch'ien.

宮人姬八子有過者，輒令嬴立擊鼓，或置樹上，久者三十日乃得衣；
或髡鉗以鉛杵舂，不中程，輒掠；或縱狼令齧殺之，建觀而大笑；或
閉不食，令餓死。凡殺不辜三十五人。建欲令人與禽獸交而生子，強
令宮人嬴四據，與羝羊及狗交。[67]

An Eighth-Rank Lady[68] of his seraglio once made a mistake; he unceremoniously ordered her to strip and stand beating a drum. Some [of his women] he would set atop a tree, forcing them to stay there for thirty days before giving them clothes. Some he would have shaved and collared, and made to pound grain with a lead pestle;[69] if they did not reach their quota, he would simply flog them. On others he would set loose wild wolves to bite them to death; Chien would watch this and laugh greatly. Some he would lock up, denying them food and causing them to starve to death. In all he killed thirty-five innocent people. Chien wanted to make someone copulate with animals and bear a child; he forced a woman of his seraglio to strip and get on all fours,[70] and copulate with rams and dogs.

This final misdeed is Liu Chien's crowning sin. There were many sadists in the imperial family—the sons of Emperor Ching were especially prominent in this regard[71]—and murdering thirty-five innocent people actually places Liu Chien fairly low on the list of the dynasty's greatest butchers. Fornicating with his sisters and stepmother was also, as we have seen, not extraordinary among his peers. But bestiality lies in a different category altogether. I know of no other reliable reference to it in the early literature,[72] and it is likely that classical readers would have taken it to be the single most immoral act that a human being could perform, because Liu Chien's desire to produce issue from a sexual union between human and animal assailed the very basis of moral philosophy as laid down by such august thinkers as Mencius (Meng K'o 孟軻, 371–289 B.C.?) and Hsün-tzu.

The difference between humans and beasts, Mencius argued, is that humans have a heart 心 (or "mind"); the gentleman preserves it, whereas the common people abandon it.[73] He goes on to show that the heart is crucial to humanity because it is the seat of our inborn morality.

所以謂人皆有不忍人之心者,今人乍見孺子將入於井,皆有怵惕惻隱之心,非所以內交於孺子之父母也,非所以要譽於鄉黨朋友也,非惡其聲而然也。由是觀之,無惻隱之心,非人也;無羞惡之心,非人也;無辭讓之心,非人也;無是非之心,非人也。惻飲之心,仁之端也。羞惡之心,義之端也。辭讓之心,禮之端也。是非之心,智之端也。人之有是四端也,猶其有四體也。[74]

To show that all human beings have a compassionate heart, suppose someone suddenly saw a child about to go into a well. Everyone [in such a situation] would have a frightened, commiserating heart, not in order to ingratiate themselves with the child's parents, not because they want praise from their neighbors and friends, and not because they hate the sound.[75] From this we see: Who does not have a commiserating heart is not a human. Who does not have a heart of shame is not a human. Who does not have a heart of deference is not a human. Who does not have a heart of right and wrong is not a human. The heart of commiseration is the beginning of humanity. The heart of shame is the beginning of righteousness. The heart of deference is the beginning of ritual. The heart of right and wrong is the beginning of wisdom. Humans have these Four Beginnings as we have our four limbs.[76]

The later philosopher Hsün-tzu—who was even more influential in Han times than Mencius—agreed that the difference between humans and animals had to do with the moral capacity of each species, though he diverged from Mencius in other respects. Hsün-tzu explicitly rejected Mencius' notion of the inborn goodness of humanity, and so he based his ethical system not on such ideas as the Four Beginnings 四端 but on the essential tendency of human beings to make distinctions.

人之所以為人者，何已也？曰：以其有辨也。飢而欲食，寒而欲煖，
勞而欲息，好利而惡害，是人之所生而有也，是無待而然者也，是
禹、桀之所同也……夫禽獸有父子而無父子之親，有牝牡而無男女之
別，故人道莫不有辨。辨莫大於分，分莫大於禮。[77]

What is it that makes humans human? I say: their making of distinctions. Desiring food when hungry, desiring warmth when cold, desiring rest when toiling, loving profit and hating harm—these are what humans have from birth; they are what is so without any development; they are what was alike in Yü and Chieh [a legendary Sage and a prodigal last king, respectively]. Birds and beasts have parents and children, but not the relationship of father and son. They have males and females, but not the separation between men and women. Thus there is nothing greater than making distinctions in the Way of Man. There are no greater distinctions than social distinctions; there are no greater social distinctions than the rituals.[78]

It was apparently conventional in Hsün-tzu's time to think of animals as beings with completely unrestrained sex drives; we have already seen lascivious humans referred to as "sows" or "boars" in this vein.[79] Zoologists today may dispute some of Hsün-tzu's assertions—we know now that animals observe very complex rituals governing the relations between males and females, for example—but his reasoning is clear. The essential attribute of humanity is to make distinctions, as between father and son, male and female, etc. This, he asserts, is a feature that no other living species shares. It is the Way of Man, and because the Way is always right, the human tendency to make distinctions is the bedrock of all morality.[80]

Given this philosophical background, we can appreciate just how abominable Liu Chien's acts are meant to seem. Instead of abiding by the natural and appropriate distinctions set down by Heaven, Liu

Chien does all he can to obscure them. And what kind of heart, in the Mencian sense, could have been possessed by the poor monster that Liu Chien was hoping to create? We sense that the benighted Liu Chien, in his zeal to gratify his diabolical curiosity, is meddling with ethical and spiritual issues that he cannot begin to comprehend—like an ancient counterpart of our Dr. Frankenstein.

Here is a character who foments "disorder" 亂 in the most literal terms. He is the antithesis of morality as his world constructed it. Sexual relations had to be orderly and regulated, because sexual aberrations—like all aberrations—threatened the fragile unity of the new empire, and so were tantamount to rebellion. This was the early imperial sex ideology; it is one of the outstanding features of the Han intellectual world.

To be sure, there had been precursors to this political conception of sexual misconduct long before the Han dynasty, stretching back all the way to the primordial world of myth itself.[81] One of the several fascinating Chinese flood myths, for example, deals with the figure of Kung Kung 共工, the debauched marplot who harmed the world by disrupting the natural courses of the rivers.

夫天地成而聚於高，歸物於下。疏為川谷，以導其氣；陂塘汙庳，以鍾其美。是故聚不崩，而物有所歸；氣不沈滯，而亦不散越。是以民生有財用，而死有所葬。然則無夭、昏、札、瘥之憂，而無飢、寒、乏、匱之患，故上下能相固，以待不虞，古之聖王唯此之慎。昔共工棄此道也，虞於湛樂，淫失其身，欲壅防百川，墮高堙庳，以害天下。皇天弗福，庶民弗助，禍亂並興，共工用滅。其在有虞，有崇伯鯀，播其淫心，稱遂共工之過，堯用殛之于羽山。其後伯禹念前之非度，釐改制量，象物天地，比類百則，儀之于民，而度之于群生。共之從孫四嶽佐之，高高下下，疏川導滯，鍾水豐物，封崇九山，決汨九川，陂鄣九澤，豐殖九藪，汨越九原，宅居九隩，合通四海。故天無伏陰，地無散陽，水無沈氣，火無災燀，神無閒行，民無淫心，時無逆數，物無害生。[82]

When Heaven and Earth were completed and [material] gathered to make highlands, the creatures[83] returned to the bottom. Riverbeds were dredged, so as to guide [the flow of] their *ch'i.* Slopes and embankments [were raised] around the marshy lowlands, so as to preserve their beauty. Therefore the gathered [earth] did not erode or cause mudslides, and the creatures had a place to return to. The *ch'i* [of the rivers] did not become heavy and blocked, but also did not disperse and encroach on [dry land]. Thus the people obtained wealth during their lives, and had a place to be buried when they died. This being the case, there were no concerns over untimely death, infant mortality,[84] pestilence, or disease; nor worries over hunger, cold, shortages, or deficiencies. Thus superiors and inferiors were able to be secure with one another, in order to anticipate the unexpected; this was all that the ancient Sage-Kings were cautious about. Long ago Kung Kung abandoned this Way, and took joy in dissolute pleasures, losing himself in licentiousness. He wanted to block up the Hundred Rivers, destroying the highlands and filling up the lowlands, in order to harm the world. August Heaven did not bestow fortune upon him, and the common people did not help him; disaster and chaos flourished together, and Kung Kung was exterminated. In the time of the possessor of Yü [i.e., Shun 舜, a legendary Sage-King], there was Kun, Earl of Ch'ung, who spread abroad his licentious heart and followed in Kung Kung's transgressions; Yao [the Sage-King whom Shun served] put him to death on Mount Yü. His scion, Earl Yü, studied his forebears' denial of standards; he regulated and corrected [the world], instituting measures. He caused things to be in the image of Heaven and Earth, and categories to match the Hundred Patterns, so that everything accorded with the people and took the flocks of living things as its measure. [Kung] Kung's descendants, the Officers of the Four Peaks,[85] assisted him. Making the highlands high and the lowlands low, they dredged the rivers, clearing a path for the blockage; and the water, thus preserved, became fertile with creatures. They piled up the several mountains, making them lofty; they opened the several rivers, so that they flowed unimpeded; they constructed slopes and dikes around the several marshes; they fertilized the several wetlands, making them fecund; they cleared the several plains, making them vast; they made the several headlands habitable; and they connected the Four Seas. Thus Heaven did not suffer from *yin*, and there was no diffusion of *yang* on Earth.[86] There was no stoppage of *ch'i* in the waters, no disastrous raging of fire; spirits did not walk about idly, and people did not have licentious hearts; there was no inversion of the sequence of seasons, no creatures harmful to the living.[87]

Thus it seems that at the very beginning of time, "licentiousness" 淫 and "dissolute pleasures" 湛樂 were already contrasted with the orderly government that preserves—and gains its strength from— the regular forces of nature. The fact that the names of both sins are based on aquatic images (overflow and dissipation) only strengthens their association with the flooding waters.[88] Kung Kung and Kun are beings who disrupt the flow of the rivers, so that "disaster and chaos flourished together" 禍亂並興; significantly, we are told point-blank that both are licentious. After Yü and the Officer of the Four Peaks succeed in reestablishing the proper condition of the world, we are again told specifically that "people did not have licentious hearts" 民無淫心.[89]

Nevertheless, although the perceived connections between licentiousness and disorder of a cosmic or political nature may be as venerable as the myth of Kung Kung and the waters, preimperial rulers did not by any means share the obsessive concern with regulating sexual conduct that marks the reigns of the Ch'in and Han emperors. This point is borne out especially well in a revealing section of a preimperial Ch'in legal handbook. The text discusses the fitting punishment for a woman who has fornicated (*chien* 奸) with two separate men, who subsequently injure each other in a fight over her. The conclusion is that she is not to be sentenced at all (whereas the men, of course, would be penalized for fighting).[90] The logical inference is that "fornication" itself was not categorically punishable by law. For readers inured to the Draconian measures of Emperors Ching, Wu, and the like, such legal restraint is stunning. Whoever was responsible for compiling the Ch'in law code evidently did not consider "fornication" to constitute a threat to public order of the magnitude that the First Emperor and his successors envisioned.

Preimperial sexual mores, as best reconstructed by the available sources, square with this permissive attitude. Remarriage was not at all uncommon among women of all social classes,[91] and *cheng* 烝, or incest with one's father's widow (an offense punishable by death in the Han),[92] seems to have been downright popular among the ancient elite—perhaps because a man's wives were seen as property that his son could freely inherit.[93] Similarly, a court jester from the fourth century B.C. recounts in almost pornographic terms communal drinking parties where men and women would choose their partners and lie together intertwined on the same mat. At the end of the night, the jester tells us, the hostess sees off all the other guests, so that she can untie her silk blouse and let him inhale her fertile odor. (The rest is left to the reader's blazing imagination.)[94] Finally, although ancient rulers were certainly criticized for their sexual excesses, many are depicted with sexual appetites that are almost endearing. King Chuang of Ch'u, for example—the same lord who wanted to make the infamous Lady Hsia his concubine (see chapter 1 in the present book)—might have considered it an act of diplomacy to embrace a courtesan from Ch'in in his left hand and a girl from Yüeh 越 in his right.[95]

The stark contrast between the totalitarian regimentation of sexual life in the early imperial era and the relatively carefree attitude of the period that immediately preceded it has been observed for centuries,[96] and most scholars rightly place the critical transition in the Ch'in dynasty, with the First Emperor's attempts to forge a "unified cosmos."[97] This means that the conception of sexuality articulated by Ssu-ma Ch'ien and others was a phenomenon peculiar to imperial times and hence must be seen as part of a larger endeavor to limit personal freedom in the new world order. Most other basic freedoms easily enumerated by those who live in a free society—freedom of speech, freedom of movement, and so on—were assaulted along with sexual freedoms for precisely the same reason: they all jeopardized the imperial ideal of unity. Of course, it had always been dangerous to express one's mind openly in ancient China, but there is far less evidence in earlier times of such organized and far-reaching efforts to control human behavior. The few outstanding cases of reforms aimed at social control—such as those of Kung-sun Yang 公孫鞅 (d. 338 B.C.) in the state of Ch'in[98]—were greeted with profound resentment and distrust at all levels. In many respects, then, the Chinese Empire was one of the first totalitarian states in human history, and its view of sexual activity was, like that of all totalitarian states, fearful and intolerant.[99]

The great achievement of the early Han dynasts was to make this repressive ideology palatable to the very people whom it was designed to control. After all, part of the dynasty's strategy of legitimation was to depict the fallen Ch'in dynasty as paradigmatic of the inevitable failure of brutally repressive policies. The scholar Chia I, for example, composed a profoundly influential essay on the demise of Ch'in, citing in particular the government's blatant disregard for the people's welfare.[100] Though probably intended simply as a warning to the emperor not to follow the "mistakes of Ch'in" 過秦, this work in effect provided policymakers with a matchless source of propaganda, which the Emperors Wen 文 (r. 180–157 B.C.) and Ching exploited to the fullest by reducing taxes, announcing several general amnesties, and abolishing all mutilating punishments, thus portraying their own rule as one of pure benevolence and restraint.[101] Capital punishment, however—like the practice of exterminating a criminal's family (mieh-tsu 滅族) when circumstances were thought to warrant it—was never abolished, and we have seen some examples of how skillfully emperors used execution and the mere threat of execution to do away with people who were politically inconvenient. This was a sanitized and vastly more sophisticated form of social control than anything the Ch'in had produced.

The Han sex ideology also proved persuasive to intellectuals because it forged a link between sexual licentiousness and moral transgression. According to the preimperial Ch'in code, as we have seen, "fornication" was not a crime; indeed, in keeping with the latitudinarian mores of the time, it was hardly seen as blameworthy. The Han government, on the other hand, by actively prosecuting high-profile cases of "acting like a beast" (*ch'in-shou hsing* 禽獸行, the standard category for sex crimes), managed to bring about an environment in which citizens themselves demanded tougher measures and more comprehensive legislation aimed at sex offenders. Like comparable sentiments today, such calls typically focused on offenders who molested victims across generational boundaries, particularly those who committed incest. The difference is that the demon of our legal system is the father (or stepfather) who forces himself on his daughter (or stepdaughter), whereas the classic profile of a Chinese sex offender was a son (or stepson) who "treated his mother as a wife" 妻母.

A famous instance of the ever-increasing complaints about the inadequacy of the law code dates to around 45 B.C.

美陽女子告假子不孝，曰：兒常以我為妻，妒笞我。尊聞之。遣吏收捕驗問，辭服。尊曰：律無妻母之法，聖人所不忍書，此經所謂造獄者也。尊於是出坐廷上，取不孝子縣磔著樹，使騎吏五人張弓射殺之，吏民驚駭。[102]

A woman of Mei-yang accused her stepson of unfiliality, saying: "My son often treats me as a wife; he flogs me out of jealousy." Tsun [i.e., Wang Tsun 王尊, the local magistrate] heard this and sent officials to arrest and interrogate him; he confessed. Tsun said: "There are no laws in the code about cohabiting with one's mother.[103] This is something that the Sages could not bear to write about; it was what the canons called an 'unprecedented case.'"[104] Tsun then went out and sat down at the head of the courthouse. He took the unfilial son and hung him from a tree, ordering five cavalrymen to draw their bows and shoot and kill him, so that the people would be terrified.

Wang Tsun's actions were to be a harbinger of intellectual attitudes in the future. First, and most obviously, he considers the crime to be abhorrent. He asserts that even the Sage-Kings could not bear to write about such topics as incest with one's stepmother, and he sees the "unfilial son" 不孝子 as such a menace to society that he makes an example of him in order that the populace would be "terrified" 驚駭. Wang Tsun thus figures as a precursor of rising popular outrage against crime in general and sex crimes in particular. He goes further in his condemnation than the imperial administration itself. (The Magistracy of Mei-yang was a thoroughly trivial position in the grand hierarchy of the Han bureaucracy, and it is nowhere stated that Wang Tsun is acting on orders from above.) We are told that he acts of his own accord and out of a profound sense of indignation and disgust. Like countless intellectuals after him, Wang Tsun complains that the laws are deficient as they stand because they do not deal effectively with moral violations as grievous as "unfiliality." Wang Tsun is an activist politician. As his own little speech makes clear, he does not execute the criminal on the authority of his administrative post, because the law does not grant him expressly the power to do what he thinks is right. He is acting on a sense of moral authority, as a concerned official who is trying to make the law more perfect.

Finally—and this is critical—Wang Tsun asserts unmistakably that he derives his moral authority from the "canons" (or "classics," *ching* 經), the infallible body of traditions handed down by the Sages. Wang Tsun believes in a time when Sages ruled on the basis of their sage wisdom, rather than their official position; when incest and similar "unprecedented cases" elicited the righteous indignation that they ought to elicit; when "unfilial sons" were dealt with as they ought to be dealt with. He believes that the world has decayed since this golden age and that it needs to be brought in line with the will of the Sages—which is to say, in concrete terms, that the laws and statutes should be scrapped and replaced by the classics. The humble Magistrate of Mei-yang, in three pithy clauses, identifies himself as a fervent Confucian revolutionary.[105]

Most of Wang Tsun's concerns are echoed more than a century later by Pan Ku in his "Treatise on Punishments and Laws" ("Hsing-fa chih" 刑法志). This later writer makes an additional point: by eliminating mutilation, the Han government has in effect left a gaping hole in the gamut of punishments available to magistrates charged with carrying out the law. Too many people are executed for lack of a more suitable sentence, whereas too many violent criminals receive the comparatively light sentence of being shaved and collared.

且除肉刑者，本欲以全民也，今去髡鉗一等，轉而入於大辟。以死罔
民，失本惠矣。故死者歲以萬數，刑重之所致也。至乎穿窬之盜，忿
怒傷人，男女淫佚，吏為姦臧，若此之惡，髡鉗之罰又不足以懲也。
故刑者歲十萬數，民既不畏，又曾不恥，刑輕之所生也。故俗之能
吏，公以殺盜為威，專殺者勝任，奉法者不治，亂名傷制，不可勝
條。是以罔密而姦不塞，刑蕃而民愈嫚……刪定律令，纂[＝撰]¹⁰⁶二
百章，以應大辟。其餘罪次，於古當生，今觸死者，皆可募行肉刑。
及傷人與盜，吏受賕枉法，男女淫亂，皆復古刑，為三千章。¹⁰⁷

The original intent of the abolition of mutilating punishments was
to keep the people intact, but now after passing the degree of "shav-
ing and collaring," one turns right to the death penalty. To trap people into the death penalty is to lose the original grace [of the aboli-
tion]. Therefore there are ten thousand killed every year; this is
brought about by the heaviness of punishments. But when we come
to robbing by "breaking and entering," injuring people in order to
vent anger, licentiousness between male and female, officials who are
treacherous and conspiratorial—evils like this—the penalty of being
shaved and collared is insufficient to punish them. Thus tens of thousands are punished every year, but the people are not awed, let alone
have a sense of shame; this arises because of the lightness of punishments. Thus officials who are known vulgarly as "capable" publicly
execute robbers in order to appear mighty; those who specialize in
killing are thought to live up to their duties, whereas those who
respect the law cannot bring about order. One cannot count the cases
where disordering the "names" [i.e., legal categories] has harmed the
legal system. Therefore the meshes [of the law] are fine, but treachery is not stopped; punishments are manifold, but the people are ever
more impertinent.... Let us erase the laws and statutes and fix new
ones, composing two hundred sections to correspond to the death
penalty. For the remaining ranks of crimes—for which [the punish-
ments] in ancient times were nonlethal, but now involve death—for
all these, [the convict] can appeal for mutilation. As for people who
injure others; robbers; officials who receive bribes or abuse the law;
men and women who engage in licentious disorder—for all such
[cases], we will revert to the ancient punishment. This will make up
3,000 sections.¹⁰⁸

Pan Ku's proposals in this "Treatise" are far more elaborate than
anything in Wang Tsun's terse speech at Mei-yang, but we can see
how the two men approached similar problems with similar attitudes.
Like Wang Tsun, Pan Ku believes that the legal code needs to be
completely rewritten, and like his forebear, he believes that following
the practices of "ancient times" 古者 is the secret to a harmonious

and moral society. For crimes such as robbery and licentiousness, to "revert to the ancient punishment" 復古刑 means reinstating penal mutilation. But Pan Ku's "ancient times" are nothing more than an idealized Never-never-land. We have seen how fornicators were dealt with by the ancients; they certainly were not routinely castrated, if they were punished at all. Traditional moralists like Pan Ku were in fact inventing their own traditional morality.[109]

Pan Ku's sister, Pan Chao 班昭 (A.D. 48–116?), is perhaps the most extraordinary "traditional" moralist of the entire dynasty. She wrote a celebrated essay called "Admonitions for Women" ("Nü-chieh" 女誡) with the express intent of instructing girls in "the rituals of women" 婦禮. Pan Chao believed that girls needed to be taught how to serve their "husband and ruler" 夫主 and lamented the fact that most families felt they had to educate only their boys.[110] "Admonitions for Women" starts from the initial supposition that males are naturally superior to females and provides straightforward behavioral guidelines for women that may allow them to fulfill their pre-destined roles as helpmates to their husbands.[111]

專心紡績，不好戲笑，絜齊酒食，以奉賓客，是謂婦功。[112]

Sew and weave with focused mind; do not be fond of games and laughter; keep pure and orderly the wine and food, in order to serve them to guests. These are called womanly achievements.[113]

Pan Chao goes through her catalog of "admonitions" with the tacit premise that she is merely encapsulating the age-old "rituals for women" in a form that women can understand. That is to say, she presents her work as though it were a summary of traditional moral precepts, and not in any respect an invention of her own. However, her essay includes recommendations that would have been shocking to the founders of the very tradition that she believes she is transmitting faithfully.

姑云不爾而是，固宜從令；姑云爾而非，猶宜順命。勿得違戾是非，爭分曲直。此則所謂曲從矣。[114]

When your mother-in-law says "No!" and she is correct, then follow her command, since it is firmly right; when your mother-in-law says "Yes!" and she is wrong, then obey her order as though it were right. Do not oppose what she says is right and wrong or fight over what she says is straight and crooked. This is what is called bending and obeying.[115]

It is a truism of Chinese sociology that the often tense relationship between daughter-in-law and mother-in-law is one of the pillars supporting the entire familial structure.[116] On the face of it, Pan Chao is merely delineating in clear-cut terms just what is expected of a daughter-in-law—namely, complete and unquestioning obedience. The young wife must do as her mother-in-law says, whether she thinks it is right or wrong, because she herself is in no position to challenge her elder's standards. Pan Chao chooses to focus here on the figure of the mother-in-law, but we can readily extend the analogy to cover all social superiors, whom a woman must obey without demurrer. In effect, this passage sets down Pan Chao's understanding of what she calls "service" (*shih* 事).[117]

However, unquestioning obedience, especially in cases in which one's superior is wrong, is *never* extolled as a virtue in early Confucian texts.[118] Confucius himself, for example, took a famous position on this issue.

子曰：事父母幾諫，見志不從，又敬不違，勞而不怨。[119]

The Master said: "In serving your father and mother, remonstrate slightly. If you see that they do not comply with your will, you should still be reverent and not disobedient. Struggle and do not complain."[120]

This utterance is vague in several respects. Commentators have continually assumed that Confucius has a male audience in mind, but in this passage, he does not necessarily exclude women. And if he does mean here to address women as well as men, then he has to disagree with Pan Chao, since he seems to posit that to "remonstrate slightly" 幾諫 is a moral duty for everyone. Moreover, just what does Confucius mean by "struggle" (*lao* 勞)? Does struggling entail trying to show one's parents their mistakes, even while maintaining a reverent and obedient posture? Can "father and mother" 父母, furthermore, be extended to include in-laws? These are contentious issues in the commentarial literature. But however we choose to interpret the details, Confucius does not generally recommend obeying wrongful commands as though they were right. On the contrary, the Confucian brand of service is not fawning obedience but a higher form of loyalty that involves criticizing one's parents or ruler with their best interests in mind.[121]

The early literature contains countless examples of this principle in action—the vast majority of which, to be sure, involve the righteous dissent of men rather than women. Nevertheless, the canons so esteemed by the Pan family also include instances in which such heroic remonstrance is placed in the mouths of female characters.

Two poems from the *Odes* illustrate this point. Consider the following stanzas.

既不我嘉	Since you did not approve it,
不能旋反	I cannot turn back.
視爾不臧	I regard you as incorrect.
我思不遠	My thoughts will not be kept at a distance.
既不我嘉	Since you did not approve it,
不能旋濟	I cannot return across the streams.
視爾不臧	I regard you as incorrect.
我思不閟	My thoughts will not be kept secret.
陟彼阿丘	I will ascend that steep hill
言采其蝱	and gather its *meng*-herbs.
女子善懷	As a girl, I am given to emotions,
亦各有行	but each one has its principles.
許人尤之	The people of Hsü are mistaken about this.
眾稚且狂	The mob is immature and rabid.

(*Mao* 54: "Tsai ch'ih" 載馳)

Evidently, this is the lament of a woman who thinks she ought to travel somewhere but is forbidden to do so by the "people of Hsü" 許人. The phrase "turn back" 旋反 implies that she is a wife or widow wishing to return to her family;[122] in other words, the "people of Hsü" are her husband's family. Repeatedly, she insists that they are "incorrect" 不臧 and "mistaken" 尤. These are certainly not the words of a woman who is content to obey blindly the dictates of her social superiors—whom, indeed, she considers to be moral inferiors. The *Tso-chuan* tells us that the poem was recited by the wife of the lord of Hsü. She was a daughter of the noble house of Wei 衛 who wished to visit her homeland after it had been sacked by a non-Chinese group known as the Ti 狄 in 660 B.C.[123] Subsequent commentators suggest that she actually composed this poem, which they all agree is intended as a woman's eloquent criticism of ignorant in-laws who succeeded in quashing her noble ambition.[124]

"The Cypress Boat" is even more crushing to Pan Chao's position. This lyric is narrated by a young widow who complains to her parents that she will not marry another man.

汎彼柏舟	It floats, that cypress boat,
在彼中河	in the middle of the river.
髧彼兩髦	He had two locks of hair over his forehead.
實維我儀	In truth, he was my only mate.
之死矢靡它	Till death I swear that there will be no other.
母也天只	Oh, mother! Oh, Heaven!
不諒人只	You do not consider other people!

(*Mao* 45: "Po-chou" 柏舟)

We must not rule out the possibility that the speaker of this poem, too, is addressing her mother-in-law rather than her natural mother, for it was common for a young widow in later imperial times to be married off as quickly as possible by her in-laws. Not only did she represent an extra mouth to feed, but she also had legal claims on her deceased husband's property that could be removed only if she could be induced to remarry.[125] For this earlier period, however, these considerations may not be relevant, and the voice of "The Cypress Boat" may well be addressing her own parents. Regardless, the significant point is that she is criticizing her elders for attempting to thwart her will, threatening darkly to commit suicide rather than betray her dead lover.[126]

Part of the reason why "The Cypress Boat" was canonized surely lies in its affirmation of a widow's chastity, an ideal that apparently has always been admired in Chinese culture. Nevertheless, we have seen that widows who refused to remarry by no means represented the rule in ancient times, and the desire of a widow's parents that she find another husband was not to be ignored flippantly. In her own day and age, the speaker of "The Cypress Boat" would have been seen as an Antigone, as an obstreperously pious young woman who is so faithful to her own moral standards that she is willing to defy her legal guardians even unto death. This is not a meek little girl who is "bending and obeying" 曲從 in the mold of Pan Chao. This is a spirited and self-confident woman whose radical opinions are socially disruptive and indeed morally precarious. And yet she is singled out as a heroine.

Pan Chao was by far the most educated woman of her day, and perhaps the most educated woman in Chinese history. She trained many important male scholars, including Ma Jung 馬融 (A.D. 79–166), one of the titans of the Confucian tradition. And her greatest achievement may well have been one which posterity has insufficiently noted, namely, her contribution to the extant *History of the Han*.[127] In spite of her undeniable scholarly accomplishments, however, her understanding of the classics as revealed by her "Admonitions to Women" is shallow. In repudiating the tradition of upright expostulation, she has debased the complex Confucian ethical system and transmogrified it into nothing more than a justification for the exploitation of females by males and of younger generations by elder generations. To purvey the view that women should know their place, serve wine in silence, and never contradict their husbands and in-laws as though it were taken straight from the classics—when in fact the classics present a view of humanity that is incomparably richer and more problematic—must qualify as a thorough falsification. The "traditional" morality that Pan Chao espouses is really a moralizing invention. But we have seen that Pan Chao is not unique among Later Han classicists in this respect.

In Pan Chao's time, "The Cypress Boat" had lost much of its original impact. The critical issue—the remarriage of widows—had already long been defused as an object of controversy. It was now unremarkable for widows to remain "chaste" 貞節 for the rest of their lives, and in the coming decades widows who took second husbands would face greater and greater stigma.[128] To Pan Chao herself, the question was not even open to discussion. "According to the rituals," she asserts, "husbands have the right to marry again, but there is no provision for women to be matched twice" 禮，夫有再娶之義，婦無二適之文.[129]

During the previous two and a half centuries of Han rule, however, countless widows of all social classes remarried in peace, some as many as five or six times. Clearly, there was no law against it.[130] The noted jurist Tung Chung-shu 董仲舒 (ca. 179–ca. 104 B.C.) found that widows without children could remarry freely—and if he meant to imply that widows with children could not, this aspect of his decision was never enforced.[131] Ch'ao Ts'o, ever the enterprising official, even went so far as to propose selling widows to men garrisoned along the frontier.[132] How can we reconcile this relatively tolerant attitude in the early Han period with Pan Chao's uncompromising rejection of remarriage for widows in the second half of the dynasty?

A closer look at the evolution of Han marriage practices suggests that this change over time from sexual permissiveness to sexual regimentation is not an isolated historical problem. No one seems to have complained, for example, when Emperor Hui made his own niece his empress in 192 B.C. In A.D. 200, however, the historian Hsün Yüeh 荀悦 (A.D. 148–209) decried Emperor Hui's action as a violation of ritual and the Way.[133] The nature of the wedding banquet also seems to have undergone a decisive shift over the course of the dynasty. At first, wedding banquets were rowdy and sexually integrated to the point of deteriorating into hymeneal orgies as the wine flowed and flowed.[134] But already by the time of Emperor Ai 哀帝 (r. 6 B.C.–A.D. 2), a bureaucrat who drank wine by a widow's gate was dismissed from office for having "thrown into disorder the separation of the sexes" 亂男女之別, when he should have known "that there are regulations pertaining to drinking wine and gorging oneself at banquets" 知飲酒飫宴有節.[135] If these unspecified "regulations" had been in force in earlier times, most families celebrating a wedding would have been carted off to prison forthwith.

Thus the picture of early Han marital customs that emerges from the sources fails utterly to conform to the idealized standards set down by later thinkers. If, as Pan Chao asserts, the rites prohibited women from remarrying, few people in the Former Han seemed to know or care. These same ritual codes prescribe in great detail the procedures necessary for a proper marriage, namely the so-called Six Rituals 六禮 that commentators have never tired of elucidating. It was assumed for centuries that Han marriages followed the Six Rituals scrupulously, simply because they are mandated by such extant codes as the *Ceremonies and Rites* (*I-li* 儀禮) and *Record of Rites*.[136] But it has now been demonstrated conclusively that most of these rituals were practiced only in the rarest of circumstances, and even then only by ambitious ideologues who wished to make a point of their extraordinary rectitude. For some of these rites, we do not have any documentation that society was aware of their existence.[137]

The spuriousness of the ritual codes is revealed further in their prescriptions regarding the proper time of the year for weddings. The *Po-hu t'ung*, for example, says,

嫁娶必以春何？春者，天地交通，萬物始生，陰陽交接之時也。[138]

Why must marriages take place in the spring? The spring is the time when Heaven and Earth meet and have congress, when the myriad things begin to live, when *yin* and *yang* meet and touch.[139]

This arrangement fits neatly with Five Phases (*wu-hsing* 五行) thought, which views spring as the season of vitality and thus the natural time for weddings. But earlier texts indicate that the proper season for weddings was thought in preimperial times to be winter. Indeed, the very next sentence in the *Po-hu t'ung* shows that the author or authors have gotten everything mixed up: "The *Odes* say: 'If a man brings home a wife, it is while the ice has not yet melted'" 詩云：士如歸妻，迨冰未泮. This is a genuine reference to the *Odes* (*Mao* 34: "P'ao yu k'u-yeh" 匏有苦葉), but it does not seem to substantiate the argument of the text. If anything, it implies that marriages should take place while there is still ice on the ground—hardly a description of springtime. The discrepancy is amplified by a passage from Hsün-tzu: "When the frost descends, one welcomes the bride; when the ice melts, [weddings] cease. Every ten days they copulate once" 霜降逆女，冰泮殺止，內十日一御.[140] This statement can be interpreted only to mean that weddings must take place during the winter. Therefore, either there were at least two accepted views in ancient times concerning the proper season for weddings (viz. winter or spring)[141]—or the authors of *Po-hu t'ung* misunderstood the *Odes* because they accepted it as a matter of course that marriages should be held in the spring. In either case, their command of the classics is revealed to be shaky at best.[142]

Similarly, several ritual codes require the use of a wild goose (*yen* 雁/鴈) in five of the six marriage rituals,[143] and it is not far-fetched to see in this stipulation an even more profound misreading of the very same poem that *Po-hu t'ung* cites as justification that weddings should take place in the spring. The poem is "The Gourds Have Bitter Leaves."

匏有苦葉	The gourds have bitter leaves.
濟有深涉	The ford has a deep crossing.
深則厲	Where it is deep, they cross with their clothes on.
淺則揭	Where it is shallow, they cross by lifting their clothes.
有瀰濟盈	Overflowing, the ford is swollen!
有鷺雉鳴	Resoundingly, the female pheasant calls!
濟盈不濡軌	The ford, though swollen, will not wet my axle.
雉鳴求其牡	The female pheasant calls to seek her male.
雝雝鳴鴈	Harmoniously, harmoniously cry the wild geese.
旭日始旦	The morning sun begins to rise.
士如歸妻	If a man brings home a wife,
迨冰未泮	it is while the ice has not yet melted.

招招舟子   He beckons, he beckons, the ferryman.
人涉卬否   Others cross, but I do not.
卬須我友   I am waiting for my friend.

(*Mao* 34: "P'ao yu k'u-yeh")

This is one of the most beautiful poems in the entire collection, and like its own image of the pregnant ford 濟盈, it is full of suggestive symbolism that can be interpreted in many different ways. One interpretation that is absolutely not warranted, however, is to link the image of the wild goose with marital bliss. As we have noted in chapter 1, the wild goose is an emblem that appears in early Chinese literature of various genres, and consistently in circumstances marked by an unwanted *separation* between lovers.[144] Thus the arousal of the wild goose symbolizes, if anything, the exact opposite of marital concord. The image fits this poem especially well. The speaker—presumably female but possibly male—is waiting for her "friend" 友 and therefore refuses to cross the ford with the others. This is what she means when she says that the ford, though swollen, will not wet her axle. The other images, such as the beckoning ferryman and the female pheasant calling for her mate, also convey frustrated attempts at union. So the literary purpose of juxtaposing the desolate image of the wild goose with the cheery remarks about the right time to find a wife is to dramatize the speaker's own longing for her friend. The reference to marriage may even explain why she is waiting for him by the ford: she has been hoping that he would take her home before the spring thaw. We are given to know by the swelling of the ford that she has waited in vain.[145]

There is good evidence, furthermore, that the earliest readers understood "The Gourds Have Bitter Leaves" in a similar spirit, as in the following passage from the Confucian *Analects*.

子擊磬於衛。有荷蕢而過孔氏之門者，曰：有心哉，擊磬乎！既而曰：鄙哉硜硜乎！莫己知也，斯己而已矣。深則厲，淺則揭。子曰：果哉，末之難矣！[146]

The Master was playing chimes in Wei. Someone carrying a basket passed by Confucius' gate and said: "There is heart in the way he strikes the chimes!" Then he said: "It is vulgar, this sound of pebbles clanging! If there is no one who knows you, then just be by yourself. 'Where it is deep, they cross with their clothes on. Where it is shallow, they cross by lifting their clothes.'" The Master said: "Indeed! There is no refuting that!"[147]

This is a very difficult passage. Commentators have debated its meaning for centuries (and there may also be some intractable problems of textual corruption).[148] Still, the basic elements are clear. The person "carrying a basket" is able to discern the emotions that Confucius expresses through his music ("There is heart" 有心哉, etc.). Confucius is evidently distraught that he has not found anyone who knows him 己知, that is, one who understands his philosophical outlook and lofty intentions. Then the critic cites a passage from "The Gourds Have Bitter Leaves," aptly enough, since he implies thereby that Confucius' anguish is comparable to that of the unwed girl by the riverbank. Probably he means to say that Confucius should simply cross his ford without worrying about who might accompany him.[149]

Therefore, given the very pointed imagery of "The Gourds Have Bitter Leaves" and its interpretation by thinkers of Confucius' age, it is surprising that ritual codices should incorporate the presentation of wild geese during the ceremonies of courtship and marriage. There is no evidence whatsoever, either in bronze inscriptions or other ancient documents, that wild geese were ever so used by the ancients or that they were even conceived as symbolic of marital union. On the contrary, every other appearance of wild geese in the *Odes* occurs in a context of marital separation, sometimes even widowhood.

How then is it possible that the *Po-hu t'ung* finds it necessary to present a litany of answers to the question: Why is it appropriate to use wild geese when we get married? They fly north and south at the right time of year; they follow the sun as the wife follows her husband; etc.[150] This is all too creative. The only plausible scenario is that the authors of *Po-hu t'ung* misunderstood the "harmoniously calling wild geese" 雝雝鳴鴈 of "The Gourds Have Bitter Leaves" as a symbol intended to prefigure the man who wants to bring home a wife before the ice has melted. In a sense, they were right: the wild geese are intended to prefigure the image of marriage in the same stanza. But the device is bitterly ironic, as we have seen. It appears as though the *Po-hu t'ung* has wrenched the figure of the wild geese from its traditional sense in the context of the *Odes*. If the misconception that ancient marriages involved the use of geese can in fact be traced to a naive reading of this particular line in the *Odes*, then this must count as a decisive blow to the credibility of ritual texts like the *Po-hu t'ung* (as well as the *Ceremonies and Rites*, a book that is usually considered to be much older).[151]

It is true that ritual codes in the genre of *Po-hu t'ung* contain hundreds, if not thousands, of genuine citations from ancient texts and that their interpretations of the classics are not always created ex nihilo. In chapter 1, for example, we saw that according to the *Tso-chuan*, Tzu-ch'an quoted from a "treatise" 志 that said: "In buying a consort, if you do not know her surname, divine it" 買妾不知其姓，則卜之; this statement appears verbatim in the *Record of Rites*.[152] This kind of correspondence between passages in the *Record of Rites* and certifiably preimperial texts is not at all uncommon, and it shows that there is much material in the *Rites* that is genuinely ancient.

But the fact that the famous ritual texts from Han times do not square with early imperial practice—let alone preimperial practice—compels us to conclude that they were compiled by the same traditional moralists who wanted to rewrite all the law codes on the basis of their own anachronistic understanding of the classics. The literati who handed down these ritual codes did so in the earnest hope of rejuvenating the crumbling dynasty with a dose of old-fashioned morality. Their project proved so successful in shaping posterity's conception of ancient history that scholars have long turned as a matter of course to the venerable *Record of Rites* and *Po-hu t'ung* for information about the distant past—when these are really the imposed products of a later age.[153] For the student of Chinese history, the problem with the late Han ritualists and their old-fashioned morality is that, like most everything else defended the world over as "old-fashioned values," none of it had much to do with the values upheld by real people in olden times.[154] In spite of the many classical quotations and allusions with which they have larded their works, the overall picture of ancient ritual life presented by these authors is fundamentally distorted. For a more accurate view of Han-dynasty conjugal relations, we must try to cast aside the false perceptions perpetuated by the ritual codes.

The two influential intellectual movements examined in this chapter share a conviction that sexual activity must be regulated. This was the hallmark of Han thinking on sexual relations. For the architects of the early imperial sex ideology, sexual activity was inseparable from political expression and therefore was subject to stringent regulation. Licentiousness was taken seriously as a malfeasance with national ramifications, and political figures who threatened the delicate "unity" that had only recently been forged—figures such as Liu Ting-kuo, Liu Chien, and Ssu-ma Ch'ien—were dealt with precisely as though they had committed sex crimes.

The reform-minded traditionalists, for their part, looked back to ancient times for moral guidance. The law codes set down by the founders of the dynasty were now thought to be ineffective, because they had not solved all of society's problems. The writings of the Pan family furnish an illustrative example of this mode of thought. It is not possible today, two thousand years later, to speculate as to the gravity of the social problems that these traditionalists sought to address; suffice it to say that they saw all around them widespread moral decay stemming from insufficient education, frequently manifesting itself in sexual misconduct. Their solution was to combat these insidious forces with the might of the ink brush and to compose ritual prescriptions designed to bring about a more orderly civilization.

From the point of view of saving the dynasty, the traditionalist movement produced few concrete results. The Han collapsed when it was ready, giving way to a protracted era of political division. One segment of the intellectual world carried on where the Han ritualists had left off, furthering the basic Chinese myth of a prehistoric utopia governed by Sage-Kings who transmitted their teachings in the form of the received canons. But others rejected completely everything that the repressive Han had stood for, advocating instead such revolutionary notions as individual autonomy, sexual freedom, and a basic right to privacy. The tensions between the two poles of this tumultuous new world form the subject of the epilogue.

Epilogue

Privacy and Other Revolutionary Notions at the End of the Han

The last century of Han rule saw a dismal succession of ineffectual emperors and a national bureaucracy paralyzed by factionalism and resentful of what it perceived as the inappropriate rise in the power of palace eunuchs. This bleak period in China's political history, which has been well documented elsewhere,[1] witnessed protracted struggles among the three prepotent and mutually antagonistic political groups: the scholar-officials; the eunuchs; and the great clans, who pretended to support the imperial structure by providing the emperors with their consorts but whose real goal was complete autonomy.

The general sense that the world was coming apart induced many writers to suggest what was wrong, who was at fault, and what might be done about it. Students at the Imperial Academy, for example, demonstrated repeatedly against the undue influence of the eunuchs, provoking the arrest of more than a thousand protesters in a crackdown in A.D. 176.[2] Other observers, such as Wang Fu 王符 (ca. A.D. 82–167),[3] denounced the spendthrift elite, who devoted their resources and energies to luxury and extravagance rather than to the traditional literati aspirations of education and government service.[4] And in line with the understanding, discussed in the previous chapter, that sexual practices were a reflection of political conditions, moralistic criticism often took the form of allegations of sexual laxity. Chung-ch'ang T'ung 仲長統 (179–219), for example, fulminated against the wine and debauchery common at wedding banquets.[5] He was convinced that the malaise of his times was a direct consequence of pervasive moral decay. In a world where the mightiest personages are interested only in gratifying their senses, Chung-ch'ang T'ung argues, one can expect only political and social fragmentation.

It is noteworthy that most of the complaints about the erosion of sexual mores were aimed specifically at well-bred women. Wang Fu, for example, notes with regret that most women no longer stay at home with their sericulture and weaving but "begin to study sorcery and incantation, serving spirits with drumming and dancing" 起學巫 祝，鼓舞事神.[6] A "Music Bureau" ballad (yüeh-fu 樂府) from the time captures the popular theme.

好婦出迎客[7]	The good wife goes out to welcome the guests,
顏色正敷愉	her countenance contented and cheerful.
伸腰再拜跪	Bending at the waist, she repeatedly pays her respects by kneeling,
問客平安不	and asks the guests whether [their trip] was pleasant.
請客北堂上	She invites the guests up to the north hall;
坐客氈氍毹	she seats the guests on a ch'ü-shu carpet.
清白各異樽	Each one has a different goblet for light and dark wine.
酒上正華疏	Over the wine there are flowery ladles.[8]
酌酒持與客	She pours the wine and hands it to the guests.
客言主人持	The guests say that the hostess should have one.
卻略再拜跪	She declines for a moment, then bows again—
然後持一栢	after which she takes a cup.
談笑未及竟	Before the chatting and laughing are finished,
左顧敕中廚	she looks to the left, and orders imperiously into the kitchen,
促令辦麤飯	hurriedly commanding them to prepare some coarse rice.
慎莫使稽留	"Make sure you don't delay!"
廢禮送客出	Letting ritual lapse, she sees the guests out.
盈盈府中趨	Gracefully she hurries across the courtyard.
送客亦不遠	In seeing the guests off, she does not go far;
足不過門樞	her foot does not cross the gate pivot.
取婦得如此	In obtaining a wife, if you get one like this,
齊姜亦不如	even a Chiang of Ch'i would not be her equal.
健婦持門戶	A vigorous wife who maintains the home
勝一大丈夫[9]	exceeds [the value of] one husband.[10]

In this clever ballad, the "good wife" 好婦 does her best to conform to the standard ideals of uxorial behavior but misses the mark tellingly. The word ch'u 出 (goes out) sets the tone for the entire poem. It was hardly proper for a good wife to go out to welcome her guests; on the contrary, she was supposed to remain within the gates of the home at all times, secluded and unseen.[11] But this wife is too "cheerful" 愉 and "vigorous" 健 to be so scrupulous about her modesty. Indeed, she revels in chatter and drink and has evidently taken great pains to prepare the goblets of light and dark wine. When the guests insist that she drink with them, she declines, but only for the sake of appearances; after a perfunctory little bow, she drains a cup. Then, in the midst of the merriment and laughter, she realizes that she has forgotten to tend to the food and quickly orders her kitchen servants to prepare some "coarse rice" 麤飯—the easiest meal to make. She has obviously taken far less care with the food than with the wine. She continues "letting ritual lapse" 廢禮 when she sees the guests off; though she does not go so far as to leave the compound, she wanders out as far as she can, all the way to the gate pivot. The narrator concludes by comparing this wife farcically to a Chiang of Ch'i 齊姜 (that is, a daughter of the noble house of Ch'i), recalling the famous usage in the *Odes*.[12]

For all of the wife's revealing gaffes, one of the most significant aspects of the poem lies in what is *not* mentioned. Where is her husband? Why should a "good wife" be entertaining a cohort of inebriated "guests" 客 inside her home—and all alone? The final line, *sheng i ta chang-fu* 勝一大丈夫 ("exceeds [the value of] one husband"), while pretending to be so laudatory, can also be read as an accusatory innuendo. She "exceeds" 勝 one husband—that is, she prefers to receive more than one man at a time. After all, her behavior does not differ appreciably from that of a madam.

Wang Fu, Chung-ch'ang T'ung, and others like them (including, perhaps, the author of this ballad) may have been certain that moral deterioration was the cause of the ongoing disintegration of the Han. But their social criticism, however stinging (and abundant), was of no use in curing the ailing dynasty. When the end finally came in A.D. 220, most people were already expecting it, but no one knew for sure what would replace the empire.

What followed was a series of short-lived dynasties and political disjunction that lasted almost four hundred years. A thorough account of this tumultuous era—known as the Six Dynasties 六朝—is beyond the scope of the present study (and there are a large number of first-rate works devoted to the subject). But the attitudes toward sexuality expressed in this period are so fascinating, and complement so strikingly the earlier material examined above, that it is worthwhile, by way of closing, to outline the competing views of sex that took shape as China was looking forward to a new world order.

The end of the Han did not bring about an end to moralism, and some writers of the Six Dynasties excoriated licentious women with a fervor that greatly exceeded anything produced by Wang Fu or Chung-ch'ang T'ung. Ko Hung 葛洪 (283–343), for example, is often cited as the most outspoken voice.

今俗婦女，休其蠶織之業，廢其玄紞之務，不績其麻，市也婆娑。舍中饋之事，修周旋之好。更相從詣，之適親戚，承星舉火，不已于行。多將侍從，曄曄盈路，婢使吏卒，錯雜如市，尋道褻謔，可憎可惡。或宿于他門，或冒夜而反。游戲佛寺，觀視漁畋，登高臨水，出境慶弔。開車褰幃，周章城邑，盃觴路酌，絃歌行奏……俗閒有戲婦之法，於稠眾之中，親屬之前，問以醜言，責以慢對，其為鄙黷，不可忍論。或蹙以楚撻，或繫腳倒懸。[13]

The vulgar women of today cease their business of sericulture and weaving; they let lapse their duty [to make] black cap-tassels; they do not spin their hemp; but they sashay around in the marketplace. They abandon matters pertaining to food and drink and cultivate their circle of friends. They pay visits to each other and go to their relatives'. When the stars come out, they bear torches and do not stop their travels. They take many servants and followers, resplendently overflowing the roads. Their maidservants, menservants, envoys, and guards form a throng as at a marketplace. On the road they jest lewdly; it is detestable and hateful. Sometimes they stay overnight at other homes; sometimes they brave the night and return. They wander and play at Buddhist monasteries; they watch fishermen and farmers;[14] they ascend peaks and draw near to the rivers; they leave their districts for celebrations and funerals. They ride in their carriages with the curtains spread open and go around the city. Cups and goblets are poured in the streets, and they play songs as they go along.... Among the vulgar, there is a way of playing with a woman. In a crowd, in front of her relatives, she is asked revolting things, and rebuked if she answers slowly, in a manner so base and vile that I cannot bear to discuss it. Sometimes she is forcibly chastised with a flogger; sometimes her feet are bound and she is suspended upside-down.[15]

It is important to keep in mind that Ko Hung cannot be considered prudish by any contemporary standard. Elsewhere, he takes pains to point out that complete abstinence from sexual pleasure is actually dangerous to one's emotional and physical health.[16] He sub-

scribed to the standard view of sexual intercourse as an exchange of
ch'i (as described in the preface in this volume) and conceded that
if one knew the proper methods, then the more one copulated, the
greater the resulting salutary benefits. Why then, did he criticize so
bitterly the women who gallivanted coquettishly through the streets
of the city? Ko Hung's complaint is that these women (and the men
who play their sadomasochistic "truth or dare" games with them) are
hardly interested in studying the arcane and respectable art of sexual
macrobiotics; they are merely giving in to their lustful impulses. Even
more important, their pleasure outings come at an intolerable price:
they cause women to abandon their proper place behind the loom
in the inner quarters. The august categories of *nei* and *wai*—for whatever they were really worth in ancient times—were being brazenly
assailed, even deliberately defied. For Ko Hung, the "vulgar" 俗 customs represent a catastrophic social breakdown.[17]

In this respect, however, Ko Hung was no longer in step with the
times. For the most characteristic attitudes of the period held that it
was not necessarily reprehensible for men and women to challenge
the received norms of behavior. It was fashionable to ask, with Juan
Chi 阮籍 (210–263), "Were the rituals established for people of our
kind?" 禮豈為我輩設也?[18] Never before, and certainly not during the
Han dynasty, could such a question have been posed. The view that
the ancient rituals need not apply to our everyday lives was revolutionary, and this dismantling of traditional morality gradually
became acceptable and even commonplace. How this momentous
change in outlook came about is worth some reflection.

The new custodians of mainstream values were scions of the mano-
rial gentry,[19] the great families that came to dominate local administration during the period of imperial weakness in the third and
fourth centuries.[20] The last thing these aristocrats wanted to see was
a resurgence of imperial power, and they devoted their energies to
consolidating their own autonomy and undermining, as much as
possible, the effectiveness of the national government.[21] The gentry
were consequently faced with two competing and irreconcilable
commitments in their role as members of the bureaucratic elite: service to the empire as government officials, and resistance to it as territorial aristocrats.[22] Their political ideal was the utopia described in
the "Record of Peach-Blossom Spring" 桃花源記, by T'ao Ch'ien 陶
潛 (365–427),[23] where an arcadian community lives undisturbed for
centuries, at peace with themselves and each other, entirely oblivious

to the rise and fall of dynasties in the world beyond the grotto.[24] In the intellectual sphere, the gentry's struggle for local hegemony manifested itself as a revolt against the tired and rigid doctrines of the Han. As the Han ideologues propounded their uniform behavioral standards in an effort to forge a unified empire centered on a single leader, the new aristocratic elite of the post-Han era, in resisting imperialist demands on their loyalty, sought to undo what they perceived as the excessive regimentation of daily life.[25]

One favorite target of attack was the empty formalism of the rituals. According to Shu Hsi 束皙 (fl. 281), for example, in an ideal society wives addressed their husbands by the familiar appellation *ch'ing* 卿, "you" (that is, instead of using some honorific phrase), and sons called their fathers by their personal names.[26] When Wang An-feng 王安豐 (i.e., Wang Jung 王戎, 234–305) reprimanded his wife for calling him *ch'ing* and thereby "being disrespectful according to the rites" 於禮為不敬, she replied disarmingly,

親卿愛卿，是以卿卿；我不卿卿，誰當卿卿？[27]

I am intimate with you and I love you; therefore I call you "you." If I do not call you "you," who should call you "you"?[28]

He never complained about it again.

The unspoken point in the above exchange, which is typical of the age, is that the rituals are dispensable when they begin to impede the expression of genuine feeling or when they interfere with deep relationships between individuals. The idea was especially well articulated by the aforementioned Juan Chi, who was one of the most celebrated examples of a so-called "urban hermit" 市隱, or a deliberate nonconformist who intended to make serious moral statements with studied idiosyncrasies.[29] Famously, Juan Chi attended parties while mourning his mother but wept excessively at the funeral of a girl that he did not even know.[30] His more conservative contemporaries wrongly deduced from his outrageous violations of the rites that he did not care for his deceased mother. In private, we are told, he cried out, expectorated several *sheng* 升 of blood, and lay ill for a long time.[31] He considered the open disregard of propriety as the surest sign of sincere devotion.[32]

But as iconoclastic as Juan Chi tried to be, his ideas soon became normal among intellectuals. Later thinkers, such as Kuo Hsiang 郭象 (d. 312), found an enduring articulation of the same notion—that ritualism merely impedes the expression of true emotions—in the ancient *Chuang-tzu*.[33] Even the august classics were not immune to reassessment. Allegedly, the wife of Hsieh An 謝安 (320–385) declared that "The *Kuan*-ing Ospreys"—which, as we have seen, was repeatedly invoked as justification for regulating sexual contact between the sexes—adopted a biased and limited point of view because it was written by a man. If a woman had written the poem, she suggested, the conventional notions of proper behavior might be completely different.[34]

The interrelated themes of nonconformism, objection to moribund ritualism, and affirmation of personal autonomy come together clearly in an anecdote about Liu Ling 劉伶 (d. after 265), who, like Juan Chi and Wang Jung, was a member of the notorious group known as the Seven Worthies of the Bamboo Grove 竹林七賢.[35]

> 劉伶恆縱酒放達，或脫衣裸形屋中，人見譏之。伶曰：我以天地為棟宇，屋室為褌衣，諸君何為入我褌中？[36]

Liu Ling always indulged in wine and let himself be uninhibited. Sometimes he would take his clothes off and stay in his house stark naked. When people saw this, they criticized him. Ling said: "I take Heaven and Earth as my pillars and roof, and the rooms of my house as my trousers. Gentlemen, what are you doing by entering my trousers?"[37]

The story must be understood in the context of Juan Chi's statement that the so-called noble men (*chün-tzu* 君子) who devote their lives solely to following the rituals are like annoying lice that inhabit one's trousers.[38] As Richard B. Mather has pointed out, Liu Ling's joke must be read as a protest "against the invasion of his personal privacy."[39] Simply put, he is declaring his right, within the confines of his home, to do anything he wants, however eccentric it may be.[40] Gone are the days when the emperor in his palace can dictate universal norms, and those hidebound conventionalists who expound the shopworn ideologies of Han times are merely trespassing in other people's personal space.[41]

It is a brilliant and cutting retort, and it is also a thoroughly aristocratic retort. Never, in imperial times, was "privacy" (*ssu* 私) conceived as a praiseworthy notion: "privacy" merely denoted those troublesome areas where imperial control (*kung* 公) was not fully established.[42] Liu Ling's comment and indeed his provocative behavior represent a calculated declaration of his rights and privileges as a member of the unfettered aristocratic class. Later figures (such as the scandalous Uninhibited Eight 八達) would take up Liu's mandate as justification for free love, nudism, drug taking, and similar affirmations of personal freedom that cannot be unfamiliar to anyone living at the beginning of the twenty-first century.[43]

Religious Taoism offered another set of alternatives to the bankrupt ideology of the Han. Part of the appeal of the sect of the Celestial Masters 天師, for example, must have been that they offered a superior celestial bureaucracy—and at times also a superior terrestrial one—while the Han bureaucracy was in the midst of ineluctable disintegration.[44] Moreover, by emphasizing the spiritual equality of men and women, the movement attracted devotees who were unsatisfied with the old sexual hierarchy of male dominance and female subservience. Female acolytes could avoid the obligation to marry husbands chosen by the male heads of their clan; indeed, they could look forward even to the possibility of ordination alongside the men in the sect.[45] The Taoist rebellions of the 180s are generally recognized as the final spark that brought about the end of the Empire,[46] and the religion went on to be a primary influence in shaping the intellectual consciousness of the Six Dynasties.

The Celestial Masters countered the prospect of sexual licentiousness by instituting highly ritualized sexual ceremonies, recorded in the so-called yellow writings (*huang-shu* 黃書), which were designed to place sexual activity within a sacrosanct cosmological framework. Like Ko Hung and the authors of the sex manuals, the Celestial Masters conceived of sexual intercourse as an exchange of *yin* and *yang ch'i*. Unlike these contemporaries, however, members of the Celestial Master sect did not practice the "union of *ch'i*" (*ho-ch'i* 合氣) for the purpose of stealing their partners' vital essences and thereby extending the measure of their own life spans. Rather, they sought a genuine union of *ch'i*, a ritualized invocation of the diverse cosmological forces.[47]

As it is prescribed in a surviving scripture, the ritual was to be carried out under the supervision of a master and only after a long sequence of preparatory steps: bathing, fasting, burning incense, saluting the officiating master, and invoking the gods.[48] The ceremony then continued through dozens of steps—which must have lasted several hours—involving massage, meditation, and recitation of liturgies. At times the man and woman linked hands, combining their fingers in numerologically significant positions; at times they rubbed specific parts of each other's body, with their hands or even with their feet. Kristofer Schipper remarks,

> The ritual was performed in a perfectly symmetrical manner. Each prayer, each gesture by the man found its symmetrical counterpart in a gesture and prayer by the woman. There was no such thing as one active and one passive partner. The text of the ritual, as it has come down to us in a version from the early Middle Ages (fourth century A.D.),[49] is very beautiful and the execution of the ritual must have been an extraordinary event. The union of *ch'i* ... must have required that the participants have perfect mastery of their bodies.[50]

The avowed purpose of the "union of *ch'i*" was to serve as a "rite of passage" (*kuo-tu* 過度)—and not to gratify the participants' carnal desires.[51] On the contrary, the Celestial Masters militated against lubricity and established Commandants of Fornication (*chien-ling* 姦令), officials whose duty was to fight against sin (which was understood as the cause of disease) by spiritual means.[52] Ironically, however, these sex rites were frequently cited by those who accused Taoism of lewdness. Some of the most effective charges came from Buddhists,[53] and eventually even Taoist patriarchs tried to distance themselves and their religion from the infamous "yellow writings."[54] Nevertheless, in the minds of many, Taoism would henceforth always be associated with secretive and questionable sex practices. In a sense, this was only fitting. As we have seen repeatedly, sexual activity was continually conceived in ancient China as an index of political activity, and it was appropriate that the Taoist church, which presented itself from the beginning as an institution with an alternative worldview to compete with the ideology of the empire, should incorporate alternative sexual norms as well.

The general spirit of the age is conveyed effectively in another famous ballad, known informally as "The Peacock Flies Southeast" 孔雀東南飛. The preface to the poem explains the story.

> 漢末建安中，廬江府小吏焦仲卿妻劉氏為仲卿母所遣。自誓不嫁，其家逼之，乃沒水而死。仲卿聞之，亦自縊于庭樹。時傷之，為詩云爾。[55]

> In the middle years of the Chien-an reign period at the end of the Han [i.e., ca. 204–212], the wife, née Liu, of Chiao Chung-ch'ing, a minor functionary in the government offices at Lu-chiang, was sent away by Chung-ch'ing's mother. [Liu] swore that she would not remarry, but her family forced her, so she drowned herself. When

Chung-ch'ing heard of this, he also hanged himself from a tree in the courtyard. At the time, one who was pained by this [event] wrote the following poem.[56]

The poem proper then begins, recounting in bathetic language how Chung-ch'ing's wife, despite her industry and modesty, is cast out cruelly by her mother-in-law, who pays no heed to Chung-ch'ing's simpering protestations. Chung-ch'ing hardly knows what to say when he faces his wife.

舉言謂新婦	He started to speak to his newlywed wife;
哽咽不能語	stammering and coughing, he could not speak.
我自不驅卿	"It's not that I am throwing you out,
逼迫有阿母	but Mommy is pressuring me.
卿但暫還家	You just go back to your family temporarily,
吾今且報府	and meanwhile I will report to the Bureau.
不久當歸還	Before long, it will be right for me to return,
還必相迎取	and when I return, I will certainly take you back.
以此下心意	Set aside your worries about this.
慎勿違吾語	Be sure not to oppose what I say."
新婦謂府吏	The newlywed wife said to the government clerk:
勿復重紛紜	"Do not keep repeating the same balderdash.
往昔初陽歲	Long ago, at the beginning of spring,
謝家來貴門	I left my family and came to your honorable gates.
奉事循公姥	Respectfully serving and obeying Mother-in-law,
進止敢自專	I was attentive and did not dare focus on myself.
晝夜勤作息	Day and night I worked and produced assiduously.
伶俜縈苦辛	Alone,[57] I am wound around in bitterness.
謂言無罪過	My words were without transgression;
供養卒大恩	I fulfilled my obligations with great kindness.
仍更被驅遣	But I am sent away nevertheless.
何言復來還[58]	Why do you speak of my coming back here?"[59]

The miserable girl then lists her worthless possessions, adding,

不足迎後人	"They are insufficient for your next wife,
留待作遺施	but I will leave them to wait for her as a hand-me-down present.[60]
於今無會因	After this, there will be no cause for us to meet.
時時為安慰	Over time, we will be consoled—
久久莫相忘[61]	And may we never forget each other."[62]

Chung-ch'ing's former wife is soon betrothed by her family to a new husband—the son of the county magistrate, no less. And Chung-ch'ing's mother, sensing her son's misery, finds a new bride for him as well. But the girl cannot bear to marry another man—to her, that would be to betray her husband—and so, as we have been warned, she drowns herself in a lake. When Chung-ch'ing hears the news, he "paces back and forth under a tree in the courtyard" 徘徊庭樹下 but then finally musters the courage to hang himself from the southeast branch.

One might dismiss this poem as a lugubrious, if not downright maudlin, sentiment piece, were it not for the astonishingly pointed conclusion. The narrator suddenly addresses us directly (people of later generations 後世人): "Be advised, and be careful not to forget!" 戒之慎勿忘.[63] What exactly are we being advised not to forget—that Chung-ch'ing brought about not only his own death but also that of his beloved, *by obeying his mother*? And that his mother lost her son by failing to appreciate his love of a girl with whom he shared no blood relation? These are absolutely revolutionary ideas, thoroughly incompatible with the old ethic of deference to one's elders and loyalty to the clan. Chung-ch'ing is not eulogized in this poem as a "filial son" who is willing to make the greatest sacrifices in order to please his mother. Rather, he is portrayed as emasculated and puerile, irresolute even in his last moments beneath the tree in the courtyard. Within the framework of a conventional love story, the poem constructs a devastating indictment of the old moral and social order. Men who prostrate themselves before the sterile ideals of "ritual" 禮, "deference" 讓, and "filial piety" 孝, while suppressing their genuine feelings, are not to be admired but to be pitied, if not condemned. If you love someone, the poem tells us, and your family stands in the way, the more difficult and praiseworthy course of action is not to overcome your heart but to overcome your family.[64]

The author of the poem may have hoped that Chung-ch'ing's death would spell the end of traditional morality and that forever after young men and women would be free to choose their lovers, to reject their parents' callous admonitions, to chart their own course of life. Of course, this was not to be. The very popularity of the theme of tragic love reveals only how pervasive such frustration must have been among real audiences. The literature of the day may have pointed out that it was a painful experience—perhaps even an unnecessary experience—to be forced to marry someone other than one's true love, but most men and women still found themselves in arranged marriages and continued in their turn to arrange marriages for their own children. Moreover, as Six Dynasties China moved on, inexorably, to the prospect of reunification under a new empire, the allure of nonconformism and antiritualism began to wear thin. Already the hopeful dynasts in the north were legislating intricate marriage codes, in the familiar belief that a kingdom where sex was regulated was a kingdom where subjects were submissive and united. When the Six Dynasties came to a close, the foundational Chinese attitudes toward love, sex, and marriage had been set in place.

Notes

Introduction

1. See, e.g., Catharine A. MacKinnon, "Does Sexuality Have a History?" *Michigan Quarterly Review* 30 (1991), reprinted in *Discourses of Sexuality: From Aristotle to AIDS*, ed. Domna C. Stanton, Ratio: Institute for the Humanities (Ann Arbor: University of Michigan Press, 1992), 117–136; David M. Halperin, "Is There a History of Sexuality?" *History and Theory* 28.3 (1989), reprinted in *Philosophy and Sex*, ed. Robert B. Baker et al., 3d ed. (Amherst, N.Y.: Prometheus, 1998), 413–431; and Robert Padgug, "Sexual Matters: On Conceptualizing Sexuality in History," *Radical History Review* 20 (1979), reprinted in Baker et al., 432–448.

2. Yin-ch'üeh-shan Han-mu chu-chien cheng-li hsiao-tsu 銀雀山漢墓竹簡整理小組, *Sun Pin Ping-fa* 孫臏兵法 (Peking: Wen-wu, 1975), 115 f.

3. See, e.g., Michel Foucault, *The History of Sexuality*, trans. Robert Hurley (New York: Random House, Vintage Books, 1978–1986), vol. 1, 105 f.

4. See, e.g., Bruce S. Thornton, *Eros: The Myth of Ancient Greek Sexuality* (Boulder, Colo.: Westview, 1997), 99–120, 201 ff.; Sue Blundell, *Women in Ancient Greece* (Cambridge: Harvard University Press, 1995), 103; and esp. K. J. Dover, *Greek Homosexuality* (repr., New York: MJF, 1989), 100–109. For a recent criticism of phallocentrism and the primacy of the distinction between penetrator and penetrated, see James N. Davidson, *Courtesans and Fishcakes: The Consuming Passions of Classical Athens* (New York: Harper Collins, 1997), 168 ff.

Even those ancient Greek works (intended for men) that discuss the relative merits of sex with women and sex with boys should not be misunderstood as comparisons between the relative merits of heterosexuality and homosexuality. See esp. David M. Halperin, "Historicizing the Sexual Body: Sexual Preferences and Erotic Identities in the Pseudo-Lucianic *Erôtes*," in Stanton, 236–261. The originality of constructionism, however, is sometimes overstated. For example, Margaret Mead, *Sex and Temperament in Three Primitive Societies* (New York: Morrow, 1935), 304 ff., discussed the cultural roots of homosexual attitudes more than six decades ago. Cf. also Bronislaw Malinowski, *Sex and Repression in Savage Society*, Meridian Books M15 (1927; repr., Cleveland: World Book Co., 1955), 161–238.

5. On the Jesuits in general and Matteo Ricci in particular, see, e.g., Howard L. Goodman and Anthony Grafton, "Ricci, the Chinese, and the Toolkits of Textualists," *Asia Major*, 3d ser., 3.2 (1990), 95–148, which is an extensive review of Jacques Gernet, *China and the Christian Impact: A Conflict of Cultures*, trans. Janet Lloyd (Cambridge: Cambridge University Press, 1985); and Jonathan D. Spence, *The Memory Palace of Matteo Ricci* (New York: Penguin, Elisabeth Sifton Books, 1984).

6. For the life and work of James Legge, see, e.g., Lindsay Ride, "Biographical Note," in James Legge, *The Chinese Classics* (n.d.; repr., Taipei: SMC, 1991), vol. 1, 1–25.

7. Arthur Waley, trans., *The Book of Songs: The Ancient Chinese Classic of Poetry*, ed. Joseph R. Allen (New York: Grove, 1996).

8. Perhaps the most infamous example of the same approach is found in the work of A. E. J. B. Terrien de Lacouperie (d. 1894), who endeavored to prove that Chinese civilization was ultimately derived from that of Mesopotamia. See his *Western Origin of the Early Chinese Civilisation from 2,300 B.C. to 200 A.D.; or, Chapters on the Elements Derived from the Old Civilisations of West Asia in the Formation of the Ancient Chinese Culture* (London: Asher, 1894). Terrien de Lacouperie's book has been roundly derided not only for its Orientalist approach but also for its implication that China is a "secondary" rather than a "primary" civilization. For an early example of such criticism, see Edward Harper Parker, *Ancient China Simplified* (London: Chapman and Hall, 1908), 186–193.

9. Cf. esp. Edward W. Said, *Orientalism* (New York: Random House, Vintage Books, 1978), 3 ff. See also Eric Hobsbawm, "The Curious History of Europe," in *On History* (London: Little, Brown and Co., Abacus, 1998), 288.

10. For the reminiscences of two scholars who undertook scholarly work on sex before most of the academy was prepared for it, see Robert B. Baker, " 'Pricks' and 'Chicks': A Plea for 'Persons,' " in Baker et al., 297 ff.; and Vern L. Bullough, "Sex in History: A Redux," in *Desire and Discipline: Sex and Sexuality in the Premodern West*, ed. Jacqueline Murray and Konrad Eisenbichler (Toronto: University of Toronto Press, 1996), 3–22.

11. See, e.g., Matthew H. Sommer, *Sex, Law, and Society in Late Imperial China*, Law, Society, and Culture in China (Stanford, Calif.: Stanford University Press, 2000); Gail Hershatter, *Dangerous Pleasures: Prostitution and Modernity in Twentieth-Century Shanghai* (Berkeley and Los Angeles: University of California Press, 1997); Frank Dikötter, *Sex, Culture, and Modernity in China: Medical Science and the Construction of Sexual Identities in the Early Republican Period* (Honolulu: University of Hawai'i Press, 1995); Keith McMahon, *Misers, Shrews, and Polygamists: Sexuality and Male-Female Relations in Eighteenth-Century Chinese Fiction* (Durham, N.C.: Duke University Press, 1995); Tonglin Lu, ed., *Gender and Sexuality in Twentieth-Century Chinese Literature and Society*, SUNY Series in Feminist Criticism and Theory (Albany, N.Y., 1993); Dian Murray, "The Practice of Homosexuality among the Pirates of Late Eighteenth and Early Nineteenth Century China," *Inter-*

national Journal of Maritime History 4.1 (1992), 121–130; M. J. Meijer, *Murder and Adultery in Late Imperial China: A Study of Law and Morality*, Sinica Leidensia 25 (Leiden: E. J. Brill, 1991) and "Homosexual Offenses in Ch'ing Law," *T'oung Pao* 71 (1985), 109–133; Vivien Ng, "Homosexuality and the State in Late Imperial China," in *Hidden from History: Reclaiming the Gay and Lesbian Past*, ed. Martin Duberman et al. (New York: Meridian, 1989), 76–89; "Ideology and Sexuality: Rape Laws in Qing China," *Journal of Asian Studies* 46.1 (1987), 57–70; and Charlotte Furth, "Androgynous Males and Deficient Females: Biology and Gender Boundaries in Sixteenth- and Seventeenth-Century China," *Late Imperial China* 9.2 (1988), 1–31.

The above list is intended to be representative rather than exhaustive. Here one may also mention Eric Chou, *The Dragon and the Phoenix: The Book of Chinese Love and Sex* (New York: Arbor House, 1971; repr., New York: Bantam, 1972), which, though not written in a scholarly style, contains some original insights.

12. R. H. van Gulik, *Sexual Life in Ancient China: A Preliminary Survey of Chinese Sex and Society from ca. 1500 B.C. till 1644 A.D.* (Leiden: E. J. Brill, 1961; repr., New York: Barnes and Noble, 1996).

13. See, e.g., Joseph Needham, *Science and Civilisation in China* (Cambridge: Cambridge University Press, 1956–), vol. 2, 147.

14. See esp. Charlotte Furth, "Rethinking van Gulik: Sexuality and Reproduction in Traditional Chinese Medicine," in *Engendering China: Women, Culture, and the State*, ed. Christina K. Gilmartin et al., Harvard Contemporary China Series 10 (Cambridge, 1994), 125–146; and Douglas Wile, *Art of the Bedchamber: The Chinese Sexual Yoga Classics, Including Women's Solo Meditation Texts* (Albany: State University of New York Press, 1992), 57 f.

15. Van Gulik, xiii passim. Compare also Janwillem van de Wetering, *Robert van Gulik: Ein Leben mit Richter Di*, trans. Klaus Schomburg (Zurich: Diogenes, 1990), 82 f. Following van Gulik's lead, Reay Tannahill, *Sex in History*, rev. ed. (n.p.: Scarborough House, 1992), 177, comments on the absence in traditional China of "practices that could be described as sadistic or masochistic." Tannahill goes on to blame "Confucianism" and "neo-Confucianism" for overpowering the "mild and indulgent philosophy of Taoism" in sexual matters (see, e.g., 183, 198).

16. See Richard von Krafft-Ebing, *Psychopathia Sexualis, with Especial Reference to the Antipathic Sexual Instinct: A Medico-Forensic Study*, trans. Franklin S. Klaf (New York: Stein and Day, 1965; repr., New York: Arcade, 1998), esp. 52–143. On the terms "sadism" and "masochism" and their invention by Krafft-Ebing, see, e.g., Vern L. Bullough et al., "Sadism, Masochism, and History, or when Is Behaviour Sado-masochistic?" in *Sexual Knowledge, Sexual Science: The History of Attitudes to Sexuality*, ed. Roy Porter and Mikuláš Teich (Cambridge: Cambridge University Press, 1994), 47 f. See also Renate Hauser's article, "Krafft-Ebing's psychological understanding of sexual behaviour," in the same volume, 210–227.

17. The standard essay on this subject is Arnold I. Davidson, "Closing Up the Corpses: Diseases of Sexuality and the Emergence of the Psychiatric Style of Reasoning," in *Meaning and Method: Essays in Honor of Hilary Putnam*, ed.

George Boolos (Cambridge: Cambridge University Press, 1990), 295–325. See also Timothy Taylor, *The Prehistory of Sex: Four Million Years of Human Sexual Culture* (New York: Bantam, 1996), 73 f.; and Foucault, vol. 1, 37 ff.

18. Van Gulik, e.g., 155 ff.

19. Julia Kristeva, *About Chinese Women*, trans. Anita Barrows (New York: Urizen, 1977), 62 ff.

20. See, e.g., Tu Yung-ming 杜永明 et al., *Hei Erh-shih-ssu shih* 黑二十四史 (Peking: Chung-kuo hua-ch'iao, 1998), vol. 1, 340 ff.; Donald Harper, *Early Chinese Medical Literature: The Mawangdui Medical Manuscripts*, The Sir Henry Wellcome Asian Series (London: Kegan Paul International, 1998), 135 ff.; Wile, 5 ff.; Li Ling 李零, *Chung-kuo fang-shu k'ao* 中國方術考 (Peking: Jen-min, 1993), 356–402; Kristofer Schipper, *The Taoist Body*, trans. Karen C. Duval (Berkeley and Los Angeles: University of California Press, 1993), 147 ff.; Li Ling and Keith McMahon, "The Content and Terminology of the Mawangdui Texts on the Arts of the Bedchamber," *Early China* 17 (1992), 179–181; van Gulik, 35 ff.; Needham, vol. 2, 146 ff.; and esp. Henri Maspero, "Les procédés de 'nourrir le principe vital' dans la religion taoïste ancienne," *Journal Asiatique* 229 (1937), reprinted in *Le Taoïsme et les religions chinoises*, Bibliothèque des histoires (Paris: Gallimard, 1971), 553–577. (The translation of Frank A. Kierman, Jr., *Taoism and Chinese Religion* [Amherst: University of Massachusetts Press, 1981], was not available to me at the time of this writing.) Cf. also Henri Maspero, "Essai sur le Taoïsme aux premiers siècles de l'ère chrétienne," in *Mélanges posthumes sur les religions et l'histoire de la Chine*, Publications du Musée Guimet; Bibliothèque de diffusion 57–59 (Paris: Civilisations du Sud, 1950), vol. 2, 114–115 (= *Le Taoïsme*, 379). Some traditions speak of *huan-ching pu-nao* 還精補腦 ("recycling the semen to nourish the brain"), which reflects the belief that injaculated semen will circulate all the way to the brain. There is a fascinating parallel to this practice in Tantric Buddhism; thus Bernard Faure, *The Red Thread: Buddhist Approaches to Sexuality*, Buddhisms: A Princeton University Press Series (Princeton, N.J., 1998), 50, describes "'coitus reservatus' with a female partner (*mudrā*)": "The trick is to stir the seminal essence without losing it through ejaculation, so that it may ascend through the central artery into the seat of Great Bliss located in the brain." This is not to suggest, of course, that the view of copulation (and of the role of the female partner) in Tantric Buddhism is comparable to that of the Chinese sex manuals. See esp. Miranda Shaw, *Passionate Enlightenment: Women in Tantric Buddhism*, Mythos (Princeton, N.J.: Princeton University Press, 1994), 140–178.

Hei Erh-shih-ssu shih (*The Black Dynastic Histories*, cited above) is the intriguing title of a new collection of twenty-four expository histories (amounting to more than four thousand large pages) covering such "black" topics as prostitution, footbinding, crime, and sex. The quality of the various essays is uneven, but the references are generally accurate, and the collection succeeds in bringing together a massive amount of information on subjects that the editors call the "blind spots of scholarship" 學術的盲點 (in their epilogue, vol. 6, 4473). For the sake of concision, I shall cite this work henceforth as merely *Hei Erh-shih-ssu shih*.

21. See esp. "Yü-fang pi-chüeh" 玉房秘決, as cited in Tamba Yasuyori 丹波康賴 (fl. A.D. 982–984), *Ishimpō* 醫心方 (Peking: Jen-min wei-sheng, 1955), 28.636, which adds that the Queen Mother of the West 西王母 became a divinity by cop-

ulating with many young boys. The text is quoted without comment in van Gulik, 158 f., and is translated in Wile, 102–108, as well as Howard S. Levy and Akira Ishihara, *The Tao of Sex: The Essence of Medical Prescriptions (Ishimpō)*, 3d ed. (Lower Lake, Calif.: Integral, 1989), 27.

22. As in the excavated text "T'ien-hsia chih-tao t'an" 天下至道談; text in Ma Chi-hsing 馬繼興, *Ma-wang-tui ku i-shu k'ao-shih* 馬王堆古醫書考釋 (Ch'ang-sha: Hu-nan k'o-hsüeh chi-shu, 1992), 1072. For a different view, see Sandra A. Wawrytko, "Prudery and Prurience: Historical Roots of the Confucian Conundrum concerning Women, Sexuality, and Power," in *The Sage and the Second Sex: Confucianism, Ethics, and Gender*, ed. Chenyang Li (Chicago: Open Court, 2000), 177, who argues that in "T'ien-hsia chih-tao t'an," "women are not perceived as sources of energy to be exploited, but rather as equal partners in the ensuing benefits of intercourse."

23. Cf. esp. Schipper, *The Taoist Body*, 148 f., and "Science, magie, et mystique du corps: Notes sur le taoïsme et la sexualité," in *Jeux des nuages et de la pluie*, ed. M. Beurdeley (Frieburg: Office du Livre, 1969), 23 ff.

It should be pointed out that van Gulik seems originally not to have held such an idealistic view of sexual relations in ancient China. Indeed, he first termed the idea of *ch'i* exchange "sexual vampirism" and was promptly criticized by Joseph Needham, who wrote in a letter to van Gulik: "on the contrary Taoism had on the whole influenced favourably the development of sexual relations, and enhanced the position of Chinese women in general" (quoted in van Gulik, xiii; see also Needham, vol. 2, 146 n). Van Gulik yielded. Needham was already a renowned scholar, van Gulik a professional diplomat who collected art and wrote books in his spare time. Cf. van de Wetering, 82. But Needham's view, as we shall see (chapter 2), is based largely on a misreading of certain passages in the *Lao-tzu*.

24. One of the oldest references appears in the "Wu-ch'eng" 武稱 chapter of the *I Chou-shu* 逸周書: "a beautiful boy undoes an older man" 美男破老; text in Chu Yu-tseng 朱右曾 (fl. 1846), *I Chou-shu chi-hsün chiao-shih* 逸周書集訓校釋 (*Kuo-hsüeh chi-pen ts'ung-shu* 國學基本叢書), 2.6.13. (Chu Yu-tseng identifies the "beautiful boy" as a catamite 外寵.) Han Fei 韓非, in his essay "Pa-chien" 八姦, also lists "lovely lads" 愛孺子 as one category of the bedfellows enjoyed by a ruler; text in Ch'en Ch'i-yu 陳奇猷, *Han Fei-tzu chi-shih* 韓非子集釋, Chung-kuo ssu-hsiang ming-chu (Peking: Chung-hua, 1958; repr., Taipei: Shih-chieh, 1991), 2.9.151, with commentary by Chiang Ch'ao-po 瑱超伯 (fl. 1845), 154 n. 4. For other early references, see, e.g., Liu Ta-lin 劉達臨, *Chung-kuo ku-tai hsing wen-hua* 中國古代性文化 (Yin-ch'uan: Ning-hsia jen-min, 1993), vol. 1, 164–169. See also *Hei Erh-shih-ssu shih*, vol. 1, 127–131; Bret Hinsch, *Passions of the Cut Sleeve: The Male Homosexual Tradition in China* (Berkeley and Los Angeles: University of California Press, 1990); and Fang-fu Ruan and Yung-mei Tsai, "Male Homosexuality in the Traditional Chinese Literature," *Journal of Homosexuality* 14.3–4 (1987), 21–33. (Liu Ta-lin's more recent work, *Chung-kuo li-tai fang-nei k'ao* 中國歷代房內考, 3 vols. [Peking: Chung-i ku-chi, 1998], was not available to me at the time of this writing.)

25. Consider the term *tui-shih* 對食 ("eating each other"), a euphemism for lesbian love. See, e.g., "Wai-ch'i chuan" 外戚傳, *Han-shu* 漢書 (Peking: Chung-

hua, 1962), 97B.3990; and esp. the commentary by Ying Shao 應劭 (d. before A.D. 204): "When palace ladies act towards each other as man and wife, it is called *tui-shih*" 宮人自相與為夫婦名對食 (3992 n. 2). Cf. also Hinsch, *Passions of the Cut Sleeve*, 174; and C. Martin Wilbur, *Slavery in China during the Former Han Dynasty*, Anthropological Series, Field Museum of Natural History 34 (Chicago, 1943), 431 n. 10. In later times, *tui-shih* came to denote an artificial marriage between a eunuch and a palace maid (presumably because the eunuch was not considered a genuine male). See *Hei Erh-shih-ssu shih*, vol. 5, 3440; and Jennifer W. Jay, "Another Side of Chinese Eunuch History: Castration, Marriage, Adoption, and Burial," *Canadian Journal of History* 28.3 (1993), 467.

1. Imagery of Copulation

1. All translations in this book are my own, except where otherwise indicated. For texts other than the *Odes*, references are provided to standard published translations for purposes of comparison. The most reliable complete translation of the *Odes* is probably Bernhard Karlgren, trans., *The Book of Odes* (Stockholm: Museum of Far Eastern Antiquities, 1950).

2. Poems in the *Shih-ching* are cited by their number in the *Mao Odes*, that is, the collection as transmitted by Mao Heng 毛亨 and Mao Ch'ang 毛萇 (both fl. 200 B.C.?). For the Chinese text of the *Odes*, I follow Ch'ü Wan-li 屈萬里, *Shih-ching shih-i* 釋義, 2 vols., Hsien-tai kuo-min chi-pen chih-shih ts'ung-shu (Taipei: Chung-kuo wen-hua, 1952–1953).

3. Wen I-to 聞一多 (1899–1946), "Shuo yü" 說魚, in *Wen I-to ch'üan-chi* 全集 (Peking: San-lien, 1982), 117–138. See also Edward L. Shaughnessy, "How the Poetess Came to Burn the Royal Chamber," in *Before Confucius: Studies in the Creation of the Chinese Classics*, SUNY Series in Chinese Philosophy and Culture (Albany, N.Y., 1997), 224 f. I Chung-t'ien 易中天, *Chung-kuo te nan-jen ho nü-jen* 中國的男人和女人, I Chung-t'ien suei-pi-t'i hsüeh-shu chu-tso, Chung-kuo wen-hua hsi-lieh 2 (Shanghai: Wen-i, 2000), 93, suggests that fish attained this symbolic significance because they were thought to resemble vulvae. Evidently not recognizing the various emblems in the poem "Hou-jen," Marcel Granet, *Fêtes et chansons anciennes de la Chine* (Paris: Ernest Leroux, 1919), 45, considers it to be "certainement déformée et d'interprétation difficile" ("certainly garbled and difficult to interpret").

Fish seem to have served a similar emblematic function in ancient Egyptian love poetry. In one fragment, for example, a seductive woman holds a red fish in her hands. (Compare the bream with the reddened tail in *Mao* 10, discussed below.) See Lise Manniche, *Sexual Life in Ancient Egypt* (London: Kegan Paul International, 1987), 88.

4. Cf., e.g., Shaughnessy, *Before Confucius*, 229 f., who cites several examples. See also Ch'ien Chung-shu 錢鍾書, *Kuan-chui pien* 管錐編, 2d ed. (Peking: Chung-hua, 1986), vol. 1, 73–74.

Excessive love of food, incidentally, was seen in the same light as sexual incontinence in ancient Greece as well. "Eating, drinking, and rutting," for example, was the fitting motto of the apolaustic King Sardanapalus. See, e.g., James N. Davidson, *Courtesans and Fishcakes: The Consuming Passions of Classical Athens* (New York: Harper Collins, 1997), 165 f., 180.

5. See the commentaries of Cheng Hsüan 鄭玄 (A.D. 127–200) and K'ung Ying-ta 孔穎達 (574–648) in *Mao-Shih cheng-i* 毛詩正義, in Juan Yüan 阮元 (1764–1849), *Shih-san ching chu-shu fu chiao-k'an chi* 十三經注疏附校勘記 (1817; repr., Peking: Chung-hua, 1980), 7A.377b.

6. This sentence is from the "Minor Preface" 小序 to the poem (*Mao-Shih cheng-i* 4C.342b) and constitutes what is sometimes called the "Upper Preface," which is attributed to Confucius' disciple Tzu-hsia 子夏 (i.e., Pu Shang 卜商, b. 507 B.C.) and is accepted by most scholars as older than the Maos. For the distinction between the "Upper Preface" and the "Lower Preface," see Steven Van Zoeren, *Poetry and Personality: Reading, Exegesis, and Hermeneutics in Traditional China* (Stanford, Calif.: Stanford University Press, 1991), 92 ff.; and Jeffrey Riegel, "Eros, Introversion, and the Beginnings of *Shijing* Commentary," *Harvard Journal of Asiatic Studies* 57.1 (1997), 147 n. 14. For more on the commentarial history of the text, see, e.g., Lin Yeh-lien 林葉連, *Chung-kuo li-tai Shih-ching hsüeh* 中國歷代詩經學, Chung-kuo wen-hsüeh yen-chiu ts'ung-k'an (Taipei: Hsüeh-sheng, 1993).

7. *Mao-Shih cheng-i*, 4C.342b ("Chài" 祭 is a place-name). The event is retold in the *Tso-chuan* 左傳; text in Yang Po-chün 楊伯峻, *Ch'un-ch'iu Tso-chuan chu* 春秋左傳注, 2d ed., Chung-kuo ku-tien ming-chu i-chu ts'ung-shu (Peking: Chung-hua, 1990), vol. 1, 132 (Huan 桓 11 = 701 B.C.). See also "Cheng shih-chia" 鄭世家, *Shih-chi* 史記 (Peking: Chung-hua, 1959), 42.1761 f. Note that in other classical texts, Chung is praised for his pragmatic decision; if he had not acceded to Sung's wishes, it is asserted, his lord and state would have been destroyed. See *Ch'un-ch'iu Kung-yang chuan chu-shu* 春秋公羊傳注疏 (*Shih-san ching chu-shu*), 5.2220a (Huan 11 = 701 B.C.). Cf., e.g., Mark Edward Lewis, *Writing and Authority in Early China*, SUNY Series in Chinese Philosophy and Culture (Albany, N.Y., 1999), 143, where the name of the minister is read as "Chi Chung."

8. See, for example, the opinions of Yen Ts'an 嚴粲 (fl. 1248) and Wang Hung-hsü 王鴻緒 (1645–1723) in Wang's *Shih-ching chuan-shuo hui-tsuan* 詩經傳說彙纂 (1868; repr., Taipei: Chung-ting wen-hua, 1967), 5.41b f. Cf. also Wei Chiung-jo 魏炯若, *Tu-Feng chih-hsin chi* 讀風知新記 (Hsi-an: Shensi jen-min, 1987), 272; and Hsieh Chin-ch'ing 謝晉青, *Shih-ching chih nü-hsing te yen-chiu* 詩經之女性的研究, 3d ed., Kuo-hsüeh hsiao ts'ung-shu (Shanghai: Shang-wu, 1934), 62, who suggests that "this poem can only be considered to be about a little lost love" 這詩只能算是一篇小小的失戀. Generally, Hsieh believes that the minor prefaces fail to comprehend the "real meaning" 真義 of the *Odes* (cf., e.g., 10 f.). For more on the commentarial history of "Chiao-t'ung," see, e.g., Ch'ien Chung-shu, vol. 1, 108–111.

9. *A History of Chinese Literature* (New York: Grove, 1923), 13. Around the same time, scholars in China were voicing similar criticisms of the commentarial tradition to the *Odes*. For two typical examples, see Ku Chieh-kang 顧頡剛 (1893–1980), "Yeh yu ssu chün" 野有死麕, in *Ku-shih pien* 古史辨, ed. Ku Chieh-kang (repr., Shanghai: Ku-chi, 1982), vol. 3, 439–443; and Hu Shih 胡適 (1891–1962), "T'an-t'an *Shih-ching*" 談談詩經, in *Ku-shih pien*, vol. 3, 576–587. A representative sample of similar opinions is presented in Pauline Yu, *The Reading of Imagery in the Chinese Poetic Tradition* (Princeton, N.J.: Princeton University Press, 1987), 45 f. For an influential argument to the contrary, see, in addition to Yu,

Ch'ü Wan-li, "Lun 'Kuo-feng' fei min-chien ko-yao te pen-lai mien-mu" 論國風非民間歌謠的本來面目, *Ku yüan-chang Hu Shih hsien-sheng chi-nien lun-wen chi* 故院長胡適先生紀念論文集, *Bulletin of the Institute of History and Philology* 34 (1963), 477–504.

10. Zhang Longxi, "The Letter or the Spirit: The *Song of Songs*, Allegoresis, and the *Book of Poetry*," *Comparative Literature* 39.3 (1987), 213.

11. *Analects* 2.2; text in Ch'eng Shu-te 程樹德 (1877–1944), *Lun-yü chi-shih* 論語集釋, ed. Ch'eng Chün-ying 程俊英 and Chiang Chien-yüan 蔣見元, Hsin-pien Chu-tzu chi-ch'eng (Peking: Chung-hua, 1990), 3.65.

12. Following the commentary of Han Yü 韓愈 (768–824) and Li Ao 李翱 (772–841). See also Ch'eng Shu-te's comments (*an* 按).

13. Compare the translation in D. C. Lau, *Confucius: The Analects* (New York: Penguin, 1979), 63. Tu Yung-ming 杜永明 et al., *Hei Erh-shih-ssu shih* 黑二十四史 (Peking: Chung-kuo hua-ch'iao, 1998) [cited henceforth as *Hei Erh-shih-ssu shih*; see note 20 in the introduction of the present volume], vol. 1, 21, insofar as I understand the argument, seems to suggest that by saying *ssu wu hsieh* 思無邪, Confucius means that there is nothing perverted about healthy sexual love.

14. See, e.g., Pauline Yu, 48f.; Donald Holzman, "Confucius and Ancient Chinese Literary Criticism," in *Chinese Approaches to Literature from Confucius to Liang Ch'i-ch'ao*, ed. Adele Austin Rickett (Princeton, N.J.: Princeton University Press, 1978), 21–41; Yau-woon Ma, "Confucius as a Literary Critic: A Comparison with the Early Greeks," in *Jao Tsung-i chiao-shou nan-yu tseng-pieh lun-wen chi* 饒宗頤教授南遊贈別論文集 (Hong Kong, 1970), 20 ff.; Zau Sinmay, "Confucius on Poetry," *T'ien Hsia Monthly* 7.2 (1938), 137–150; and Ku Chieh-kang, "*Shih-ching* tsai Ch'un-ch'iu Chan-kuo chien te ti-wei" 詩經在春秋戰國間的地位, in Ku, *Ku-shih pien*, vol. 3, 345–352, for reviews of Confucius' statements regarding the *Odes*. Cf. also Christoph Harbsmeier, "Eroticism in Early Chinese Poetry: Sundry Comparative Notes," in *Das andere China: Festschrift für Wolfgang Bauer zum 65. Geburtstag*, ed. Helwig Schmidt-Glintzer, Wolfenbütteler Forschungen 62 (Wiesbaden: Harrassowitz, 1995), 333 ff., for another view of Confucius' response to eroticism in the *Odes*.

15. Cheng Hsüan's gloss on *ts'u* 徂 is that it means no more than "go" (*hsing* 行). Hence the traditional understanding of the couplet: "Ah, without diverging, may these horses walk ahead!" But as Ch'ü Wan-li points out, *ts'u* was frequently interchanged with *ch'ieh* 且, "become manifold." For an overview of exegesis on the poem "Chiung," see Haun Saussy, *The Problem of a Chinese Aesthetic*, Meridian: Crossing Aesthetics (Stanford, Calif.: Stanford University Press, 1993), 67–73.

16. There are a few notable exceptions to this consensus in the commentarial tradition. Yü Yüeh 俞樾 (1821–1907) suggests that Confucius used *ssu* exactly as in the *Odes*; thus "Ah, may there be no digression" (*Lun-yü chi-shih* 3.65). Cheng Hao 鄭浩 (fl. 1933), on the other hand, provides a long and tenuous philological argument designed to show that *hsieh* 邪 here is not to be taken in its normal sense, but that it should be read *hsü* 徐 (which he takes to mean *hsü* 虛, "may the horses not jade"). In other words, Confucius means only that we should not let our energies flag. Compare also Bernhard Karlgren's narrow objection to "all forced speculations" in "Glosses on the Ta ya and Sung Odes," *Bulletin of the Museum of Far Eastern Antiquities* 18 (1946), 174: "The whole ode is

nothing but a praise of the prince's fine horses." Karlgren's three collections of *Shih-ching* glosses have been reprinted together as *Glosses on the Book of Odes* (Stockholm: Museum of Far Eastern Antiquities, 1964).

17. See his *Mao-Shih chuan-chien t'ung-shih* 毛詩傳箋通釋 (*Huang-Ch'ing ching-chieh hsü-pien* 皇清經解續編), 2.4af.

18. *Analects* 3.20, *Lun-yü chi-shih* 6.198.

19. Compare the translation in Lau, *Analects*, 70.

20. Compare the statement in *Ch'un-ch'iu Tso-chuan chu*, vol. 3, 1145 (Hsiang 襄 28 = 545 B.C.), in which the speaker takes it as a matter of course that one may bypass the ostensible sense of the *Odes* in order to extract a particular meaning from them: "In reciting my ode, I have broken the stanzas, taking what I seek from them" 賦詩斷章，余取所求焉. Cf. Lewis, *Writing and Authority*, 158. See also *Mencius* 5A.4: "One who interprets the *Odes* does not take the words to distort the lyric, or the lyric to distort [the poet's] intention. To engage this intention with one's own faculties—that is to comprehend it" 故說詩者，不以文害辭，不以辭害志，以意逆志，是為得之. Text in Chiao Hsün 焦循 (1763–1820), *Meng-tzu cheng-i* 孟子正義, ed. Shen Wen-cho 沈文倬, Hsin-pien Chu-tzu chi-ch'eng (Peking: Chung-hua, 1987), 18.638.

21. Note that the guest is lucky (*chia* 嘉) because he confers luck on the speaker (as in a "lucky penny"), not because he is lucky himself.

22. For more on the poetic technique of *hsing*, see Ch'en Shih-hsiang, "The *Shih Ching*: Its Generic Significance in Chinese Literary History and Poetics," *Ch'ing-chu Li Fang-kuei hsien-sheng liu-shih-wu sui lun-wen chi* 慶祝李方桂先生六十五歲論文集, *Bulletin of the Institute of History and Philology* 39 (1969), 371–413, reprinted in *Studies in Chinese Literary Genres*, ed. Cyril Birch (Berkeley and Los Angeles: University of California Press, 1974), 8–41; and Ying-hsiung Chou, "The Linguistic and Mythical Structure of *Hsing* as a Combinational Model," in *Chinese-Western Comparative Literature Theory and Strategy*, ed. John J. Deeney (Hong Kong: Chinese University Press, 1980), 51–78.

23. See Donald Harper, "The Sexual Arts of Ancient China as Described in a Manuscript of the Second Century B.C.," *Harvard Journal of Asiatic Studies* 47.2 (1987), 570 ff.; and Edward L. Shaughnessy, "Marriage, Divorce, and Revolution: Reading between the Lines of the *Book of Changes*," *Journal of Asian Studies* 51.3 (1992), reprinted in *Before Confucius*, 17 f.

24. Cf., e.g., K. C. Chang, "Shang Shamans," in *The Power of Culture: Studies in Chinese Cultural History*, ed. Willard J. Peterson et al. (Hong Kong: Chinese University Press, 1994), 19 f., and *Art, Myth, and Ritual: The Path to Political Authority in Ancient China* (Cambridge: Harvard University Press, 1983), 54 f.; and, most recently, David N. Keightley, "Shamanism, Death, and the Ancestors: Religious Mediation in Neolithic and Shang China (ca. 5000–1000 B.C.)," *Asiatische Studien/Etudes Asiatiques* 52.3 (1998), 808 ff., whose purpose is to challenge the suggestion that the hosting ceremony was shamanistic. (Keightley refers to his more extensive study of *pin* in an unpublished paper that was not available to me.)

According to the *Shuo-wen chieh-tzu* 說文解字, the great dictionary by Hsü Shen 許慎 (ca. A.D. 55–ca. 149), the basic meaning of *pin* is "union with the otherworld" 冥合; it is unclear whether this union is intended to have a sexual connotation. Text in Chiang Jen-chieh 蔣人傑, *Shuo-wen chieh-tzu chi-chu* 集注,

ed. Liu Jui 劉銳 (Shanghai: Ku-chi, 1996), 7B.1539, where *pin* is cited by the older form of the graph, 丂.

25. Cf. Shirakawa Shizuka 白川靜, *Shikyō* 詩經 (Tokyo: Chūō Kōronsha, 1970), 190.

The following discussion, incidentally, addresses only cases in which the hierogamous union is desired and cherished by the human participant. A recently discovered apotropaic text from the third century B.C., however, sheds light on the possibility of undesired or forcible cohabitation with spirits: "When a ghost continually follows someone's daughter and cohabits with her, saying, 'The son of Ti Above has descended to frolic'—if you wish to expel it, bathe yourself in the excrement of a dog and beat [the ghost] with reeds; then it will die" 鬼恒從人女，與居，曰：上帝子下游。欲去，自浴以犬屎，擊以葦，則死矣 (the character *chi* 擊 may also be interpreted as *hsi* 繫; thus "tie it with reeds"); text in "Chieh-chiu" 詰咎, *Shui-hu-ti Ch'in-mu chu-chien* 睡虎地秦墓竹簡 (Peking: Wen-wu, 1990), 215; and Liu Lo-hsien 劉樂賢, *Shui-hu-ti Ch'in-chien* Jih-shu *yen-chiu* 睡虎地秦簡日書研究, Ta-lu ti-ch'ü po-shih lun-wen ts'ung-k'an 76 (Taipei: Wen-chin, 1994), 231. (The 1990 version of *Shui-hu-ti Ch'in-mu chu-chien* is the most recent appearance of a title that has been used more than once since the 1970s.) Compare the translation in Donald Harper, "*Spellbinding*," in *Religions of China in Practice*, ed. Donald S. Lopez, Jr., Princeton Readings in Religions (Princeton, N.J., 1996), 249; and the discussion in "Warring States, Qin, and Han Manuscripts Related to Natural Philosophy and the Occult," in *New Sources of Early Chinese History: An Introduction to the Reading of Inscriptions and Manuscripts*, ed. Edward L. Shaughnessy, Early China Special Monograph Series 3 (Berkeley, Calif., 1997), 245 f. Compare also the item immediately following in the text: "When a ghost continually tells one, 'Give me your daughter,' it cannot be answered. This is a spirit from above descending to take a wife. Beat it with reeds; then it will die. If you do not defend against it, it will come five times and the girl will die" 鬼恒謂人：予我而女。不可辭。是上神下娶妻，擊以葦，則死矣。弗禦，五來，女子死矣。 (Once again, *chi* may also be interpreted as *hsi*.) For more on "Chieh-chiu," see Donald Harper, "A Chinese Demonography of the Third Century B.C.," *Harvard Journal of Asiatic Studies* 45.2 (1985), 459–498. Harper calls the text simply "Chieh," which he translates as "Spellbinding."

26. For more on this subject, see, e.g., John S. Major, "Characteristics of Late Chu Religion," in *Defining Chu: Image and Reality in Ancient China*, ed. Constance A. Cook and John S. Major (Honolulu: University of Hawai'i Press, 1999), 136; Gopal Sukhu, "Monkeys, Shamans, Emperors, and Poets: The *Chuci* and Images of Chu during the Han Dynasty," in Cook and Major, esp. 157–165; Wai-yee Li, *Enchantment and Disenchantment: Love and Illusion in Chinese Literature* (Princeton, N.J.: Princeton University Press, 1993), 1–10; Hsiao Ping 蕭兵, *Ch'u-tz'u te wenhua p'o-i* 楚辭的文化破譯, Chung-kuo wen-hua te jen-lei-hsüeh p'o-i (Hu-pei: Hupei jen-min, 1991), esp. 234 ff.; David Hawkes, *The Songs of the South: An Ancient Chinese Anthology of Poems by Qu Yuan and Other Poets* (New York: Penguin, 1985), 42 ff.; Edward H. Schafer, *The Divine Woman: Dragon Ladies and Rain Maidens in T'ang Literature* (San Francisco: North Point, 1980), 48–53; David Hawkes, "The Quest of the Goddess," *Asia Major*, n.s., 13 (1967), 71–94; Hoshikawa Kiyotaka

星川清孝, *Soji no kenkyū* 楚辭の研究 (Tokyo: Yōtokusha, 1963), 227–255; and Arthur Waley, *Chiu Ko—The Nine Songs: A Study of Shamanism in Ancient China* (London: Allen and Unwin, 1955).

27. See, e.g., Li Ling, "An Archaeological Study of Taiyi (Grand One) Worship," trans. Donald Harper, *Early Medieval China* 2 (1995–1996), 22; Hsü Chih-hsiao 徐志嘯, *Ch'u-tz'u tsung-lun* 楚辭綜論, Ts'ang-hai ts'ung-k'an (Taipei: Tung-ta, 1994), 105 ff.; and Yang Ts'ai-hua 楊采華, *Ch'ü Yüan chi-ch'i tz'u-fu hsin-chieh* 屈原及其辭賦新解 (Wu-han: Wu-han Ta-hsüeh, 1994), 222 f. The excavated manuscript "T'ai-i sheng shui" 太一生水, discovered at Kuo-tien 郭店, may refer to this god. For the text, see Ching-men Shih Po-wu-kuan 荊門市博物館, *Kuo-tien Ch'u-mu chu-chien* 郭店楚墓竹簡 (Peking: Wen-wu, 1998), 125–126; see also Li Ling, "Tu Kuo-tien Ch'u-chien 'T'ai-i sheng shui'" 讀郭店楚簡太一生水, *Tao-chia wen-hua yen-chiu* 道家文化研究 17 (1999), 316–331. Sun Xiaochun and Jacob Kistemaker, *The Chinese Sky during the Han: Constellating Stars and Society*, Sinica Leidensia 38 (Leiden: Brill, 1997), 50, have identified T'ai-i with the star 8 Dra.

28. Note the chiasmus.

29. "Chiu-ko" 九歌; text in Hung Hsing-tsu 洪興祖 (1090–1155), *Ch'u-tz'u chang-chü pu-chu* 章句補注, in *Ch'u-tz'u chu pa-chung* 注八種, Chung-kuo wen-hsüeh ming-chu (Taipei: Shih-chieh, 1990), 2.33 f. Some scholars recommend the more modern edition by Chiang Liang-fu 姜亮夫 (b. 1901), *Ch'ü Yüan fu chiao-chu* 屈原賦校註 (Peking: Jen-min wen-hsüeh, 1957), but I find that I continually disagree with his judgments. Moreover, Chiang does not reproduce all the comments by Wang I and Hung Hsing-tsu. My translation of this poem relies throughout on the glosses in Geoffrey R. Waters, *Three Elegies of Ch'u: An Introduction to the Traditional Interpretation of the* Ch'u Tz'u (Madison: University of Wisconsin Press, 1985), 44–82. Compare the translation in Hawkes, *Songs of the South*, 102.

30. Scholars disagree as to whether the "Chiu-ko" were real liturgies or merely literary works in liturgical style. See the well-annotated discussion in Lewis, *Writing and Authority*, 184 f. For our purposes, however, the difference is not crucial, because it is clear that the "Chiu-ko" use hierogamic imagery to literary effect, whether or not they were genuine invocations in their own right. Moreover, it is remarkable how well the names of gods in "Chiu-ko" square with those invoked in recently discovered divinatory material from the ancient state of Ch'u. See, e.g., Li Ling, "The Formulaic Structure of Chu Divinatory Bamboo Slips," *Early China* 15 (1990), 71–86.

31. See Chiang Liang-fu, *Ch'u-tz'u t'ung-ku* 楚辭通故 (K'un-ming: Yün-nan jen-min, 2000), vol. 1, 212 f.; *Hei Erh-shih-ssu shih*, vol. 3, 1752; Hoshikawa, 325 ff.; M. Kaltenmark, "*Ling-pao*: note sur un terme du Taoïsme religieux," *Mélanges publiés par l'Institut des Hautes Études Chinoises* 2 (1960), 559–588; Wang Shu-nu 王書奴, *Chung-kuo ch'ang-chi shih* 中國娼妓史, Chiu-chi hsin-k'an (Shanghai: Sheng-huo, 1934; repr., Ch'ang-sha: Yüeh-lu, 1998), 14; and Henri Maspero, *China in Antiquity*, trans. Frank A. Kierman, Jr. ([Amherst]: University of Massachusetts Press, 1978), 116 ff. See also the dissenting opinion of Wu Chou 武舟, *Chung-kuo chi-nü sheng-huo shih* 中國妓女生活史 (Ch'ang-sha: Hu-nan wen-i, 1990), 32–42. I Chung-t'ien, 215 ff., suggests that the terms *ch'ang* 娼 and *ch'ang-*

chi 娼妓 (which now both mean "prostitute") may have originally denoted a singer or performer (*ch'ang-chi* 倡伎) in a shamanic ritual.

32. This story is included in the commentary of Yen Shih-ku 顏師古 (581–645) to "Wu-ti chi" 武帝紀, *Han-shu* 漢書 (Peking: Chung-hua, 1962), 6.190 n. 2, where it is attributed to the *Huai-nan-tzu* 淮南子. It is not to be found in the received version of that text, however. See Anne Birrell, *Chinese Mythology: An Introduction* (Baltimore: Johns Hopkins University Press, 1993), 122 f., for a discussion of this passage and the question of its authenticity. For a discussion of the myth and its implications, see Paul Rakita Goldin, "Reflections on Irrationalism in Chinese Aesthetics," *Monumenta Serica* 44 (1996), 184; Edward H. Schafer, *Pacing the Void: T'ang Approaches to the Stars* (Berkeley and Los Angeles: University of California Press, 1977), 237 ff.; Bernhard Karlgren, "Legends and Cults of Ancient China," *Bulletin of the Museum of Far Eastern Antiquities* 18 (1946), 310; and Marcel Granet, *Danses et légendes de la Chine ancienne*, Bibliothèque de philosophie contemporaine, Travaux de l'Année sociologique (Paris: Félix Alcan, 1926), vol. 2, 549 ff., and "Remarques sur le Taoïsme Ancien," *Asia Major*, 1st ser., 2.1 (1925), 149. See also Wolfram Eberhard's review of Karlgren in *Artibus Asiae* 9 (1946), 360.

33. In the *Ch'u-tz'u*, Yü's relations with the woman from T'u-shan are also portrayed in terms of eating: "How did he obtain the girl from T'u-shan and have intercourse with her at T'ai-sang? He encouraged her to unite with him as his mate, and her body gave him an heir. How did they come to lust after extraordinary tastes and satiate themselves with a breakfast of joy?" 焉得嵞山女而通之於台桑？閔妃匹合，厥身是繼。胡維嗜不同味而快鼂[= 朝]飽? Text in "T'ien-wen" 天問, *Ch'u-tz'u chang-chü pu-chu* 3.56 f. Compare the translation in Hawkes, *Songs of the South*, 129. Wang I and others note that some editions omit *pu* 不 (thus *t'ung-wei*, "the same tastes," instead of *pu-t'ung wei*, "extraordinary tastes"); Hawkes follows this variant, although it must count as the simpler, and hence less likely, reading.

34. According to *Ch'un-ch'iu Tso-chuan chu*, vol. 2, 535 (Wen 文 4 = 623 B.C.), "T'ung-kung" was recited (*fu* 賦; see n. 47, below) on the occasion of a visit to Lu by Ning Wu-tzu 甯武子 of Wei 衛 (whom Confucius mentions in *Analects* 5.21). Wu-tzu goes on to explain that in ancient times, the king would give vassals who had attacked his enemy one red-lacquered bow and one hundred red-lacquered arrows. Probably on the basis of this speech, the "Minor Preface" interprets "T'ung-kung" as "the Son of Heaven rewarding the several meritorious vassals" 天子錫有功諸侯也, *Mao-Shih cheng-i* 10A.421c. See also *Ch'un-ch'iu Tso-chuan chu*, vol. 3, 960 (Hsiang 8 = 565 B.C.). But for evidence supporting the interpretation of "T'ung-kung" as a hierogamic invocation, consider, for example, the "ornamented bows" 敦弓 of *Mao* 246 ("Hsing-wei" 行葦), which are used in a ritual cultivating the ancestral spirits.

35. Bernhard Karlgren, "Some Fecundity Symbols in Ancient China," *Bulletin of the Museum of Far Eastern Antiquities* 2 (1930), 1–66, suggests that the ancestral cult was originally combined with a phallic fertility cult. See also Siegfried Englert, *Materialien zur Stellung der Frau und zur Sexualität im vormodernen und modernen China*, Heidelberger Schriften zur Ostasienkunde 1 (Frankfurt:

Haag und Herchen, 1980), 2; and Eduard Erkes, "Some Remarks on Karlgren's 'Fecundity Symbols in Ancient China,' " *Bulletin of the Museum of Far Eastern Antiquities* 3 (1931), 63–68.

36. For more on this topic, see, e.g., Wang Kuo-wei 王國維 (1877–1927), *Sung-Yüan hsi-ch'ü k'ao* 宋元戲曲考 (1912), in *Wang Kuan-t'ang hsien-sheng ch'üan-chi* 王觀堂先生全集 (Taipei: Wen-hua, 1968), vol. 14, 5977 ff.; C. H. Wang, "The Lord Impersonator: *Kung-shih* and the First Stage of Chinese Drama," in *The Chinese Text: Studies in Comparative Literature*, ed. Ying-hsiung Chou (Hong Kong: Chinese University Press, 1986), reprinted in Wang's *From Ritual to Allegory: Seven Essays in Early Chinese Poetry* (Hong Kong: Chinese University Press, 1988), 42–51; and Maspero, *China in Antiquity*, 130 f.

37. For the *kung-chu* 工祝 ("officiating priest"), see, e.g., "Shao-lao k'uei-shih li" 少牢饋食禮, *I-li chu-shu* 儀禮注疏 (*Shih-san ching chu-shu*), 48.1202c.; John Steele, *The I-li, or Book of Etiquette and Ceremonial*, Probsthain's Oriental Series 8–9 (London, 1917), vol. 2, 172, translates the term there as "official liturgist." Cf. also Bernhard Karlgren, "Glosses on the Siao ya Odes," *Bulletin of the Museum of Far Eastern Antiquities* 16 (1944), 135.

38. Ch'ien Chung-shu, vol. 1, 156–158, suggests that *shen-pao* 神保 refers to a dancing invocator (like a *ling-pao* 靈保).

39. According to Cheng Hsüan (*Mao-Shih cheng-i* 1A.273b), who is later followed by most orthodox commentators, the phrase *yao-t'iao* 窈窕 indicates the lady's chastity and virtue. He does not take the "fine girl" to be a goddess. In later usage, *yao-t'iao* comes to mean "sluttish"; see, e.g., "Lieh-nü chuan" 列女傳, *Hou-Han shu* 後漢書 (Peking: Chung-hua, 1965), 84.2790.

40. See Riegel, "Eros," 149 ff.; Mark Laurent Asselin, "The Lu-School Reading of 'Guanju' as Preserved in an Eastern Han *fu*," *Journal of the American Oriental Society* 117.3 (1997), 427–443; and Pauline Yu, 47 ff., for an overview of exegesis on "The *Kuan*-ing Ospreys."

41. This is the "Upper Preface," *Mao-Shih cheng-i* 6A.361c.

42. Following the Mao commentary for *chiao-chiao*. The phrase will be discussed in greater detail in the text. Karlgren, *The Book of Odes*, 84, renders it as "crosswise." Waley, *The Book of Songs*, 103, takes it onomatopoetically ("'Kio' sings the oriole"), an interpretation that is also discussed in Bernhard Karlgren, "Glosses on the Kuo feng Odes," *Bulletin of the Museum of Far Eastern Antiquities* 14 (1942), 215.

43. Reconstructions of rhyming words are adapted from William H. Baxter, *A Handbook of Old Chinese Phonology*, Trends in Linguistics 64 (Berlin: Mouton de Gruyter, 1992), 634.

44. Recently, Yuri Pines, "Intellectual Change in the Chunqiu Period: The Reliability of the Speeches in the *Zuo Zhuan* as Sources of Chunqiu Intellectual History," *Early China* 22 (1997), 77–132, has presented trenchant evidence to suggest that despite its relatively late date of compilation, the *Tso-chuan* is far more reliable than previously thought as a source of Springs and Autumns history. For the purposes of this book, all material in the *Tso-chuan* is considered to date from ca. 300 B.C. at the latest, with the possibility that some of it may indeed be centuries older than that.

45. *Ch'un-ch'iu Tso-chuan chu*, vol. 2, 546 f. (Wen 6 = 621 B.C.). The story is retold in "Ch'in pen-chi" 秦本紀, *Shih-chi* 5.194, with the one variant that the surname of the three brothers is given there as "Tzu-yü" 輿. The *Shih-chi* also says explicitly that the poem was composed (*tso* 作) for this occasion; the *Tso-chuan* only implies this.

46. On the "citizens" (*kuo-jen* 國人), or the denizens of the capital precinct, see Cho-yun Hsu, "The Spring and Autumn Period," in *The Cambridge History of Ancient China: From the Origins of Civilization to 221 B.C.*, ed. Michael Loewe and Edward L. Shaughnessy (Cambridge, 1999), 549; Yang K'uan 楊寬, *Chan-kuo shih* 戰國史, 3d ed. (Shanghai: Jen-min, 1998), 151 ff.; *Hei Erh-shih-ssu shih*, vol. 6, 4035 ff.; T'ien Ch'ang-wu 田昌五 and Tsang Chih-fei 臧知非, *Chou Ch'in she-hui chieh-kou yen-chiu* 周秦社會結構研究, Chou Ch'in Han T'ang yen-chiu shu-hsi (Hsi-an: Hsi-pei Ta-hsüeh, 1996), 38–53; Chao Shih-ch'ao 趙世超, *Chou-tai kuo-yeh kuan-hsi yen-chiu* 周代國野關係研究 (Taipei: Wen-chin, 1993); Mark Edward Lewis, *Sanctioned Violence in Early China*, SUNY Series in Chinese Philosophy and Culture (Albany, N.Y., 1990), 48 ff.; T'ung Shu-yeh 童書業, *Ch'un-ch'iu Tso-chuan yen-chiu* 春秋左傳研究 (Shanghai: Jen-min, 1980), 132–146, 366–367, and 371–372; Kaizuka Shigeki 貝塚茂樹, "Chūgoku kodai toshi ni okeru minkai no seido" 中國古代都市における民會の制度, in *Kaizuka Shigeki chosaku shū* 著作集 (Tokyo: Chūō Kōronsha, 1978), vol. 2, 95–118; and Masubuchi Tatsuo 增淵龍夫, "Shunjū Sengoku jidai no shakai to kokka" 春秋戰國時代の社會と國家, in *Iwanami kōza sekai rekishi* 岩波講座世界歷史 (Tokyo: Iwanami, 1970), vol. 4, 139–179. The *kuo* and the *kuo-jen* are distinguished from the *yeh* 野 (the area beyond the city wall) and its inhabitants, the *yeh-jen*.

47. The term *fu* 賦 does not necessarily mean "compose" in this context (although it certainly *may*); Chang Su-ch'ing 張素卿, *Tso-chuan ch'eng-Shih yen-chiu* 左傳稱詩研究, Kuo-li T'ai-wan Ta-hsüeh wen-shih ts'ung-k'an 89 (Taipei, 1991), esp. 51–65, demonstrates that a rendering such as "recite" is usually more appropriate. See also K'ung Ying-ta's commentary to *Ch'un-ch'iu Tso-chuan cheng-i* (*Shih-san ching chu-shu*), 3.1724a (Yin 隱 3 = 720 B.C.); as well as Tseng Ch'in-liang 曾勤良, *Tso-chuan yin-Shih fu-Shih chih Shih-chiao yen-chiu* 左傳引詩賦詩之詩教研究, Wen-shih-che ta-hsi 61 (Taipei: Wen-chin, 1993); and Nakajima Chiaki 中島千秋, *Fu no seiritsu to tenkai* 賦の成立と展開 (Matsuyama: Kan'yoshi, 1963), 1–94.

48. Compare the translation in Legge, vol. 5, 244.

49. Cf., e.g., Yeh Shan 葉珊 (i.e., C. H. Wang), "*Shih-ching* 'Kuo-feng' te ts'ao-mu ho shih te piao-hsien chi-ch'iao" 詩經國風的草木和詩的表現技巧, *Hsien-tai wen-hsüeh* 現代文學 33 (1967), reprinted in *Chung-kuo ku-tien wen-hsüeh yen-chiu ts'ung-k'an: Shih-ko chih pu* 中國古典文學研究叢刊：詩歌之部, ed. K'o Ch'ing-ming 柯慶明 and Lin Ming-te 林明德 (Taipei: Chü-liu), vol. 1, 20. For a general study of the poetic uses of rhyme in the *Odes*, see Haun Saussy, "Repetition, Rhyme, and Exchange in the *Book of Odes*," *Harvard Journal of Asiatic Studies* 57.2 (1997), 519–542.

50. Cf. esp. Chai Hsiang-chün 翟相君, "'Huang-niao' chih hsing-i" 黃鳥之興義, *Hsi-pei Ta-hsüeh hsüeh-pao* 西北大學學報 1984.4, reprinted in *Shih-ching hsin-chieh* 新解 (Cheng-chou: Chung-chou ku-chi, 1993), 378–381; and C. H. Wang, *The Bell and the Drum: Shih Ching as Formulaic Poetry in an Oral Tradition* (Berke-

ley and Los Angeles: University of California Press, 1974), 115. Granet, *Danses et légendes*, vol. 1, 220 n, notes that the yellow bird is an "emblème du mariage" (symbol of marriage), but he does not comment further.

51. Compare also such poems as *Mao* 40 ("Pei-men" 北門) and *Mao* 169 ("Ti-tu" 杕杜), in which the language of a woman longing for her lover is interwoven with the plaint of a soldier or minister burdened by "the king's affairs" 王事.

52. Shaughnessy, *Before Confucius*, 21 f.

53. See, e.g., Pauline Yu, 66.

54. For the dates, see Edward L. Shaughnessy, *Sources of Western Zhou History: Inscribed Bronze Vessels* (Berkeley and Los Angeles: University of California Press, 1991), 241 f.

55. See *Mao-Shih cheng-i* 8C.399b.

56. See, e.g., Edward L. Shaughnessy, "The Duke of Zhou's Retirement in the East and the Beginnings of the Minister-Monarch Debate in Chinese Political Philosophy," *Early China* 18 (1973), 41–72, reprinted in *Before Confucius*, 101–136.

57. The *wa* 瓦 is explained by Mao and Cheng Hsüan as a loom: *Mao-Shih cheng-i* 11B.438a.

58. Cf., e.g., I Chung-t'ien, 57 f.; and *Hei Erh-shih-ssu shih*, vol. 1, 17, 665.

59. The reduplicative *t'o-t'o* (or *tui-tui*) 脫脫 is usually taken as an attribute ("gently," etc.); see the commentaries of Mao and Cheng Hsüan, *Mao-Shih cheng-i* 1E.293a. Cf. also Karlgren, "Glosses on the Kuo feng Odes," 105. But there are numerous instances where reduplicatives function as verbs, and there is no reason why *t'o* cannot carry its basic sense of "undress" here.

60. Granet, *Fêtes et chansons*, 125 n. 10, notes astutely that the maiden's *shui* 帨 (kerchief) plays a crucial role in the rituals of marriage. It is kept intact from the day of her birth and is finally torn on the wedding night. Thus the kerchief functions here as a metaphor for the girl's maidenhead. See also Hu Shih, "Lun 'Yeh yu ssu chün' shu" 論野有死麋書, *Ku-shih pien*, vol. 3, 442, and the extended discussion of the term in the articles immediately following.

61. Shaughnessy, *Before Confucius*, 232 ff.

62. See, e.g., Ch'en Ping-liang 陳炳良, "Shuo 'Ju-fen': Chien-lun *Shih-ching* chung yu-kuan lien-ai ho hun-yin te shih" 説汝墳：兼論詩經中有關戀愛和婚姻的詩, *Chung-wai wen-hsüeh* 中外文學 7.12 (1979), 138–155.

63. *Ch'un-ch'iu Tso-chuan chu*, vol. 1, 146 f. (Huan 16 = 696 B.C.). The story is retold in "Wei K'ang-shu shih-chia" 衛康叔世家, *Shih-chi* 37.1593.

64. Following the commentary of Yang Po-chün.

65. Compare the translations in Burton Watson, trans., *The Tso chuan: Selections from China's Oldest Narrative History*, Translations from the Oriental Classics (New York: Columbia University Press, 1989), 13 f.; and Legge, vol. 5, 66 f.

66. Traditional commentators take three important poems in the *Odes, Mao* 34 ("P'ao yu k'u-yeh" 匏有苦葉), *Mao* 43 ("Hsin-t'ai" 新臺), and *Mao* 44 ("Erh-tzu ch'eng chou" 二子乘舟), as allusions to this affair. Donald Holzman, "The Place of Filial Piety in Ancient China," *Journal of the American Oriental Society* 118.2 (1998), 189 f., rightly observes that Chi-tzu's extreme filial devotion "may seem irrational" to modern readers.

67. *Ch'un-ch'iu Tso-chuan chu*, vol. 4, 1597 (Ting 定 14 = 497 B.C.).

68. Her reputation was such that Confucius himself felt obligated to justify himself for having had an interview with her (*Analects* 6.26). See Siegfried Englert and Roderich Ptak, "Nan-tzu, or Why Heaven Did Not Crush Confucius," *Journal of the American Oriental Society* 106.4 (1986), 679–686, for a review of the sources pertaining to Nan-tzu. See also *Hei Erh-shih-ssu shih*, vol. 1, 123 f., 351.

69. *Ch'un-ch'iu Tso-chuan chu*, vol. 4, 1597 (Ting 14 = 497 B.C.).

70. Compare the translations in Watson, *Tso chuan*, 195 f.; and Legge, vol. 5, 788.

71. An abbreviated version of the story—omitting Nan-tzu's incest—appears in "Wei K'ang-shu shih-chia," *Shih-chi* 37.1598 f.

72. *Ch'un-ch'iu Tso-chuan chu*, vol. 2, 853 (Ch'eng 成 11 = 580 B.C.). Cf. Li Meng-ts'un 李孟存 and Li Shang-shih 李尚師, *Chin-kuo shih* 晉國史, San-Chin wen-hua yen-chiu ts'ung-shu (T'ai-yüan: Shan-hsi ku-chi, 1999), 440; and *Hei Erh-shih-ssu shih*, vol. 1, 19.

73. Compare the translation in Legge, vol. 5, 376.

74. On Tzu-ch'an in general, see, e.g., V. A. Rubin, "Tzu-ch'an and the City-State of Ancient China," *T'oung Pao* 52 (1965), 8–34. For a similar opinion, see the speech by Shu-chan 叔詹 (i.e., Cheng Chan 鄭詹, fl. 677–637 B.C., who was the younger brother of Lord Wen of Cheng, r. 672–628 B.C.) in *Ch'un-ch'iu Tso-chuan chu*, vol. 1, 408 (Hsi 僖 23 = 637 B.C.): "When men and women have the same surname, their offspring do not prosper" 男女同姓，其生不蕃; and the parallel in "Cheng Wen-kung pu-li Ch'ung-erh" 鄭文公不禮重耳, *Kuo-yü* 國語 (Shanghai: Ku-chi, 1978; repr., Taipei: Li-jen, 1981), 10.349. "Cheng shih-chia," *Shih-chi* 42.1765, recounts the same episode in brief. Cf. also I Chung-t'ien, 105; *Hei Erh-shih-ssu shih*, vol. 1, 15; and Sheng I 盛義, *Chung-kuo hun-su wen-hua* 中國婚俗文化, Yü nei-wai min-su hsüeh ts'ung-k'an (Shanghai: Wen-i, 1994), 18, 382, though the last work misquotes both the *Tso-chuan* and *Kuo-yü* passages. (Regardless of its minor errors, Sheng's book is now the first study to which one should turn for a discussion of marriage in ancient China.)

75. *Ch'un-ch'iu Tso-chuan chu*, vol. 4, 1220 f. (Chao 昭 1 = 541 B.C.).

76. This injunction appears verbatim in "Ch'ü-li shang" 曲禮上, *Li-chi cheng-i* 禮記正義 (*Shih-san ching chu-shu*), 2.1241a, and "Fang-chi" 坊記, *Li-chi cheng-i* 51.1622b; compare the commentary of Ku Yen-wu 顧炎武 (1613–1682) to "Ch'ü-li shang" in Sun Hsi-tan 孫希旦 (1736–1784), *Li-chi chi-chieh* 集解, ed. Shen Hsiao-huan 沈嘯寰 and Wang Hsing-hsien 王星賢, Shih-san ching Ch'ing-jen chu-shu (Peking: Chung-hua, 1989), 2.1A.46 f.; as the well as the commentary of Chu Pin 朱彬 (1753–1843) in his *Li-chi hsün-tsuan* 訓纂, ed. Jao Ch'in-nung 饒欽農, Shih-san ching Ch'ing-jen chu-shu (Peking: Chung-hua, 1996), 1.23 f. See also *Hei Erh-shih-ssu shih*, vol. 4, 2607. Compare the translations in S. Couvreur, S.J., *Li Ki ou Mémoires sur les bienséances et les cérémonies*, 2d ed. (Ho Kien Fou: Mission Catholique, 1913), vol. 1, 31; and Richard Wilhelm, *Li Gi: Das Buch der Riten, Sitten, und Bräuche*, 2d ed., Diederichs Gelbe Reihe 31 (Munich, 1994), 314. It is of course impossible to know whether Tzu-ch'an is quoting from the "Ch'ü-li" (or "Fang-chi") or whether the received version of that text borrows this passage from an older source, to which Tzu-ch'an refers here. The same quotation is attributed to the "Ch'ü-li" in the "Chia-ch'ü" 嫁娶 chapter of the *Po-hu t'ung* 白

虎通; see Ch'en Li 陳立 (1809–1869), *Po-hu t'ung shu-cheng* 疏證, ed. Wu Tse-yü 吳則虞, Hsin-pien Chu-tzu chi-ch'eng (Peking: Chung-hua, 1994), 10.477. Compare the translation in Tjan Tjoe Som, *Po Hu T'ung: The Comprehensive Discussions in the White Tiger Hall*, Sinica Leidensia 6 (Leiden: E. J. Brill, 1949), vol. 1, 255.

Chao I 趙翼 (1727–1814) points out, however, that the prohibition against marrying a woman with the same surname was often violated during the Springs and Autumns period. See "T'ung-hsing wei hun" 同姓為婚, in *Kai-yü ts'ung-k'ao* 陔餘叢考 (1790), 31.2b f.; cf. also Sheng I, 382 ff.; Liu Tseng-kuei 劉增貴, "Shih-lun Han-tai hun-yin kuan-hsi chung te li-fa kuan-nien" 試論漢代婚姻關係中的禮法觀念, in *Chung-kuo fu-nü shih lun-chi hsü-chi* 中國婦女史論集續集, ed. Pao Chia-lin 鮑家麟 (Taipei: Tao-hsiang, 1991), 23 n. 23; and T'ung Shu-yeh, 212.

77. Compare the translation in Legge, vol. 5, 580.

78. *Ch'un-ch'iu Tso-chuan chu*, vol. 4, 1324 (Chao 11 = 531 B.C.).

79. Compare the translation in Legge, vol. 5, 634.

80. Cf. *Hei Erh-shih-ssu shih*, vol. 1, 364. For a review of these and similar accounts in the *Tso-chuan*, see, e.g., Yuvoon Chen, "Zur Frage der Ausschweifung in der Ch'un-ch'iu Periode (771–480 v.Chr.)," *Oriens Extremus* 19 (1972), 23–26; and R. H. van Gulik, *Sexual Life in Ancient China: A Preliminary Survey of Chinese Sex and Society from ca. 1500 B.C. till 1644 A.D.* (Leiden: E. J. Brill, 1961; repr., New York: Barnes and Noble, 1996), 30 ff. For a more general discussion of ritualism in the *Tso-chuan*, see Burton Watson, *Early Chinese Literature* (New York: Columbia University Press, 1962), 44 ff.

81. See, e.g., Terry F. Kleeman, "Licentious Cults and Bloody Victuals: Sacrifice, Reciprocity, and Violence in Traditional China," *Asia Major*, 3d ser., 7.1 (1994): 185–211; and Rolf A. Stein, "Religious Taoism and Popular Religion from the Second to Seventh Centuries," in *Facets of Taoism: Essays in Chinese Religion*, ed. Holmes Welch and Anna Seidel (New Haven, Conn.: Yale University Press, 1979), 57. For an overview of Han-dynasty usage of the term, see Mu-chou Poo, *In Search of Personal Welfare: A View of Ancient Chinese Religion*, SUNY Series in Chinese Philosophy and Culture (Albany, N.Y., 1998), 185–192.

82. *Ch'un-ch'iu Tso-chuan chu*, vol. 1, 334 (Hsi 10 = 650 B.C.). A parallel version of the story appears in "Chin shih-chia" 晉世家, *Shih-chi* 39.1651.

83. Compare the translations in Watson, *Tso chuan*, 28 f.; and Legge, vol. 5, 157.

84. See the commentary of K'ung Ying-ta, as summarized by Yang Po-chün. K'ung was evidently relying on the testimony of Fu Ch'ien 服虔 (ca. 125–ca. 95 B.C.), cited in the commentary to "Chin shih-chia," *Shih-chi* 39.1651 n. 2.

85. It is curious, however, that a mere mortal is more informed regarding the procedures of worship than Shen-sheng's own spirit, whose plan, furthermore, has ostensibly been approved by Ti, the highest god. Cf. Watson, *Tso chuan*, 28; and Maspero, *China in Antiquity*, 97.

86. *Ch'un-ch'iu Tso-chuan chu*, vol. 4, 1291 f. (Chao 7 = 535 B.C.).

87. Compare the translation in Legge, vol. 5, 618.

88. Cf., e.g., Granet, *Danses et légendes*, vol. 1, 224 n. 2; and Maspero, *China in Antiquity*, 167 f. On vengeful ghosts in general, see, e.g., Poo, *In Search of Personal Welfare*, 53 ff.; "The Completion of an Ideal World: The Human Ghost in Early-Medieval China," *Asia Major*, 3d ser., 10.1–2 (1997), 71–73; Alvin P. Cohen,

"Avenging Ghosts and Moral Judgement in Ancient China: Three Examples from the *Shih-chi*," in *Legend, Lore, and Religions in China: Essays in Honor of Wolfram Eberhard on His Seventieth Birthday*, ed. Sarah Allan and Alvin P. Cohen (San Francisco: Chinese Materials Center, 1979), 97–108.

89. Note that Tzu-ch'an and Liang Hsiao (Po-yu) were cousins. They shared a common ancestor in Lord Mu of Cheng (r. 627–605 B.C.).

90. "Ch'ü-li hsia" 下, *Li-chi cheng-i* 5.1268c; compare the translation in Couvreur, vol. 1, 100 (this section is not translated by Richard Wilhelm). See also "Chiao-ssu chih" 郊祀志, *Han-shu* 25A.1194: "For each [kind of worship], there are codes and rituals, and there is a prohibition against licentious worship" 各有典禮，而淫祀有禁. Cf. Stein, "Religious Taoism," 77 f. The idea is also echoed in *Analects* 2.24, *Lun-yü chi-shih* 132: "If it is not one's ghost [i.e., one's familial spirit], and one sacrifices to it—this is toadying" 非其鬼而祭之，諂也; in his commentary ad loc., Cheng Hsüan refers to such sacrifices by the same phrase, "licentious worship." See Wang Su 王素, *T'ang hsieh-pen Lun-yü Cheng-shih chu chi-ch'i yen-chiu* 唐寫本論語鄭氏注及其研究 (Peking: Wen-wu, 1991), 14.

91. See the entry for *yin* 淫 in *Shuo-wen chieh-tzu chi-chu* 11A.2348 f., with the commentaries of Ch'en Ch'i-yüan 陳啟源 (d. 1689) and Chu Chün-sheng 朱駿聲 (1788–1858). Cf. also the entry for *yin* 婬, 12B.2655, and the commentary of Wang Yün 王筠 (1784–1854). The "Hsiao Erh-ya" 小爾雅 chapter of the *K'ung-ts'ung-tzu* 孔叢子 preserves both senses of *yin* in its two definitions: *mo* 沒 ("to sink") and *nan-nü pu i li chiao* 男女不以禮交 ("intercourse without ritual between males and females"); text in Ch'eng Jung 程榮 (1447–1520), *Han-Wei ts'ung-shu* 漢魏叢書 (1592; repr., Ch'ang-ch'un: Chi-lin Ta-hsüeh, 1992), A.11.339c and 340a, respectively. See also Yoav Ariel, K'ung-ts'ung-tzu: *A Study and Translation of Chapters 15–23 with a Reconstruction of the* Hsiao Erh-ya *Dictionary*, Sinica Leidensia 35 (Leiden: E. J. Brill, 1996), 152.

92. Chü of Chiao 椒舉 (i.e., Wu 伍 Chü, fl. 545–540 B.C.), the grandfather of the famous Wu Tzu-hsü 子胥 (d. 484 B.C.), recounts briefly the circumstances of Yü-shu's marriage to Lady Hsia in "Ts'ai Sheng-tzu lun Ch'u ts'ai Chin yung" 蔡聲子論楚材晉用, *Kuo-yü*, 17.539; compare the commentary by Wei Chao 韋昭 (A.D. 204–273). See Lisa Raphals, *Sharing the Light: Representations of Women and Virtue in Early China*, SUNY Series in Chinese Philosophy and Culture (Albany, N.Y., 1998), 66–68, for the traditions concerning Lady Hsia. Cf. also *Hei Erh-shih-ssu shih*, vol. 1, 111, 352 f., 643 f.

I estimate Wu Chü's floruit based on the fact that he had audiences with Kings K'ang 康 (r. 559–545 B.C.) and Ling 靈 (r. 540–529 B.C.) of Ch'u. Ssu-ma Ch'ien 司馬遷 (145?–86? B.C.) asserts that he became "noteworthy by serving King Chuang [r. 613–591 B.C.] with upright remonstrance" 以直諫事莊王有顯, "Wu Tzu-hsü lieh-chuan" 列傳, *Shih-chi* 66.2171. However, as Yü Yu-ting 余有丁 (1527–1584) and others have pointed out, Ssu-ma has mistaken Wu Chü for his father, Wu Ts'an 參. See Takigawa Kametarō 瀧川龜太郎 (b. 1865), *Shiki kaichū kōshō* 史記會注考證 (Tokyo: Tōhō Bunka Gakuin, 1932–1934; repr., Taipei: Hung-shih, 1986), 66.2.

93. *Ch'un-ch'iu Tso-chuan chu*, vol. 2, 701 f. (Hsüan 宣 9 = 600 B.C.).

94. Following the commentary of Tu Yü.

95. Following the commentary of Tu Yü.

96. Compare the translation in Legge, vol. 5, 305.

97. *Ch'un-ch'iu Tso-chuan chu*, vol. 2, 707 f. (Hsüan 10 = 599 B.C.).

98. Compare the translation in Legge, vol. 5, 308.

99. It was evidently common in ancient China to impugn a man's legitimacy by observing that he looked like someone other than his supposed father. For another example, see, e.g., *Ch'un-ch'iu Ku-liang chuan chu-shu* 3.2375a (Huan 6 = 706 B.C.): "In the ninth month, on *ting-mao* day, the [Marquis's] son T'ung was born. There was some doubt [as to his legitimacy]; thus there is a record of it. At the time, it was said, 'He resembles [*t'ung*] another man'" 九月，丁卯，子同生。疑，故志之。時曰：同乎人也.

100. *Ch'un-ch'iu Tso-chuan chu*, vol. 2, 713 f. (Hsüan 11 = 598 B.C.).

101. Compare the translation in Legge, vol. 5, 310.

102. The story is retold, with few significant differences, in "Ch'en Ch'i shih-chia" 陳杞世家, *Shih-chi* 36.1579 f.

103. See, e.g., *Ch'un-ch'iu Tso-chuan chu*, vol. 2, 804 (Ch'eng 2 = 589 B.C.); and esp. vol. 4, 1492 (Chao 28 = 514 B.C.), where she is accused of having "killed three husbands, one lord, one son, and destroyed one country and two officers" 殺三夫、一君、一子，而亡一國、兩卿矣. By the lord is meant Lord Ling; the son, Hsia Cheng-shu; the country, Ch'en; and the two officers, K'ung Ning and I Hang-fu.

104. *Ch'un-ch'iu Tso-chuan chu*, vol. 2, 803 (Ch'eng 2 = 589 B.C.).

105. Compare the translation in Legge, vol. 5, 347.

106. This is also why it is said of Chòu 紂, the prodigal last king of the Shang 商 dynasty, that the most abominable consequence of his lewd sexual games was that he ended up neglecting the sacrifices. Cf., e.g., Lewis, *Sanctioned Violence*, 33, and the classical texts he cites on 260 n. 77.

107. For a discussion of Ch'ü Yüan's dates, see, e.g., Hawkes, *Songs of the South*, 51 ff., and Maspero, *China in Antiquity*, 483 n. 2.

108. The following discussion is an expansion of Paul Rakita Goldin, "Reading Po Chü-i," *T'ang Studies* 12 (1994), 64 ff.

109. *Ch'u-tz'u chang-chü pu-chu* 1.4.

110. Note that this line contains two telltale features of relatively late grammar: the use of *chih* 之 as an indicator of the possessive after a personal pronoun (*yü* 余); and the use of *ch'ing* 情 in the sense of "passion," "emotion." Both uses are rare in compositions from before the third century B.C.

111. *Ch'u-tz'u chang-chü pu-chu* 1.5.

112. Following the commentary of Kung Ching-han 龔景瀚 (1747–1803), in Yu Kuo-en 游國恩 (1899–1978), *Li-sao tsuan-i* 離騷纂義, ed. Chin K'ai-ch'eng 金開誠 et al., *Ch'u-tz'u chu-shu ch'ang-pien* (Peking: Chung-hua, 1980), 69. See also Yu's comments (70), as well as Chiang Liang-fu, *Ch'u-tz'u t'ung-ku*, vol. 4, 91.

113. *Ch'u-tz'u chang-chü pu-chu* 1.9.

114. Cf. also Laurence A. Schneider, *A Madman of Ch'u: The Chinese Myth of Loyalty and Dissent* (Berkeley and Los Angeles: University of California Press, 1980), 32 f. and 217 nn. 26–27.

115. On this goddess, see, e.g., Wolfgang Münke, *Die klassische chinesische Mythologie* (Stuttgart: Ernst Klett, 1976), 100 ff.; and Granet, *Danses et légendes*, vol. 2, 481, 513.

116. Commentators disagree over the meaning of this verse. See *Li-sao tsuan-i*, 309 ff.

117. *Ch'u-tz'u chang-chü pu-chu* 1.17 f.

118. *Ch'u-tz'u chang-chü pu-chu* 1.20.

119. *Ch'u-tz'u chang-chü pu-chu* 1.27.

120. For the various possibilities of the phrase *p'eng-hsien* 彭咸, see, e.g., Hawkes, *Songs of the South*, 84 ff.; Hoshikawa, 295–313; and Lin Keng 林庚, "P'eng-hsien shih shei?" 彭咸是誰 (1948), in *Shih-jen Ch'ü Yüan chi-ch'i tso-p'in yen-chiu* 詩人屈原及其作品研究, Chung-kuo ku-tai wen-hsüeh yen-chiu ts'ung-k'an (Shanghai, 1952), 63–73. See also *Li-sao tsuan-i*, 499 ff. Compare Hawkes' translation of the entire poem (*Songs of the South*, 68–95), with notes on such figures as Fu-fei and Chien-hsiu.

121. Cf., e.g., Hsü Chih-hsiao, 183 ff.; and Chu Pi-lien 朱碧蓮, "'Li-sao' san ch'iu-nü chieh" 離騷三求女解, in Chu's *Ch'u-tz'u lun-kao* 論稿 (Shanghai: San-lien, 1993), 123–133. Yu Kuo-en, *Tu-Sao lun-wei ch'u-chi* 讀騷論微初集, Jen-jen wen-k'u 441–442 (Taipei: Shang-wu, 1967), 117 ff., reads "beauty" as a metaphor for the idea of resisting the might of the state of Ch'in.

122. Pauline Yu, 89 ff., points out that there is a parallel dynamic in the many fragrances that arise in the poem. The observation that fragrant flowers are used in "Encountering Sorrow" as a metaphor for virtue goes back to Wang I. See also Chou Chien-chung 周建忠, "'Li-sao' hsiang-ts'ao lun" 離騷香草論, in *Ch'u-tz'u lun-kao* (Cheng-chou: Chung-chou ku-chi, 1994), 116–139. For the idea of "fragrant virtue" 馨香德, see also "Lü-hsing" 呂刑, *Shang-shu cheng-i* 尚書正義 (*Shih-san ching chu-shu*), 19.247c; cf. also Thomas H. C. Lee, "The Idea of Social Justice in Ancient China," in *Social Justice in the Ancient World*, ed. K. D. Irani and Morris Silver, Contributions in Political Science 354: Global Perspectives in History and Politics (Westport, Conn.: Greenwood, 1995), 128.

123. For other connections between the *Chuang-tzu* and the *Ch'u-tz'u*, see, e.g., Isabelle Robinet, *Taoism: Growth of a Religion*, trans. Phyllis Brooks (Stanford, Calif.: Stanford University Press, 1997), 35; Paul Demiéville, "Enigmes taoïstes," in *Silver Jubilee Volume of the Zimbun-Kagaku-Kenkyusyo* (Kyoto, 1954), 54–60, reprinted in *Choix d'études sinologiques (1921–1970)* (Leiden: E. J. Brill, 1973), 141–147; and Marcel Granet, *La pensée chinoise*, L'évolution de l'humanité: Synthèse collective 25b (Paris: Albin Michel, 1950), 549 f.

124. Following the commentary of Hsi T'ung 奚侗 (fl. 1916), in Wang Shu-min 王叔岷, *Chuang-tzu chiao-ch'üan* 莊子校詮, 2d ed., Chung-yang Yen-chiu-yüan Li-shih Yü-yen Yen-chiu-so chuan-k'an 88 (Taipei, 1994), vol. 1, 189 n. 14.

125. "Te-ch'ung fu" 德充符; text in Kuo Ch'ing-fan 郭慶藩 (1844–1896), *Chuang-tzu chi-shih* 集釋, ed. Wang Hsiao-yü 王孝魚, Hsin-pien Chu-tzu chi-ch'eng (Peking: Chung-hua, 1961), 2C.5.206.

126. Following the commentary of Ch'eng Hsüan-ying 成玄英 (fl. 630–660); *ch'ang* 唱 here is to be taken in the sense of *ch'ang* 倡.

127. Following the commentaries of Ch'eng Hsüan-ying and others.

128. Compare the translation in Victor H. Mair, trans., *Wandering on the Way: Early Taoist Tales and Parables of Chuang Tzu* (New York: Bantam, 1994), 46 f. Mair calls Ai-t'ai T'o "Nag the Hump."

129. "Te-ch'ung fu," *Chuang-tzu chi-shih* 2C.5.214f. Compare the translation in Mair, *Wandering on the Way*, 48.

130. On the philosophy of the *Chuang-tzu* in general, see, e.g., A. C. Graham, *Disputers of the Tao: Philosophical Argument in Ancient China* (La Salle, Ill.: Open Court, 1989), 170–211.

131. These two lines are not easy to construe, and Hawkes (*Songs of the South*, 121), considering them to be interpolations, omits them.

132. Admittedly, the translation of this line is ungrammatical, but it is very difficult to render the phrase *hsin hsiang chih* 新相知 idiomatically.

133. "Chiu-ko," *Ch'u-tz'u chang-chü pu-chu* 2.42f.

134. Cf. Chiang Liang-fu, *Ch'u-tz'u t'ung-ku*, vol. 3, 409ff.; and Yu Kuo-en, *Li-sao tsuan-i*, 70. Hung Hsing-tsu suggested that *ch'üan* 荃 and *sun* 蓀 actually denote the same plant; see *Ch'u-tz'u chang-chü pu-chu* 1.5.

135. Cf., e.g., Lewis, *Sanctioned Violence*, 73ff. The trope is especially well attested in the *Chan-kuo ts'e* 戰國策. J. I. Crump, *Intrigues: Studies of the Chan-kuo Ts'e* (Ann Arbor: University of Michigan Press, 1964), 86f., discusses two related episodes in that collection, in which the minister Ch'en Chen 陳軫 convinces King Hui-wen of Ch'in 秦惠文王 (r. 337–311 B.C.) of his loyalty by continually comparing himself to a faithful woman. See "Chang I yu wu Ch'en Chen yü Ch'in-wang" 張儀又惡陳軫於秦王 and "Ch'en Chen ch'ü Ch'u chih Ch'in" 陳軫去楚之秦, in *Chan-kuo ts'e* (Shanghai: Ku-chi, 1978; repr., Taipei: Li-jen, 1990), 3.127–132. See also Crump's translation of the two anecdotes in *Chan-kuo ts'e*, rev. ed., Michigan Monographs in Chinese Studies 77 (Ann Arbor, 1996), secs. 54 and 55.

For this reason, we must take care in assessing ancient passages that describe in sexual terms a ruler's relationship with a male inferior. These should not necessarily be understood as instances of homosexuality (as discussed in the introduction of this book), because it was conventional to conceive of a ruler's relationship with any of his ministers in sexual terms. The standard term *ch'ung* 寵, for example, meaning "to favor," could be applied indiscriminately to cases where the ruler "favors" an inferior in a sexual or nonsexual sense. See, e.g., Hinsch, *Passions of the Cut Sleeve*, 21.

136. *Chou-I cheng-i* 周易正義 (*Shih-san ching chu-shu*), 1.19a. Compare also *Mencius* 3B.2, *Meng-tzu cheng-i* 12.417: "To take compliance as one's rule is the Way of the wife" 以順為正者，妾婦之道也. See especially the commentary of Chiao Hsün on p. 419.

137. The seminal work on Shen Pu-hai is Herrlee G. Creel, *Shen Pu-hai: A Chinese Political Philosopher of the Fourth Century B.C.* (Chicago: University of Chicago Press, 1974). Cf. also Léon Vandermeersch, *La formation du légisme: Recherche sur la constitution d'une philosophie politique caractéristique de la Chine ancienne*, Publications de l'Ecole Française d'Extrême-Orient 56 (Paris, 1965), 41ff.

138. Creel, *Shen Pu-hai*, 343f., fragment 1(1); the source text is Wei Cheng 魏徵 (580–643), *Ch'ün-shu chih-yao* 群書治要 (*Kuo-hsüeh chi-pen ts'ung-shu*), 36.629. The first two sentences (up to *p'o-kuo* 破國) also appear in Ma Tsung 馬總 (d. 823), *I-lin* 意林 (*Ssu-pu pei-yao* 四部備要), 2.10b, with minor variations. Compare Creel's translation.

139. "Chu-tao" 主道, *Han Fei-tzu chi-shih* 1.5.68.

140. The word is *chien* 姦, which, tellingly, can mean either "to fornicate" or "to conspire" (typically against a ruler). In this respect, *chien* parallels our word "skulduggery" (or "skulduddery"), which today generally means "trickery" or "deceit" but which originally was a euphemistic alteration of "adultery" and denoted illicit sexual intercourse.

141. Commentators are troubled by this phrase, as it does not entirely make sense. T'ao Hung-ch'ing 陶鴻慶 (1859–1918) suggests that *wei chien-ch'en* 為姦臣 ("they are treacherous ministers") is excrescent and is probably the remnant of an ancient commentary. For *wen ch'i chu chih t'e* 聞其主之忒 ("hearing of their ruler's errors"), T'ao suggests *hsien* 閒 *ch'i chu chih t'e* ("spying out their ruler's errors"), although the meaning is still not materially different. Ku Kuang-ch'i 顧廣圻 (1776–1835) proposes that *ch'en* in *wei chien-ch'en* might be a graphic error for *i* 以. Although he is right that this change would make the sentence read more fluidly ("They practice treachery by spying out/hearing their ruler's errors"), there is no text-critical reason for such an emendation. Thus I prefer to leave the original as it stands.

142. On the technique of matching "forms and names" 刑名, see, e.g., John Makeham, "The Legalist Concept of *Hsing-ming*: An Example of the Contribution of Archeological Evidence to the Re-Interpretation of Transmitted Texts," *Monumenta Serica* 39 (1990–1991): 87–114; and Herrlee G. Creel, "The Meaning of *Hsing-ming*," in *Studia Serica Bernhard Karlgren Dedicata*, ed. Søren Egerod and Else Glahn (Copenhagen, 1959), 199–211, reprinted in *What Is Taoism? and Other Studies in Chinese Cultural History*, Midway Reprint (Chicago: University of Chicago Press, 1970), 79–91.

143. Compare the translation in Burton Watson, trans., *Basic Writings of Han Fei Tzu*, in *Basic Writings of Mo Tzu, Hsün Tzu, and Han Fei Tzu*, Records of Civilization: Sources and Studies 74 (New York: Columbia University Press, 1963), 18.

144. Omitting excrescent *ssu* 死, with Ku Kuang-ch'i.

145. "Pei-nei" 備內, *Han Fei-tzu chi-shih* 5.17.289. In a massive study of the compilation of the *Han Fei-tzu*, Cheng Liang-shu 鄭良樹, *Han Fei chih chu-shu chi ssu-hsiang* 韓非之著述及思想, Chung-kuo che-hsüeh ts'ung-shu 35 (Taipei: Hsüeh-sheng, 1993), 26–37 and 183–195, concludes that both the "Chu-tao" and "Pei-nei" chapters were written by Han Fei toward the end of his life.

146. Compare the translation in Watson, *Han Fei Tzu*, 85.

147. Cf. Harper, *Early Chinese Medical Literature*, 414 n. 3, and "Sexual Arts," 579; and Li and McMahon, 161.

148. "Nei-tse" 內則, *Li-chi cheng-i* 28.1468c; compare the translations in Couvreur, vol. 1, 661, and Richard Wilhelm, 326. The rule is repeated in "Chia-ch'ü," *Po-hu t'ung shu-cheng* 10.492. Cf. also *Hei Erh-shih-ssu shih*, vol. 1, 329 f.; Englert, 2; Tjan, vol. 1, 262 and 360 nn. 593 ff.; van Gulik, 60 and 78; and Marcel Granet, *La polygynie sororale et le sororat dans la Chine féodale: Etude sur les formes anciennes de la polygamie chinoise* (Paris: Ernest Leroux, 1920), reprinted in *Études sociologiques sur la Chine*, Bibliothèque de sociologie contemporaine (Paris: Presses Universitaires de France, 1953), 26.

Compare also the statement in the "Ta-lüeh" 大略 chapter of the *Hsün-tzu* 荀子: "When the frost descends, one welcomes the bride; when the ice breaks, [weddings] cease. Every ten days there is one driving" 霜降逆女，冰泮殺止，內十日一御; text in Wang Hsien-ch'ien 王先謙 (1842–1918), *Hsün-tzu chi-chieh* 集解, ed. Shen Hsiao-huan and Wang Hsing-hsien, Hsin-pien Chu-tzu chi-ch'eng (Peking: Chung-hua, 1988), 19.27.496. My interpretation of this passage follows the commentary of Wang Yin-chih 王引之 (1766–1834): Hsün-tzu means to say that marriages must take place during the winter. As we shall see in chapter 3, this statement goes against received wisdom and has, for that reason, long been misunderstood. See, e.g., *Mao* 34 ("P'ao yu k'u-yeh"): "If a man brings home a wife, it is while the ice has not yet melted" 士如歸妻，迨冰未泮, and the commentaries by Cheng Hsüan and K'ung Ying-ta, *Mao-Shih cheng-i* 2B.303bf. Some modern scholars (e.g., Sheng I, 255) read *kuei-ch'i* 歸妻 as "go back with the wife," and they see this poem as evidence of uxorilocal marriage.

Thus, despite the translation by, e.g., John Knoblock, *Xunzi: A Translation and Study of the Complete Works* (Stanford, Calif.: Stanford University Press, 1988–1994), vol. 3, 217, the phrase *sha-chih* 殺止 in this passage from Hsün-tzu does not refer to executions and means no more than "finish." For other examples of this usage of *sha*, see, e.g., Morohashi Tetsuji 諸橋轍次, *Dai Kan-Wa jiten* 大漢和辭典, rev. ed. (Tokyo: Daishūkan, 1986), entry 16638, vol. 6, 776, row 2, under the definition そぐ.

149. "Hun-i" 昏義, *Li-chi cheng-i* 61.1681c. Couvreur, vol. 2, 648, misses the substance of the title by translating *yü-ch'i* as "autres femmes de l'empereur … du cinquième rang" ("other women of the Emperor … of the fifth rank"). Granet, *Etudes sociologiques*, 25, calls them simply "femmes de palais" (palace women). Robert Joe Cutter and William Gordon Crowell, *Empresses and Consorts: Selections from Chen Shou's* Records of the Three States *with Pei Songzhi's Commentary* (Honolulu: University of Hawai'i Press, 1999), 28, translate *yü-ch'i* as "royal wives" (taking *yü* in the sense of "imperial" or "royal," which is also possible). The *yü-ch'i* are known as *nü-yü* 女御 in the *Chou-li* 周禮. See, e.g., "Nü-yü," *Chou-li chu-shu (Shih-san ching chu-shu)*, 8.689c; and the commentary of Sun Hsi-tan, *Li-chi chi-chieh* 58.44.1422. Cf. also *Hei Erh-shih-ssu shih*, vol. 1, 666; and Ch'en Ku-yüan 陳顧遠, *Chung-kuo hun-yin shih* 中國婚姻史, Chiu-chi hsin-k'an (1936; repr., Ch'ang-sha: Yüeh-lu, 1998), 40. (Ch'en's book is bound together with that of Wang Shu-nu into one volume.)

150. According to the "schedule of driving the flock of consorts" 群妃御見之法 put forward by Cheng Hsüan, the Emperor is to copulate with nine *nü-yü* daily for the first and last nine days of each month; see his commentary to "Chiu-p'in" 九嬪, *Chou-li chu-shu* 8.687b. Sheng I, 324, notes soberly that such an effort is hardly possible.

151. *Tu-tuan* 獨斷 (*Han-Wei ts'ung-shu*), A.180c.

152. *Ch'u-tz'u chang-chü pu-chu* 5.96.

153. See Hawkes, *Songs of the South*, 199f., for the apotheosis of the ancient diviner Fu Yüeh and the third-century medicine man Han Chung. "Attaining the One" 得一 is a basic idea in late Warring States thought. See, e.g., Schipper, *The Taoist Body*, 130–159, for an overview of the concept and its later development.

154. Following the commentary of Hung Hsing-tsu.

155. *Ch'u-tz'u chang-chü pu-chu* 5.97.

156. *Ch'u-tz'u chang-chü pu-chu* 5.98 f.

157. *Ch'u-tz'u chang-chü pu-chu* 5.100.

158. For the phrase *lieh-ch'üeh* 列缺 (which is the same as *lieh-ch'üeh* 缺), I follow the commentaries of Wang I and Hung Hsing-tsu (the latter also cites the opinion of Ying Shao). See also Chiang Liang-fu, *Ch'u-tz'u t'ung-ku*, vol. 1, 152.

159. *Ch'u-tz'u chang-chü pu-chu* 5.103. Compare Hawkes' translation of the entire poem in *Songs of the South*, 193–203. Kuo Mo-jo 郭沫若 (1892–1978), *Ch'ü Yüan yen-chiu* 屈原研究, 2d rev. ed. (Shanghai: Hsin wen-i, 1952), 42, suggested that "Yüan-yu" was actually the first draft of Ssu-ma Hsiang-ju's 司馬相如 (ca. 179–117 B.C.) "Ta-jen fu" 大人賦, which appears in "Ssu-ma Hsiang-ju lieh-chuan," *Shih-chi* 117.3056–3062. Cf. also Hawkes, *Songs of the South*, 191 ff., who concurs that whether or not Kuo Mo-jo is right about the specifics, "Yüan-yu" is clearly later than Ch'ü Yüan and is "obviously influenced" (39) by "Li-sao." It is not entirely clear why both scholars are so sure that "Yüan-yu" is a much later work. Perhaps their reason lies in that poem's reference to the *tao* 道 (*Ch'u-tz'u chang-chü pu-chu* 5.98), for Hawkes suggests that there is too much evidence of Han Taoism in "Yüan-yu" for it to be a genuine Warring States piece. Similarly, Hoshikawa, 439, writes that "Yüan-yu" contains "Lao-Chuang" 老莊 ideas (by which he means the Taoism of *Lao-tzu* and *Chuang-tzu*) and hence cannot be the work of Ch'ü Yüan. But scholars are no longer so comfortable in talking about Taoism (not to mention Lao-Chuang) in this early period. See esp. Nathan Sivin, "On the Word 'Taoist' as a Source of Perplexity: With Special Reference to the Relations of Science and Religion in Traditional China," *History of Religion* 17 (1978), 303–330; and Michel Strickmann, "On the Alchemy of T'ao Hung-ching," in Welch and Seidel, 164 ff. Furthermore, the author of "Li-sao" too—whether Ch'ü Yüan or not—was certainly active long after it had become possible to speak of the *tao* in its extended senses. (One piece of evidence that seems to argue in favor of a Han date for "Yüan-yu" is the reference to a figure named Han Chung 韓眾 at *Ch'u-tz'u chang-chü pu-chu* 5.97. If, as is often surmised, this Han Chung is the same as the Han Chung 韓終 who appears in "Ch'in Shih-huang pen-chi" 秦始皇本紀, *Shih-chi* 6.252 and 258, then "Yüan-yu" cannot possibly be a preimperial document.) In any case, Kuo Mo-jo and Hawkes are right to point out that the "Li-sao," "Yüan-yu," and "Ta-jen fu" have many things in common. Cf. also Paul W. Kroll, "On 'Far Roaming,'" *Journal of the American Oriental Society* 116.4 (1996), 654; Yang Ts'ai-hua, 304 f.; and Fukunaga Mitsuji 福永光司, "'Taijin fu' no shisōteki keifu: Jifu no bungaku to Rō-Sō no tetsugaku 大人賦の思想的系譜：楚辭の文學と老莊の哲學, *Tōhō gakuhō* 東方學報 41 (1970), 100 ff.

160. Cf. Goldin, "Reflections," 186.

161. Cf., e.g., Roger Walsh, *The Spirit of Shamanism* (Los Angeles: Tarcher, 1990), 120 ff.

162. Translated from Mircea Eliade, *Le chamanisme et les techniques archaïques de l'extase*, 2d ed. (Paris: Payot, 1974), 164. Willard Trask's translation, *Shaman-*

ism and the Archaic Techniques of Ecstasy, Bollingen Series 76 (New York: Pantheon, 1964), is based on the first edition of this study and is now out of date.

163. For a sociological account of shamanism, see, e.g., I. M. Lewis, *Ecstatic Religion: An Anthropological Study of Spirit Possession and Shamanism*, Pelican Anthropology (New York: Penguin, 1971). See also Åke Hultkrantz, "A Definition of Shamanism," *Temenos* 9 (1973), 25–37.

164. Text in Kuo-chia Wen-wu-chü Ku-wen-hsien Yen-chiu-Shih 國家文物局古文獻研究室, *Ma-wang-tui Han-mu po-shu* 馬王堆漢墓帛書 (Peking: Wen-wu, 1985), vol. 4, 155. The text is emended in accordance with Harper, *Early Chinese Medical Literature*, 412 ff.; and "Sexual Arts," 567. Compare also the annotation in Ma Chi-hsing 馬繼興, *Ma-wang-tui ku i-shu k'ao-shih* 馬王堆古醫書考釋 (Ch'ang-sha: Hu-nan k'o-hsüeh chi-shu, 1992), 977 ff.; as well as Wei Ch'i-p'eng 魏啟鵬 and Hu Hsiang-hua 胡翔驊, *Ma-wang-tui Han-mu i-shu chiao-shih* 馬王堆漢墓醫書校釋, Erh-shih shih-chi ch'u-t'u Chung-kuo ku i-shu chi-ch'eng (Ch'eng-tu: Ch'eng-tu ch'u-pan-she, 1992), vol. 2, 130 f.

165. Trans. Harper, *Early Chinese Medical Literature*, 412 ff. Compare also the translations in Douglas Wile, *Art of the Bedchamber: The Chinese Sexual Yoga Classics, Including Women's Solo Meditation Texts* (Albany: State University of New York Press, 1992), 78; and Harper, "Sexual Arts," 566.

166. Li and McMahon, 167 f., however, interpret the "receiving canister" in this context as a reference to the shoulders.

167. "Yangism" is the term used to denote the philosophy of those who followed a shadowy figure named Yang Chu 楊朱. What Yang Chu actually taught (if he even existed) is not clear, but the position attributed to him and his group emphasizes the well-being of the body over all other concerns, especially wealth and political power. For example, the "Fan-lun" 氾論 chapter of the *Huai-nan-tzu* states, "Keeping one's nature whole and protecting one's purity, not tying down one's form with [material] objects—this is what Master Yang proposed" 全性保真，不以物累形，楊子之所立也. Text in Liu Wen-tien 劉文典, *Huai-nan Hung-lieh chi-chieh* 淮南鴻烈集解, ed. Feng I 馮逸 and Ch'iao Hua 喬華, Hsin-pien Chu-tzu chi-ch'eng (Peking: Chung-hua, 1989), 13.436. Cf. also Graham, *Disputers of the Tao*, 53–64.

2. Women and Sex Roles

1. See, e.g., Julia Ching, *Mysticism and Kingship in China: The Heart of Chinese Wisdom*, Cambridge Studies in Religious Traditions 11 (Cambridge, 1997), 94–97; and Richard W. Guisso, "Thunder over the Lake: The Five Classics and the Perception of Woman in Early China," in *Women in China: Current Directions in Historical Scholarship*, ed. Richard W. Guisso and Stanley Johannesen, Historical Reflections/Réflexions Historiques: Directions 3 (Youngstown, N.Y.: Philo Press, 1981), 59 f. Recently, Lisa Raphals, *Sharing the Light: Representations of Women and Virtue in Early China* (SUNY Series in Chinese Philosophy and Culture, Albany, N.Y., 1998), 259, has questioned such "widely held assumptions about women in traditional China." However, most of her arguments rely on the *Lieh-nü chuan* 列女傳, which, as she concedes (105–112), is a spurious text from mid-Han times at the very earliest, and so she fails to reexamine such scholarly clichés on the

basis of genuine preimperial material. (Raphals redresses some of these problems in her more recent essay, "Gendered Virtue Reconsidered: Notes from
the Warring States and Han," in Chenyang Li, ed., *The Sage and the Second Sex:
Confucianism, Ethics, and Gender* [Chicago: Open Court, 2000], 223–247.) In this
chapter, there appear only accounts from the most ancient texts, though later
versions of some stories will be mentioned in the notes.

2. Cf. also Siegfried Englert, *Materialien zur Stellung der Frau und zur Sexualität
im vormodernen und modernen China*, Heidelberger Schriften zur Ostasienkunde 1
(Frankfurt: Haag und Herchen, 1980), 32 f.

3. This poem has become the standard source that contemporary scholars
recite as an example of ancient Chinese misogyny. See, e.g., Henry Rosemont,
Jr., "Classical Confucian and Contemporary Feminist Perspectives on the Self:
Some Parallels and Their Implications," in *Culture and Self: Philosophical and Reli-
gious Perspectives, East and West*, ed. Douglas Allen (Boulder, Colo.: Westview,
1997), 65; Alison H. Black, "Gender and Cosmology in Chinese Correlative
Thinking," in *Gender and Religion: On the Complexity of Symbols*, ed. Caroline Walker
Bynum et al. (Boston: Beacon, 1986), 171; and R. H. van Gulik, *Sexual Life in
Ancient China: A Preliminary Survey of Chinese Sex and Society from ca. 1500 B.C. till
1644 A.D.* (Leiden: E. J. Brill, 1961; repr., New York: Barnes and Noble, 1996), 29.

4. This line highlights the two meanings of the term *jen* 人: "people" in general and "elite people" in particular. Thus *jen yu min-jen*: "The elite people had
people [as followers]." The *jen* who are disenfranchised in this stanza are to be
understood, therefore, as members of the feudal aristocracy. See, e.g., A. C.
Graham, *Disputers of the Tao: Philosophical Argument in Ancient China* (La Salle, Ill.:
Open Court, 1989), 19, for the various meanings of *jen*.

5. The *hsiao* 梟 is an unfilial bird that eats its mother before it can fly. See,
e.g., text in Chiang Jen-chieh 蔣人傑, *Shuo-wen chieh-tzu chi-chu* 集注, ed. Liu Jui
劉銳 (Shanghai: Ku-chi, 1996), 6A.1266; and the commentary of Meng K'ang
孟康 (fl. ca. A.D. 225–250) to "Chiao-ssu chih," *Han-shu* 漢書 (Peking: Chung-
hua, 1962), 25A.1219 n. 4. On owls in general, see Marcel Granet, *Danses et légendes de la Chine ancienne*, Bibliothèque de philosophie contemporaine, Travaux de
l'Année sociologique (Paris: Félix Alcan, 1926), vol. 2, 515–548.

6. Following the commentary of Cheng Hsüan, *Mao-Shih cheng-i* 18E.578a.
Legge and Karlgren (as well as Raphals, *Sharing the Light*, 64) both take *ssu* 寺
(which should be taken as though it were written *shih* 侍, "attend") to mean
"eunuchs"; thus they all construe the couplet to mean that women and eunuchs
cannot be taught or instructed (or that they cannot teach or instruct). Similarly, Shih-shan Henry Tsai, *The Eunuchs in the Ming Dynasty*, SUNY Series in
Chinese Local Studies (Albany, N.Y., 1996), 12, translates *ssu* as "those without
balls." However, I suspect that the "eunuchs" represent something of an
anachronism. Moreover, Cheng Hsüan's interpretation has the added advantage that it easily accounts for the word *shih* 時, "constantly," whereas other
readings force it into the sense of *shih* 是, "are [women and eunuchs]." Karlgren, "Glosses on the Ta Ya and Sung Odes," in *Glosses on the Book of Odes* (Stockholm: Museum of Far Eastern Antiquities, 1964), 139 and 141 f., misrepresents
Cheng Hsüan's explanation of *ssu*. On the other hand, the phrase *ssu-jen* 寺人,
"attendant," appears in *Mao* 200 ("Hsiang-po" 巷伯), *Mao-Shih cheng-i* 12C.456c,

and here the commentaries all agree that the person in question is a eunuch. Cf. Tu Yung-ming 杜永明 et al., *Hei Erh-shih-ssu shih* 黑二十四史 (Peking: Chung-kuo hua-ch'iao, 1998), vol. 5, 3223, 3236 f., 3243 f. [this work cited hereafter as *Hei Erh-shih-ssu shih*; see note 20 in the introduction of the present volume].

7. Thus the "Minor Preface," *Mao-Shih cheng-i* 18E.577b. See also the commentaries of Cheng Hsüan and K'ung Ying-ta, and cf. *Hei Erh-shih-ssu shih*, vol. 1, 643. Pao was a minor state vanquished by Chou. *Ssu* 姒 is usually explained as Pao Ssu's surname but can also mean "elder sister."

8. See, e.g., "Shih Su lun Hsien-kung fa Li-Jung sheng erh pu-chi" 史蘇論獻公伐驪戎勝而不吉, *Kuo-yü* 國語 (Shanghai: Ku-chi, 1978; repr., Taipei: Li-jen, 1981), 7.255; "Shih Po wei Huan-kung lun hsing-shuai" 史伯為桓公論興衰, *Kuo-yü* 16.519; "Chou pen-chi" 周本紀, *Shih-chi* 史記 (Peking: Chung-hua, 1959), 4.147 ff.; and "Cheng shih-chia," *Shih-chi* 42.1757 ff. Pao Ssu is also the subject of a biography in *Lieh-nü chuan*; text in "Chou Yu Pao Ssu" 周幽褒姒, in Wang Chao-yüan 王照圓 (fl. 1879–1884), *Lieh-nü chuan pu-chu* 列女傳補註 (*Kuo-hsüeh chi-pen ts'ung-shu*), 7.127–129. See also Jianfei Kralle, with Roderich Ptak and Dennis Schilling, "Böse Brut: Bao Si [褒姒] und das Ende von König You [幽王]," *Zeitschrift der deutschen morgenländischen Gesellschaft* 149.1 (1999), 145–172; Edward L. Shaughnessy, "Western Zhou History," in *The Cambridge History of Ancient China: From the Origins of Civilization to 221 B.C.*, ed. Michael Loewe and Edward L. Shaughnessy (Cambridge, 1999), 349 f.; Raphals, *Sharing the Light*, 64 ff.; Wolfgang Münke, *Die klassische chinesische Mythologie* (Stuttgart: Ernst Klett, 1976), 255–257; Herrlee G. Creel, *The Origins of Statecraft in China* (Chicago: University of Chicago Press, 1970), 438 f.; and Granet, *Danses et légendes*, vol. 2, 558 f.

9. See, e.g., Wang Lei-sheng 王雷生, "P'ing-wang tung-ch'ien yüan-yin hsin-lun—Chou P'ing-wang tung-ch'ien shou-pi yü Ch'in, Chin, Cheng chu-hou shuo" 平王東遷原因新論—周平王東遷受逼於秦、晉、鄭諸侯説, *Jen-wen tsa-chih* 人文雜誌 1998.1, 86–90, for an overview of relations between King P'ing and the most powerful feudal lords.

10. *Wu* 無 is usually explained as an "empty particle" 發語詞, but Karlgren, "Glosses on the Ta Ya and Sung Odes," 101, suggests persuasively that its function is to turn a clause into an "oratorical question." Following Cheng Hsüan, *Mao-Shih cheng-i* 18A.554c, most commentators take *ching* 競 to mean simply "strong" 強, but I prefer to retain its basic sense of "struggle" or "compete."

11. See David S. Nivison's pathbreaking study of the notion of *te* in early Chinese thought: " 'Virtue' in Bone and Bronze," in *The Ways of Confucianism: Investigations in Chinese Philosophy*, ed. Bryan W. Van Norden (Chicago: Open Court, 1996), 17–30. Cf. also Vassili Kryukov, "Symbols of Power and Communication in Pre-Confucian China (on the Anthropology of *De*): Preliminary Assumptions," *Bulletin of the School of Oriental and African Studies* 58 (1995), 314–332.

12. Thus the "Minor Preface," *Mao-Shih cheng-i* 18A.554b. For the dates of King Li's reign, see Shaughnessy, "Western Zhou History," 342 ff., and *Sources of Western Zhou History: Inscribed Bronze Vessels* (Berkeley and Los Angeles: University of California Press, 1991), 272–286. He seems to have acceded in 857 B.C. and started to rule in his own name in 853. He was exiled in 842 and died in 828.

13. Chen Zhi, "A New Reading of 'Yen-yen,'" *T'oung Pao* 85.1–3 (1999), 18 f., argues that this "Chung-shih Jen" 仲氏任 refers not to T'ai Jen but to the wife of the Duke of Chou. However, the rest of the stanza, and especially the line *nai chi wang Chi* 乃及王季 ("and she, with King Chi"), is hard to reconcile with this novel suggestion. In any case, it is clear that at least part of this poem deals with T'ai Jen.

14. Because of the possible sexual dimensions of the term *te* 德 (discussed later in this chapter), this line is sometimes understood as a reference to sexual intercourse between King Wen's parents. See, e.g., Pertti Nikkilä, *Early Confucianism and Inherited Thought in the Light of Some Key Terms of the Confucian Analects, Studia Orientalia* 53 (1982), 181.

15. As in *Mao* 236 ("Ta Ming").

16. The three "mothers of Chou" have their own biographical section in the *Lieh-nü chuan*: "Chou-shih san-mu" 周室三母, *Lieh-nü chuan pu-chu* 1.6–7. Cf. *Hei Erh-shih-ssu shih*, vol. 1, 646. Consider also the figure of Mencius' mother, one of the most venerated women in Confucian lore. See, e.g., *Han-Shih wai-chuan* 韓詩外傳 (*Ssu-pu ts'ung-k'an* 四部叢刊), 9.1a, 8b f.; and "Tsou Meng K'o mu" 鄒孟軻母, *Lieh-nü chuan pu-chu* 1.15–18; see also Raphals, *Sharing the Light*, 33–35. The traditional image of Mencius' virtuous mother is in line with the appreciative view of the wives and mothers of Chou.

17. Dorothy Ko, *Teachers of the Inner Chambers: Women and Culture in Seventeenth-Century China* (Stanford, Calif.: Stanford University Press, 1994), 53. Cf. also Guisso, 48; and Julia Kristeva, *About Chinese Women*, trans. Anita Barrows (New York: Urizen, 1977), 76, who states that according to Confucianism, a woman either "leaves the bedchamber to be acknowledged—but only as genetrix—the mother of the father's sons; or she gains access to the social order (as poet, dancer, singer) but behind the door of the bedchamber, an unacknowledgeable sexual partner." In other words, the only morally acceptable role for women is that of wife and mother.

18. This point is made forcefully in the context of a discussion of Confucianism and feminist philosophy in Rosemont, "Classical Confucian and Contemporary Feminist Perspectives," 71 ff. See also Chenyang Li, "The Confucian Concept of *Jen* and the Feminist Ethics of Care: A Comparative Study," *Hypatia* 9.1 (1994), reprinted in idem, *The Sage and the Second Sex*, 24.

19. "Chung-yung," *Li-chi cheng-i* 52.1627a f.

20. Compare the translations in S. Couvreur, S.J., *Li Ki ou Mémoires sur les bienséances et les cérémonies*, 2d ed. (Ho Kien Fou: Mission Catholique, 1913), vol. 2, 437, and Richard Wilhelm, *Li Gi: Das Buch der Riten, Sitten, und Bräuche*, 2d ed., Diederichs Gelbe Reihe 31 (Munich, 1994), 30.

21. E.g., *Analects* 5.12, text in Ch'eng Shu-te 程樹德 (1877–1944), *Lun-yü chi-shih* 論語集釋, ed. Ch'eng Chün-ying 程俊英 and Chiang Chien-yüan 蔣見元, Hsin-pien Chu-tzu chi-ch'eng (Peking: Chung-hua, 1990), 9.316; and *Analects* 15.24, *Lun-yü chi-shih* 32.1106. For more on *shu*, see, e.g., Herbert Fingarette, "Following the 'One Thread' of the *Analects*," in *Studies in Classical Chinese Thought*, ed. Henry Rosemont, Jr., and Benjamin I. Schwartz, *Journal of the American Academy of Religion* 47.3, Thematic Issue S (1979), 373–405. Fingarette's essay is discussed in Philip J. Ivanhoe, "Reweaving the 'One Thread' in the

Analects," *Philosophy East and West* 40.1 (1990), 17–33; see also See Yee Chan, "Disputes on the One Thread of *Chung-Shu,*" *Journal of Chinese Philosophy* 26.2 (1999), 165–186; and David S. Nivison, "Golden Rule Arguments in Chinese Moral Philosophy," in *Ways of Confucianism,* 66.

22. *Analects* 17.25, *Lun-yü chi-shih* 35.1244.

23. Compare the translation in Lau, *Analects,* 148.

24. See, e.g., Bettina L. Knapp, *Images of Chinese Women: A Westerner's View* (Troy, N.Y.: Whitston, 1992), 2; Daniel L. Overmyer, "Women in Chinese Religions: Submission, Struggle, Transcendence," in *From Benares to Beijing: Essays on Buddhism and Chinese Religion in Honour of Prof. Jan Yün-hua,* ed. Koichi Shinohara and Gregory Schopen (Oakville, Ont.: Mosaic, 1991), 93; Black, 171; and Kristeva, 75 (with an idiosyncratic translation). David L. Hall and Roger T. Ames, *Thinking from the Han: Self, Truth, and Transcendence in Chinese and Western Culture* (Albany: State University of New York Press, 1998), 88, adduce the quote without comment. Chenyang Li, 83, sees Confucius' remark as an example of "social prejudice" and not "an inevitable consequence of his general philosophy."

25. *Mencius* 7B.35, text in Chiao Hsün 焦循 (1763–1820), *Meng-tzu cheng-i* 孟子正義, ed. Shen Wen-cho 沈文倬, Hsin-pien Chu-tzu chi-ch'eng (Peking: Chung-hua, 1987), 29.1017. Compare also the famous usage in *Mencius* 2A.2, *Meng-tzu cheng-i* 6.199: "I am good at nourishing my flood-like *ch'i*" 我善養吾浩然之氣.

26. See, e.g., *Mencius* 4B.19, *Meng-tzu cheng-i* 16.567; and *Mencius* 4B.28, *Meng-tzu cheng-i* 17.595.

27. In this connection, scholars sometimes cite Hsün-tzu's famous statement that a mother is not fit to educate her own children. See, e.g., Raphals, *Sharing the Light,* 21; and Anne Behnke Kinney, "Dyed Silk: Han Notions of the Moral Development of Children," in Kinney, ed., *Chinese Views of Childhood* (Honolulu: University of Hawai'i Press, 1995), 27. However, the passage in question should not be misread as a blanket indictment of women's abilities. The context, which Raphals and Kinney both ignore, is an explanation of why the mourning period for a deceased lord should last three years. The text ("Li-lun" 禮論, in Wang Hsien-ch'ien 王先謙 (1842–1918), *Hsün-tzu chi-chieh* 集解, ed. Shen Hsiao-huan and Wang Hsing-hsien, Hsin-pien Chu-tzu chi-ch'eng (Peking: Chung-hua, 1988), 13.19.374) says,

詩曰：愷悌君子，民之父母。彼君子者，固有為民父母之説焉。父能生之，不能養之，母能食之，不能教誨之，君者，已能食之矣，又能教誨之者也，三年畢矣哉。

The *Odes* say: "The kind and courteous noble man is the father and mother of the people" [*Mao* 251: "Chiung-cho" 泂酌]. The term "noble man" surely has the meaning of acting as the people's father and mother. A father can beget [a child] but cannot nourish it; a mother can feed it but cannot instruct and admonish it. One who is a lord not only can feed it but also can instruct and admonish it. And [the mourning period for a lord] is finished after just three years!

Thus Hsün-tzu means to say not that women are generally incapable of teaching their children but that any parent who does not live up to the author's concept of the *chün-tzu* cannot go beyond simply begetting and feeding his or her children to "nourish" 養 or "instruct and admonish" 教誨 them. Hsün-tzu is implying, furthermore, that the mourning period of three years is appropriate for a moral *chün-tzu*, and not just any lord.

A more difficult case (which neither Raphals nor Kinney cite) is *Mencius* 3B.2, *Meng-tzu cheng-i* 12.415 ff., where Mencius compares the conduct of a "great man" 大丈夫 to "the way of maids and women" 妾婦之道, which he explains disparagingly as nothing more than "compliance" 順. Mencius' argument is that morality requires one to disagree with one's superiors when they are wrong, and that women cannot reach this level of excellence because they merely obey their husbands in all matters. (Cf. chapter 1, n. 136, in this volume.)

28. This is the position attributed to "the standard interpreters" by Arthur Waley, trans., *The Analects of Confucius* (New York: Random House, Vintage Books, 1938), 217 n. 1. Waley is probably thinking of Chu Hsi 朱熹 (1130–1200), who writes that *hsiao-jen* refers to *p'u-li hsia-jen* 僕隸下人 (by which he means male servants), and *nü-tzu* to *ch'ieh* 妾 (which can mean either "concubines" or "handmaidens"). See his commentary to *Lun-yü chi-shih* 35.1244.

29. E. Bruce Brooks and A. Taeko Brooks, *The Original Analects: Sayings of Confucius and His Successors*, Translations from the Asian Classics (New York: Columbia University Press, 1998), 166, report this reading without attribution.

30. Thus Brooks and Brooks, e.g., 240. The idea that the *Analects* are made up of separate strata goes back several centuries. See, e.g., John Makeham, "The Formation of *Lunyu* as a Book," *Monumenta Serica* 44 (1996), esp. 6 ff.

31. See, e.g., "Hsing o" 性惡, *Hsün-tzu chi-chieh* 17.23.442 ff., where he discusses the aphorism that "a person in the street can become Yü" 塗之人可以為 禹, but only with difficulty.

32. This example and those that follow should qualify as what Hall and Ames, 88, have called the "promotion [of] females to the status of *honorary males*" (emphasis in original), which they go on to associate with characteristically Western forms of sexism. They assert that in China, by contrast (where sexism, in their parlance, is "correlative"), it is not considered a constructive goal for females to take on male "gender traits." However, Hall and Ames do not consider the passages discussed here, which throw into question their generalizing distinction between sexism in China and in the West.

33. *Analects* 8.20, *Lun-yü chi-shih* 16.552–556.

34. For the dates, see Shaughnessy, *Sources of Western Zhou History*, 241.

35. Following the commentary of Liu Pao-nan 劉寶楠 (1791–1855). Most earlier commentators take *chi* 際 to mean the time during which Yao and Shun had contact with each other.

36. Compare the translation in D. C. Lau, *Confucius: The Analects* (New York: Penguin, 1979), 95.

37. In an earlier version of this chapter ("The View of Women in Early Confucianism," in *The Sage and the Second Sex: Confucianism, Ethics, and Gender*, in Chenyang Li, 140), I mistakenly took "Wen-mu" to mean "King Wen's mother." For the problem of the identity of "Wen-mu," see *Lun-yü chi-shih* 16.555. Cf. Raphals, "Gendered Virtue Reconsidered," 239 n. 11.

38. *Lun-yü chi-shih* 16.558.

39. "Kung-fu Wen-po tsu ch'i mu chieh ch'i ch'ieh" 公父文伯卒其母戒其妾, *Kuo-yü* 5.211.

40. Commentators disagree over the significance of the final *fu* 夫 in this sentence. Wei Chao takes it to mean "husband" or "man" (as in the translation here); Sung Hsiang 宋庠 (996–1066), on the other hand, interprets it as merely an exclamatory particle. See Tung Tseng-ling 董增齡, *Kuo-yü cheng-i* 國語正義 (n.p.: Chang-shih shih-hsün t'ang, 1880; repr., [Ch'eng-tu:] Pa-shu, 1985), 5.31a f. On *fu* as a final particle, see, e.g., Edwin G. Pulleyblank, *Outline of Classical Chinese Grammar* (Vancouver: UBC Press, 1995), 17 and 145; A. C. Graham, "The Final Particle *Fwu* 夫," *Bulletin of the School of Oriental and African Studies* 17.1 (1955), 120–132; as well as the excellent new *Ku-tai Han-yü hsü-tz'u tz'u-tien* 古代漢語虛詞詞典 (Peking: Shang-wu, 2000), 158 f.

41. On the textual history of the *Kuo-yü*, see, e.g., Chang I-jen et al., "*Kuo-yü*," in *Early Chinese Texts: A Bibliographical Guide*, ed. Michael Loewe, Early China Special Monograph Series 2 (Berkeley, Calif., 1993), 263–268; William G. Boltz, "Notes on the Textual Relationships between the *Kuo Yü* and the *Tso Chuan*," *Bulletin of the School of Oriental and African Studies* 53 (1990), 491–502; Chang I-jen 張以仁, "Lun *Kuo-yü* yü *Tso-chuan* te kuan-hsi" 論國語與左傳的關係, *Bulletin of the Institute of History and Philology* 33 (1962), reprinted in Chang I-jen, *Kuo-yü Tso-chuan lun-chi* 國語左傳論集, Tung-sheng hsüeh-jen chuan-k'an 2 (Taipei: Tung-sheng, 1980), 19–108, and "Ts'ung wen-fa, yü-hui te ch'a-i cheng *Kuo-yü Tso-chuan* erh-shu fei i-jen so-tso" 從文法、語彙的差異證國語左傳二書非一人所作, *Ku yüan-chang Hu Shih hsien-sheng chi-nien lun-wen chi*, *Bulletin of the Institute of History and Philology* 34 (1962), reprinted in *Kuo-yü Tso-chuan lun-chi*, 109–162; and Bernhard Karlgren, *The Authenticity and Nature of the Tso Chuan* (Göteborg, Sweden: Elanders, 1926).

42. See, in addition to the above, "Kung-fu Wen-po chih mu tui Chi K'ang-tzu wen" 公父文伯之母對季康子問, *Kuo-yü* 5.202; "Kung-fu Wen-po chih mu lun lao-i" 公父文伯之母論勞逸, *Kuo-yü* 5.208; "Kung-fu Wen-po chih mu pieh yü nan-nü chih li" 公父文伯之母別於男女之禮, *Kuo-yü* 5.209; "Kung-fu Wen-po chih mu yü shih Wen-po" 公父文伯之母欲室文伯, *Kuo-yü* 5.210 (where she is praised by "Music-Master Hai" 師亥); and "K'ung Ch'iu wei Kung-fu Wen-po chih mu chih li" 孔丘謂公父文伯之母知禮, *Kuo-yü* 5.212. She is also the subject of a biography in the *Lieh-nü chuan*; see "Lu Chi Ching-chiang" 魯季敬姜, *Lieh-nü chuan pu-chu* 1.10–14. Cf. also Raphals, *Sharing the Light*, 92–98.

43. For other classical versions of this anecdote, see (in addition to *Lieh-nü chuan*): *Han-Shih wai-chuan* 1.6b–7a; "P'ing-yüan chün Yü Ch'ing lieh-chuan" 平原君虞卿列傳, *Shih-chi* 76.2373; "Ch'in kung Chao yü Ch'ang-p'ing" 秦攻趙於長平, *Chan-kuo ts'e* 戰國策 (Shanghai: Ku-chi, 1978; repr., Taipei: Li-jen, 1990), 20.692 f.; "T'an-kung hsia" 檀弓下, *Li-chi cheng-i* 9.1304b; and "Chi-i" 記義, *K'ung-ts'ung-tzu* 孔叢子 (*Han-Wei ts'ung-shu*) 漢魏叢書 (1592; repr., Ch'ang-ch'un: Chi-lin Ta-hsüeh, 1992), A.3.333a.

44. See, e.g., *Analects* 6.12, 9.23, and especially 14.43.

45. "Kung-fu Wen-po tsu ch'i mu chieh ch'i ch'ieh," *Kuo-yü* 5.211.

46. *Ssu-chih* 死之 is sometimes taken in this passage to mean the opposite, i.e., that he will die for women or for men. Grammatically, this reading is unjustifiable. Moreover, the parallel account in *Chan-kuo ts'e* says that sixteen of

his women committed suicide on his account after his passing; see "Ch'in kung Chao yü Ch'ang-p'ing," *Chan-kuo ts'e* 20.692.

47. For more on *nei* and *wai*, see, e.g., Raphals, *Sharing the Light*, 195–234; Tu Yung-ming 杜永明 et al., *Hei Erh-shih-ssu shih* 黑二十四史 (Peking: Chung-kuo hua-ch'iao, 1998), vol. 1, 18, 29, 660 [cited henceforth as *Hei Erh-shih-ssu shih*; see note 20 in the introduction]; and Black, 169 and 191 n. 11. Ancient Greek ideology maintained a similar distinction between *hypaithria erga exō* ("work outside in the open air") for men and *ta endon* ("things within") for women. See, e.g., Sue Blundell, *Women in Ancient Greece* (Cambridge: Harvard University Press, 1995), 135–138; Elaine Fantham et al., *Women in the Classical World: Image and Text* (New York: Oxford University Press, 1994), 71; Lesley Dean-Jones, "The Cultural Construct of the Female Body in Classical Greek Science," in *Women's History and Ancient History*, ed. Sarah B. Pomeroy (Chapel Hill: University of North Carolina Press, 1991), 112 f.; Anne Carson, "Putting Her in Her Place: Woman, Dirt, and Desire," in *Before Sexuality: The Construction of Erotic Experience in the Ancient Greek World*, ed. David M. Halperin et al. (Princeton, N.J.: Princeton University Press, 1990), 156 ff.; R. Padel, "Women: Model for Possession by Greek Daemons," in *Images of Women in Antiquity*, ed. Averil Cameron and Amélie Kuhrt (Detroit: Wayne State University Press, 1983), 3–19; and Hans Licht, *Sexual Life in Ancient Greece*, trans. J. H. Freese, ed. Lawrence H. Dawson (repr., New York: Dorset, 1993), 28 ff.

48. The excavated sex manual "T'ien-hsia chih-tao t'an," for example, offers its own creative understanding of the *nei/wai* distinction: males should be stimulated sexually on the outside and females on the inside. In other words, the male is the penetrator and the female the penetrated. For the text and commentary, see Ma Chi-hsing, 馬繼興, *Ma-wang-tui ku i-shu k'ao-shih* 馬王堆古醫書考釋 (Ch'ang-sha: Hu-nan k'o-hsüeh chi-shu, 1992), 1071.

49. "Nei hsiao-ch'en," *Chou-li chu-shu* (*Shih-san ching chu-shu*), 7.686b. Compare the translation in Édouard Biot, *Le Tcheou-li ou Rites des Tcheou* (Paris: Imprimerie Nationale, 1851), vol. 1, 148. The *nei hsiao-ch'en* is often taken to be a eunuch; see, e.g., *Hei Erh-shih-ssu shih*, vol. 5, 3236.

50. *Ch'un-ch'iu Tso-chuan chu*, 春秋左傳注, 2d ed., Chung-kuo ku-tien ming-chu i-chu ts'ung-shu (Peking: Chung-hua, 1990), vol. 3, 1145 (Hsiang 28＝545 B.C.). Cf. *Hei Erh-shih-ssu shih*, vol. 1, 111. Incidentally, this is not the only reference to wife swapping in the *Tso-chuan*; see also *Ch'un-ch'iu Tso-chuan chu*, vol. 4, 1491 (Chao 28＝514 B.C.).

51. Chou Fa-kao 周法高, *Chou Ch'in ming-tzu chieh-ku hui-shih* 周秦名字解詁彙釋, Chung-hua ts'ung-shu (Taipei, 1958), 48, recommends the pronunciation "Ch'ing Pang" (as though the second character were 邦).

52. This is clearly what the context demands and what the commentators all suggest. One might speculate that the original text read *yü Ch'ing She she cheng* 與慶舍舍政, which would mean exactly that "he gave over the government to Ch'ing She" and that the second *she* was at some point mistakenly deleted.

53. Compare the translation in Legge, vol. 5, 541.

54. He was also a political opportunist and a murderer. See the relevant entries in *Ch'un-ch'iu Tso-chuan chu*, vol. 3, 1099 (Hsiang 25＝548 B.C.) and 1137 f. (Hsiang 27＝546 B.C.).

55. "Nei-tse," *Li-chi cheng-i* 27.1462c; see the commentary of Sun Hsi-tan 孫希旦 (1736–1784), *Li-chi chi-chieh* 集解, ed. Shen Hsiao-huan 沈嘯寰 and Wang Hsing-hsien 王星賢, Shih-san ching Ch'ing-jen chu-shu (Peking: Chung-hua, 1989), 27.735 f. Compare also the "T'uan" 彖 commentary to hexagram 37 (*chia-jen* 家人) in the *I-ching*: "The correct position for females is inside; the correct position for males is outside" 女正位乎內，男正位乎外; text in *Chou-I cheng-i (Shih-san ching chu-shu)* 4.50a.

56. "Yang Chen lieh-chuan," *Hou-Han shu* 後漢書 (Peking: Chung-hua, 1965), 54.1761. Cf. also van Gulik, 86 f., although the translation there silently omits whole sections of the original.

57. Cf. Mark Edward Lewis, *Sanctioned Violence in Early China*, SUNY Series in Chinese Philosophy and Culture (Albany, N.Y., 1990), 73 ff.

58. For similar attitudes in ancient Greece, see, e.g., James N. Davidson, *Courtesans and Fishcakes: The Consuming Passions of Classical Athens* (New York: Harper Collins, 1997), 165 f.

59. *Ch'un-ch'iu Tso-chuan chu*, vol. 1, 425 (Hsi 24 = 636 B.C.). See also the parallel account in "Fu Ch'en chien Hsiang-wang i Ti fa Cheng chi i Ti-nü wei hou" 富辰諫襄王以狄伐鄭及以狄女為后, *Kuo-yü* 2.48 ff., where Fu Ch'en constructs a different argument: marriage is an affair that can bring about fortune or disaster, and by marrying an alien, the king is courting disaster. Cf. *Hei Erh-shih-ssu shih*, vol. 1, 326.

60. Compare the translation in Legge, vol. 5, 192.

61. "I Ho shih P'ing-kung chi" 醫和視平公疾, *Kuo-yü* 14.473–474. See also the parallel account in *Ch'un-ch'iu Tso-chuan chu*, vol. 4, 1221 ff. (Chao 1 = 541 B.C.). The doctor goes on to explain that *ku* is derived from "worms," namely, the larvae that infest grain and fly away as insects. Eating food contaminated by such worms can be fatal. Compare also the usage in *Ch'un-ch'iu Tso-chuan chu*, vol. 1, 241 (Chuang 莊 28 = 666 B.C.), where one Tzu-yüan 子元 desires to "expend himself" 蟲 with the widow of King Wen of Ch'u 楚文王 (r. 689–677), his deceased brother. The several meanings of the term are explained in the commentaries to the *I-ching* entry for the hexagram by the same name, *Chou-I cheng-i* 3.35b f.; as well as the commentaries to the entry in Chiang Jen-chieh 蔣人傑, *Shuo-wen chieh-tzu chi-chu* 集注, ed. Liu Jui 劉銳 (Shanghai: Ku-chi, 1996), 13B.2836. For one of the oldest uses, see Chang Ping-ch'üan 張秉權, *Hsiao-t'un ti-erh pen: Yin-hsü wen-tzu ping-pien* 小屯第二本：殷虛文字丙編 (Taipei, 1957–1972), 415.5. The excavated text "Wu-shih-erh ping-fang" 五十二病方 contains a section dealing with remedies for *ku*; see Ma Chi-hsing, 631–635. Cf. further *Hei Erh-shih-ssu shih*, vol. 3, 1722 f.; Donald Harper, *Early Chinese Medical Literature: The Mawangdui Medical Manuscripts*, The Sir Henry Wellcome Asian Series (London: Kegan Paul International, 1998), 300 n. 5; Kidder Smith, Jr., "*Zhouyi* Divination from Accounts in the *Zuozhuan*," *Harvard Journal of Asiatic Studies* 49.2 (1989), 444 f.; Paul L-M. Serruys, "Towards a Grammar of the Language of the Shang Bone Inscriptions," *Proceedings of the International Sinological Conference* (Taipei: Academia Sinica, 1982), 349; H. Y. Feng and J. K. Shryock, "The Black Magic in China Known as *Ku*," *Journal of the American Oriental Society* 55 (1935), 1–30; and especially J. J. M. de Groot, *The Religious System of China* (Leiden: E. J. Brill, 1892–1910; repr., Taipei: Southern Materials Center, 1989), vol. 5, 826–869.

62. Compare also the usage in "Tu Chou chuan" 杜周傳, *Han-shu* 60.2668 (in a memorial by Tu Ch'in 杜欽). See the commentary of Tung Tseng-liang, *Kuo-yü cheng-i* 14.22b f.

63. Once again, ancient China was by no means the only civilization to express such opinions. For the ancient Greek case, see, e.g., Bruce S. Thornton, *Eros: The Myth of Ancient Greek Sexuality* (Boulder, Colo.: Westview, 1997), 70 ff.; Blundell, 100 ff.; Fantham et al., 169 ff.; Lesley Dean-Jones, "The Politics of Pleasure: Female Sexual Appetite in the Hippocratic Corpus," in *Discourses of Sexuality: From Aristotle to AIDS*, ed. Domna C. Stanton, Ratio: Institute for the Humanities (Ann Arbor: University of Michigan Press, 1992), 48–77; Carson, 138 f.; and K. J. Dover, "Classical Greek Attitudes to Sexual Behavior," *Arethusa* 6 (1973), reprinted in *Women in the Ancient World: The* Arethusa *Papers*, ed. John Peradotto and J. P. Sullivan, SUNY Series in Classical Studies (Albany, N.Y., 1984), 149.

64. "Huan-che chuan" 宦者傳, *Hsin Wu-tai shih* 新五代史 (Peking: Chunghua, 1974), 26.406. On the deteriorating position of women in Sung China, see, e.g., Patricia Buckley Ebrey, *The Inner Quarters: Marriage and the Lives of Chinese Women in the Sung Period* (Berkeley and Los Angeles: University of California Press, 1993), esp. 267–270; and James T. C. Liu, *Ou-yang Hsiu: An Eleventh-Century Neo-Confucianist* (Stanford, Calif.: Stanford University Press, 1967), 23.

65. "Chin shih-chia," *Shih-chi* 39.1658. Cf. *Hei Erh-shih-ssu shih*, vol. 1, 326.

66. *Analects* 9.18, *Lun-yü chi-shih* 18.611; and *Analects* 15.13, *Lun-yü chi-shih* 32.1094. Cf. also *Analects* 1.7, *Lun-yü chi-shih* 2.30, where we read that an attribute of a learned person is "to value [moral] worth as readily as sex" 賢賢易色.

67. Compare the translation in Lau, *Analects*, 98 and 134.

68. *Mencius* 6B.1, *Meng-tzu cheng-i* 24.809.

69. Compare the translation in Lau, *Mencius*, 171.

70. Cf. *Hei Erh-shih-ssu shih*, vol. 1, 324 ff.; and Jeffrey Riegel, "Eros, Introversion, and the Beginnings of *Shijing* Commentary," *Harvard Journal of Asiatic Studies* 57.1 (1997): 151.

71. See esp. "Li-lun," *Hsün-tzu chi-chieh* 13.19.346–378. For more on this issue, see, e.g., Paul Rakita Goldin, *Rituals of the Way: The Philosophy of Xunzi* (Chicago: Open Court, 1999), 65 ff. "Ta-lüeh," *Hsün-tzu chi-chieh* 19.27.511, also addresses directly the problem of eroticism in the *Odes*: "There is a tradition about the lustfulness of the 'Airs of the States': 'They are replete with desire but do not pass beyond the [correct] stopping-point'" 國風之好色也，傳曰：盈其欲而不愆其止. According to the commentary of Yang Liang 楊倞 (fl. A.D. 818), this means that the *Odes* teach us to rein in our desires even when they are about to overflow. Cf. *Hei Erh-shih-ssu shih*, vol. 1, 332.

72. *Mao-Shih cheng-i* (*Shih-san ching chu-shu*) 1A.273b. For similar statements in the classics, see, e.g., *Hei Erh-shih-ssu shih*, vol. 1, 660.

73. Compare the translations in Steven Van Zoeren, *Poetry and Personality: Reading, Exegesis, and Hermeneutics in Traditional China* (Stanford, Calif.: Stanford University Press, 1991), 87; and Pauline Yu, *The Reading of Imagery in the Chinese Poetic Tradition* (Princeton, N.J.: Princeton University Press, 1987), 50.

74. Riegel, "Eros," 150 ff., points out that the commentary to "Kuan-chü" in the recently excavated *Wu-hsing p'ien* 五行篇 emphasizes the importance of

observing ritual "in spite of strong sexual urgings" to the contrary. See the text in *Ma-wang-tui Han-mu po-shu*, vol. 1, 24. Cf. also Mark Laurent Asselin, "The Lu-School Reading of 'Guanju' as Preserved in an Eastern Han *fu*." *Journal of the American Oriental Society* 117.3 (1997): 433.

75. This notion of overcoming one's sexual desires was so basic to ancient writers that it led to a novel understanding of the phrase *nü-te* 女德 (or *fu-te* 婦德), namely "female virtue," or the virtue that a woman attains in chastity—which is effectively the opposite of *nü-te* as it is used in Physician Ho's diagnosis (discussed in the text, above). Cf., e.g., *Hei Erh-shih-ssu shih*, vol. 1, 18. Wei Chao, for example, misinterprets the doctor's advice in an amusingly creative way. He glosses the phrase *hsiao ching nü-te* 宵靜女德 (which, in the context, clearly means "diminish female potency at night," or stop copulating with women at night) as follows: "that is to say, at night one should take one's peace with females who possess virtue and moderate themselves with ritual, in order to expel one's own disease of *ku*" 言夜當安女之有德者以禮自節，以去己蠱害之疾. Thus Wei Chao, misreading *nü-te* as "female virtue," seems to suggest that the ailing lord should treat his disease by sleeping next to chaste maidens. See his commentary to "I Ho shih P'ing-kung chi," *Kuo-yü* 14.475 n. 22. Wei Chao was not the most brilliant of the ancient commentators, and part of the reason for the unusual difficulty of the *Kuo-yü* text is that his is the only surviving classical commentary.

76. *Mao* 247 ("Chi tsui" 既醉). Compare also *Mencius* 1B.5, *Meng-tzu cheng-i* 4.139, where Mencius explains to King Hsüan of Ch'i 齊宣王 (r. 319–301 B.C.) that the latter's fondness for sex 好色 is not necessarily blameworthy, as long as he channels it properly by cherishing his wife and encouraging his subjects to marry and be fruitful. Cf. *Hei Erh-shih-ssu shih*, vol. 1, 325 f.

77. Even contemporary essays in the philosophy of sex have been criticized for treating the sex act as merely a means to some end (whether it be procreation, interpersonal communication, etc.) and not coming to grips with the consequences of sex for the sake of sexual pleasure. See especially Alan Goldman, "Plain Sex," *Philosophy and Public Affairs* 6.3 (1977), 267–287.

78. *Analects* 18.4, *Lun-yü chi-shih* 36.1258.

79. Compare the translation in Lau, *Analects*, 149.

80. "Kung-fu Wen-po chih mu lun nei-ch'ao yü wai-ch'ao" 公父文伯之母論內朝與外朝, *Kuo-yü* 5.203–204.

81. For the references, see, e.g., Lau, *Analects*, 237. He was the son of Chi Huan-tzu (mentioned above in the text).

82. In *Han-Shih wai-chuan* 9.8b f., Mencius' mother criticizes him for entering his wife's bedroom unannounced and thus catching her in a compromising position. (There is a parallel account in "Tsou Meng K'o mu," *Lieh-nü chuan pu-chu* 1.16.) Cf. Eric Henry, "The Social Significance of Nudity in Early China," *Fashion Theory* 3.4 (1999), 481 f.

83. "Kung-fu Wen-po chih mu tui Chi K'ang-tzu chih wen," *Kuo-yü* 5.202.

84. "Kung-fu Wen-po chih mu lun lao-i," *Kuo-yü* 5.205.

85. The language of this passage is archaic and difficult; I suspect that Lady Ching might be quoting from a lost ritual codex. For administrative titles, I follow Charles O. Hucker, *A Dictionary of Official Titles in Imperial China* (Stanford,

Calif.: Stanford University Press, 1985). My translation is based largely on the commentaries of Yü Fan 虞翻 (A.D. 164–233), Wei Chao, and others in *Kuo-yü* 5.206 f., with one major exception. Wei Chao adduces the following quote from the "*Rites*" 禮: "The Son of Heaven salutes the sun in the spring" 天子以春分朝日. This evidence then leads Wei Chao to the deduction that the Son of Heaven sacrifices to the moon in the autumn. However, I think this interpretation is unwarranted here, given that the text clearly describes the ruler's daily activities from morning to night. Thus I take *chao* 朝 and *hsi* 夕 in their basic senses of "morning" and "evening."

Incidentally, Wei Chao's quote is not to be found in the received versions of any of the classical ritual texts but may represent a paraphrase of "Pao-fu" 保傅, *Ta-Tai Li-chi* 大戴禮記; text in Wang P'in-chen 王聘珍 (eighteenth century), *Ta-Tai Li-chi chieh-ku* 解詁, ed. Wang Wen-chin 王文錦, Shih-san ching Ch'ing-jen chu-shu (Peking: Chung-hua, 1983), 3.48.53: "The Son of Heaven salutes the sun on a spring morning" 天子春朝朝日. See also the commentary of Tung Tseng-ling, *Kuo-yü cheng-i* 5.23a. For an insightful early discussion of this issue, see the memorial by Ho T'ung-chih 何佟之 (449–503) in Hsiao Tzu-hsien 蕭子顯 (489–537), *Nan-Ch'i shu* 南齊書 (Peking: Chung-hua, 1972), 9.140 f. ("Li-chih shang" 禮志上). See also the commentary of P'ei Sung-chih 裴松之 (A.D. 372–451) to Ch'en Shou 陳壽 (233–297), *San-kuo chih* 三國志 (Peking: Chung-hua, 1959), 2.77 n. 1 (*Wei-shu* 魏書, "Wen-ti P'i" 文帝丕); as well as Shen Yüeh 沈約 (441–513) et al., *Sung-shu* 宋書 (Peking: Chung-hua, 1974), 14.348 ("Li-chih i" 禮志一); and Wei Cheng 魏徵 (580–643) et al., *Sui-shu* 隋書 (Peking: Chung-hua, 1973), 7.140 ("Li-i chih erh" 禮儀志二).

86. *Mencius* 6B.6, *Meng-tzu cheng-i* 24.831.

87. Compare the translation in Lau, *Mencius*, 175.

88. Albert Richard O'Hara, *The Position of Woman in Early China*, Catholic University of America Studies in Sociology 16 (Washington, D.C., 1945), 113, gives Chuang's reign dates as 794–731 B.C. He has the wrong Lord Chuang of Ch'i, of which there were two.

89. See *Ch'un-ch'iu Tso-chuan chu*, vol. 3, 1084 f. (Hsiang 23 = 550 B.C.). Hua Chou's personal name is given here as Huan 還.

90. See, e.g., the commentaries of Tu Yü and K'ung Ying-ta, *Ch'un-ch'iu Tso-chuan cheng-i* (*Shih-san ching chu-shu*), 35.1978b f. Cf. also Bernt Hankel, *Der Weg in den Sarg: Die ersten Tage des Bestattungsrituals in den konfuzianischen Riten-klassikern*, Münstersche Sinologische Mitteilungen: Beiträge zur Geschichte und Kultur des alten China 4 (Bad Honnef: Bock und Herchen, 1995), 164 f.

91. For other early accounts of this story, see "T'an-kung hsia," *Li-chi cheng-i* 10.1312a f.; "Li-chieh" 立節, *Shuo-yüan* 説苑 4.402c; "Shan-shui" 善説, *Shuo-yüan* 11.428c; and "Ch'i Ch'i Liang ch'i" 齊杞梁妻, *Lieh-nü chuan pu-chu* 4.68–469. In the later versions, the widow's weeping causes a wall to collapse, which impresses bystanders. Cf. also Englert, 36 ff.

92. The "T'an-kung," for example, includes both stories.

93. *Ch'un-ch'iu Tso-chuan chu*, vol. 1, 407 (Hsi 23 = 637 B.C.). See also "Ts'ao Kung-kung pu-li Ch'ung-erh erh kuan ch'i p'ien-hsieh" 曹共公不禮重耳而觀其 駢脅, *Kuo-yü* 10.346–347 (as well as the commentary of Tung Tseng-ling, *Kuo-yü cheng-i* 10.8b f.); "Shang-te" 上德, in Ch'en Ch'i-yu, *Lü-shih ch'un-ch'iu chiao-shih*

呂氏春秋校釋 (Shanghai: Hsüeh-lin, 1984), 19.1256; "Shih-kuo" 十過, in *Han Fei-tzu chi-shih* 韓非子集釋, Chung-kuo ssu-hsiang ming-chu (Peking: Chung-hua, 1958; repr., Taipei: Shih-chieh, 1991), 3.10.200; "Jen-chien" 人間, in Liu Wen-tien 劉文典, *Huai-nan Hung-lieh chi-chieh* 淮南鴻烈集解, ed. Feng I 馮逸 and Ch'iao Hua 喬華, Hsin-pien Chu-tzu chi-ch'eng (Peking: Chung-hua, 1989), 18.614; "Chin shih-chia," *Shih-chi* 39.1658; and "Ts'ao Hsi-shih ch'i" 曹僖氏妻, *Lieh-nü chuan pu-chu* 3.44. Cf. Raphals, *Sharing the Light*, 102–104.

94. Compare the translations in Burton Watson, trans., *The Tso chuan: Selections from China's Oldest Narrative History*, Translations from the Oriental Classics (New York: Columbia University Press, 1989), 42; and Legge, vol. 5, 187.

95. See, e.g., *Ch'un-ch'iu Tso-chuan chu*, vol. 1, 451 ff. (Hsi 28 = 632 B.C.). In the heat of the battle, Lord Wen remembers Hsi Fu-chi and his wife, and orders that no one enter their dwelling, but his command is disobeyed by his underlings, who burn it down.

96. Cf. Raphals, *Sharing the Light*, 27.

97. See, for example, the castigations of the Mohists in "Fei-Ju hsia" 非儒下; text in Wu Yü-chiang 吳毓江, *Mo-tzu chiao-chu* 墨子校注, ed. Sun Ch'i-chih 孫啟治, Hsin-pien Chu-tzu chi-ch'eng (Peking: Chung-hua, 1993), 9.39.436 f.

98. Even supporters of the tradition sometimes consider it sexist; see, e.g., Henry Rosemont, Jr., *A Chinese Mirror: Moral Reflections on Political Economy and Society* (La Salle, Ill.: Open Court, 1991), 74 f.

99. Cf., e.g., Tu Wei-ming, "Probing the 'Three Bonds' and 'Five Relationships' in Confucian Humanism," in *Confucianism and the Family*, ed. Walter H. Slote and George A. De Vos, SUNY Series in Chinese Philosophy and Culture (Albany, N.Y., 1998), 123.

100. Wing-tsit Chan, *A Source Book in Chinese Philosophy* (Princeton, N.J.: Princeton University Press, 1963), 47.

101. For some examples, see, e.g., Marina H. Sung, "The Chinese Lieh-nü Tradition," in Guisso and Johannesen, 66 ff. The work of Pan Chao 班昭 is discussed in chapter 3.

102. *Lao-tzu* 6; text in Kao Ming 高明, *Po-shu Lao-tzu chiao-chu* 帛書老子校注, Hsin-pien Chu-tzu chi-ch'eng (Peking: Chung-hua, 1996), 6.247 ff. This is a convenient variorum edition of the received *Lao-tzu* and the Ma-wang-tui versions, with collected commentary. The quotation here is from the received text.

103. Compare the translation in Victor Mair, *Tao Te Ching: The Classic Book of Integrity and the Way* (New York: Bantam, 1990), 65.

104. *Lao-tzu* 61, *Po-shu Lao-tzu chiao-chu* 61.121 ff.

105. Compare the translation in Mair, *Tao Te Ching*, 31.

106. See, e.g., Black, 173 f.; Joseph Needham, *Science and Civilisation in China* (Cambridge: Cambridge University Press, 1956), vol. 2, 59; and Max Kaltenmark, *Lao Tzu and Taoism*, trans. Roger Greaves (Stanford, Calif.: Stanford University Press, 1969), 59 f.

107. *Lao-tzu* 28, *Po-shu Lao-tzu chiao-chu* 28.369.

108. Compare the translation in Mair, *Tao Te Ching*, 93.

109. Cf. esp. Chad Hansen, *A Daoist Theory of Chinese Thought: A Philosophical Interpretation* (New York: Oxford University Press, 1992), 223 ff.; Graham, *Disputers of the Tao*, 228 ff.; and Roger T. Ames, "Taoism and the Androgynous Ideal," in

Guisso and Johannesen, 21–45. For a comparable case in Socratic philosophy, see David M. Halperin, "Why Is Diotima a Woman? Platonic *Erōs* and the Figuration of Gender," in Halperin et al., 257–308.

110. Cf. esp. Overmyer, 92.

111. *Ma-wang-tui Han-mu po-shu*, vol. 1, 70. Not all of the editors' emendations seem necessary; thus I retain *hsiang* 鄉, for example, in the sense of "provinces," rather than change it to *hsiang* 向 (which the editors probably understand as "directions").

112. Compare the translation in Robin D. S. Yates, *Five Lost Classics: Tao, Huang-Lao, and Yin-Yang in Han China*, Classics of Ancient China (New York: Ballantine, 1997), 129. Yates renders *chieh* 節 as "tally" where I have "mode." For more on this other possible sense, see, e.g., Lao Kan, "The Early Use of the Tally in China," in *Ancient China: Studies in Early Civilization*, ed. David T. Roy and Tsuen-hsuin Tsien (Hong Kong: Chinese University Press, 1978), 97.

113. *Ma-wang-tui Han-mu po-shu*, vol. 1, 49.

114. Compare the translation in Yates, 67f.

115. "Wang-cheng" 亡徵, *Han Fei-tzu chi-shih* 5.15.269. Yates, 227 n. 72, refers to this chapter erroneously as 王徵.

116. Compare the translation in W. K. Liao, *The Complete Works of Han Fei Tzu: A Classic of Chinese Legalism*, Probsthain's Oriental Series 25 (London, 1939), vol. 1, 139.

3. Sex, Politics, and Ritualization

1. Li Ling's biography appears in "Li Kuang Su Chien chuan" 李光蘇建傳, *Han-shu* 漢書 (Peking: Chung-hua, 1962), 54.2450–2459. For more on his campaigns, see Michael Loewe, "The Campaigns of Han Wu-ti," in *Chinese Ways in Warfare*, ed. Frank A. Kierman, Jr., and John K. Fairbank, Harvard East Asian Series 74 (Cambridge, Mass., 1974), 90f. and 119–122. See also Ts'ui Ming-te 崔明德, *Li Ling* 李陵, Li-shih cheng-i jen-wu hsi-lieh 2 (Taipei: Wen-chin, 1994), esp. 75–82.

2. Cf. Kuo Shuang-ch'eng 郭雙成, Shih-chi *jen-wu chuan-chi lun kao* 史記人物傳記論稿 ([Cheng-chou]: Chung-chou ku-chi, 1985), 25.

3. Cf., e.g., Stephen W. Durrant, *The Cloudy Mirror: Tension and Conflict in the Writings of Sima Qian*, SUNY Series in Chinese Philosophy and Culture (Albany, N.Y., 1995), 8 ff.; and Hsiao Li 肖黎, *Ssu-ma Ch'ien p'ing-chuan* 司馬遷評傳, Chung-kuo li-shih jen-wu ts'ung-shu (n.p.: Chi-lin wen-shih, 1986), 48–51. Ssu-ma Ch'ien tells his version of the story in a famous epistle to Jen An 任安 (d. 91 B.C.?), an imprisoned official who was himself executed for treachery. See "Ssu-ma Ch'ien chuan," *Han-shu* 62.2725 ff. The problems associated with dating this letter are complex and are discussed in Kuo Shuang-ch'eng, 350–355; Burton Watson, *Ssu-ma Ch'ien: Grand Historian of China* (New York: Columbia University Press, 1958), 194–198 (with a translation of the entire letter on pp. 57–67); and Edouard Chavannes, *Les Mémoires historiques de Se-ma Ts'ien* (Paris: Ernest Leroux, 1895–1905), vol. 1, xlii ff. Incidentally, Li Kuang-li himself fell into disgrace in 90 B.C.; cf. Michael Loewe, *Crisis and Conflict in Han China: 104 B.C. to A.D. 9* (London: George Allen and Unwin, 1974), 45; and J.J. M. de Groot, *The Religious System of China* (Leiden: E. J. Brill, 1892–1910; repr., Taipei: Southern Materials Center, 1989), vol. 5, 840 ff.

4. Consider, for example, the case of the historian Tung Hu 董狐, who earned the praise of Confucius because he recorded that "Chao Tun [the chief minister of Chin] assassinated his lord" 趙盾弒其君, even though the actual assailant was someone else; the point was that Chao Tun did nothing to stop the crime. The mighty Chao Tun contested Tung Hu's statement, but the historian would not be cowed, and the chief minister eventually acknowledged his fault. See *Ch'un-ch'iu Tso-chuan chu* 春秋左傳注, 2d ed., Chung-kuo ku-tien ming-chu i-chu ts'ung-shu (Peking: Chung-hua, 1990), vol. 2, 662 f. (Hsüan 2 = 607 B.C.). A similar theme appears in *Ch'un-ch'iu Tso-chuan chu*, vol. 3, 1099 (Hsiang 25 = 548 B.C.), where four successive historians (the first three of whom were executed) write that Ts'ui Shu 崔杼 (d. 546 B.C.) assassinated his lord, when in fact the culprits were members of Ts'ui Shu's bodyguard. Speaking one's mind truthfully, regardless of the consequences, has long been prized in the Chinese tradition as a mark of a minister's true loyalty, and Ssu-ma Ch'ien made ample use of this theme in his biographies of ancient worthies. See, e.g., Paul Rakita Goldin, "Some Commonplaces in the *Shiji* Biographies of Talented Men," in *Studies on the* Shiji: *A Volume of Essays on Sima Qian*, ed. Michael Puett (forthcoming); and David Schaberg, "Remonstrance in Eastern Zhou Historiography," *Early China* 22 (1997), 133–179.

5. "Cheng-lun" 正論, in Wang Hsien-ch'ien 王先謙 (1842–1918), *Hsün-tzu chi-chieh* 集解, ed. Shen Hsiao-huan and Wang Hsing-hsien, Hsin-pien Chu-tzu chi-ch'eng (Peking: Chung-hua, 1988), 12.18.328: "When punishments match the gravity of crimes, there is order; when they do not match the gravity of crimes, there is chaos" 刑稱罪則治，不稱罪則亂; cf. also J. L. Kroll, "Notes on Ch'in and Han Law," in *Thought and Law in Qin and Han China: Studies Dedicated to Anthony Hulsewé on the Occasion of His Eightieth Birthday*, ed. W. L. Idema and E. Zürcher, Sinica Leidensia 24 (Leiden: E. J. Brill, 1990), 64; and A. F. P. Hulsewé, *Remnants of Han Law*, vol. 1 (*Introductory Studies and an Annotated Translation of Chapters 22 and 23 of the History of the Former Han Dynasty*), Sinica Leidensia 9 (Leiden: E. J. Brill, 1955), 347 f. (Note that J. L. Kroll's name is given erroneously as "J. K. Kroll" in the table of contents of *Thought and Law*.)

6. Cf., e.g., Hulsewé, *Remnants of Han Law*, 385 n. 185.

7. "Fu-hsing" 甫刑; text in D. C. Lau and Chen Fong Ching, *A Concordance to Shangshudazhuan*, ICS Ancient Chinese Texts Concordance Series: Classical Works 5 (Hong Kong: Commercial Press, 1994), 22. The above statement is also cited by Cheng Hsüan in his commentary to "Ssu-hsing" 司刑, *Chou-li chu-shu* (*Shih-san ching chu-shu*), 36.880b. Cf. Matthew H. Sommer, *Sex, Law, and Society in Late Imperial China*, Law, Society, and Culture in China (Stanford, Calif.: Stanford University Press, 2000), 33; Tu Yung-ming 杜永明 et al., *Hei Erh-shih-ssu shih* 黑二十四史 (Peking: Chung-kuo hua-ch'iao, 1998), vol. 5, 3222, 3672 [this work cited hereafter as *Hei Erh-shih-ssu shih*; see note 20 in the introduction of the present volume]; and Édouard Biot, *Le Tcheou-li ou Rites des Tcheou* (Paris: Imprimerie Nationale, 1851), vol. 2, 354 n. 1.

8. Though most other works are cited in the body of the text by their English translations, *Po-hu t'ung* will appear by its Chinese name, since *Comprehensive Discussions in the White Tiger Hall* is too long and clumsy. The editors of the *Ssu-k'u ch'üan-shu* 四庫全書 pointed out that the Chinese title is more properly called *Po-hu t'ung-i* 義, but that the abbreviated title *Po-hu t'ung* is centuries old. See Chi

Yün 紀昀 (1724–1805) et al., *Ssu-k'u ch'üan-shu tsung-mu t'i-yao* 總目提要 (*Kuo-hsüeh chi-pen ts'ung-shu*), 23.1468–1469. Cf. also Tjan Tjoe Som, *Po Hu T'ung: The Comprehensive Discussions in the White Tiger Hall*, Sinica Leidensia 6 (Leiden: E. J. Brill, 1949), vol. 1, 9 f.

9. "Wu-hsing" 五刑, in Ch'en Li 陳立 (1809–1869), *Po-hu t'ung shu-cheng* 疏證, ed. Wu Tse-yü 吳則虞, Hsin-pien Chu-tzu chi-ch'eng (Peking: Chung-hua, 1994), 9.441; see also Cheng Hsüan's explanation of *kung* in his commentary to "Ssu-hsing," *Chou-li chu-shu* 36.880b (which may actually be older than the *Po-hu t'ung*): "In the case of a man, one severs his genitals; a woman is closed inside a room" 丈夫則割其勢，女子閉於宮中 (cf. Biot, vol. 2, 354 n. 1). Why the word *kung* (room) should also be used for castration is not clear; Wang Yin-chih suggests ingeniously that *kung* is a sort of abbreviation for the fuller term *kung-ko* 宮割 ("incarcerating [a woman] or severing [a man's genitals]"). See his commentary to *Po-hu t'ung shu-cheng* 9.441. Although the relevant texts all declare, straightforwardly enough, that the corresponding punishment for women is simply to be locked inside a room, scholars have speculated for centuries that some more gruesome punishment was actually inflicted. Cf., e.g., *Hei Erh-shih-ssu shih*, vol. 5, 3221 f., 3563; and Hulsewé, *Remnants of Han Law*, 127.

10. Compare the translation in Tjan, vol. 2, 604 f.

11. Ma Tuan-lin 馬端臨 (1254–1325), *Wen-hsien t'ung-k'ao* 文獻通考 (*Shih T'ung* 十通), 163.1414c.

12. Hulsewé, *Remnants of Han Law*, 127 ff.

13. "Lü T'ai-hou pen-chi" 呂太后本紀, *Shih-chi* 史記 (Peking: Chung-hua, 1959), 9.397. Cf. also the account in "Wai-ch'i chuan," *Han-shu* 97A.3937 f., which adds that when Empress Dowager Lü first imprisoned Lady Ch'i, she had her "shaved, collared, clad in red garments, and ordered her to be a grain-pounder" 髡鉗衣赭衣，令舂. "Grain-pounders" (*ch'ung* 舂) were female convicts sentenced to pound grain in a penal labor camp. We know from a Ch'in-dynasty jurist's manual that *ch'ung* wore red uniforms and were fettered. See "Ssu-k'ung" 司空, *Shui-hu-ti Ch'in-mu chu-chien* 睡虎地秦墓竹簡 (Peking: Wen-wu, 1990), 51; and A. F. P. Hulsewé, *Remnants of Ch'in Law: An Annotated Translation of the Ch'in Legal and Administrative Rules of the Third Century B.C. Discovered in Yün-meng Prefecture, Hu-pei Province, in 1975*, Sinica Leidensia 17 (Leiden: E. J. Brill, 1985), A 70. Cf. also *Hei Erh-shih-ssu shih*, vol. 5, 3584. It should be pointed out that this too constituted unusually humiliating treatment for Lady Ch'i, because it appears to have been extremely rare in Han times for any woman, let alone an imperial consort, to be shaved and collared even if she was a grain-pounder. Cf. Hulsewé, *Remnants of Han Law*, 129.

14. Following the suggestion in Ch'ien Chung-shu, vol. 1, 282. *Ts'e* 廁 is usually translated as "privy" or "latrine."

15. Compare the translations in Burton Watson, trans., *Records of the Grand Historian: Han Dynasty*, rev. ed., Records of Civilization: Sources and Studies 65 (Hong Kong: Columbia University Press, 1993), vol. 1, 269; and T'ung-tsu Ch'ü, *Han Social Structure*, ed. Jack L. Dull, Han Dynasty China 1 (Seattle: University of Washington Press, 1972), 259 f.

16. The crucial conclusion to the story, in which the emperor resigns himself to a life of dissipation, is generally omitted in recent studies, as in Raphals, *Sharing the Light*, 72.

17. The pronunciation follows the phonological gloss of Lu Te-ming 陸德明 (556–627); see his commentary to "Chih-fang shih" 職方氏, *Chou-li chu-shu* 33.862a; and *Ch'un-ch'iu Tso-chuan cheng-i* (*Shih-san ching chu-shu*), 57.2154b (Ai 哀 1 = 494 B.C.). The name is commonly pronounced as "K'uai-chi," however, and it is possible that this reading is superior. At the first appearance of the name in the *Shih-chi*, the text tells us that the hero Yü 禹 convened the various lords at this mountain and that the name means *k'uai-chi* 會計 ("planning meeting" or "caucus"); see "Hsia pen-chi" 夏本紀, *Shih-chi* 2.89. As far as I know, none of the commentaries give a phonological gloss at this point, implying strongly that they took the name to be a homophone of *k'uai-chi*. Indeed, the *Shih-chi chi-chieh* 集解, by P'ei Yin 裴駰 (fl. A.D. fifth century), cites a text explaining that the mountain was called 會稽 precisely because it was the site of Yü's great convocation. For a review of early references to the mountain, see, e.g., Ku Tsu-yü 顧祖禹 (1631–1692), *Tu-shih fang-yü chi-yao* 讀史方輿紀要 (repr., Shanghai: Shanghai shu-tien, 1998), 89.2b f. Yü's assembly is discussed in Marcel Granet, *Danses et légendes de la Chine ancienne*, Bibliothèque de philosophie contemporaine, Travaux de l'Année sociologique (Paris: Félix Alcan, 1926), vol. 1, 341–350.

Finally, it is important to keep in mind that the mountain was originally in the territory of Yüeh 越, and so the name 會稽 (perhaps Old Chinese *koopskəəy) may, like other bisyllabic names from that region, represent nothing more than the Chinese approximation of some ancient non-Chinese (possibly Austronesian) word. For more on the language of Wu 吳 and Yüeh, see, e.g., Donald B. Wagner, "The Language of the Ancient Chinese State of Wu," in *The Master Said: To Study and . . . : To Søren Egerod on the Occasion of His Sixty-seventh Birthday*, ed. Birthe Arendrup et al., East Asian Institute Occasional Papers 6 (Copenhagen: University of Copenhagen, 1990), 161–176.

18. On the so-called "Vertical Alliance" 合從 of lesser states united against Ch'in, see, e.g., Yang K'uan, 楊寬, *Chan-kuo shih* 戰國史, 3d ed. (Shanghai: Jenmin, 1998), 386 ff.; and Henri Maspero, "Le roman historique dans la littérature chinoise de l'antiquité," in idem, *Mélanges posthumes sur les religions et l'histoire de la Chine*, Publications du Musée Guimet; Bibliothèque de diffusion 57–59 (Paris: Civilisations du Sud, 1950), vol. 3, 55–62.

19. Following the commentary of Yü Yu-ting and others, *Shiki kaichū kōshō* 6.63.

20. Takigawa Kametarō, *Shiki kaichū kōshō* 6.63, notes that Sung Ch'ao, who was famous for his incestuous relationship with his sister Nan-tzu, is called a "fine boar" 艾豭 in *Ch'un-ch'iu Tso-chuan chu*, vol. 4, 1597 (Ting 14 = 497 B.C.). (The passage was discussed in chapter 1 of the present volume.) Thus it appears that humans who could not control their sexual desires were commonly likened to pigs. See also n. 79, below.

21. Following the commentary of Shen Chia-pen 沈家本 (1840–1913), *Shiki kaichū kōshō* 6.64.

22. "Ch'in Shih-huang pen-chi," *Shih-chi* 6.261 f.

23. Compare the translation in Burton Watson, trans., *Records of the Grand Historian: Qin Dynasty* (Hong Kong: Columbia University Press, 1993), 60 f.

24. Cf. Liu Tseng-kuei, 劉增貴, "Shih-lun Han-tai hun-yin kuan-hsi chung te li-fa kuan-nien" 試論漢代婚姻關系中的禮法觀念, in *Chung-kuo fu-nü shih lun-chi*

hsü-chi 中國婦女史論集續集, ed. Pao Chia-lin 鮑家麟 (Taipei: Tao-hsiang, 1991), 17.

25. For more on the inscription at Kuei-chi, see, e.g., Sheng I, 盛義, *Chung-kuo hun-su wen-hua* 中國婚俗文化, Yü nei-wai min-su hsüeh ts'ung-k'an (Shanghai: Wen-i, 1994), 336; Wu Chou, 武舟, *Chung-kuo chi-nü sheng-huo shih* 中國妓女生活史 (Ch'ang-sha: Hu-nan wen-i, 1990), 8; Jack L. Dull, "Marriage and Divorce in Han China: A Glimpse at 'Pre-Confucian' Society," in *Chinese Family Law and Social Change in Historical and Comparative Perspective*, ed. David C. Buxbaum, Asian Law Series 3 (Seattle: University of Washington Press, 1978), 67 f.; and Ch'en Ku-yüan, 陳顧遠, *Chung-kuo hun-yin shih* 中國婚姻史, Chiu-chi hsin-k'an (1936; repr., Ch'ang-sha: Yüeh-lu, 1998), 119. Miao Wen-yüan 繆文遠, *Chan-kuo chih-tu t'ung-k'ao* 戰國制度通考 (Ch'eng-tu: Pa-Shu, 1998), 273, cites a passage from the inscription but identifies it mistakenly as from the inscription at Mount T'ai 泰山.

One of the most insightful discussions is still that of Ku Yen-wu (*Shiki kaichū kōshō* 6.64), who points out that the First Emperor probably selected Kuei-chi as the site for this inscription because it lay in the ancient state of Yüeh—for the most successful monarch of that state, King Kou-chien 越王勾踐 (r. 496–465 B.C.), is famous for having encouraged his subjects to reproduce in order to increase his population. See, e.g., "Kou-chien mieh Wu" 句踐滅吳, *Kuo-yü* 20.635; and "Kou-chien fa Wu wai-chuan" 勾踐伐吳外傳, in Chou Sheng-ch'un 周生春, *Wu-Yüeh ch'un-ch'iu chi-chiao hui-k'ao* 吳越春秋輯校匯考 (Shanghai: Ku-chi, 1997), 10.160. Ku Yen-wu then goes on to cite another section that is not found in the extant *Wu-Yüeh ch'un-ch'iu*, wherein we are told further that Kou-chien would transport licentious widows to a mountaintop ("Mount Single-Girl" 獨女山) and let his anxious troops gratify their desires with them (cf. *Hei Erh-shih-ssu shih*, vol. 2, 881 f., vol. 4, 2629). As Chou Sheng-ch'un points out ("*Wu-Yüeh ch'un-ch'iu* i-wen" 佚文, *Wu-Yüeh ch'un-ch'iu chi-chiao hui-k'ao*, 271), this passage is preserved in Li Fang 李昉 (925–996) et al., *T'ai-p'ing yü-lan* 太平御覽 (*Kuo-hsüeh chi-pen ts'ung-shu*), 47.1b; see also "Ti-chuan" 地傳, *Yüeh-chüeh shu* 越絕書 (*Ssu-pu ts'ung-k'an*), 8.10.11b. In other words, according to Ku Yen-wu (who vigorously applauds this inscription), the First Emperor was emphasizing that he would no longer tolerate such behavior. Ku Yen-wu then argues that the rules set down at Kuei-chi represent one of the many precedents set by Ch'in that were later followed by the Han and indeed all subsequent dynasties: "Those Confucians in the world who say, concerning the Ch'in, that their policies were those of a doomed state—oh, they have not investigated this very deeply!" 世之儒者言及於秦，既以為亡國之法，亦未之深考乎. Cf. also Mu-chou Poo, *In Search of Personal Welfare: A View of Ancient Chinese Religion*, SUNY Series in Chinese Philosophy and Culture (Albany, 1998), 186 f.; Chou Chen-ho 周振鶴, "Ts'ung 'Chiu-chou i-su' tao 'Liu-ho t'ung-feng'—Liang-Han feng-su ch'ü-hua te pien-ch'ien" 從九州異俗到六合同風—兩漢風俗區劃的變遷, *Chung-kuo wen-hua yen-chiu* 中國文化研究 1997.4, 61 and 65 f.; Ch'ien Mu 錢穆, *Ch'in Han shih* 秦漢史 (Hong Kong: Hsin-hua, 1957), 16; and Wang Shu-nu, 王書奴, *Chung-kuo ch'ang-chi shih* 中國娼妓史, Chiu-chi hsin-k'an (Shanghai: Sheng-huo, 1934; repr., Ch'ang-sha: Yüeh-lu, 1998), 26.

26. Some of the more famous examples will come up in the course of the following discussion. Consider also the figure of Queen Dowager Hsüan 宣太后 (d. after 311 B.C.), who was the mother of King Chao of Ch'in 秦昭王 (r. 310–251

B.C.) and who is said to have fornicated with the ruler of the I-ch'ü 義渠 barbarians, before betraying him and thereby engineering a major military victory for Ch'in over his people ("Hsiung-nu lieh-chuan" 匈奴列傳, *Shih-chi* 110.2885). Elsewhere in the text, King Chao cites this affair when he apologizes to his client Fan Sui 范睢 (fl. 266–256 B.C.) for having overlooked him ("Fan Sui Ts'ai Tse lieh-chuan" 范睢蔡澤列傳, *Shih-chi* 79.2406). In his ensuing lectures to the king, Fan Sui begins to focus more and more on the manipulative behavior of the Queen Dowager, as well as that of her younger brother, Marquis Jang 穰侯 (i.e., Wei Jan 魏冉, fl. 300–271 B.C.), who was Prime Minister of Ch'in. Finally he accuses them both of plotting to usurp the throne ("Fan Sui Ts'ai Tse lieh-chuan," *Shih-chi* 79.2411 f.). Fan Sui does not mention the Queen Dowager's sexual misconduct, but in having the king himself refer to her affair with the ruler of the I-ch'ü, Ssu-ma Ch'ien discloses his own conviction that her various forms of insubordination count as different manifestations of the same rebellious character. It may also not be a coincidence that Queen Dowager Hsüan was from the state of Ch'in; as we shall see, Ssu-ma Ch'ien repeatedly employs the theme of sexual transgression in order to attack the legitimacy of Ch'in's rule. Finally, it is alleged elsewhere and in a completely different context that the same Queen Dowager carried on a shameful affair with a younger lover after her husband's death (see n. 91, below), so her reputation for lechery was probably well known to Ssu-ma Ch'ien. Wu Shih-tao 吳師道 (1283–1344), for example, in his commentary to "Ch'u wei Yung-shih wu-Yüeh" 楚圍雍氏五月, *Chan-kuo ts'e* 戰國策 (Shanghai: Ku-chi, 1978; repr., Taipei: Li-jen, 1990), 27.970 n.7 (where Queen Dowager Hsüan declares, in effect, that she enjoyed being mounted by her late husband), opines that her "words are filthy and vulgar in the extreme" 言汙鄙甚 and that she is a fitting precursor of the First Emperor's slatternly mother (whose case is discussed in the text below). Compare J.I. Crump's remarks in *Legends of the Warring States: Persuasions, Romances, and Stories from* Chan-kuo Ts'e, Michigan Monographs in Chinese Studies 83 (Ann Arbor, 1999), 103.

27. "Ssu-ma Ch'ien chuan," *Han-shu* 漢書 (Peking: Chung-hua, 1962), 62.2736.

28. Compare the translation in Watson, *Ssu-ma Ch'ien*, 67.

29. For a slightly different ancient account of this affair, see "P'u-yang jen Lü Pu-wei ku yü Han-tan" 濮陽人呂不韋賈於邯鄲, *Chan-kuo ts'e* 7.275–81. See also *Hei Erh-shih-ssu shih*, vol. 6, 4064 ff.

30. "Lü Pu-wei lieh-chuan," *Shih-chi* 85.2508.

31. Following the commentary of Liang Yü-sheng 梁玉繩 (1745–1819), *Shiki kaichū kōshō* 85.7, who notes astutely that the phrase *ta-ch'i* 大期 ("great period") is defined by K'ung Ying-ta as the ten (lunar) months during which a woman carries a child; see K'ung's subcommentary to *Ch'un-ch'iu Tso-chuan cheng-i* 14.1809b (Hsi 17 = 643 B.C.). (On the ten lunar months of pregnancy, see, e.g., Timothy Taylor, *The Prehistory of Sex: Four Million Years of Human Sexual Culture* (New York: Bantam, 1996), 159 f.) The phrase *ta-ch'i* is almost always taken by other commentators to mean an unusually long confinement (of eleven months or more). Hence this passage is frequently adduced as evidence that the story of the First Emperor's illegitimacy is spurious.

32. Compare the translation in Watson, *Records: Qin*, 161 f.

33. "Lü Pu-wei lieh-chuan," *Shih-chi* 85.2511.

34. Ssu-ma Ch'ien uses his future title; at this point Cheng had not yet unified China and assumed the title of emperor.

35. Literally, "with his penis closing [the hole] of a wheel of *t'ung*-wood."

36. Following the commentary of Ts'ui Shih 崔適, *Shiki kaichū kōshō* 85.12.

37. Compare the translation in Watson, *Records: Qin*, 163 f.

38. "Lü Pu-wei chuan," *Shih-chi* 85.2512. A parallel account of Lao Ai appears in "Cheng-chien" 正諫, *Shuo-yüan* 説苑 (*K'ung-ts'ung-tzu* 孔叢子 *Han-Wei ts'ung-shu* 漢魏叢書 [1592; repr., Ch'ang-ch'un: Chi-lin Ta-hsüeh, 1992]), 9.420b f.; see also "Ch'in Shih-huang pen-chi," *Shih-chi* 6.227. Note that in "Ch'in kung Wei chi," 秦攻魏急, *Chan-kuo ts'e* 25.920, Lü Pu-wei and Lao Ai are presented as arch-enemies rather than as coconspirators. Some scholars (cf. n. 42, below) cite this point as reason to disbelieve the *Shih-chi*, but it is not impossible that Lao Ai, with the Dowager in his clutches, indeed went on to become Lü Pu-wei's greatest rival, after having served him originally as his retainer. Cf. *Hei Erh-shih-ssu shih*, vol. 5, 3249 f., 3565, 3579. There is a parallel to the *Chan-kuo ts'e* version in "Lun-shih" 論勢, *K'ung-ts'ung-tzu* B.16.344b f. See Yoav Ariel, *K'ung-ts'ung-tzu: A Study and Translation of Chapters 15–23 with a Reconstruction of the* Hsiao Erh-ya *Dictionary*, Sinica Leidensia 35 (Leiden: E. J. Brill, 1996), 50 n. 72.

39. Compare the translation in Watson, *Records: Qin*, 164; and the bowdlerized version in T'ung-tsu Ch'ü, 325 ff. Cf. *Hei Erh-shih-ssu shih*, vol. 1, 124, 359.

40. It is noteworthy that the Dowager's fame is due entirely to her having copulated with the most powerful men in Ch'in: Lü Pu-wei, Tzu-ch'u, and then Lao Ai. She thus embodies totally Han Fei's cynical image of dangerously libidinous palace ladies (see chapter 1 in the present volume). Indeed, many readers take her to have been an entertainer or prostitute before Lü Pu-wei took her into his house (thus, e.g., *Hei Erh-shih-ssu shih*, vol. 2, 881). The support for this reading comes in the statement that she was the loveliest and most skilled at dancing among the various *chi* 姬 of Han-tan; *chi* can mean "courtesan" or "mistress." However, I think the sense of "lady" is more typical of Han usage.

41. This appears in a section that is now appended to "Ch'in Shih-huang pen-chi," *Shih-chi* 6.291.

42. Cf., e.g., Hung Chia-i 洪家義, *Lü Pu-wei p'ing-chuan* 呂不韋評傳, Chung-kuo ssu-hsiang chia p'ing-chuan ts'ung-shu 11 (Nan-ching: Nan-ching Ta-hsüeh, 1995), 80 f.; Derk Bodde, *Statesman, Patriot, and General in Ancient China: Three* Shih-chi *Biographies of the Ch'in Dynasty (255–206 B.C.)*, American Oriental Series 17 (New Haven, Conn.: American Oriental Society, 1940), 15 ff.; and "The State and Empire of Ch'in," in *The Cambridge History of China*, vol. 1 *(The Ch'in and Han Empires, 221 B.C.-A.D. 220)*, ed. Denis Twitchett and Michael Loewe (Cambridge, 1986), 95. Bodde's arguments are based largely on Ch'ien Mu, *Hsien-Ch'in chu-tzu hsi-nien* 先秦諸子繫年, 2d ed., Ts'ang-hai ts'ung-k'an (Hong Kong: Hong Kong University Press, 1956; repr., Taipei: Tung-ta, 1990), secs. 159 and 161. Ch'ien points out that the account in the *Shih-chi* biography of Lü Pu-wei differs materially from that in the *Chan-kuo ts'e* and other texts (including other portions of the *Shih-chi* itself), adding that the motif of the pregnant concubine appears in at least one other well-known tale of royal bastardy and hence may not be believable. Bodde, "The State and Empire of Ch'in," also notes that the period of the Dowager's confinement is not made clear, but this reflects a mis-

understanding of the text that was cleared up long ago by Liang Yü-sheng (see note 31, above).

43. "Ch'in Shih-huang pen-chi," *Shih-chi* 6.223. Ku Yen-wu, *Shiki kaichū kōshō* 6.2, complains that Ssu-ma Ch'ien always conflates the *hsing* 姓 and the *shih* 氏 (of which the former is determined by blood, the latter by any number of criteria); cf. also Sheng I, 384. Thus the First Emperor took "Chao" as his *shih* (and not his *hsing*), either because he was born in Chao or because the denizens of Ch'in all took "Chao" as their *shih* since they considered themselves to be the descendants of Tsao Fu 造父, the legendary charioteer who was enfeoffed in the city of Chao. Cf. "Ch'in pen-chi," *Shih-chi* 5.175.

44. Cf. Paul Rakita Goldin, "Personal Names in Early China—A Research Note," *Journal of the American Oriental Society* 120.1 (2000), 78 f.

45. Ting Tu 丁度 (990–1053) et al., *Sung-k'o Chi-yün* 宋刻集韻 (1037; repr., Peking: Chung-hua, 1989), 8.15b, states that *lao* can be a surname, but I suspect that the authors specifically have Lao Ai in mind. Some editions of the *Shih-chi* give Lao Ai's surname as Chiu 摎; see Mizusawa Toshitada 水澤利忠, *Shiki kaichū kōshō kōho* 史記會注考證校補 (Tokyo: *Shiki kaichū kōshō kōho* kankō kai, 1957–1970; repr., Taipei: Kuang-wen, 1972), 85.7 (=2713 in the repr. ed.). Similarly, Ch'en Chih 陳直, *Shih-chi hsin-cheng* 史記新證 (T'ien-chin: Jen-min, 1979), 143, attempts to connect Lao Ai with two figures known from other texts, namely Prime Minister Chiu 相邦摎 and General Chiao/Chiu 將軍摎, on the basis of the graphic similarity of their names. Ch'en Chih does not acknowledge that Ch'ien Ta-hsin 錢大昕 (1728–1804), *Nien-erh shih k'ao-i* 廿二史考異 (*Shih-hsüeh ts'ung-shu* 史學叢書), 1.7b, had the same idea two hundred years ago. Yen Shih-ku, in his commentary to "Wu-hsing chih" 五行志, *Han-shu* 27B2.1422 n. 3, also remarks that some people read 嫪 as "Chiu" (居虯反; in other words, as though it were written 摎). Finally, Lu Ts'ang-yung 盧藏用 (ca. A.D. 660–ca. 715), *Shiki kaichū kōshō* 85.11, asserts that Lao Ai's name should be written 摎毐 but then adds that 摎 should be pronounced "Lao"! So no one has ever adequately explained Lao Ai's surname—or, if it really was originally Chiu 摎, why he should have used such a unique variant.

46. Chiang Jen-chieh 蔣人傑, *Shuo-wen chieh-tzu chi-chu* 集注, ed. Liu Jui 劉銳 (Shanghai: Ku-chi, 1996), 12B.2660.

47. Cf. *Shuo-wen chieh-tzu chi-chu* 12B.2642, and the various commentaries ad loc. For other connections between poison and sexual transgression, see, e.g., chapter 2, n. 60, above.

48. Morohashi Tetsuji 諸橋轍次, *Dai Kan-Wa jiten* 大漢和辭典, rev. ed. (Tokyo: Daishūkan, 1986), entry 6669.1, vol. 3, 753, quotes the *K'ung-ts'ung-tzu* as speculating that Lao Ai earned this epithet because of his misbehavior with his penis. However, I cannot find this statement in any edition, and I suspect that Morohashi has conflated a commentarial remark with the original text. Tuan Yü-ts'ai 段玉裁 (1735–1815), *Shuo-wen chieh-tzu Tuan chu* (*Ssu-pu pei-yao*), 12B.21b, was evidently aware of the uncanny appropriateness of Lao Ai's name; he writes: "['Misdeed'] is the basic meaning of *ai*. It is not the case that this character was created for Lao Ai" 毐之本義如此。非為嫪毐造此字也.

49. This is related by Hsü Shen in *Shuo-wen chieh-tzu chi-chu* 12B.2660. According to Ssu-ma Chen 司馬貞 (fl. early eighth century), the author of the *So-yin*

索隱 commentary to the *Shih-chi*, Wang Shao 王劭 (fl. early sixth century) cited an almost identical remark, also attributing it to Chia I; see his commentary to "Ch'in Shih-huang pen-chi," *Shih-chi* 6.227 n. 1.

50. See, for example, the comments by Chai Hao 翟灝 (1736–1788) in "Chuang-mao" 狀貌, *T'ung-su pien* 通俗編 (Wu-pu-i chai 無不宜齋 ed., 1751), 34.8a f. The Wu-pu-i chai edition of *T'ung-su pien* is on deposit in the Rare Book Room of Harvard-Yenching Library (T9301/1138). The two most common editions of this work (viz., *Han-hai* 函海 and *Ts'ung-shu chi-ch'eng* 叢書集成) are both incomplete and do not contain this chapter.

51. *Yin* 陰, "sex organ" or "conspiracy," is completely unrelated to *yin* 淫, "licentiousness."

52. Cf. Kuo Hsing-wen 郭興文, *Chung-kuo ch'uan-t'ung hun-yin feng-su* 中國傳統婚姻風俗, Chung-kuo feng-su ts'ung-shu (Hsi-an: Shensi jen-min, 1994), 193 ff.

53. "Ching Yen shih-chia" 荊燕世家, *Shih-chi* 51.1997; "Ching Yen Wu chuan" 荊燕吳傳, *Han-shu* 35.1903.

54. Cf. Sheng I, 231; and Liu Tseng-kuei, "Han-tai hun-yin kuan-hsi," 6.

55. Cf. Dull, 69.

56. "P'ing-chin Hou Chu-fu lieh-chuan" 平津侯主父列傳, *Shih-chi* 112.2962; "Yen Chu Wu-ch'iu Chu-fu Hsü Yen Chung Wang Chia chuan" 嚴朱吾丘主父徐嚴終王賈傳, *Han-shu* 64A.2803 f.

57. See, e.g., "Wu-tsung shih-chia" 五宗世家, *Shih-chi* 59.2098 f. In addition to other crimes, the Prince of Chao took the former concubine of his deceased cousin as his own. This lady, for her part, was notorious for having slept with her husband's son.

58. For an insightful, if somewhat dated, account of Chou-dynasty feudalism, see Herrlee G. Creel, *The Origins of Statecraft in China* (Chicago: University of Chicago Press, 1970). The classic study of feudalism in Europe is Marc Bloch, *Feudal Society*, trans. L. A. Manyon (Chicago: University of Chicago Press, 1961).

59. On the policies of Emperors Ching and Wu, see, e.g., Lin Chien-ming 林劍鳴, *Hsin-pien Ch'in Han shih* 新編秦漢史 (Taipei: Wu-nan, 1992), vol. 1, 389 ff. and 484–493; Michael Loewe, "The Former Han Dynasty," in Twitchett and Loewe, vol. 1, 137 ff. and 156 f; T'ung-tsu Ch'ü, 165 ff.; Dull, 69 f.; Tao Tien-yi, "Vassal Kings and Marquises of the Former Han Dynasty," *Bulletin of the Institute of History and Philology* 46.1 (1974), 170 ff.; and Ch'ien Mu, *Ch'in Han shih*, 229 ff.

60. "P'ing-chin Hou Chu-fu lieh-chuan," *Shih-chi* 112.2961; "Yen Chu Wu-ch'iu Chu-fu Hsü Yen Chung Wang Chia chuan," *Han-shu* 64A.2802.

61. See Ch'ao Ts'o's biographies in "Yüan Ang Ch'ao Ts'o lieh-chuan" 袁盎晁錯列傳, *Shih-chi* 101.2742–2748; and "Yüan Ang Ch'ao Ts'o chuan" 爰盎晁錯傳, *Han-shu* 49.2276–2305.

62. Compare the translation in Watson, *Records: Han*, vol. 2, 203 f.

63. "Wu-tsung shih-chia," *Shih-chi* 59.2096.

64. For an account of these rebellious princes, see, e.g., Benjamin E. Wallacker, "Liu An, Second King of Huai-nan (180?–122 B.C.), *Journal of the American Oriental Society* 92 (1972), 36–51.

65. Compare the translation in Watson, *Records: Han*, vol. 1, 391 f.

66. Cf., e.g., *Hei Erh-shih-ssu shih*, vol. 1, 19; Kuo Hsing-wen, 70 ff.; Sheng I, 229 ff. and 334 ff.; Stephen Durrant, "Smoothing Edges and Filling Gaps: *Tso*

chuan and the 'General Reader,'" *Journal of the American Oriental Society* 112.1 (1992), 40; T'ung Shu-yeh, 童書業, *Ch'un-ch'iu Tso-chuan yen-chiu* 春秋左傳研究 (Shanghai: Jen-min, 1980), 209 ff. and 347 f.; and Liu Te-han 劉德漢, *Tung-Chou fu-nü sheng-huo* 東周婦女生活 (Taipei: Hsüeh-sheng, 1976), 52 f. Melvin P. Thatcher, "Marriages of the Ruling Elite in the Spring and Autumn Period," in *Marriage and Inequality in Chinese Society*, ed. Rubie S. Watson and Patricia Buckley Ebrey, Studies on China 12 (Berkeley and Los Angeles: University of California Press, 1991), 48 n. 2, argues that *cheng* 烝 (i.e., copulating with one's father's wife or concubine) was "regarded as aberrant and unacceptable" in the Spring and Autumn period, but the texts that he cites as justification all date from centuries later.

In its characteristic debunking fashion, "Chung-hsiao" 忠孝, in Ch'en Ch'i-yu, *Han Fei-tzu chi-shih* 韓非子集釋, Chung-kuo ssu-hsiang ming-chu (Peking: Chung-hua, 1958; repr., Taipei: Shih-chieh, 1991), 20.51.1108, suggests that the Sage-King Shun "took his mother as a concubine" 妾其母. Cf. Eduard Erkes, "Zur Sage von Shun," *T'oung Pao* 34.4 (1938–1939), 315 f., who explains this information as evidence of an ancient practice akin to the levirate, whereby sons would inherit their widowed mothers. Wolfgang Münke, *Die klassische chinesische Mythologie* (Stuttgart: Ernst Klett, 1976), 295 f., argues that *ch'ieh* 妾 in this context does not connote a sexual relationship. The commentary of Hosaka Seisō 蒲坂青莊 (1775–1834), *Han Fei-tzu chi-shih* 20.51.1113 n. 24, is equivocal; he glosses *ch'ieh* as *pi* 婢 (female slave, maid), which also may or may not be the designation of sexual slave. (On *ch'ieh* as a general term for a female slave, see also T'ung Shu-yeh, 312.) Ch'en Ch'i-yu refers to Hosaka as Shōkōen 松皋圓, one of his many appellations. The commentary is taken from Hosaka's *Teihon Kampishi sammon* 定本韓非子纂聞 (1809).

67. "Ching shih-san wang chuan" 景十三王傳, *Han-shu* 53.2416. Incidentally, *Hei Erh-shih-ssu shih*, vol. 5, 3699, recounts all of these transgressions, omitting only the last and most shocking: bestiality.

68. Following the commentary of Yen Shih-ku; cf. also *Hei Erh-shih-ssu shih*, vol. 1, 666; and Charles O. Hucker, *A Dictionary of Official Titles in Imperial China* (Stanford, Calif.: Stanford University Press, 1985), 4385. *Pa-tzu* 八子 was a title in the harem hierarchy. See, e.g., Robert Joe Cutter and William Gordon Crowell, *Empresses and Consorts: Selections from Chen Shou's* Records of the Three States *with Pei Songzhi's Commentary* (Honolulu: University of Hawai'i Press, 1999), 13 f.; and Hans Bielenstein, *The Bureaucracy of Han Times*, Cambridge Studies in Chinese History, Literature, and Institutions (Cambridge, 1980), 73.

69. This detail makes the reader think immediately of Empress Dowager Lü and her treatment of Lady Ch'i (cf. n. 13, above).

70. Following the commentary of Wang Hsien-ch'ien, *Han-shu pu-chu* 漢書補注, Erh-shih-ssu shih k'ao-ting ts'ung-shu chuan-chi (1900; repr., Peking: Shu-mu wen-hsien, 1995), 53.6a.

71. See esp. R. H. van Gulik, *Sexual Life in Ancient China: A Preliminary Survey of Chinese Sex and Society from ca. 1500 B.C. till 1644 A.D.* (Leiden: E. J. Brill, 1961; repr., New York: Barnes and Noble, 1996), 61 f.

72. Van Gulik, 167, cites a solitary reference from the T'ang dynasty: Li Yin 李隱 (fl. ca. 865–870), *Hsiao-hsiang lu* 瀟湘錄 (*Ku-chin shuo-hai* 古今説海), 5b f.

(i.e., the last item in this small collection). Cf. also de Groot, vol. 4, 256 ff. Van Gulik notes that even this case is different, because the woman involved copulated with a dog of her own free will, whereas the bestiality of Liu Chien's harem ladies was coerced (though van Gulik does not appear to take into account the statement in *Hsiao-hsiang lu* that the woman yielded to the dog's advances out of "fear" 懼). Liu Ta-lin, 劉達臨, *Chung-kuo ku-tai hsing wen-hua* 中國古代性文化 (Yin-ch'uan: Ning-hsia jen-min, 1993), vol. 1, 306 ff., discusses early notices of bestiality, including that of Li Yin; most appear in Ch'ing-dynasty sources. An ancient demonography discusses a horror that may be understood as the visitation of a canine incubus who copulates with men's wives: "When a dog continually enters someone's apartment at night, seizing the men and playing with the women, and cannot be apprehended, this is Spirit-Hound acting as a ghost" 犬恒夜入人室，執丈夫，戲女子，不可得也，是神狗偽為鬼; text in "Chieh-chiu," *Shui-hu-ti Ch'in-mu chu-chien*, 212; and Liu Lo-hsien, 劉樂賢, *Shui-hu-ti Ch'in-chien Jih-shu yen-chiu* 睡虎地秦簡日書研究, Ta-lu ti-ch'ü po-shih lun-wen ts'ung-k'an 76 (Taipei: Wen-chin, 1994), 227. Compare the translation in Donald Harper, "Spellbinding," in *Religions of China in Practice*, ed. Donald S. Lopez, Jr., Princeton Readings in Religions (Princeton, 1996), 245; and the discussion in Hsü Fu-ch'ang 徐富昌, "Shui-hu-ti Ch'in-mu *Jih-shu* chung te kuei-shen hsin-yang" 睡虎地秦墓日書中的鬼神信仰, in *Chang I-jen hsien-sheng ch'i-chih shou-ch'ing lun-wen chi* 張以仁先生七秩壽慶論文集 (Taipei: Hsüeh-sheng, 1999), vol. 2, 899 ff.

There is also an important nexus of myths that link the origins of various "barbarian" peoples to the sexual union of a woman and an animal (such as a monkey, snake, dog, or wolf). See esp. de Groot, vol. 4, 253–271; and cf. also Victor H. Mair, "Canine Conundrums: Dog Ancestor Myths of Origin in Ethnic Perspective," *Sino-Platonic Papers* 87 (1998); Anne Birrell, *Chinese Mythology: An Introduction* (Baltimore: Johns Hopkins University Press, 1993), 118–119; and N. J. Girardot, *Myth and Meaning in Early Taoism: The Theme of Chaos (hun-tun)*, Hermeneutics: Studies in the History of Religions (Berkeley and Los Angeles: University of California Press, 1983), 188 ff. and 320–322.

73. See, e.g., chapter 2, n. 26, in this volume.

74. *Mencius* 2A.6, *Meng-tzu cheng-i* 7.233 ff.

75. I. A. Richards, *Mencius on the Mind: Experiments in Multiple Definition* (London: Routledge and Kegan Paul, 1932), 19, suggests that the "sound" refers to "the unpleasant sound of the child thudding down into the well, not the mere rumour or report of what has happened." Traditional commentators since at least Chao Ch'i 趙崎 (d. A.D. 201), however, take it to mean a bad reputation. See also the commentary of Chiao Hsün ad loc.

76. Compare the translation in D. C. Lau, *Mencius* (New York: Penguin, 1970), 82 f. For more on this aspect of Mencius' philosophy, see, e.g., A. C. Graham, *Disputers of the Tao: Philosophical Argument in Ancient China* (La Salle, Ill.: Open Court, 1989), 123–132; and Kwong-loi Shun, *Mencius and Early Chinese Thought* (Stanford, Calif.: Stanford University Press, 1997), 48 ff.

77. "Fei-hsiang" 非相, *Hsün-tzu chi-chieh* 3.5.78 f.

78. Compare the translation in John Knoblock, *Xunzi: A Translation and Study of the Complete Works* (Stanford, Calif.: Stanford University Press, 1988–1994), vol. 1, 206.

79. Compare also the "Li-cheng chiu-pai chieh" 立政九敗解 chapter of the *Kuan-tzu* 管子: "Thus they pursue their desires and behave recklessly; men and women, not being separated, revert to being animals" 然則從欲妄行，男女無別，反於禽獸; text in Tai Wang 戴望 (1783–1863), *Kuan-tzu chiao-cheng* 校正, in *Chu-tzu chi-ch'eng* 諸子集成 (1935; repr., Peking: Chung-hua, 1954), 21.65.338.

80. For a more extended discussion of these issues in Mencius and Hsün-tzu, see, e.g., Paul Rakita Goldin, *Rituals of the Way: The Philosophy of Xunzi* (Chicago: Open Court, 1999), 1 ff. and 72 ff.

81. Scholars often cite the legends surrounding Chòu 紂, the last King of Shang, but unfortunately the well-known references to his sexual transgressions in the *Shang-shu* (cited in Mark Edward Lewis, *Sanctioned Violence in Early China*, SUNY Series in Chinese Philosophy and Culture [Albany, N.Y., 1999], 260 n. 77) all appear in spurious chapters. The most explicit account, "Yin pen-chi" 殷本紀, *Shih-chi* 3.105 ff., dates, of course, from the Han dynasty. This is where we read of his carousals at Sha-ch'iu 沙丘: "He would make a pond of wine and suspend meat to make a forest, causing men and women to chase each other naked therein, and making an all-night drinking party of it" 以酒為池，縣肉為林，使男女倮相逐其閒，為長夜之飲. Cf. also Raphals, *Sharing the Light*, 63; and Granet, *Danses et légendes*, vol. 2, 395 n. 1. We should keep in mind, however, that Chòu is already described as "licentious and dissolute" 淫泆 in the earliest stratum of the *Shang-shu* 尚書; see, e.g., "To-shih" 多士, *Shang-shu cheng-i* (*Shih-san ching chu-shu*), 16.220a. The specific crimes of Chòu enumerated there are impiety and disregard of the plight of his people, but the term *yin* may imply that there was some sexual element to his crimes as well.

82. "T'ai-tzu Chin chien Ling-wang yung Ku-shui" 太子晉諫靈王壅穀水, *Kuo-yü* 3.102–104. The myth is related in the context of a speech by Crown Prince Chin (who died before taking the throne; see the commentary of Tung Tseng-ling, *Kuo-yü cheng-i* 3.11b) criticizing the plan of his father, King Ling of Chou (r. 571–545 B.C.), to dam a river that was threatening to flood the royal palace. The entire speech is translated and analyzed in James A. Hart, "The Speech of Prince Chin: A Study of Early Chinese Cosmology," in *Explorations in Early Chinese Cosmology: Papers Presented at the Workshop on Classical Chinese Thought Held at Harvard University, August 1976*, ed. Henry Rosemont, Jr., *Journal of the American Academy of Religion Thematic Studies* 50.2 (Chico, Calif.: Scholars Press, 1984), 35–65.

83. The word *wu* 物, though commonly used to mean any kind of "thing," seems to refer consistently to living creatures in this passage (as it does elsewhere in the *Kuo-yü*); see, e.g., K. C. Chang, *Art, Myth, and Ritual: The Path to Political Authority in Ancient China* (Cambridge: Harvard University Press, 1983), 63 ff. The presence of the *niu* 牛 (ox) radical in the graph suggests that something close to "animal" was indeed the original sense.

84. Following Tu Yü and K'ung Ying-ta, who both gloss *hun* 昏 as the death of an infant who has not lived three months and consequently has not been named; see their commentaries to *Ch'un-ch'iu Tso-chuan cheng-i* 48.2087c (Chao 19 = 523 B.C.). Wang Nien-sun 王念孫 (1744–1832) and others take the term to mean *mo* 沒 (demise); see the corresponding section in *Ch'un-ch'iu Tso-chuan chu*, vol. 4, 1402 f. However, the older explanation (which Yang Po-chün does not reproduce) fits the context more closely. Compare also the commentary in I

Chung-t'ien 易中天 and Hou Nai-hui 侯迺慧, *Kuo-yü tu-pen* 讀本, Ku-chi chin-chu hsin-i ts'ung-shu; Li-shih lei (Taipei: San-min, 1995), 120 n. 8. (Despite the implication of the title, this is a very serious work with insightful commentary.) Wei Chao glosses *hun* as "madness" 狂惑, which is an acceptable sense, though it ruins the parallelism of the sentence.

85. See especially the commentary of Tung Tseng-ling, *Kuo-yü cheng-i* 3.14b; Takigawa Kametarō in *Shiki kaichū kōshō* 1.29; as well as Cheng Hsüan's commentaries to "Sung-kao" 崧高 (*Mao* 259), *Mao-Shih cheng-i* (*Shih-san ching chu-shu*), 18C.565c; and "Wu-ti pen-chi" 五帝本紀, *Shih-chi* 1.21 n. 6 (as quoted by P'ei Yin). Cf. Karlgren, "Legends and Cults," 258 f.

86. Commentators since Wei Chao have regularly taken *fu-yin* 伏陰 in the sense of "summer frost" (and *san-yang* 散陽 as winter heat), because *fu* can also refer to a period in midsummer. For this sense of *fu*, see, e.g., Poo, *In Search of Personal Welfare*, 130 f.; and Derk Bodde, *Festivals in Classical China* (Princeton, N.J.: Princeton University Press, 1975), 317 ff. But it is not clear to me how this interpretation can account for the evident parallelism between Heaven and Earth in this sentence; for how are we to comprehend "There was no summer frost in Heaven, no winter heat-waves on Earth"? Moreover, it is not obvious that the phrase *san-yang* (diffusion of *yang*), though clearly in parallel position to *fu-yin*, must refer specifically to abnormal warmth in winter. Morohashi, entry 13265.232, vol. 5, 529, defines *san-yang* as "the absence of frost in winter" 冬に凍らなかつたり, but relies precisely on Wei Chao's commentary to this passage as evidence. More likely is the intended contrast between Heaven and *yin* on the one hand, and Earth and *yang* on the other, because Heaven was regarded as the supreme instantiation of *yang*, and Earth as that of *yin*. But see the commentary of Tung Tseng-ling, *Kuo-yü cheng-i* 3.15b and 16a.

87. Compare the translation in Hart, 39 f.; and the partial translation in Anne Birrell, "The Four Flood Myth Traditions of Classical China," *T'oung Pao* 83.4–5 (1997), 234 and 248 f. (Hart confuses the graphs *yü* 虞 and *yü* 禹.)

88. Cf. Birrell, "Flood Myth Traditions," 234. As we have seen in chapter 2, the phrase *chan-lo* 湛樂 also appears tellingly in *Mao* 256 ("I"), in which rulers given to "dissolute pleasures" are criticized for offending against Heaven and thereby bringing about their own ruination.

89. Note that Kung Kung and Kun both appear in several other versions of the flood myth, and Kun is sometimes portrayed sympathetically as a hero who simply failed in his task to control the floods. See, e.g., Birrell, *Chinese Mythology*, 79 ff. and 97 f. For more on Kung Kung as marplot, see esp. William G. Boltz, "Kung Kung and the Flood: Reverse Euhemerism in the *Yao tien*," *T'oung Pao* 67.3–5 (1981), 141–153. Cf. also Münke, 219–232; Marcel Granet, *La pensée chinoise*, L'évolution de l'humanité: Synthèse collective 25b (Paris: Albin Michel, 1950), 344 ff.; Granet, *Danses et légendes*, vol. 2, 485 f.; and Bernhard Karlgren, "Legends and Cults in Ancient China," *Bulletin of the Museum of Far Eastern Antiquities* 18 (1946), 218 ff.

90. "Fa-lü ta-wen" 法律答問, *Shui-hu-ti Ch'in-mu chu-chien*, 134; cf. Hulsewé, *Remnants of Ch'in Law*, D 152. The same text, incidentally, affirms that a woman may leave her husband with impunity if she (or if the relationship) has not yet been *kuan* 官—the meaning of which is unclear. (If she has been *kuan*, the run-

away wife is liable to be "sentenced" 論.) The editors of *Shui-hu-ti Ch'in-mu chu-chien*, 132, surmise that *kuan* signifies official recognition of the marriage, in which case one must conclude that the law allowed unmarried men and women to cohabit freely. Cf. Hulsewé, *Remnants of Ch'in Law*, D 145. Another article in the same text mandates the punishment of a certain woman who leaves her husband, takes another lover, and does not inform her husband for two years. This passage is also tantalizing, because the text does not say whether or how she should be punished if she informed her husband immediately. See "Fa-lü ta-wen," *Shui-hu-ti Ch'in-mu chu-chien*, 132; and Hulsewé, *Remnants of Ch'in Law*, D 146. Finally, "Feng-chen shih" 封診式, *Shui-hu-ti Ch'in-mu chu-chien*, 163, contains the model testimony of a private citizen who has fettered and delivered to the authorities a man and a woman that he has discovered "fornicating" 姦. Once again, however, we are not provided with a precise protocol as to what does and does not constitute punishable fornication. Cf. Miao Wen-yüan, 273; Hulsewé, *Remnants of Ch'in Law*, E 25; and Katrina C. D. McLeod and Robin D. S. Yates, "Forms of Ch'in Law: An Annotated Translation of the *Feng-chen shih*," *Harvard Journal of Asiatic Studies* 41.1 (1981), 162.

91. The "Sang-fu" 喪服 section of the *I-li* 儀禮, for example, far from condemning remarriage, requires that if one's widowed stepmother remarries, and one accompanies her to her new husband's house, then one must wear sackcloth for an entire year after her death, in order to show respect for mothers who love their children to the end. See "Sang-fu," *I-li chu-shu* (*Shih-san ching chu-shu*), 30.1104c; and the commentary in Hu P'ei-hui 胡培翬 (1782–1849), *I-li cheng-i* (*Kuo-hsüeh chi-pen ts'ung-shu*), 10.22.42 f.

Incidentally, the ancient literature contains not a few ribald stories about women who have more than one husband or lover during their lifetimes; this seems to have been a favorite theme for jokes and witticisms. Howard S. Levy, *Chinese Sex Jokes in Traditional Times*, Asian Folklore and Social Life Monographs 58, Sino-Japanese Sexology Classics Series 5 (Taipei, 1973), has collected and translated 456 anecdotes that he calls sex jokes (the vast majority of which date from the Ming dynasty or later). It is remarkable that virtually all of the ancient material has to do with adulterous women or women who wish to remarry. See especially items 30, 51, 185, and 209. Levy does not include the amusing story in "Ch'in Hsüan t'ai-hou ai Wei Ch'ou-fu" 秦宣太后愛魏醜夫, *Chan-kuo ts'e* 4.167, in which the widowed Queen Dowager Hsüan of Ch'in, on her deathbed, is persuaded not to have her young lover buried alive with her, lest she thereby enrage her deceased husband in the afterworld. See also *Hei Erh-shih-ssu shih*, vol. 1, 123 f., 354. Other notorious women, such as Lady Hsia and Nan-tzu, were discussed in chapter 1 of the present volume.

92. Cf., e.g., Shen Chia-pen, "Yü hou-mu luan" 與後母亂 and "Chia-tzu i mu wei ch'i" 假子以母為妻, *Han-lü chih-i* 漢律摭遺, in *Shen Chi-i hsien-sheng i-shu* 沈寄簃先生遺書 (n.d.; repr., Taipei: Wen-hai, 1964), 8.9a f.

93. See n. 66, above.

94. "Ku-chi lieh-chuan" 滑稽列傳, *Shih-chi* 126.3199. For the meaning of the term *ku-chi*, see, e.g., Ch'ien Chung-shu, vol. 1, 316–317; see also Lai Han-p'ing 賴漢屏, *Shih-chi p'ing-shang* 史記評賞, San-min ts'ung-k'an 159 (Taipei, 1998), 283.

The jester, named "Ch'un-yü the Shaved" 淳于髡, is also noteworthy because he is one of the most famous early examples of a *chui-hsü* 贅婿 (excrescent son-in-law), that is, a husband who is forced on account of indigence to reside with his wife's family. Chia I explains the term in "Chia I chuan," *Han-shu* 48.2244. Cf. further Goldin, "Personal Names," 79; *Hei Erh-shih-ssu shih*, vol. 4, 2635, 2648; Bret Hinsch, "Women, Kinship, and Property as Seen in a Han Dynasty Will," *T'oung Pao* 84.1–3 (1998), 5 ff.; Sheng I, 254 ff.; Hellmut Wilhelm, "Notes on Chou Fiction," in *Transition and Permanence: Chinese History and Culture*, ed. David C. Buxbaum and Frederick W. Mote (Hong Kong: Cathay, 1972), 265 n. 25; T'ung-tsu Ch'ü, 252 n. 8; and Ch'en Ku-yüan, 70. This man is usually referred to as Ch'un-yü K'un (or Shun-yü K'un, a variant that I do not understand), but *k'un* 髡 is probably an epithet ("shaved," like a slave). See Sheng I, 258 f.; and David R. Knechtges, "Riddles as Poetry: The '*Fu*-Chapter' of the *Hsün-tzu*," in *Wen-lin: Studies in the Chinese Humanities*, ed. Tse-tsung Chow (Madison: University of Wisconsin Press, 1968–1989), vol. 2, 22 n. 98. The surname Ch'un-yü was taken from the name of the capital of the ancient state of Chou 州; see *Ch'un-ch'iu Tso-chuan chu* I, 108 (Huan 5 = 707 B.C.). See also the comments by Ying Shao in "Hsing-shih" 姓氏 (as reconstructed from surviving fragments); text in Wang Li-ch'i 王利器, *Feng-su t'ung-i chiao-chu* 風俗通義校注 (Taipei: Ming-wen, 1982), 509. (So "Ch'un-yü K'un" might actually just mean "the shaved man from Ch'un-yü.") Granet, *Danses et légendes*, vol. 1, 17 n. 1, misconstrues the name totally and reads it as though it were "Shun Yü-k'un."

A contemporaneous Ch'un-yü K'un appears in several contexts as one of the world's leading rhetoricians. See, e.g., *Mencius* 4A.17, text in Chiao Hsün 焦循 (1763–1820), *Meng-tzu cheng-i* 孟子正義, ed. Shen Wen-cho 沈文倬, Hsin-pien Chu-tzu chi-ch'eng (Peking: Chung-hua, 1987), 15.520–522; *Mencius* 6B.6, *Meng-tzu cheng-i* 24.829–838; "Pao-keng" 報更, in Ch'en Ch'i-yu, *Lü-shih ch'un-ch'iu chiao-shih* (Shanghai: Hsüeh-lin, 1984), 15.894 f.; "Wei shih-chia" 魏世家, *Shih-chi* 44.1847; "Meng-tzu Hsün Ch'ing lieh-chuan" 孟子荀卿列傳, *Shih-chi* 74.2347; *Han-Shih wai-chuan* 韓詩外傳 (*Ssu-pu ts'ung-k'an* 四部叢刊), 6.7b–8a; "Fu-en" 復恩, *Shuo-yüan* 6.410a; "Tsun-hsien" 尊賢, *Shuo-yüan* 8.418c; and "Chih-shih" 知實, in Huang Hui 黃暉, *Lun-heng chiao-shih (fu Liu P'an-sui chi-chieh)* 論衡校釋 (附劉盼遂集解), Hsin-pien Chu-tzu chi-ch'eng (Peking: Chung-hua, 1990), 26.79. 1098 f. He is also the subject of several articles in the *Chan-kuo ts'e*: "Meng-ch'ang chün tsai Hsüeh" 孟嘗君在薛, *Chan-kuo ts'e* 10.376–377; "Ch'un-yü K'un i-jih erh hsien ch'i-jen yü Hsüan-wang" 淳于髡一日而見七人於宣王, *Chan-kuo ts'e* 10.388–389; "Ch'i yü fa Wei" 齊欲伐魏, *Chan-kuo ts'e* 10.390; "Ch'i yü fa Wei," *Chan-kuo ts'e* 24.865–866; and "Su Tai wei Yen shui Ch'i" 蘇代為燕說齊, *Chan-kuo ts'e* 30.1092. Since this Ch'un-yü K'un, like the jester, was in the service of King Wei of Ch'i 齊威王 (r. 357–320 B.C.), commentators have continually assumed that "Ch'un-yü K'un" always refers to the same man; see, e.g., the commentaries of Yen Jo-ch'ü 閻若璩 (1636–1704) and Chou Kuang-yeh 周廣業 (1730–1798) to *Meng-tzu cheng-i* 15.521; as well as Wilhelm, 252–258; and Ch'ien Mu, *Hsien-Ch'in chu-tzu hsi-nien*, sec. 118. However, it is very strange that Ssu-ma Ch'ien should have included two separate biographies of Ch'un-yü K'un, as though there were two contemporary personages by the same appellation: "Ku-chi lieh-chuan," *Shih-chi* 126.3197–3199; and "Meng-tzu Hsün Ch'ing lieh-chuan," *Shih-chi* 74.2347.

The only other person in the *Shih-chi* who has more than one biography is Tuan-mu Tz'u 端木賜 (b. 520 B.C.), better known as Tzu-kung 子貢. See the commentary of Chao I in *Shiki kaichū kōshō* 67.17.

95. "Wang Liao shih kung-tzu Kuang chuan" 王僚使公子光傳, *Wu-Yüeh ch'un-ch'iu chi-chiao hui-k'ao* 3.23. It has been demonstrated solidly that rulers of various states routinely exchanged pleasure women for diplomatic purposes (and also used them to reward loyal vassals). Cf., e.g., Wu Chou, 5 ff.; and Wang Shu-nu, 23 f.

We have seen earlier (ch. 2, n. 76) that Mencius did not condemn King Hsüan of Ch'i for his sexual appetite. Similarly, in "Hsiao-k'uang" 小匡, *Kuan-tzu chiao-cheng* 8.20.129, the figure of Kuan Chung 管仲 surprises his lord by declaring that the latter's love of sex is not a crucial shortcoming.

96. See, e.g., Wang Mao 王楙 (1151–1213), "Ku-che nan-nü hsiang-chien wu-hsien" 古者男女相見無嫌, *Yeh-k'o ts'ung-shu* 野客叢書, ed. Wang Wen-chin 王文錦, *Hsüeh-shu pi-chi ts'ung-k'an* (Peking: Chung-hua, 1987), 1.4 f., an early attempt to show that males and females were not embarrassed to see each other naked in ancient times, as an illustration of how early society was less restrictive from a sexual point of view. Wang's specific examples do not always stand up to scrutiny, but his larger point is valid.

97. See, e.g., *Hei Erh-shih-ssu shih*, vol. 1, 488 f.; Sheng I, 336; Liu Ta-lin, *Chung-kuo ku-tai hsing wen-hua*, vol. 1, 238 f.; Liu Tseng-kuei, "Han-tai hun-yin kuan-hsi," 9; and Wu Chou, 8.

98. On the reforms of Kung-sun Yang (i.e., Lord Shang 商君, putative author of the *Shang-chün shu* 書), see, e.g., T'ien Ch'ang-wu 田昌五 and Tsang Chih-fei 臧知非, *Chou Ch'in she-hui chieh-kou yen-chiu* 周秦社會結構研究, *Chou Ch'in Han T'ang yen-chou shu-hsi* (Hsi-an: Hsi-pei Ta-hsüeh, 1996), 278 ff.; Lewis, *Sanctioned Violence*, 61 ff.; Cheng Liang-shu, *Shang Yang p'ing-chuan* 商鞅評傳, Chung-kuo ssu-hsiang chia p'ing-chuan ts'ung-shu 5 (Nan-ching: Nan-ching Ta-hsüeh, 1998), 103–170, and *Shang Yang chi-ch'i hsüeh-p'ai* 商鞅及其學派 (Shanghai: Ku-chi, 1989), esp. 169–182; Moriya Mitsuo 守屋美都雄, *Chūgoku kodai no kazoku to kokka* 中國古代の家族と國家 (Kyoto: Tōyōshi Kenkyūkai, 1968), 3–138; and Yang K'uan, *Shang Yang pien-fa* 商鞅變法 (Shanghai: Jen-min, 1955). The popular opprobrium leading to his demise is described in "Wei Yang wang Wei ju Ch'in" 衛鞅亡魏入秦, *Chan-kuo ts'e* 3.75 ff.; and "Shang-chün lieh-chuan," *Shih-chi* 68.2227–2240.

99. For the illustrative example of Nazi sexual ideology, see Hans Peter Bleuel, *Das saubere Reich* (Bern: Scherz, 1972). Compare the more tendentious account in Magnus Hirschfeld et al., *The Sexual History of the World War* (New York: Cadillac, 1946), 270–318. (For its information on sexual life during World War I, on the other hand, Hirschfeld's work is an unparalleled classic.) Some modern Asian regimes have displayed similar attitudes. See, e.g., Sabine Frühstück, "Managing the Truth of Sex in Imperial Japan," *Journal of Asian Studies* 59.2 (2000), 332–358; and M. J. Meijer, *Marriage Law and Policy in the Chinese People's Republic* (Hong Kong: Hong Kong University Press, 1971).

100. The oldest extant version of this essay is in "Ch'in Shih-huang pen-chi," *Shih-chi* 6.276–284. The work also appears in the *Hsin-shu* 新書, which is attributed to Chia I; see the annotated edition in Wang Chou-ming 王洲明 and Hsü

Ch'ao 徐超, *Chia I chi chiao-chu* 賈誼集校注, Hsin-chu ku-tai wen-hsüeh ming-chia chi (Peking: Jen-min wen-hsüeh, 1996), 1–22.

101. Cf., e.g., Loewe, "The Former Han Dynasty," 148 ff.; and Ch'ien Mu, *Ch'in Han shih*, 61 ff. On the abrogation of mutilation, see the memorial in "Hsing-fa chih" 刑法志, *Han-shu* 23.1099; which is translated with commentary in Hulsewé, *Remnants of Han Law*, 335 f. Castration was reinstituted as a substitute for the death penalty in such extreme cases as that of Ssu-ma Ch'ien. Cf., e.g., Hulsewé, *Remnants of Han Law*, 385 n. 185; and Shen Chia-pen, "Kung" 宮, *Han-lü chih-i* 9.12a f. Oskar Weggel, *Chinesische Rechtsgeschichte*, Handbuch der Orientalistik 4.6 (Leiden: E. J. Brill, 1980), 31, erroneously attributes the abolition of mutilating punishments to Emperor Wu. On the Han portrayal of the Ch'in in general, see, e.g., Yü Tsung-fa 余宗發, *Hsien-Ch'in chu-tzu hsüeh-shuo tsai Ch'in-ti chih fa-chan* 先秦諸子學說在秦地之發展, Wen-shih-che ta-hsi 133 (Taipei: Wen-chin, 1998), 9–19.

102. "Chao Yin Han Chang liang-Wang chuan" 趙尹韓張兩王傳, *Han-shu* 76.3227.

103. Following the interpretation in Dull, 70, who argues compellingly that there really were no such laws in Wang Tsun's time. But *lü wu ch'i-mu chih fa* 律無妻母之法 could also mean something like, "The code does not countenance the practice of cohabiting with one's mother." Note also that Ho Hsiu 何休 (A.D. 129–182), in his commentary to *Ch'un-ch'iu Kung-yang chuan chu-shu* 4.2216c (Huan 6 = 706 B.C.), seems to cite a law allowing one to kill with impunity a son who fornicates with his mother; cf. Kuo Hsing-wen, 74, who mistakenly attributes the commentary to Hsiang Hsiu 向休 (A.D. 221?–300?). (Such errors are frequent in books published in the People's Republic of China and are almost always typographical; Kuo Hsing-wen's work is otherwise very careful and learned.)

104. This translation represents a best guess. In fact, the received classics do *not* contain the phrase *tsao-yü* 造獄, which is not easily construed in any case. Chin Cho 晉灼 (Chin 晉 dynasty) notes that "this matter of *tsao-yü* is in the Ou-yang *Shang-shu*" 歐陽尚書有此造獄之事也, which is a long-lost tradition of the *Shang-shu* (see e.g. "I-wen chih" 藝文志, *Han-shu* 30.1705).

105. Wang Tsun went on to have an eventful official career. The inclusion of this episode in his official biography is manifestly intended to show that he was destined for greatness. He was very much a child of his times; Loewe, *Crisis and Conflict*, esp. 92 ff. and 158 ff., traces the rise of this kind of ahistorical traditionalism (which he calls Reformism) to this same period.

106. Essentially following the commentary of Meng K'ang. *Chuan* 籑 (usually meaning "to offer food") might also be an error for *tsuan* 纂; but see, e.g., Hulsewé, *Remnants of Han Law*, 416 n. 337, who argues that *chuan* 籑 was originally written 饌, which is itself a mistake here for the homophone *chuan* 撰.

107. "Hsing-fa chih," *Han-shu* 23.1112.

108. Compare the translation in Hulsewé, *Remnants of Han Law*, 348 f.

109. Thus it may well be asked why Pan Ku was so critical of the usurper Wang Mang 王莽 (d. A.D. 23), the most notorious such "traditionalist" in the entire Han period, when the two men's intellectual dispositions actually had far

more in common than Pan Ku would have cared to admit. One persuasive answer is that as a historian who believed in Heaven's Mandate 天命, Pan Ku was compelled to stigmatize Wang Mang for no other reason than that he had failed, and therefore his praising any of Wang Mang's opinions was out of the question. See Hans Bielenstein, "Pan Ku's Accusations against Wang Mang," in *Chinese Ideas about Nature and Society: Studies in Honour of Derk Bodde*, ed. Charles Le Blanc and Susan Blader (Hong Kong: Hong Kong University Press, 1987), 265–270; cf. also Clyde Bailey Sargent, *Wang Mang: A Translation of the Official Account of His Rise to Power as Given in the* History of the Former Han Dynasty (Shanghai, 1947), 11–24, who does not consider any possible intellectual motive on the part of Pan Ku.

110. "Lieh-nü chuan," *Hou-Han shu* 84.2788. "Chia-ch'ü," *Po-hu t'ung shu-cheng* 10.485 f., states explicitly that women must have a teacher so that they can "learn the way of serving others" 學事人之道. The fact that Pan Chao felt the need to justify herself thus implies that few people in her world knew or cared about the prescriptions in the *Po-hu t'ung*—a conclusion corroborated by other evidence (discussed further below).

111. Cf., e.g., Pao Chia-lin, "Yin-yang hsüeh-shuo yü fu-nü ti-wei" 陰陽學説與婦女地位, *Han-hsüeh yen-chiu* 漢學研究 5.2 (1987), reprinted in *Chung-kuo fu-nü shih lun-chi hsü-chi* 中國婦女史論集續集 (Taipei: Tao-hsiang, 1991), 42.

112. "Lieh-nü chuan," *Hou-Han shu* 84.2789.

113. Compare the translation in Nancy Lee Swann, *Pan Chao: Foremost Woman Scholar of China* (New York: Century, 1932), 86.

114. "Lieh-nü chuan," *Hou-Han shu* 84.2790.

115. Compare the translation in Swann, 88.

116. Cf., e.g., Fei Xiaotong, *From the Soil: The Foundations of Chinese Society*, trans. Gary G. Hamilton and Wang Zheng (Berkeley and Los Angeles: University of California Press, 1992), 85.

117. Compare the interpretation of this passage in Yu-shih Chen, "The Historical Template of Pan Chao's *Nü Chieh*," *T'oung Pao* 82 (1996), 257, which is radically different from that offered here.

118. Cf. also Siegfried Englert, *Materialien zur Stellung der Frau und zur Sexualität im vormodernen und modernen China*, Heidelberger Schriften zur Ostasienkunde 1 (Frankfurt: Haag und Herchen, 1980), 51 f., and his criticism of Joanna F. Handlin, "Lü K'un's New Audience: The Influence of Women's Literacy on Sixteenth-Century Thought," in *Women in Chinese Society*, ed. Margery Wolf and Roxane Witke, Studies in Chinese Society (Stanford, Calif.: Stanford University Press, 1975), 13–38.

119. *Analects* 4.17; text in Ch'eng Shu-te 程樹德 (1877–1944), *Lun-yü chi-shih* 論語集釋, ed. Ch'eng Chün-ying 程俊英 and Chiang Chien-yüan 蔣見元, Hsin-pien Chu-tzu chi-ch'eng (Peking: Chung-hua, 1990), 8.270.

120. Compare the translation in Lau, *Analects*, 74.

121. See esp. *Analects* 14.7, *Lun-yü chi-shih* 28.958: "in being loyal to someone, can one fail to instruct?" 忠焉，能勿誨乎? Similarly, in the recently excavated text, "Lu Mu-kung wen Tzu-ssu" 魯穆公問子思, Lord Mu of Lu (r. 415–383 B.C.) asks Confucius' grandson Tzu-ssu (483–402 B.C.) the definition of a "loyal vassal" 忠臣 and is told, "one who constantly cites his lord's faults" 恆稱其君之惡者; text

in Ching-men Shih Po-wu-kuan 荊門市博物館, *Kuo-tien Ch'u-mu chu-chien* 郭店楚墓竹簡 (Peking: Wen-wu, 1998), 141. Compare also "Chien-cheng" 諫諍, *Hsiao-ching chu-shu* 孝經注疏 (*Shih-san ching chu-shu*), 7.15.2558ab; as well as *Mencius* 4A.18, *Meng-tzu cheng-i* 15.522–24, and 4B.30, *Meng-tzu cheng-i* 17.598–601, where it is taken for granted that fathers and sons will have serious disagreements over moral issues that can even lead to estrangement between the two. Therefore it is asserted in both Mencian passages that fathers and sons do not "consider it a duty to be good to each other" 責善, that is, to gloss over each other's mistakes in the interest of saving their relationship. Cf. Huang Jen-erh 黃人二, "Kuo-tien Ch'u-chien 'Lu Mu-kung wen Tzu-ssu' k'ao-shih" 郭店楚簡魯穆公問子思考釋, in *Chang I-jen hsien-sheng ch'i-chih shou-ch'ing lun-wen chi*, vol. 1, 403f.

122. Compare, e.g., *Mao* 187: "Huang-niao," discussed in chapter 1 in the present volume.

123. *Ch'un-ch'iu Tso-chuan chu*, vol. 1, 267 (Min 閔 2 = 660 B.C.).

124. See, e.g., the "Minor Preface," *Mao-Shih cheng-i* 3B.320a. The same interpretation is accepted implicitly in *Han-Shih wai-chuan* 韓詩外傳 (*Ssu-pu ts'ung-k'an* 四部叢刊), 2.2bf.; and "Hsü Mu fu-jen" 許穆夫人, in Wang Chao-yüan 王照圓 (fl. 1879–1884), *Lieh-nü chuan pu-chu* 列女傳補註 (*Kuo-hsüeh chi-pen ts'ung-shu*), 3.43; cf. James Robert Hightower, trans., *Han Shih Wai Chuan: Han Ying's Illustrations of the Didactic Application of the* Classic of Songs, Harvard-Yenching Institute Monograph Series 11 (Cambridge, 1952), 40f.

125. Cf. Sommer, 172ff.

126. C. H. Wang, *The Bell and the Drum: Shih Ching as Formulaic Poetry in an Oral Tradition* (Berkeley and Los Angeles: University of California Press, 1974), 110ff., points out that the "cypress boat" is a *hsing* 興 in the *Odes* that consistently symbolizes a woman oppressed by her kin. He suggests further that the word *po* 柏 (cypress) may be intended as a play on words with *p'o* 迫 (press, coerce).

127. The best study of Pan Chao is still Swann; see also Bettina L. Knapp, *Images of Chinese Women: A Westerner's View* (Troy, N.Y.: Whitston, 1992), 18–40. O. B. van der Sprenkel discusses the *Han-shu* as a family project of the Pan clan in *Pan Piao, Pan Ku, and the Han History*, Centre for Oriental Studies Occasional Paper 3 (Canberra: Australian National University, 1964).

128. As late as the fourth century, however, it was still possible for Fan Ning to complain of childless widows who do not remarry as symptomatic of a decadent age. See Fang Hsüan-ling 房玄齡 (578–648) et al., *Chin-shu* 晉書 (Peking: Chung-hua, 1974), 75.1985f. Cf. Charles Holcombe, *In the Shadow of the Han: Literati Thought and Society at the Beginning of the Southern Dynasties* (Honolulu: University of Hawai'i Press, 1994), 54.

129. "Lieh-nü chuan," *Hou-Han shu* 84.2790. Because Pan Chao goes on to compare a woman's husband to her Heaven, it is possible that she has in mind the similar passage in "Sang-fu," *I-li chu-shu* 30.1106c. (As we have seen in n. 91, however, that text does not prohibit remarriage.) Other ritual texts also forbid women from marrying twice; see "Chiao t'e sheng" 郊特牲, *Li-chi cheng-i* 禮記正義 (*Shih-san ching chu-shu*), 26.1456b; and "Chia-ch'ü," *Po-hu t'ung shu-cheng* 10.467. Cf. *Hei Erh-shih-ssu shih*, vol. 1, 483, 661.

130. Cf., e.g., Sheng I, 337ff.; Liu Tseng-kuei, "Han-tai hun-yin kuan-hsi," 16ff.; "Han-tai te hao-men hun-yin" 漢代的豪門婚姻, in *Chung-kuo fu-nü shih*

lun-wen chi 中國婦女史論文集, ed. Li Yu-ning 李又寧 and Chang Yü-fa 張玉法 (Taipei: Shang-wu, 1981), 21 f.; Dull, 65 ff.; Ch'en Tung-yüan 陳東原, *Chung-kuo fu-nü sheng-huo shih* 中國婦女生活史 (Shanghai: Shang-wu, 1937), 55; Ch'en Ku-yüan, 148 ff.; and Tung Chia-tsun 董家遵, "Ts'ung Han tao Sung kua-fu tsai-chia hsi-su k'ao" 從漢到宋寡婦再嫁習俗考, *Chung-shan Ta-hsüeh Wen-shih hsüeh Yen-chiu-so yüeh-k'an* 中山大學文史學研究所月刊 3.1 (1934), 193–213. For more general discussions of the issue of remarriage, see, e.g., *Hei Erh-shih-ssu shih*, vol. 1, 35 f.; Hsieh Pao-fu 謝寶富, *Pei-ch'ao hun-sang li-su yen-chiu* 北朝婚喪禮俗研究 (Peking: Shou-tu Shih-fan Ta-hsüeh, 1998), 64–69; and Kuo Hsing-wen, 196 ff.

As is often observed, the "Hsiao-k'uang" (*Kuan-tzu chiao-cheng* 8.20.124) proposes that women who marry three times should be made into "grain pounders" 春穀. Cf., e.g., *Hei Erh-shih-ssu shih*, vol. 1, 19; Kung-chuan Hsiao, *A History of Chinese Political Thought*, vol. 1 (*From the Beginnings to the Sixth Century A.D.*), trans. F. W. Mote, Princeton Library of Asian Translations (Princeton, N.J.: 1979), 350; and Ch'en Ku-yüan, 151. Significantly, however, the parallel in "Kuan Chung tso Huan-kung wei cheng" 管仲佐桓公為政, *Kuo-yü* 6.235, which is otherwise virtually identical to the "Hsiao-k'uang," does not contain this stipulation. Therefore, the divergent passage in the "Hsiao-k'uang" may be an interpolation from Han times.

131. Tung Chung-shu, *Chüeh-yü* 決獄; text in *T'ai-p'ing yü-lan* 640.8a. Cf. Sarah A. Queen, *From Chronicle to Canon: The Hermeneutics of the* Spring and Autumn, *According to Tung Chung-shu*, Cambridge Studies in Chinese History, Literature, and Institutions (Cambridge, 1996), 141 f.; Benjamin E. Wallacker, "The Spring and Autumn Annals as a Source of Law in Han China," *Journal of Chinese Studies* 2.1 (1985), 65; and Dull, 68.

132. "Yüan Ang Ch'ao Ts'o chuan," *Han-shu* 49.2286. *Hei Erh-shih-ssu shih*, vol. 4, 2629, cites the event narrated in "Li Kuang Su Chien chuan," *Han-shu* 54.2453, in which the aforementioned Li Ling discovers that a group of convict women have been hiding among his troops (whereupon he beheads them), as another example of state-sponsored prostitution in the military. But the original text does not imply that the women were forced into prostitution as part of their sentence. Moreover, *Hei Erh-shih-ssu shih* cites the phrase *chan-shou san-ch'ien yü chi* 斬首三千餘級 ("He cut off more than three thousand heads") as though this means that Li Ling executed three thousand prostitutes, but it is clear in the *Han-shu* that the three thousand heads belonged to enemy soldiers killed the next day by his victorious troops. The authors of the *Hei Erh-shih-ssu shih* are usually not as careless as this.

133. *Han-chi* 漢紀 (*Kuo-hsüeh chi-pen ts'ung-shu*), 5.41; the marriage is recorded in "Hui-ti chi" 惠帝紀, *Han-shu* 2.90, and "Wai-ch'i chuan," *Han-shu* 97A.3940. This example is cited by both Kuo Hsing-wen, 86, and Liu Tseng-kuei, "Han-tai hun-yin kuan-hsi," 3 ff., but is perhaps not entirely convincing. The union was orchestrated by Empress Dowager Lü and was part of a series of impious acts (which also included her treatment of Lady Ch'i, discussed above) condemned in "Wu-hsing chih," *Han-shu* 27A.1330 f. So the lack of any objection to this marriage in the oldest sources may be only a reflection of Empress Dowager Lü's reign of terror. Cf. Homer H. Dubs, *History of the Former Han Dynasty* (Baltimore: Waverly, 1938–1955), vol. 1, 168 ff. and 181 f. T'ung Shu-yeh, 212, suggests that

Emperor Hui's marriage may be a vestige of an older marital system whereby such unions were common.

134. The source that is most frequently cited for such statements is Chung-ch'ang T'ung 仲長統 (A.D. 179–219), *Ch'ang-yen* 昌言; text in *Ch'ün-shu chih-yao* 群書治要 (*Kuo-hsüeh chi-pen ts'ung-shu*), 45.791. Cf., e.g., Liu Tseng-kuei, "Han-tai hun-yin kuan-hsi," 8; and Dull, 50. Surviving fragments of the *Ch'ang-yen* are collected in Yen K'o-chün 嚴可均 (1762–1843), *Ch'üan Shang-ku San-tai Ch'in Han San-kuo Liu-ch'ao wen* 全上古三代秦漢三國六朝文 (1893; repr., Peking: Chung-hua, 1958), *Ch'üan Hou-Han wen* 全後漢文, 88.1a–89.12a (this passage appears in 89.1a). But Chung-ch'ang T'ung composed this work at the very end of the Han dynasty, and so his testimony obviously cannot be taken as a reliable account of early Han society. Moreover, the author was a self-conscious moralist who saw signs all around him that civilization was coming to an end. Cf. Kuo Hsing-wen, 273; and esp. Etienne Balazs, "La crise sociale et la philosophie politique à la fin des Han," *T'oung Pao* 39 (1949), trans. as "Political Philosophy and Social Crisis at the End of the Han Dynasty," in *Chinese Civilization and Bureaucracy: Variations on a Theme*, trans. H. M. Wright, ed. Arthur F. Wright (New Haven, Conn.: Yale University Press, 1964), 213 ff. Nevertheless, Yang Shu-ta 楊樹達, *Han-tai hun-sang li-su k'ao* 漢代婚喪禮俗考 (Shanghai: Shang-wu, 1933), 22 ff., provides ample evidence from primary texts that early Han wedding banquets were indeed uproarious affairs.

135. "Yu-hsia chuan" 游俠傳, *Han-shu* 92.3712.

136. "Shih hun-li" 士昏禮, *I-li chu-shu* 4.961b–63a; and "Hun-i," *Li-chi cheng-i* 61.1680b. See also the commentary by Chu Pin 朱彬 (1753–1843) in his *Li-chi hsün-tsuan* 訓纂, ed. Jao Ch'in-nung 饒欽農, Shih-san ching Ch'ing-jen chu-shu (Peking: Chung-hua, 1996), 44.877 f.

137. Dull, 42 ff. This piece was so far ahead of its time that it implicitly refuted much of the article immediately following it in the volume, i.e., Tai Yen-hui, "Divorce in Traditional Chinese Law," in Buxbaum, 75–106. (Note, on the other hand, that *Mencius* 6B.1, *Meng-tzu cheng-i* 24.805, refers to one of the Six Rituals, namely *ch'in-ying* 親迎, or "personally welcoming [the bride]," as paradigmatic of a ritually correct marriage; cf. *Hei Erh-shih-ssu shih*, vol. 1, 331.) Dull goes on to show that divorce procedures in Han times also bear little resemblance to the prescriptions found in traditional ritual codes. For other recent studies of the Six Rituals, see, e.g., *Hei Erh-shih-ssu shih*, vol. 1, 16 f.; Kuo Chen-hua 郭振華, *Chung-kuo ku-tai jen-sheng li-su wen-hua* 中國古代人生禮俗文化, Ch'uan-t'ung wen-hua yü hsien-tai wen-hua wen-ts'ung (Hsi-an: Shensi jen-min, 1998), 94 ff.; Kuo Hsing-wen, 236–239; Sheng I, 104 ff.; Ma Chih-su 馬之驌, "Wo-kuo ch'uan-t'ung chieh-hun te p'in-li" 我國傳統結婚的聘禮, in Li Yu-ning and Chang Yü-fa, 2 ff.; and Ch'en Ku-yüan, 99 ff. Finally, for an incisive view of differences between women's quotidian lives in Han times and the idealized lives laid out for them in ritual codes, see Michael Nylan, "Golden Spindles and Axes: Elite Women in the Achaemenid and Han Empires," in Chenyang Li, ed., *The Sage and the Second Sex: Confucianism, Ethics, and Gender* (Chicago: Open Court, 2000), 203 ff.

138. "Chia-ch'ü," *Po-hu t'ung shu-cheng* 10.466.

139. Compare the translation in Tjan, vol. 1, 250.

140. "Ta-lüeh," *Hsün-tzu chi-chieh* 19.27.496. The interpretation of *sha-chih* 殺 止 follows the commentary of Wang Yin-chih.

141. Other ritual texts also stipulate that weddings should take place in the second month of spring; see, e.g., "Mei-shih" 媒氏, *Chou-li chu-shu* 14.733b; and "Hsia hsiao-cheng" 夏小正, in Wang P'in-chen 王聘珍 (eighteenth century), *Ta-Tai Li-chi chieh-ku* 大戴禮記解詁, ed. Wang Wen-chin 王文錦, Shih-san ching Ch'ing-jen chu-shu (Peking: Chung-hua, 1983), 2.47.31. (Cf. Biot, vol. 1, 307 n. 6.) I have not found a similar comment in the *Li-chi*, but it cannot be a coincidence that "Yüeh-ling" 月令, *Li-chi cheng-i* 15.1361c, calls for sacrifices to the god of matchmaking 禖 precisely in the second month of spring. This passage also appears verbatim in "Chung-ch'un chi" 仲春紀, *Lü-shih ch'un-ch'iu chiao-shih* 2.63 (see also the rich commentary at 67 n. 12). Because the *Lü-shih ch'un-ch'iu* is a reliable pre-Han text, there appears to be good reason to date both the traditions of vernal and hibernal marriages to ancient times. Cf. also Kuo Hsing-wen, 176 ff; and Chow Tse-tung, "The Childbirth Myth and Ancient Chinese Medicine: A Study of Aspects of the *Wu* Tradition," in Roy and Tsien, 54 f.

142. Commentators have tried to solve this conundrum for almost two millennia. The fullest exposition of the relevant issues appears in the commentary of Sun I-jang 孫詒讓 (1848–1908) to the *Chou-li*; text in "Mei-shih," *Chou-li cheng-i* 周禮正義 (*Kuo-hsüeh chi-pen ts'ung-shu*), 7.26.68 ff.

Another notorious problem with the received ritual codes has to do with the appropriate ages for men and women to marry. The rule that men should marry at the age of thirty *sui* (i.e., twenty-eight or twenty-nine, by our reckoning) and women at twenty (or, in some cases, at any time between the ages of fifteen and twenty), goes back to such texts as "Mei-shih," *Chou-li chu-shu* 14.733a; *Ch'un-ch'iu Ku-liang chuan chu-shu* 春秋穀梁傳注疏 (*Shih-san ching chu-shu*), 11.2408c (Wen 12 = 615 B.C.); and "Yao-tien" 堯典, *Shang-shu ta-chuan* (Lau and Chen, 2). Similarly, "Chieh-yung shang" 節用上, *Mo-tzu chiao-chu* 6.20.248, complains that men and women should be married at twenty and fifteen, respectively, but that now the people "do as they please" 次 [= 恣] (following the commentary of Sun I-jang). Consequently, later ritual texts did not fail to incorporate this injunction as well; see, e.g., "Nei-tse," *Li-chi cheng-i* 28.1471b; "Pen-ming" 本命, *Ta-Tai Li-chi chieh-ku* 13.80.251; and "Chia-ch'ü, *Po-hu t'ung shu-cheng* 10.453–457. However, many classical writers disputed the authenticity of this rule, pointing out numerous counterexamples in the ancient records. One of the oldest such dissenting voices is that of Wang Ch'ung 王充 (A.D. 27–ca. 100); see "Ch'i-shih," 齊世, *Lun-heng chiao-shih* 18.804. Similarly, "Fan-lun," in Liu Wen-tien 劉文典, *Huai-nan Hung-lieh chi-chieh* 淮南鴻烈集解, ed. Feng I 馮逸 and Ch'iao Hua 喬華, Hsin-pien Chu-tzu chi-ch'eng (Peking: Chung-hua, 1989), 13.424, points out that King Wen was already a father by the age of fifteen. More orthodox commentators later began to express doubts as well (though they never cite Wang Ch'ung, who was not considered a major thinker until recent times): see, e.g., the sub-commentary of Chia Kung-yen 賈公彥 (fl. A.D. 650) to *Chou-li chu-shu* 14.733a, citing the opinion of Wang Su 王肅 (A.D. 195–256); and the commentary of Fan Ning 范甯 (A.D. 339–401) to *Ch'un-ch'iu Ku-liang chuan chu-shu* 11.2408c, citing the opinion of Ch'iao Chou 譙周 (A.D. 199–270). Once again, the best overview of commentarial opinions on this issue is Sun I-jang's commentary to "Mei-shih," *Chou-li cheng-i* 7.26.64 ff. See also *Hei Erh-shih-ssu shih*, vol. 1, 15, 34 f., 337 f.; Sheng I, 49 ff.; Englert, 18 ff.; Ch'en Ku-yüan, 80–85; and Liang Chang-chü 梁章鉅 (1775–1849), "Chia-li i" 家禮一, *T'ui-an sui-pi* 退庵隨筆 (*Ssu-pu pei-yao*), 9.2a.

For obvious reasons, these authors were all unaware of the recently excavated text "T'ang Yü chih tao" 唐虞之道, which asserts that the "Sages of the past" 古者聖人 were capped at the age of twenty and "possessed families" 有家 at thirty; text in *Kuo-tien Ch'u-mu chu-chien*, 158.

143. "Shih hun-li," *I-li chu-shu* 4.961b ff.; "Chia-ch'ü," *Po-hu t'ung shu-cheng* 10.457.

144. Cf. Edward L. Shaughnessy, *Before Confucius: Studies in the Creation of the Chinese Classics*, SUNY Series in Chinese Philosophy and Culture (Albany, N.Y., 1997), 21 f.; and idem, *I Ching: The Classic of Changes*, Classics of Ancient China (New York: Ballantine, 1996), 10 ff. *Mao* 181 ("Hung-yen" 鴻鴈) is especially illustrative; see also *Mao* 159 ("Chiu-yü"), discussed in chapter 1, above. Finally, compare the appearance of the emblem in *Chou-I cheng-i* 5.63c, hexagram *Chien* 漸: "The wild geese gradually advance to the land. The husband campaigns and does not return. The wife is pregnant but does not give birth" 鴻漸于陸。夫征不復，婦孕不育.

145. According to Cheng Hsüan, *Mao-Shih cheng-i* 2B.302c, the deep crossings in the ford indicate a setting in midautumn. But he is more or less forced into this reading, since he believes that the rites of marriage should begin in the autumn and culminate in the spring. Cf. also Marcel Granet, *Fêtes et chansons anciennes de la Chine* (Paris: Ernest Leroux, 1919), 102.

146. *Analects* 14.39; *Lun-yü chi-shih* 30.1031–1035.

147. Compare the translation in Lau, *Analects*, 130.

148. Most notably in the phrase *ssu chi erh i i* 斯己而已矣, which is sometimes taken as an error for *ssu i erh i i* 斯已而已矣 ("then just stop," or the like).

149. It is impossible to tell whether Confucius' final comment is intended sincerely or sarcastically. For further exegesis on "P'ao yu k'u-yeh" and its use in this passage from the *Analects*, see Steven Van Zoeren, *Poetry and Personality: Reading, Exegesis, and Hermeneutics in Traditional China* (Stanford, Calif.: Stanford University Press, 1991), 27 and 36; and Jeffrey K. Riegel, "Poetry and the Legend of Confucius's Exile," in *Sinological Studies Dedicated to Edward H. Schafer*, ed. Paul W. Kroll, *Journal of the American Oriental Society* 106.1 (1986), 15 f.

150. In his commentary to "Chia-ch'ü," *Po-hu t'ung shu-cheng* 10.457, Ch'en Li lists several other early explanations of this sort; see also Sheng I, 105 ff. The oldest surviving explanation is probably that of Cheng Chung 鄭眾 (d. A.D. 83) in his *Hun-li* 婚禮; text in Ou-yang Hsün 歐陽詢 (557–641) et al., *I-wen lei-chü* 藝文類聚 (Taipei: Hsin-hsing, 1969), 91.4b. Many early calendrical texts list the arrival of wild geese as a regular feature of the second or third month of autumn. See, e.g., "Chi-ch'iu chi" 季秋紀, *Lü-shih ch'un-ch'iu chiao-shih* 9.467; "Shih-tse" 時則, *Huai-nan Hung-lieh chi-chieh* 5.175, 5.177; and "Yüeh-ling," *Li-chi cheng-i* 16.1373c, 17.1379a. Given these parallels, it is possible also that the statement *hou niao-lai* 候鳥來 ("we expect the birds to arrive") in "Chung-ch'iu chi"

仲秋紀, *Lü-shih ch'un-chiu chiao-shih* 8.421, may be a graphic error for *hou yen-lai* 候鴈來 ("we expect the wild geese to arrive").

P'eng Ta-i 彭大翼 (fl. 1573–1595), "T'ien-wen" 天文, *Shan-t'ang ssu-k'ao* 山堂肆考 (*Ying-yin Wen-yüan ko Ssu-k'u ch'üan-shu* 影印文淵閣四庫全書), 5.3a, observes that the wild geese were said to arrive when "the frost descends" 霜降; this is noteworthy in view of Hsün-tzu's statement that one should welcome the bride precisely when the frost descends. Cf. also Sheng I, 106; and Ma Chih-su, 4. The same calendrical texts also place the "descending of frost" in the second or third month of autumn: "Chung-ch'iu chi," *Lü-shih ch'un-ch'iu chiao-shih* 8.422; "Chi-ch'iu chi," *Lü-shih ch'un-ch'iu chiao-shih* 9.467; "T'ien-wen" 天文, *Huai-nan Hung-lieh chi-chieh* 3.106; "Shih-tse," *Huai-nan Hung-lieh chi-chieh* 5.178; "Yüeh-ling," *Li-chi cheng-i* 17.1379b. (Similarly, "Yüan-yu," in Hung Hsing-tsu 洪興祖 (1090–1155), *Ch'u-tz'u chang-chü pu-chu* 章句補注, in *Chu'u-tz'u chu pa-chung* 注八種, Chung-kuo wen-hsüeh ming-chu [Taipei: Shih-chieh, 1990], 5.97, places the time of "descending frost" after the "falling of the fragrant herbs" 芳草之先零.) The ritual texts, however, do not make the connection between the arrival of wild geese and the descent of frost. The point is irrelevant to their purposes, because they agree that marriages should take place in the spring.

151. Tjan's careful study of the *Po-hu t'ung* (esp. vol. 1, 57 ff.) confirms that its handling of classical texts could be astonishingly sloppy; at times the authors even confused classical commentaries with the words of the classics themselves. Furthermore, Chung Wen-cheng 鍾文烝 (1818–1877), *Ku-liang pu-chu* 穀梁補注 (*Kuo-hsüeh chi-pen ts'ung-shu*), 14.369 (Wen 12 = 615 B.C.), has pointed out another case of careless reading that most other scholars have missed. "Chia-ch'ü," *Po-hu t'ung shu-cheng* 10.456, quotes the *Ku-liang* as follows: "At twenty-five a male's heart is bound; at fifteen a female may be married. They are stimulated by *yin* and *yang*" 男二十五繫心，女十五許嫁，感陰陽也. In fact, the *Ku-liang* contains no such passage, and Chung Wen-cheng suggests that it must have appeared in some ancient commentary.

152. *Ch'un-ch'iu Tso-chuan chu*, vol. 4, 1220 f. (Chao 1 = 541 B.C.); "Ch'ü-li shang," *Li-chi cheng-i* 2.1241a.

153. On the authenticity of the *Po-hu t'ung*, see esp. Tjan, vol. 1, 1–66. The traditional attribution to Pan Ku can hardly be upheld; Tjan points out many passages in the text that may be as late as post-Han. The *Li-chi*, similarly, is a *mixtum compositum* that may well have coalesced after the *Po-hu t'ung*; see Jeffrey K. Riegel, "*Li chi*," in *Early Chinese Texts: A Bibliographic Guide*, ed. Michael Loewe, Early China Monograph Series 2 (Berkeley, Calif., 1993), 294 f. (Riegel apparently accepts without comment the traditional date of A.D. 79 for the *Po-hu t'ung*); and especially Wang Meng-ou 王夢鷗, "Tsung-hsü" 總敘, *Li-chi chiao-cheng* 校證 (Taipei: I-wen, 1976), 1–11. Cf. also Kanaya Osamu 金谷治, *Shin Kan shisōshi kenkyū* 秦漢思想史研究 (Tokyo: Heirakuji, 1960), 338–353, who sees certain chapters of the *Li-chi* (including "Hun-i," "Chiao t'e sheng," and other chapters considered here) as the work of Han Confucians who attempted to clarify and expand on late Warring States notions of "ritual" 禮. However, he dates these works to the early Han period, on the basis of their frequent citations from pre-Ch'in texts and evident indebtedness to Hsün-tzu.

154. For a general discussion of the practice of reinventing history for contemporary moral or political purposes, see Eric Hobsbawm, "The Social Function of the Past: Some Questions," *Past and Present* 55 (1972), reprinted as "The Sense of the Past" in *On History* (London: Little, Brown and Co., Abacus, 1998), esp. 18 ff.

Epilogue

1. See, e.g., Lin Chien-ming 林劍鳴, *Hsin-pien Ch'in Han shih* 新編秦漢史 (Taipei: Wu-nan, 1992), vol. 2, 1247–1320; Cho-yun Hsu, "The Roles of the Literati and of Regionalism in the Fall of the Han Dynasty," in *The Collapse of Ancient States and Civilizations*, ed. Norman Yoffee and George L. Cowgill (Tucson: University of Arizona Press, 1988), 176–195; Michael Loewe, "The Conduct of Government and the Issues at Stake (A.D. 57–167)," in *The Cambridge History of China*, vol. 1 (*The Ch'in and Han Empires, 221 B.C.–A.D. 220*), ed. Denis Twitchett and Michael Loewe (Cambridge, 1986), 291–316; B.J. Mansvelt Beck, "The Fall of Han," in Twitchett and Loewe, 317–376; Ch'en Ch'i-yün 陳啟雲, "Kuan-yü Tung-Han shih te chi-ko wen-t'i: ch'ing-i, tang-ku, huang-chin" 關於東漢史的幾個問題：清議、黨錮、黃巾, in *Yen-yüan lun-hsüeh chi* 燕園論學集 (Peking: Peking University, 1984), reprinted in *Han Chin Liu-ch'ao wen-hua, she-hui, chih-tu—Chung-hua chung-ku ch'ien-ch'i shih yen-chiu* 漢晉六朝文化、社會、制度—中華中古前期史研究 (Taipei: Hsin wen-feng, 1996), 55–73; Wang Chung-lo 王仲犖, *Wei Chin Nan-pei-ch'ao shih* 魏晉南北朝史 (Shanghai: Jen-min, 1979), vol. 1, 1–29; T'ung-tsu Ch'ü, *Han Social Structure*, ed. Jack L. Dull, Han Dynasty China 1 (Seattle: University of Washington Press, 1972), 202–247; and Lü Ssu-mien 呂思勉, *Ch'in Han shih* 秦漢史 (n.p.: K'ai-ming, 1947; repr., Hong Kong: T'ai-p'ing, 1962), vol. 1, 296–334.

2. See, e.g., T'ung-tsu Ch'ü, 241 ff. It is not incorrect to trace the origin of Chinese student movements, which have once again made headlines in recent years, to these demonstrations more than 1,800 years ago. Protesting, when circumstances call for it, is regarded as a basic element of students' identity and self-consciousness.

3. For the dates, see Liu Wen-ying 劉文英, *Wang Fu p'ing-chuan fu Ts'ui Shih Chung-ch'ang T'ung p'ing-chuan* 王符評傳附崔寔、仲長統評傳, Chung-kuo ssu-hsiang chia p'ing-chuan ts'ung-shu 27 (Nan-ching: Nan-ching Ta-hsüeh, 1993), 2 ff. See also Chin Fa-ken 金發根, "Wang Fu sheng-tsu nien-sui te k'ao-cheng chi *Ch'ien-fu lun* hsieh-ting shih-chien te t'uei-lun" 王符生卒年歲的考證及潛夫論寫定時間的推論, *Kung-chu tsung-t'ung Chiang-kung pa-chih chin erh hua-tan Li-shih Yü-yen Yen-chiu-so ch'eng-li ssu-shih chou-nien chi-nien* 恭祝總統蔣公八秩晉二華誕歷史語言研究所成立四十周年紀念, *Bulletin of the Institute of History and Philology* 40 (1969), 781–799.

4. See esp. his essay "Fou-ch'ih" 郅侈; text in P'eng To 彭鐸, *Ch'ien-fu lun chiao-cheng* 潛夫論校正, Hsin-pien Chu-tzu chi-ch'eng (Peking: Chung-hua, 1985), 3.12.120–142. See also Patricia Ebrey, "The Economic and Social History of Later Han," in Twitchett and Loewe, 609 ff.; Ch'en Ch'i-yün, "Confucian, Legalist, and Taoist Thought in Later Han," in Twitchett and Loewe, 789–794; and Etienne Balazs, *Chinese Civilization and Bureaucracy: Variations on a Theme*,

trans. H. M. Wright, ed. Arthur F. Wright (New Haven, Conn.: Yale University Press, 1964), 198–205.

5. For the reference, see chapter 3, n. 134, above. See also Sheng I, 118 f.; and Michael Loewe, "The Failure of the Confucian Ethic in Later Han Times," in *China: Dimensionen der Geschichte*, ed. Peter Kuhfus (Tübingen, 1991), reprinted in Michael Loewe, *Divination, Mythology, and Monarchy in Han China*, University of Cambridge Oriental Publications 48 (Cambridge, 1994), 266. For more on Chung-ch'ang T'ung, see, e.g., Horiike Nobuo 堀池信夫, *Kan Gi shisōshi kenkyū* 漢魏思想史研究 (Tokyo: Meiji, 1988), 402–418; Uchiyama Toshihiko 內山俊彥, *Chūgoku kotai shisōshi ni okeru shizen ninshiki* 中國古代思想史における自然認識, Tōyōgaku sōsho 31 (Tokyo: Sōbunsha, 1987), 364–393; Kung-chuan Hsiao, *A History of Chinese Political Thought*, vol. 1 (*From the Beginnings to the Sixth Century A.D.*), trans. F. W. Mote, Princeton Library of Asian Translations (Princeton, N.J., 1979), 545 ff.; Balazs, 213–225; and Alfred Forke, *Geschichte der mittelalterlichen chinesischen Philosophie*, Abhandlungen aus dem Gebiet der Auslandskunde 41 (repr., Hamburg: Cram, de Gruyter, and Co., 1964), 172–175.

6. "Fou-ch'ih," *Ch'ien-fu lun chiao-cheng* 3.12.125.

7. The first eight lines of the poem, which describe the speaker's vantage point high in the skies, are omitted.

8. This line may be garbled in the original. One edition reads *chih* 止 for *shang* 上; the sense is far from transparent in either case.

9. "Lung-hsi hsing" 隴西行; text in Hsü Ling 徐陵 (A.D. 507–583), *Yü-t'ai hsin-yung* 玉臺新詠, ed. Wu Chao-i 吳兆宜 (*Kuo-hsüeh chi-pen ts'ung-shu*), 1.9–11. See also Kuo Mao-ch'ien 郭茂倩 (fl. 1084), *Yüeh-fu shih-chi* 樂府詩集 (Peking: Chung-hua, 1979), 37.542–543. The poem probably dates from the late Eastern Han.

10. Compare the translations in Anne Birrell, *Popular Songs and Ballads of Han China* (London: Unwin Hyman, 1988; repr., Honolulu: University of Hawai'i Press, 1993), 173–174 (with insightful comments); and *New Songs from a Jade Terrace: An Anthology of Early Chinese Love Poetry* (London: George Allen and Unwin, 1982; repr., New York: Penguin, 1986), 35–36.

11. The locus classicus for this rule (which is related to the idea of *nei* and *wai*, discussed in chapter 2 of the present volume) is *Ch'un-ch'iu Tso-chuan chu* 春秋左傳注, 2d ed., Chung-kuo ku-tien ming-chu i-chu ts'ung-shu (Peking: Chung-hua, 1990), vol. 1, 399 (Hsi 22 = 638 B.C.): "When welcoming or seeing off [guests], a wife does not go out of the gate" 婦人送迎不出門. The line is repeated in the "Chi-miu" 疾謬 chapter of the *Pao-p'u-tzu* 抱朴子; text in Yang Ming-chao 楊明照, *Pao-p'u-tzu wai-p'ien chiao-chien* 外篇校箋, Hsin-pien Chu-tzu chi-ch'eng (Peking: Chung-hua, 1991), 25.614. In her "Nü-chieh" ("Lieh-nü chuan," *Hou-Han shu* 後漢書 [Peking: Chung-hua, 1965], 84.2790), Pan Chao expressly forbids women to "watch at the gates" 看視門戶. Compare also the poem "K'u-hsiang p'ien" 苦相篇, by Fu Hsüan 傅玄 (217–278), *Yü-t'ai hsin-yung* 2.61: "Pity me, that I am a girl! / My lowliness is hard to convey. / Boys can stand at the gate" 苦相身為女，卑陋難再陳，男兒當門戶. Similar injunctions are found in ritual manuals from later dynasties; for the example of the *T'ai-kung chia-chiao* 太公家教, a popular text discovered at Tun-huang 敦煌, see, e.g., Paul Demiéville, *L'œuvre de Wang le zélateur (Wang Fan-tche) suivie des Instructions domes-*

tiques de l'Aïeul (T'ai-kong kia-kiao): Poèmes populaires des T'ang (VIIIe–Xe siècles), Bibliothèque de l'Institut des Hautes Études Chinoises 26 (Paris, 1982), 694 and 696 (=secs. 10A and 10D).

Incidentally, in ancient Greece—which maintained a concept of inner and outer sex roles comparable to that of ancient China (cf. chapter 2, n. 47 in the present volume)—it was also considered shameful for a woman to open the front door herself or to stand in the doorway and talk to passersby. In one text, leaning out the door is taken to be a sign that a woman is an adulteress. See James N. Davidson, *Courtesans and Fishcakes: The Consuming Passions of Classical Athens* (New York: Harper Collins, 1997), 128; cf. also Sue Blundell, *Women in Ancient Greece* (Cambridge: Harvard University Press, 1995), 135.

12. *Mao* 138 (discussed in chapter 1 in the present volume).

13. "Chi-miu," *Pao-p'u-tzu wai-p'ien* 25.616–618 and 628.

14. *T'ien* 畋 could also denote hunters.

15. Compare the translation in Jay Sailey, *The Master Who Embraces Simplicity: A Study of the Philosopher Ko Hung, A.D. 283–343*, Asian Library Series 9 (San Francisco: Chinese Materials Center, 1978), 142–143 and 148.

16. See, e.g., "Wei-chih" 微旨 and "Shih-tai" 釋滯; text in Wang Ming 王明, *Pao-p'u-tzu nei-p'ien chiao-shih* 內篇校釋, 2d ed., Hsin-pien Chu-tzu chi-ch'eng (Peking: Chung-hua, 1985), 6.129 and 8.150, respectively.

17. Cf., e.g., Hsü K'ang-sheng 許抗生, *Wei Chin ssu-hsiang shih* 魏晉思想史, Kuei-kuan ts'ung-k'an 28 (Taipei, 1992), 496–498; Ying-shih Yü, "Individualism and the Neo-Taoist Movement in Wei-Chin China," in *Individualism and Holism: Studies in Confucian and Taoist Values*, ed. Donald J. Munro, Michigan Monographs in Chinese Studies 52 (Ann Arbor, 1985), 125; Siegfried Englert, *Materialien zur Stellung der Frau und zur Sexualität im vormodernen und modernen China*, Heidelberger Schriften zur Ostasienkunde 1 (Frankfurt: Haag und Herchen, 1980), 63 f.; Beatrice Spade, "The Education of Women in China during the Southern Dynasties," *Journal of Asian History* 13.1 (1979), 33; and Kung-chuan Hsiao, 635 f. and 655. Cf. also *Chin-shu* 晉書 (Peking: Chung-hua, 1974), 5.136.

For a recent critique of the historiographical trope of "individualism" in Wei-Chin China, see Michael Nylan, "Confucian Piety and Individualism in Han China," *Journal of the American Oriental Society* 116.1 (1996), esp. 22–26.

18. As cited in the "Jen-tan" 任誕 chapter of the *Shih-shuo hsin-yü* 世說新語; text in Yü Chia-hsi 余嘉錫, *Shih-shuo hsin-yü chien-shu* 箋疏, ed. Chou Tsu-mo 周祖謨 et al., rev. ed. (Shanghai: Ku-chi, 1993), 23.730. Compare the translation in Richard B. Mather, *Shih-shuo Hsin-yü: A New Account of Tales of the World* (Minneapolis: University of Minnesota Press, 1976), 374. See also *Chin-shu* 49.1361.

19. Scholars disagree over the appropriateness of the terms "gentry," "aristocracy," "nobility," "oligarchy," "literati," etc. (The most common Chinese terms are *shih-ta-fu* 士大夫 and *kuei-tsu* 貴族.) See, e.g., Albert E. Dien, "Introduction," in *State and Society in Early Medieval China* (Stanford, Calif.: Stanford University Press, 1990), 4 ff.; Patricia Buckley Ebrey, *The Aristocratic Families of Early Imperial China: A Case Study of the Po-ling Ts'ui Family*, Cambridge Studies in Chinese History, Literature and Institutions (Cambridge, 1978), 1 ff.; David G. Johnson, *The Medieval Chinese Oligarchy*, Westview Special Studies on China and East Asia (Boulder, Colo., 1977), 1 ff.; Wolfram Eberhard, *Conquerors and Rulers: Social*

Forces in Medieval China, 2d ed. (Leiden: E. J. Brill, 1970), 42 f. In what follows, these various terms are used more or less interchangeably, because the controversial issues are not directly relevant to this study.

20. See, e.g., Charles Holcombe, *In the Shadow of the Han: Literati Thought and Society at the Beginning of the Southern Dynasties* (Honolulu: University of Hawai'i Press, 1994), 17; and Nakamura Keiji 中村圭爾, "'Kyōri' no ronri: Rikuchō kizoku shakai no ideorogii" 鄉里の論理：六朝貴族社會のイデオロギー, *Tōyōshi kenkyū* 東洋史研究 41.1 (1982), 1–27.

21. For one of the most influential accounts of this topic, see Tanigawa Michio, *Medieval Chinese Society and the Local "Community,"* trans. Joshua A. Fogel (Berkeley and Los Angeles: University of California Press, 1985). See also Nakamura Keiji, "Rikuchōshi to 'chiiki shakai'" 六朝史と地域社會, in *Chūgoku chū- shishi kenkyū: Zokuhen* 中國中世史研究：續編, ed. Chūgoku chūshishi kenkyūkai 中國中世史研究會 (Kyoto: Kyōtō Daigaku gakujutsu, 1995), 36–60; Wang Chung-lo, vol. 1, 378–507; and Ch'en Ch'i-yün, "Chung-kuo chung-ku 'shih-tsu cheng-chih' yüan-yüan k'ao" 中國中古士族政治淵源考, *Hsin-Ya hsüeh-pao* 新亞學報 12 (1977), reprinted in Ch'en, *Han Chin Liu-ch'ao wen-hua,* 129–169.

22. This point was first articulated by Chao I in his *Nien-erh shih cha-chi* 廿二 史札記 (1795; repr., Taipei: Hua-shih, 1977), 12.254. See also Holcombe, 13 and 39; Richard B. Mather, "Individualist Expressions of the Outsiders during the Six Dynasties," in Munro, 210; and Helwig Schmidt-Glintzer, "Der Buddhismus im frühen Mittelalter und der Wandel der Lebensführung bei der Gentry im Süden," *Saeculum* 23 (1972), 289.

23. Kung Pin 龔斌, *T'ao Yüan-ming chi chiao-chien* 陶淵明集校箋, Chung-kuo ku-tien wen-hsüeh ts'ung-shu (Shanghai: Ku-chi, 1996), 6.402–403.

24. Cf., e.g., Holcombe, 55; Hsü Cho-yün, "Comparisons of Idealized Societies in Chinese History: Confucian and Taoist Models," in *Sages and Filial Sons: Mythology and Archaeology in Ancient China,* ed. Julia Ching and R. W. L. Guisso (Hong Kong: Chinese University Press, 1991), 54–57; Ying-shih Yü, 123; Kuo Yin-t'ien 郭銀田, *T'ien-yüan shih-jen T'ao Ch'ien* 田園詩人陶潛 (repr., Taipei: San-jen, 1974), 185 f.; and Ch'en Yin-k'o 陳寅恪, "'T'ao-hua yüan chi' p'ang-cheng" 桃花 源記旁證, *Ch'ing-hua hsüeh-pao* 清華學報 11 (1938), 79–88.

25. Cf., e.g., Liu Chen-tung 劉振東, *Chung-kuo Ju-hsüeh shih: Wei Chin Nan-pei-ch'ao chüan* 中國儒學史：魏晉南北朝卷 (Kuang-chou: Kuang-tung chiao-yü, 1998), 130 ff.

26. "Chin-yu fu" 近遊賦, reconstructed from fragments in *Ch'üan Chin-wen* 全晉文 (Yen K'o-chün, 嚴可均 [1762–1843], *Ch'üan Shang-ku San-tai Ch'in Han San-kuo Liu-ch'ao wen* 全上古三代秦漢三國六朝文 [1893; repr., Peking: Chung-hua, 1958]), 87.2a. Cf. Ying-shih Yü, 129; and Spade, 31.

27. "Huo-ni" 惑溺, *Shih-shuo hsin-yü chien-shu* 35.922. Cf. also I Chung-t'ien, 易中天, *Chung-kuo te nan-jen ho nü-jen* 中國的男人和女人, I Chung-t'ien suei-pi-t'i hsüeh-shu chu-tso, Chung-kuo wen-hua hsi-lieh 2 (Shanghai: Wen-i, 2000), 157; Tu Yung-ming 杜永明 et al., *Hei Erh-shih-ssu shih* 黑二十四史 (Peking: Chung-kuo hua-ch'iao, 1998) [cited henceforth as *Hei Erh-shih-ssu shih*; see n. 20 in the introduction of the present volume], vol. 1, 31; and Hsü Shih-ying 許世瑛, "*Shih-shuo hsin-yü* chung ti-erh shen ch'eng tai-tz'u yen-chiu" 世說新語中第二身稱代詞研 究, *Chi-nien Tung Tso-pin Tung T'ung-ho liang hsien-sheng lun-wen chi* 紀念董作賓、

董同龢兩先生論文集, *Bulletin of the Institute of History and Philology* 36.1 (1965), 211.

28. Compare the translation in Mather, *Shih-shuo Hsin-yü,* 488.

29. For more on the "urban hermits," see esp. Wakatsuki Toshihide 若槻俊秀, "Chūgoku ni okeru injakan no hensen: Sanrin no inja kara shichō no inja e" 中國における隱者觀の變遷：山林の隱者から市朝の隱者へ, *Bungei ronsō* 文藝論叢 8 (1964), 13–20, and 9 (1964), 65–73; as well as Aat Vervoorn, *Men of the Cliffs and Caves: The Development of the Chinese Eremitic Tradition to the End of the Han Dynasty* (Hong Kong: Chinese University Press, 1990), 203–227; Wolfgang Bauer, "The Hidden Hero: Creation and Disintegration of the Ideal of Eremitism," in Munro, 169; and Li Chi, "The Changing Concept of the Recluse in Chinese Literature," *Harvard Journal of Asiatic Studies* 24 (1962–1963), 241 ff.

30. "Jen-tan," *Shih-shuo hsin-yü chien-shu* 23.727, 731, and 733. For his grief over a girl whom he did not know, see the passage from the lost *Chin-shu* 晉書 of Wang Yin 王隱 (fl. fourth century) cited in the commentary of Liu Chün 劉峻 (462–521) to "Jen-tan," *Shih-shuo hsin-yü chien-shu* 23.730.

31. See the passage from the lost *Chin-chi* 晉紀 of Teng Ts'an 鄧粲 (fl. fourth century) cited in the commentary of Liu Chün to "Jen-tan," *Shih-shuo hsin-yü chien-shu* 23.731.

32. Cf., e.g., Ning Chia 寧稼, *Wei Chin feng-tu—Chung-ku wen-jen sheng-huo hsing-wei te wen-hua i-yün* 魏晉風度—中古文人生活行為的文化意蘊, Ko-lun-pu hsüeh-shu wen-k'u (Peking: Tung-fang, 1996), 169 f.; Holcombe, 93; Sun Shu-ch'i 孫述圻, *Liu-ch'ao ssu-hsiang shih* 六朝思想史, Liu-ch'ao ts'ung-shu (Nanching: Nan-ching ch'u-pan-she, 1992), 310; Ying-shih Yü, 140; Bauer, 169; Mather, "Individualist Expressions," 203; Donald Holzman, *Poetry and Politics: The Life and Works of Juan Chi, A.D. 210–263* (Cambridge: Cambridge University Press, 1976), 73 ff.; and Etienne Balazs, "Entre Révolte nihiliste et évasion mystique: Les courants intellectuels en Chine au IIIe siècle de notre ère," *Etudes Asiatiques* 2 (1948), 27–55, trans. H. M. Wright as "Nihilistic Revolt or Mystical Escapism: Currents of Thought in China during the Third Century A.D.," in Balazs, *Chinese Civilization and Bureaucracy,* 236 ff.

33. See, e.g., Kuo Hsiang's commentary to "Ta tsung-shih" 大宗師, *Chuang-tzu chi-shih* 3A.6.267 n. 1.

34. See the passage of the lost *Tu-chi* 妒記 by Yü T'ung-chih 虞通之 (fl. fifth century) cited in the commentary of Liu Chün to "Hsien-yüan" 賢媛, *Shih-shuo hsin-yü chien-shu* 19.694. Yü Chia-hsi thinks the anecdote might be fabricated, because he doubts that anyone in Hsieh An's household would have attributed "Kuan-chü" to the Duke of Chou. For our purposes, however, it is sufficient that *someone* wrote the story in the Six Dynasties period. Cf. also *Hei Erh-shih-ssu shih,* vol. 1, 135; Jean Pierre Diény, *Portrait anecdotique d'un gentilhomme Chinois: Xie An (320–385) d'après le* Shishuo xinyu, Bibliothèque de l'Institut des Hautes Études Chinoises 28 (Paris, 1993), 91; Englert, 65; and Howard S. Levy, *Chinese Sex Jokes in Traditional Times,* Asian Folklore and Social Life Monographs 58, Sino-Japanese Sexology Classics Series 5 (Taipei, 1973), item 75.

The most famous attack on the Confucian classics was that of Hsi K'ang 嵇康 (223–262). See especially his "Nan 'Tzu-jan hao-hsüeh lun'" 難自然好學論; text in Tai Ming-yang 戴明揚, *Hsi K'ang chi chiao-chu* 集校注 (Peking: Jen-min, 1962),

7.259–264. See also Donald Holzman, *La vie et la pensée de Hi K'ang (223–262 ap. J.-C.)* (Leiden: E.J. Brill, 1957), 74 f.

35. See "Jen-tan," *Shih-shuo hsin-yü chien-shu* 23.726. On this club, see, e.g., Mather, "Individualist Expressions," 200 f.; Ho Ch'i-min 何啟民, *Chu-lin ch'i-hsien yen-chiu* 竹林七賢研究 (Taipei: Shang-wu, 1965); Balazs, 236 ff.; and Henri Maspero, "Le poète Hi K'ang et le Club des Sept Sages de la Forêt de Bambous," in *Mélanges posthumes sur la religions et l'histoire de la Chine*. Publications du Musée Guimet; Bibliothèque de diffusion, vol. 2, 57–59 (Paris: Civilisations du Sud, 1950), 59–69 (= *Le Taoïsme*, 331–340).

36. "Jen-tan," *Shih-shuo hsin-yü chien-shu* 23.730.

37. Compare the translation in Mather, *Shih-shuo Hsin-yü*, 374.

38. "Ta-jen hsien-sheng chuan" 大人先生傳; text in Ch'en Po-chün 陳伯君, *Juan Chi chi chiao-chu*, Chung-kuo ku-tien wen-hsüeh chi-pen ts'ung-shu (Peking: Chung-hua, 1987), A.165 f. See also *Chin-shu* 49.1362. Cf., e.g., Balazs, 238.

39. "Individualist Expressions," 204. See also Ning Chia, 167; and Sun Shu-ch'i, 310.

40. Despite, e.g., Christina B. Whitman, "Privacy in Early Confucian and Taoist Thought," in Munro, 91.

41. Moreover, the sexual dimensions of this exchange are readily apparent; the trousers are, after all, the garment that houses one's genitals. (The story would have been much less effective had Liu Ling complained that his visitors were entering his shirt or his shoes.) Eric Henry, "The Social Significance of Nudity in Early China," *Fashion Theory* 3.4 (1999), 482 ff., explains insightfully that Liu Ling's nudity could have been interpreted as an affront to his guests because of an early Chinese "fear of the destructive emanations of revealed body parts."

42. See esp. "Chu-shu" 主術, in Liu Wen-tien 劉文典, *Huai-nan Hung-lieh chi-chieh* 淮南鴻烈集解, ed. Feng I 馮逸 and Ch'iao Hua 喬華, Hsin-pien Chu-tzu chi-ch'eng (Peking: Chung-hua, 1989), 9.295, which laid the groundwork for the Han imperial ideology. Cf. Paul Rakita Goldin, "Insidious Syncretism in the Political Philosophy of *Huai-nan-tzu*," *Asian Philosophy* 9.3 (1999), 171; and, more generally, Chiang Jung-ch'ang 蔣榮昌, "Chung-kuo wen-hua te kung-ssu kuan" 中國文化的公私觀, *Hsi-nan Min-tsu Hsüeh-yüan hsüeh-pao: Che-she pan* 西南民族學院學報：哲社版 1998.4, esp. 11–17. Even during the Six Dynasties, more conservative thinkers objected to the rise of *ssu* at the expense of *kung*. See, e.g., the "T'ung-chih" 通志 chapter of the lost *Fu-tzu* 傅子 of Fu Hsüan, reconstructed from fragments in *Ch'üan Chin-wen* (Yen K'o-chün), 48.4a–5b. Cf. Holcombe, 36; and Jordan D. Paper, *The Fu-tzu: A Post-Han Confucian Text*, Monographies du T'oung Pao 13 (Leiden: E.J. Brill, 1987), 25 and 46–51.

Incidentally, Hsi K'ang's usage of the terms in his "Shih-ssu lun" 釋私論, *Hsi K'ang chi chiao-chu* 6.233–243, is peculiar. Robert G. Henricks, *Philosophy and Argumentation in Third-Century China: The Essays of Hsi K'ang*, Princeton Library of Asian Translations (Princeton, 1983), 107, explains: "*Kung* in the essay is 'unselfish,' and *ssu* is 'self-interest.' But Hsi K'ang also uses *kung* to mean 'be open,' 'go public,' while *ssu* means to keep things to oneself." These are not the normal senses of the words, and Hsi K'ang would not have characterized Liu Ling's ideals (with which he sympathized) as *ssu*.

43. See, e.g., Ning Chia, 171 f.; Mather, "Individualist Expressions," 205; Rudolf G. Wagner, "Lebensstil und Drogen im chinesischen Mittelalter," *T'oung Pao* 59 (1973), 79–178; E. Zürcher, *The Buddhist Conquest of China*, Sinica Leidensia 11 (Leiden: E.J. Brill, 1972), vol. 1, 79; Balazs, 247 ff.; and Fung Yu-lan, *A History of Chinese Philosophy*, trans. Derk Bodde (Princeton, N.J.: Princeton University Press, 1952–1953), vol. 2, 190.

44. Cf., e.g., Holcombe, 96; and Anna Seidel, "Taoist Messianism," *Numen* 31.2 (1984), 173.

45. See Stephan Peter Bumbacher, "Abschied von Heim und Herd: Die Frau im mittelalterlichen Daoismus und Buddhismus," *Asiatische Studien/Etudes Asiatiques* 52.3 (1998), 682 ff.; Overmyer, 97–103; and Catherine Despeux, "L'ordination des femmes taoïstes sous les Tang," *Etudes Chinoises* 5 (1986), 56.

46. See, e.g., Ōfuchi Ninji 大淵忍爾, *Shoki no Dōkyō* 初期の道教, Tōyōgaku sōsho 38 (Tokyo: Sōbunsha, 1991), 13–76; Mansvelt Beck, 367 ff.; Rolf A. Stein, "Remarques sur les mouvements du taoïsme politico-religieux au IIe siècle ap. J.-C.," *T'oung Pao* 50.1–3 (1963), 1–78; Paul Michaud, "The Yellow Turbans," *Monumenta Serica* 17 (1958), 47–127; Werner Eichhorn, "T'ai-p'ing und T'ai-p'ing Religion," *Mitteilungen des Instituts für Orientforschung* 5 (1957), 113–140; idem, "Bemerkungen zum Aufstand des Chang Chio und zum Staate des Chang Lu," *Mitteilungen des Instituts für Orientforschung* 3 (1955), 291–327; and Howard S. Levy, "Yellow Turban Religion and Rebellion at the End of the Han," *Journal of the American Oriental Society* 76 (1956), 214–227.

47. Ōfuchi, 330–334, and Kobayashi Masayoshi 小林正美, *Rikuchū Dōkyōshi kenkyū* 六朝道教史研究, Tōyōgaku sōsho 37 (Tokyo: Sōbunsha, 1990), 199 ff., both argue that sexual practices were unknown to the first Celestial Masters during the Han dynasty and that they were incorporated only during the Chin 晉 or later, when the movement came into contact with the traditions of *ch'i* exchange as they are known from the writings of Ko Hung. Moreover, Ōfuchi and Kobayashi both contend that the macrobiotic dimensions of *ho-ch'i* have nothing to do with the Celestial Masters' earliest doctrines, which centered on faith healing and exorcism. But see Stephen R. Bokenkamp, "Traces of Early Celestial Master Physiological Practice in the *Xiang'er* Commentary," *Taoist Resources* 4.2 (1993), 37–51, and *Early Daoist Scriptures*, Taoist Classics (Berkeley and Los Angeles: University of California Press, 1997), 44 ff.

48. *Shang-ch'ing huang-shu kuo-tu i* 上清黃書過度儀 (*Tao-tsang* 道藏, *HY* 1284), 1a. The entire ritual is described in Wile, 25 f.; Kobayashi, 357–366; and Kristofer Schipper, *The Taoist Body*, trans. Karen C. Duval (Berkeley and Los Angeles: University of California Press, 1993), 150 ff. As far as I know, the text has never been translated in its entirety, perhaps because of its extremely complicated technical vocabulary. Evidently not knowing the *Shang-ch'ing huang-shu kuo-tu i*, Henri Maspero, *Le Taoïsme et les religions chinoises*, Bibliothèque de histoires (Paris: Gallimard, 1971), 571, writes, "Le rituel de cette fête ne nous est parvenu: il a probablement été éliminé du *Tao-tsang*" ("The ritual of this festival has not come down to us; it was probably excised from the Taoist canon"; and consequently his discussion of the *huang-shu* relies on the very dubious testimony of Buddhist critics). Incidentally, Schipper, *The Taoist Body*, 241 n. 56 and 252, gives the wrong *HY* index number of the text.

49. Schipper disagrees with Kobayashi, 357, who dates the text to the end of the Liu-Sung 劉宋 dynasty (A.D. 420–478).

50. *The Taoist Body*, 151.

51. Cf., e.g., Bumbacher, 688.

52. Cf., e.g., Bokenkamp, *Early Daoist Scriptures*, 258 n. 43; Ōfuchi, 143; and Levy, "Yellow Turban Religion," 217.

53. The most famous example is probably that of Chen Luan 甄鸞 (fl. 570), *Hsiao-tao lun* 笑道論, in *Kuang Hung-ming chi* 廣弘明集 (*Taishō shinshū Daizōkyō* 大正新修大藏經 52), 2103.152a, which is the same as Fa-lin 法琳 (572–640), *Pien-cheng lun* 辯正論 (*Taishō* 52), 2110.545cf. See also Hsüan-kuang 玄光 (fl. sixth century), *Pien-huo lun* 辯惑論, in *Hung-ming chi* (*Taishō* 52), 2102.48bf. Cf., e.g., Livia Kohn, *Laughing at the Tao: Debates among Buddhists and Taoists in Medieval China* (Princeton, N.J.: Princeton University Press, 1995), 149f.; Richard B. Mather, "K'ou Ch'ien-chih and the Taoist Theocracy at the Northern Wei Court, 425–451," in *Facets of Taoism: Essays in Chinese Religion*, ed. Holmes Welch and Anna Seidel (New Haven, Conn.: Yale University Press, 1979), 109ff.; R. H. van Gulik, *Sexual Life in Ancient China: A Preliminary Survey of Chinese Sex and Society from ca. 1500 B.C. till 1644 A.D.* (Leiden: E. J. Brill, 1961; repr., New York: Barnes and Noble, 1996), 88ff.; and Michaud, 94f.

54. For the example of K'ou Ch'ien-chih 寇謙之 (d. 448), see, e.g., *Lao-chün yin-sung chieh-ching* 老君音誦戒經 (*Tao-tsang, HY* 784), 2a; and "Shih-Lao chih" 釋老志, *Wei-shu* 魏書 (Peking: Chung-hua, 1974), 114.3051. See also T'ao Hung-ching 陶弘景 (456–536), *Chen-kao* 真誥 (*Tao-tsang, HY* 1010), 2.1a.

55. "Ku-shih wei Chiao Chung-ch'ing ch'i tso" 古詩為焦仲卿妻作, *Yü-t'ai hsin-yung* 1.34; Kuo Mao-ch'ien, *Yüeh-fu shih-chi* 73.1034.

56. Compare the translation in Birrell, *New Songs from a Jade Terrace*, 53. She misunderstands the phrase *Lu-chiang fu hsiao-li* 廬江府小吏 as "magistrate of Luchiang prefecture." *Hsiao-li* (minor functionary) is not an official term and definitely does not signify a position as high as magistrate. We must bear in mind that Chung-ch'ing is greatly outranked by the son of the county magistrate (*hsien-ling* 縣令), to whom his former wife is later promised. Moreover, Lu-chiang was not a prefecture in its own right but was a "commandery" (*chün* 郡) in Yang Prefecture 揚州; see "Chün-kuo ssu" 郡國四, *Hou-Han shu, chih* 志 22, 3487. Finally, *fu* in this context means simply "government offices," as in the line in the poem below: "And meanwhile I will report to the Bureau" 吾今且報府. Cf. Burton Watson, trans., *The Columbia Book of Chinese Poetry: From Early Times to the Thirteenth Century* (New York: Columbia University Press, 1984), 83.

57. Following the commentary of Wu Chao-i. *Ling-p'ing* 伶俜 (which is the same as *ling-ting* 伶/零丁), "lonely," is evidently an indivisible binome.

58. "Ku-shih wei Chiao Chung-ch'ing ch'i tso," *Yü-t'ai hsin-yung* 1.36f.; Kuo Mao-ch'ien, *Yüeh-fu shih-chi* 73.1035.

59. Compare the translations in Watson, *Columbia Book of Chinese Poetry*, 83f.; Birrell, *New Songs from a Jade Terrace*, 54f.; and Arthur Waley, *Chinese Poems*, paperback ed. (London: George Allen and Unwin, 1961), 80.

60. Wu Chao-i's edition has *ch'ien-shih* 遣施, which does not make much sense, but he notes that one text reads *i-shih* 遺施, which is intelligible as "hand-

me-down present." Confusion between *ch'ien* 遣 and *i* 遺 is not surprising, especially since the former appears repeatedly in this poem.

61. "Ku-shih wei Chiao Chung-ch'ing ch'i tso," *Yü-t'ai hsin-yung* 1.37; Kuo Mao-ch'ien, *Yüeh-fu shih-chi* 73.1035.

62. Compare the translations in Watson, *Columbia Book of Chinese Poetry*, 84; Birrell, *New Songs from a Jade Terrace*, 55; and Waley, *Chinese Poems*, 80 f.

63. "Ku-shih wei Chiao Chung-ch'ing ch'i tso," *Yü-t'ai hsin-yung* 1.45; Kuo Mao-ch'ien, *Yüeh-fu shih-chi* 73.1038.

64. Cf., e.g., Liu Ta-lin 劉達臨, *Chung-kuo ku-tai hsing wen-hua* 中國古代性文化 (Yin-ch'uan: Ning-hsia jen-min, 1993), vol. 1, 272 f.

Bibliography

1. Classical Chinese Texts

Note: Texts from the Sung and later are listed in section 3, where they are alphabetized by author's surname. Where more than one edition is listed for a given work, the edition regularly cited in the text is listed first; the others have been consulted for variants and additional commentaries. Archaeologically excavated texts are found in section 2.

Chan-kuo ts'e 戰國策. Redacted by Liu Hsiang 劉向 (79–8 B.C.).
Chan-kuo ts'e. 2 vols. Shanghai: Ku-chi, 1978; repr., Taipei: Li-jen, 1990.

Chen-kao 真誥. By T'ao Hung-ching 陶弘景 (A.D. 456–536).
Chen-kao. *Tao-tsang* 道藏, *HY* 1010.

Ch'ien-fu lun 潛夫論. By Wang Fu 王符 (ca. A.D. 82–167).
P'eng To 彭鐸. *Ch'ien-fu lun chiao-cheng* 校正. Hsin-pien Chu-tzu chi-ch'eng. Peking: Chung-hua, 1985.

Chin-shu 晉書. By Fang Hsüan-ling 房玄齡 (578–648) and others.
Chin-shu. Peking: Chung-hua, 1974.

Chou-li 周禮. Ritual text from the mid–Warring States period.
Chou-li chu-shu 注疏. *Shih-san ching chu-shu fu chiao-k'an chi* 十三經注疏附校勘記. 1817; repr., Peking: Chung-hua, 1980.
Sun I-jang 孫詒讓 (1848–1908). *Chou-li cheng-i* 正義. 4 vols. *Kuo-hsüeh chi-pen ts'ung-shu* 國學基本叢書.

Ch'u-tz'u 楚辭. Attributed to Ch'ü Yüan 屈原 (third century B.C.) and others.
Hung Hsing-tsu 洪興祖 (1090–1155). *Ch'u-tz'u chang-chü pu-chu* 章句補注. In *Ch'u-tz'u chu pa-chung* 八種. Chung-kuo wen-hsüeh ming-chu. Taipei: Shih-chieh, 1990.

193

Yu Kuo-en 游國恩 (1899–1978). *Li-sao tsuan-i* 離騷纂義. Ed. Chin K'ai-ch'eng 金開誠 et al. *Ch'u-tz'u* chu-shu ch'ang-pien. Peking: Chung-hua, 1980.

Chiang Liang-fu 姜亮夫 (b. 1901). *Ch'ü Yüan fu chiao-chu* 屈原賦校註. Peking: Jen-min wen-hsüeh, 1957.

———. *Ch'u-tz'u t'ung-ku* 通故. 4 vols. K'un-ming: Yün-nan jen-min, 2000.

Chuang-tzu 莊子. Attributed to Chuang Chou 莊周 (fourth century B.C.) but of composite authorship over several centuries.

Kuo Ch'ing-fan 郭慶藩 (1844–1896). *Chuang-tzu chi-shih* 集釋. Ed. Wang Hsiao-yü 王孝魚. 4 vols. Hsin-pien Chu-tzu chi-ch'eng. Peking: Chung-hua, 1961.

Wang Shu-min 王叔岷. *Chuang-tzu chiao-ch'üan* 校詮. 2d edition. 3 vols. Chung-yang Yen-chiu-yüan Li-shih Yü-yen Yen-chiu-so chuan-k'an 88. Taipei, 1994.

Ch'un-ch'iu Ku-liang chuan 春秋穀梁傳. Attributed to Ku-liang Shu 穀梁淑 (fifth century B.C.) but not written down until the Western Han.

Ch'un-ch'iu Ku-liang chuan chu-shu. Shih-san ching chu-shu.

Chung Wen-cheng 鍾文烝 (1818–1877). *Ku-liang pu-chu* 補注. 2 vols. *Kuo-hsüeh chi-pen ts'ung-shu.*

Ch'un-ch'iu Kung-yang chuan 公羊傳. Attributed to Kung-yang Kao 公羊高 (fifth century B.C.) but not written down until the Western Han.

Ch'un-ch'iu Kung-yang chuan chu-shu. Shih-san ching chu-shu.

Ch'un-ch'iu Tso-chuan 左傳. Attributed to Tso Ch'iu-ming 左丘明 (fifth century B.C.) but probably dating from the fourth century B.C.

Ch'un-ch'iu Tso-chuan cheng-i. Shih-san ching chu-shu.

Yang Po-chün 楊伯峻. *Ch'un-ch'iu Tso-chuan chu* 注. 2d ed. 4 vols. Chung-kuo ku-tien ming-chu i-chu ts'ung-shu. Peking: Chung-hua, 1990.

Ch'ün-shu chih-yao 群書治要. Excerpts from primary texts collected by Wei Cheng 魏徵 (580–643).

Ch'ün-shu chih-yao. Ssu-pu ts'ung-k'an 四部叢刊.

Feng-su t'ung-i 風俗通義. By Ying Shao 應劭 (d. before A.D. 204).

Wang Li-ch'i 王利器. *Feng-su t'ung-i chiao-chu* 校注. Taipei: Ming-wen, 1982.

Han-chi 漢紀. By Hsün Yüeh 荀悦 (A.D. 148–209).

Han-chi. Kuo-hsüeh chi-pen ts'ung-shu.

Han Fei-tzu 韓非子. By Han Fei 韓非 (d. 233 B.C.).

Ch'en Ch'i-yu 陳奇猷. *Han Fei-tzu chi-shih* 韓非子集釋. 2 vols. Chung-kuo ssu-hsiang ming-chu. Peking: Chung-hua, 1958; repr., Taipei: Shih-chieh, 1991.

Han-Shih wai-chuan 韓詩外傳. By Han Ying 韓嬰 (ca. 200–ca. 120 B.C.).

Han-Shih wai-chuan. Ssu-pu ts'ung-k'an.

Han-shu 漢書. By Pan Ku 班固 (A.D. 32–92) and others.

Han-shu. 12 vols. Peking: Chung-hua, 1962.

Wang Hsien-ch'ien 王先謙 (1842–1918). *Han-shu pu-chu* 漢書補注. 2 vols. Erh-shih-ssu shih k'ao-ting ts'ung-shu chuan-chi. 1900; repr., Peking: Shu-mu wen-hsien, 1995.

Hou-Han shu 後漢書. By Fan Yeh 范曄 (A.D. 398–445).

Hou-Han shu. 12 vols. Peking: Chung-hua, 1965.

Hsi K'ang chi 嵇康集. Collected works of Hsi K'ang (A.D. 223–262).

Tai Ming-yang 戴明揚. *Hsi K'ang chi chiao-chu.* Peking: Jen-min, 1962.

Hsiao-ching 孝經. Attributed to Confucius but probably dating from the fourth century B.C. at the earliest.

Hsiao-ching chu-shu. Shih-san ching chu-shu.

Hsiao-hsiang lu 瀟湘錄. Collection of stories by Li Yin 李隱 (fl. ca. A.D. 865–870).

Hsiao-hsiang lu. Ku-chin shuo-hai 古今説海.

Hsin-shu 新書. Attributed to Chia I 賈誼 (201–169 B.C.).

Wang Chou-ming 王洲明 and Hsü Ch'ao 徐超. *Chia I chi chiao-chu* 賈誼集校注. Hsin-chu ku-tai wen-hsüeh ming-chia chi. Peking: Jen-min wen-hsüeh, 1996.

Hsün-tzu 荀子. By Hsün K'uang 荀況 (ca. 310–ca. 210 B.C.).

Wang Hsien-ch'ien. *Hsün-tzu chi-chieh* 集解. Ed. Shen Hsiao-huan 沈嘯寰 and Wang Hsing-hsien 王星賢. Hsin-pien Chu-tzu chi-ch'eng. Peking: Chung-hua, 1988.

Huai-nan-tzu 淮南子. Commissioned by Liu An 劉安 (d. 122 B.C.).

Liu Wen-tien 劉文典. *Huai-nan Hung-lieh chi-chieh* 淮南鴻烈集解. Ed. Feng I 馮逸 and Ch'iao Hua 喬華. 2 vols. Hsin-pien Chu-tzu chi-ch'eng. Peking: Chung-hua, 1989.

Hung-ming chi 弘明集. Anthology of primary texts collected by Seng-yu 僧祐 (A.D. 445–518).

Hung-ming chi. Taishō shinshū Daizōkyō 大正新修大藏經 52, 2102.

I-ching 易經. Western Chou divinatory text, with later appendices.

Chou-I cheng-i 周易正義. *Shih-san ching chu-shu.*

I Chou-shu 逸周書. Miscellaneous text composed of a core from the third century B.C. or earlier, and other chapters of varying date.

Chu Yu-tseng 朱右曾 (fl. 1846). *I Chou-shu chi-hsün chiao-shih* 集訓校釋. Kuo-hsüeh chi-pen ts'ung-shu.

I-li 儀禮. Ritual text of unknown origin.

I-li chu-shu. Shih-san ching chu-shu.

Hu P'ei-hui 胡培翬 (1782–1849). *I-li cheng-i. Kuo-hsüeh chi-pen ts'ung-shu.*

I-wen lei-chü 藝文類聚. Excerpts from primary texts compiled by Ou-yang Hsün 歐陽詢 (557–641) and others.
I-wen lei-chü. 4 vols. Taipei: Hsin-hsing, 1969.

Juan Chi chi 阮籍集. Collected works of Juan Chi (A.D. 210–263).
Ch'en Po-chün 陳伯君. *Juan Chi chi chiao-chu.* Chung-kuo ku-tien wen-hsüeh chi-pen ts'ung-shu. Peking: Chung-hua, 1987.

Kuan-tzu 管子. Anthology named after Kuan Chung 管仲 (d. 645 B.C.) but dating from centuries later.
Tai Wang 戴望 (1783–1863). *Kuan-tzu chiao-cheng* 校正. Chu-tzu chi-ch'eng 諸子集成. 1935; repr., Peking: Chung-hua, 1954.

Kuang Hung-ming chi 廣弘明集. Anthology of primary texts collected by Tao-hsüan 道宣 (596–667).
Kuang Hung-ming chi. Taishō shinshū Daizōkyō 52, 2103.

K'ung-ts'ung-tzu 孔叢子. Miscellaneous text forged by Wang Su 王肅 (A.D. 195–256) or an associate.
K'ung-ts'ung-tzu. Han-Wei ts'ung-shu 漢魏叢書. 1592; repr., Ch'ang-ch'un: Chi-lin Ta-hsüeh, 1992.

Kuo-yü 國語. Attributed to Tso Ch'iu-ming and of similar date to *Tso-chuan.*
Kuo-yü. Shanghai: Ku-chi, 1978; repr., Taipei: Li-jen, 1981.
Tung Tseng-ling 董增齡. *Kuo-yü cheng-i.* 2 vols. N.p.: Chang-shih shih-hsün t'ang, 1880; repr., [Ch'eng-tu:] Pa-shu, 1985.
I Chung-t'ien 易中天 and Hou Nai-hui 侯迺慧. *Kuo-yü tu-pen* 讀本. Ku-chi chin-chu hsin-i ts'ung-shu; Li-shih lei. Taipei: San-min, 1995.

Lao-chün yin-sung chieh-ching 老君音誦戒經. Attributed to K'ou Ch'ien-chih 寇謙之 (d. A.D. 448).
Lao-chün yin-sung chieh-ching. Tao-tsang, HY 784.

Lao-tzu 老子. Otherwise known as *Tao-te ching* 道德經, a *mixtum compositum* that may have taken its final shape in the third century B.C.
Kao Ming 高明. *Po-shu Lao-tzu chiao-chu* 帛書老子校注. Hsin-pien Chu-tzu chi-ch'eng. Peking: Chung-hua, 1996.

Li-chi 禮記. Composite text from the Eastern Han or later.
Li-chi cheng-i. Shih-san ching chu-shu.
Sun Hsi-tan 孫希旦 (1736–1784). *Li-chi chi-chieh.* Ed. Shen Hsiao-huan and Wang Hsing-hsien. 3 vols. Shih-san ching Ch'ing-jen chu-shu. Peking: Chung-hua, 1989.
Chu Pin 朱彬 (1753–1843). *Li-chi hsün-tsuan* 訓纂. Ed. Jao Ch'in-nung 饒欽農. 2 vols. Shih-san ching Ch'ing-jen chu-shu. Peking: Chung-hua, 1996.
Wang Meng-ou 王夢鷗. *Li-chi chiao-cheng* 校證. Taipei: I-wen, 1976.

Lieh-nü chuan 列女傳. By Liu Hsiang.
Wang Chao-yüan 王照圓 (fl. 1879–1884). *Lieh-nü chuan pu-chu* 補註. *Kuo-hsüeh chi-pen ts'ung-shu.*

Lun-heng 論衡. By Wang Ch'ung 王充 (A.D. 27–ca. 100).
Huang Hui 黃暉. *Lun-heng chiao-shih (fu Liu P'an-sui chi-chieh)* 論衡校釋 (附劉盼遂集解). 4 vols. Hsin-pien Chu-tzu chi-ch'eng. Peking: Chung-hua, 1990.

Lun-yü 論語 (i.e., *Analects*). Sayings attributed to K'ung Ch'iu 孔丘 (i.e., Confucius, 551–479 B.C.).
Ch'eng Shu-te 程樹德 (1877–1944). *Lun-yü chi-shih* 論語集釋. Ed. Ch'eng Chün-ying 程俊英 and Chiang Chien-yüan 蔣見元. 4 vols. Hsin-pien Chu-tzu chi-ch'eng. Peking: Chung-hua, 1990.
Wang Su 王素. *T'ang hsieh-pen Lun-yü Cheng-shih chu chi-ch'i yen-chiu* 唐寫本論語鄭氏注及其研究. Peking: Wen-wu, 1991.

Lü-shih ch'un-ch'iu 呂氏春秋. Encyclopaedic text commissioned by Lü Pu-wei 呂不韋 (d. 235 B.C.).
Ch'en Ch'i-yu. *Lü-shih ch'un-ch'iu chiao-shih.* 2 vols. Shanghai: Hsüeh-lin, 1984.

Meng-tzu 孟子 (i.e., *Mencius*). Sayings attributed to Meng K'o 孟軻 (i.e., Mencius, 371–289 B.C.).
Chiao Hsün 焦循 (1763–1820). *Meng-tzu cheng-i.* Ed. Shen Wen-cho 沈文倬. 2 vols. Hsin-pien Chu-tzu chi-ch'eng. Peking: Chung-hua, 1987.

Mo-tzu 墨子. Essays and sayings from the philosophical school founded by Mo Ti 墨翟 (ca. 480–ca. 390 B.C.)
Wu Yü-chiang 吳毓江. *Mo-tzu chiao-chu* 校注. Ed Sun Ch'i-chih 孫啟治. 2 vols. Hsin-pien Chu-tzu chi-ch'eng. Peking: Chung-hua, 1993.

Nan-Ch'i shu 南齊書. By Hsiao Tzu-hsien 蕭子顯 (489–537).
Nan-Ch'i shu. 3 vols. Peking: Chung-hua, 1972.

Pao-p'u-tzu 抱朴子. By Ko Hung 葛洪 (A.D. 283–343).
Wang Ming 王明. *Pao-p'u-tzu nei-p'ien chiao-shih* 內篇校釋. 2d ed. Hsin-pien Chu-tzu chi-ch'eng. Peking: Chung-hua, 1985.
Yang Ming-chao 楊明照. *Pao-p'u-tzu wai-p'ien chiao-chien* 外篇校箋. 2 vols. Hsin-pien Chu-tzu chi-ch'eng. Peking: Chung-hua, 1991.

Pien-cheng lun 辯正論. By Fa-lin 法琳 (572–640).
Pien-cheng lun. Taishō shinshū Daizōkyō 52, 2110.

Po-hu t'ung 白虎通. Attributed to Pan Ku and others but probably from the second century A.D. at the earliest.
Ch'en Li 陳立 (1809–1869). *Po-hu t'ung shu-cheng* 疏證. Ed. Wu Tse-yü 吳則虞. 2 vols. Hsin-pien Chu-tzu chi-ch'eng. Peking: Chung-hua, 1994.

San-kuo chih 三國志. By Ch'en Shou 陳壽 (A.D. 233–297).
San-kuo chih. 5 vols. Peking: Chung-hua, 1959.

Shang-ch'ing huang-shu kuo-tu i 上清黃書過度儀. Anonymous text from the fourth
or fifth century A.D.
Shang-ch'ing huang-shu kuo-tu i. Tao-tsang, HY 1284.

Shang-shu 尚書. Anthology of documents purportedly from the most ancient
times; some chapters are significantly older than others.
Shang-shu cheng-i. Shih-san ching chu-shu.

Shang-shu ta-chuan 尚書大傳. Attributed to Fu Sheng 伏勝 (fl. third–second century B.C.).
Lau, D. C., and Chen Fong Ching. *A Concordance to Shangshudazhuan.* ICS Ancient Chinese Texts Concordance Series: Classical Works 5. Hong Kong:
Commercial Press, 1994.

Shen-tzu 申子. Sayings of Shen Pu-hai 申不害 (fl. 354–340 B.C.).
Creel, Herrlee G. *Shen Pu-hai: A Chinese Political Philosopher of the Fourth Century
B.C.* Chicago: University of Chicago Press, 1974.

Shih-chi 史記. By Ssu-ma Ch'ien 司馬遷 (145?–86? B.C.) and others.
Shih-chi. 10 vols. Peking: Chung-hua, 1959.
Takigawa Kametarō 瀧川龜太郎 (b. 1865). *Shiki kaichū kōshō* 史記會注考證.
Tokyo: Tōhō Bunka Gakuin, 1932–1934; repr., Taipei: Hung-shih, 1986.
Mizusawa Toshitada 水澤利忠. *Shiki kaichū kōshō kōho* 校補. Tokyo: *Shiki kaichū
kōshō kōho* kankō kai, 1957–1970; repr., Taipei: Kuang-wen, 1972.

Shih-ching 詩經. An ancient redaction of traditional odes.
Ch'ü Wan-li 屈萬里. *Shih-ching shih-i* 釋義. 2 vols. Hsien-tai kuo-min chi-pen chih-
shih ts'ung-shu. Taipei: Chung-kuo wen-hua, 1952–1953.
Mao-Shih cheng-i. Shih-san ching chu-shu.
Ma Jui-ch'en 馬瑞辰 (1782–1853). *Mao-Shih chuan-chien t'ung-shih* 毛詩傳箋通釋.
Huang-Ch'ing ching-chieh hsü-pien 皇清經解續編.
Wang Hung-hsü 王鴻緒 (1645–1723). *Shih-ching chuan-shuo hui-tsuan* 傳說彙纂.
1868; repr., Taipei: Chung-ting wen-hua, 1967.

Shih-shuo hsin-yü 世說新語. Attributed to Liu I-ch'ing 劉義慶 (A.D. 403–444).
Yü Chia-hsi 余嘉錫. *Shih-shuo hsin-yü chien-shu* 箋疏. Ed. Chou Tsu-mo 周祖謨, et
al. Rev. ed. Shanghai: Ku-chi, 1993.

Shuo-wen chieh-tzu 説文解字. By Hsü Shen 許慎 (ca. A.D. 55–ca. 149).
Chiang Jen-chieh 蔣人傑. *Shuo-wen chieh-tzu chi-chu* 集注. Ed. Liu Jui 劉銳. 3 vols.
Shanghai: Ku-chi, 1996.
Tuan Yü-ts'ai 段玉裁 (1735–1815). *Shuo-wen chieh-tzu Tuan chu. Ssu-pu pei-yao* 四
部備要.

Shuo-yüan 説苑. Anecdotes compiled by Liu Hsiang.
Liu Hsiang. *Shuo-yüan*. Han-Wei ts'ung-shu.

Sui-shu 隋書. By Wei Cheng and others.
Sui-shu. 6 vols. Peking: Chung-hua, 1973.

Sung-shu 宋書. By Shen Yüeh 沈約 (441–513) and others.
Sung-shu. 8 vols. Peking: Chung-hua, 1974.

Ta-Tai Li-chi 大戴禮記. Composite ritual text attributed spuriously to Tai Te
    戴德 (fl. first century B.C.).
Wang P'in-chen 王聘珍 (eighteenth century). *Ta-Tai Li-chi chieh-ku* 解詁. Ed.
    Wang Wen-chin 王文錦. Shih-san ching Ch'ing-jen chu-shu. Peking: Chung-
    hua, 1983.

T'ai-p'ing yü-lan 太平御覽. Excerpts from primary texts compiled by Li Fang
    李昉 (925–996) and others.
T'ai-p'ing yü-lan. 12 vols. Kuo-hsüeh chi-pen ts'ung-shu.

T'ao Yüan-ming chi 陶淵明集. Collected works of T'ao Ch'ien 陶潛 (A.D. 365–427).
Kung Pin 龔斌. *T'ao Yüan-ming chi chiao-chien* 校箋. Chung-kuo ku-tien wen-
    hsüeh ts'ung-shu. Shanghai: Ku-chi, 1996.

Tu-tuan 獨斷. By Ts'ai Yung 蔡邕 (A.D. 132–192).
Tu-tuan. Han-Wei ts'ung-shu.

Wei-shu 魏書. By Wei Shou 魏收 (A.D. 506–572).
Wei-shu. 5 vols. Peking: Chung-hua, 1974.

Wu-Yüeh ch'un-ch'iu 吳越春秋. Attributed to Chao Yeh 趙曄 (fl. A.D. 40) but may
    date from as late as the T'ang.
Chou Sheng-ch'un 周生春. *Wu-Yüeh ch'un-chiu chi-chiao hui-k'ao* 輯校匯考.
    Shanghai: Ku-chi, 1997.

Yü-t'ai hsin-yung 玉臺新詠. Anthology of poems collected by Hsü Ling 徐陵 (A.D.
    507–583).
Yü-t'ai hsin-yung. Ed Wu Chao-i 吳兆宜. Kuo-hsüeh chi-pen ts'ung-shu.

Yüeh-chüeh shu 越絕書. Early gazetteer of unknown authorship, probably from
    the Eastern Han.
Yüeh-chüeh shu. Ssu-pu ts'ung-k'an.

2. Archaeologically Excavated Texts
From Hsiao-t'un 小屯

Chang Ping-ch'üan 張秉權. *Hsiao-t'un ti-erh pen: Yin-hsü wen-tzu ping-pien* 小屯第
    二本：殷虛文字丙編. Taipei, 1957–1972.

From Ma-wang-tui 馬王堆

Kuo-chia Wen-wu-chü Ku-wen-hsien Yen-chiu-shih 國家文物局古文獻研究室. *Ma-wang-tui Han-mu po-shu* 馬王堆漢墓帛書. 6 vols. Peking: Wen-wu, 1980–.

Ma Chi-hsing 馬繼興. *Ma-wang-tui ku i-shu k'ao-shih* 馬王堆古醫書考釋. Ch'ang-sha: Hu-nan k'o-hsüeh chi-shu, 1992.

Wei Ch'i-p'eng 魏啟鵬 and Hu Hsiang-hua 胡翔驊. *Ma-wang-tui Han-mu i-shu chiao-shih* 馬王堆漢墓醫書校釋. 2 vols. Erh-shih shih-chi ch'u-t'u Chung-kuo ku i-shu chi-ch'eng. Ch'eng-tu: Ch'eng-tu ch'u-pan-she, 1992.

From Yin-ch'üeh-shan 銀雀山

Yin-ch'üeh-shan Han-mu chu-chien cheng-li hsiao-tsu 銀雀山漢墓竹簡整理小組. *Sun Pin Ping-fa* 孫臏兵法. Peking: Wen-wu, 1975.

From Shui-hu-ti 睡虎地

Shui-hu-ti Ch'in-mu chu-chien cheng-li hsiao-tsu 睡虎地秦墓竹簡整理小組. *Shui-hu-ti Ch'in-mu chu-chien* 睡虎地秦墓竹簡. Peking: Wen-wu, 1990.

Liu Lo-hsien 劉樂賢. *Shui-hu-ti Ch'in-chien* Jih-shu *yen-chiu* 睡虎地秦簡日書研究. Ta-lu ti-ch'ü po-shih lun-wen ts'ung-k'an 76. Taipei: Wen-chin, 1994.

From Kuo-tien 郭店

Ching-men Shih Po-wu-kuan 荊門市博物館. *Kuo-tien Ch'u-mu chu-chien* 郭店楚墓竹簡. Peking: Wen-wu, 1998.

3. Secondary Works

Allan, Sarah, and Alvin P. Cohen, eds. *Legend, Lore, and Religions in China: Essays in Honor of Wolfram Eberhard on His Seventieth Birthday.* San Francisco: Chinese Materials Center, 1979.

Allen, Douglas, ed. *Culture and Self: Philosophical and Religious Perspectives, East and West.* Boulder, Colo.: Westview, 1997.

Ames, Roger T. "Taoism and the Androgynous Ideal." In Guisso and Johannesen, 21–45.

Arendrup, Birthe et al., eds. *The Master Said: To Study and . . . : To Søren Egerod on the Occasion of His Sixty-seventh Birthday.* East Asian Institute Occasional Papers 6. Copenhagen: University of Copenhagen, 1990.

Ariel, Yoav. *K'ung-ts'ung-tzu: A Study and Translation of Chapters 15–23 with a Reconstruction of the* Hsiao Erh-ya *Dictionary.* Sinica Leidensia 35. Leiden: E. J. Brill, 1996.

Asselin, Mark Laurent. "The Lu-School Reading of 'Guanju' as Preserved in an Eastern Han *fu.*" *Journal of the American Oriental Society* 117.3 (1997): 427–443.

Baker, Robert B. "'Pricks' and 'Chicks': A Plea for 'Persons.'" In Baker et al., 281–305.

Baker, Robert B., et al., eds. *Philosophy and Sex.* 3d ed. Amherst, N.Y.: Prometheus, 1998.

Balazs, Etienne. *Chinese Civilization and Bureaucracy: Variations on a Theme.* Trans. H. M. Wright. Ed. Arthur F. Wright. New Haven, Conn.: Yale University Press, 1964.

Bauer, Wolfgang. "The Hidden Hero: Creation and Disintegration of the Ideal of Eremitism." In Munro, 157–197.

Baxter, William H. *A Handbook of Old Chinese Phonology.* Trends in Linguistics 64. Berlin: Mouton de Gruyter, 1992.

Beurdeley, M., ed. *Jeux des nuages et de la pluie.* Frieburg: Office du Livre, 1969.

Bielenstein, Hans. *The Bureaucracy of Han Times.* Cambridge Studies in Chinese History, Literature, and Institutions. Cambridge, 1980.

———. "Pan Ku's Accusations against Wang Mang." In Le Blanc and Blader, 265–270.

Biot, Édouard, trans. *Le Tcheou-li ou Rites des Tcheou.* Paris: Imprimerie Nationale, 1851.

Birch, Cyril, ed. *Studies in Chinese Literary Genres.* Berkeley and Los Angeles: University of California Press, 1974.

Birrell, Anne. *Chinese Mythology: An Introduction.* Baltimore: Johns Hopkins University Press, 1993.

———. *Popular Songs and Ballads of Han China.* London: Unwin Hyman, 1988; repr., Honolulu: University of Hawai'i Press, 1993.

———. "The Four Flood Myth Traditions of Classical China." *T'oung Pao* 83.4–5 (1997): 213–259.

———, trans. *New Songs from a Jade Terrace: An Anthology of Early Chinese Love Poetry.* London: George Allen and Unwin, 1982; repr., New York: Penguin, 1986.

Black, Alison H. "Gender and Cosmology in Chinese Correlative Thinking." In Bynum et al., 166–195.

Bleuel, Hans Peter. *Das saubere Reich.* Bern: Scherz, 1972.

Bloch, Marc. *Feudal Society.* Trans. L. A. Manyon. 2 vols. Chicago: University of Chicago Press, 1961.

Blundell, Sue. *Women in Ancient Greece.* Cambridge: Harvard University Press, 1995.

Bodde, Derk. *Statesman, Patriot, and General in Ancient China: Three Shih-chi Biographies from the Ch'in Dynasty (255–206 B.C.).* American Oriental Series 17. New Haven, Conn.: American Oriental Society, 1940.

———. *Festivals in Classical China.* Princeton, N.J.: Princeton University Press, 1975.

———. "The State and Empire of Ch'in." In Twitchett and Loewe, 20–102.

Bokenkamp, Stephen R. "Traces of Early Celestial Master Physiological Practice in the *Xiang'er* Commentary." *Taoist Resources* 4.2 (1993): 37–51.

———. *Early Daoist Scriptures.* Taoist Classics. Berkeley and Los Angeles: University of California Press, 1997.

Boltz, William G. "Kung Kung and the Flood: Reverse Euhemerism in the *Yao tien.*" *T'oung Pao* 67.3–5 (1981): 141–153.

———. "Notes on the Textual Relationships between the *Kuo Yü* and the *Tso Chuan.*" *Bulletin of the School of Oriental and African Studies* 53 (1990): 491–502.

Boolos, George, ed. *Meaning and Method: Essays in Honor of Hilary Putnam.* Cambridge: Cambridge University Press, 1990.

Brooks, E. Bruce, and A. Taeko Brooks. *The Original Analects: Sayings of Confucius and His Successors.* Translations from the Asian Classics. New York: Columbia University Press, 1998.

Bullough, Vern L. "Sex in History: A Redux." In Murray and Eisenbichler, 3–22.

Bullough, Vern L., et al. "Sadism, Masochism, and History, or when Is Behaviour Sado-masochistic?" In Porter and Teich, 47–62.

Bumbacher, Stephan Peter. "Abschied von Heim und Herd: Die Frau im mittelalterlichen Daoismus und Buddhismus." *Asiatische Studien/Etudes Asiatiques* 52.3 (1998): 673–694.

Buxbaum, David C., ed. *Chinese Family Law and Social Change in Historical and Comparative Perspective.* Asian Law Series 3. Seattle: University of Washington Press, 1978.

Buxbaum, David C., and Frederick W. Mote, eds. *Transition and Permanence: Chinese History and Culture.* Hong Kong: Cathay, 1972.

Bynum, Caroline Walker et al., eds. *Gender and Religion: On the Complexity of Symbols.* Boston: Beacon, 1986.

Cameron, Averil, and Amélie Kuhrt, eds. *Images of Women in Antiquity.* Detroit: Wayne State University Press, 1983.

Carson, Anne. "Putting Her in Her Place: Woman, Dirt, and Desire." In Halperin et al., 135–169.

Chai Hao 翟灝 (1736–1788). *T'ung-su pien* 通俗編. Wu-pu-i chai 無不宜齋, 1751.

Chai Hsiang-chün 翟相君. *Shih-ching hsin-chieh* 詩經新解. Cheng-chou: Chungchou ku-chi, 1993.

Chan, See Yee. "Disputes on the One Thread of *Chung-Shu.*" *Journal of Chinese Philosophy* 26.2 (1999): 165–186.

Chan, Wing-tsit. *A Source Book in Chinese Philosophy.* Princeton, N.J.: Princeton University Press, 1963.

Chang I-jen 張以仁. *Kuo-yü Tso-chuan lun-chi* 國語左傳論集. Tung-sheng hsüehjen chuan-k'an 2. Taipei: Tung-sheng, 1980.

Chang I-jen et al. *"Kuo-yü."* In Loewe, *Early Chinese Texts,* 263–268.

Chang I-jen hsien-sheng ch'i-chih shou-ch'ing lun-wen chi 張以仁先生七秩壽慶論文集. 2 vols. Taipei: Hsüeh-sheng, 1999.

Chang, K. C. *Art, Myth, and Ritual: The Path to Political Authority in Ancient China.* Cambridge: Harvard University Press, 1983.

———. "Shang Shamans." In Peterson et al., 10–36.

Chang Su-ch'ing 張素卿. *Tso-chuan ch'eng-Shih yen-chiu* 左傳稱詩研究. Kuo-li T'aiwan Ta-hsüeh wen-shih ts'ung-k'an 89. Taipei, 1991.

Chao I 趙翼 (1727–1814). *Kai-yü ts'ung-k'ao* 陔餘叢考. N.p., 1790.

———. *Nien-erh shih cha-chi* 廿二史札記. (1795; repr., Taipei: Hua-shih, 1977).

Chao Shih-ch'ao 趙世超. *Chou-tai kuo-yeh kuan-hsi yen-chiu* 周代國野關係研究. Taipei: Wen-chin, 1993.

Chavannes, Edouard. *Les Mémoires historiques de Se-ma Ts'ien.* 6 vols. Paris: Ernest Leroux, 1895–1905.

Chen, Yu-shih. "The Historical Template of Pan Chao's *Nü Chieh.*" *T'oung Pao* 82 (1996): 229–257.

Chen, Yuvoon. "Zur Frage der Ausschweifung in der Ch'un-ch'iu Periode (771–480 v.Chr.)." *Oriens Extremus* 19 (1972): 23–26.

Chen Zhi. "A New Reading of 'Yen-yen.'" *T'oung Pao* 85.1–3 (1999): 1–28.

Ch'en Ch'i-yün [陳啟雲]. "Confucian, Legalist, and Taoist thought in Later Han." In Twitchett and Loewe, 766–807.

———. *Han Chin Liu-ch'ao wen-hua, she-hui, chih-tu—Chung-hua chung-ku ch'ien-ch'i shih yen-chiu* 漢晉六朝文化、社會、制度—中華中古前期史研究. Taipei: Hsin wen-feng, 1996.

Ch'en Chih 陳直. *Shih-chi hsin-cheng* 史記新證. T'ien-chin: Jen-min, 1979.

Ch'en Ku-yüan 陳顧遠. *Chung-kuo hun-yin shih* 中國婚姻史. Chiu-chi hsin-k'an. 1936; repr., Ch'ang-sha: Yüeh-lu, 1998. [This book is bound together with that of Wang Shu-nu.]

Ch'en Ping-liang 陳炳良. "Shuo 'Ju-fen': Chien-lun *Shih-ching* chung yu-kuan lien-ai ho hun-yin te shih" 説汝墳：兼論詩經中有關戀愛和婚姻的詩. *Chung-wai wen-hsüeh* 中外文學 7.12 (1979): 138–155.

Ch'en Shih-hsiang. "The *Shih-Ching*: Its Generic Significance in Chinese Literary History and Poetics." *Ch'ing-chu Li Fang-kuei hsien-sheng liu-shih-wu sui lun-wen chi* 慶祝李方桂先生六十五歲論文集. *Bulletin of the Institute of History and Philology* 39 (1969): 371–413. Reprinted in Birch, 8–41.

Ch'en Tung-yüan 陳東原. *Chung-kuo fu-nü sheng-huo shih* 中國婦女生活史. Shanghai: Shang-wu, 1937.

Ch'en Yin-k'o 陳寅恪. "'T'ao-hua yüan chi' p'ang-cheng" 桃花源記旁證. *Ch'ing-hua hsüeh-pao* 清華學報 11 (1938): 79–88.

Cheng Liang-shu 鄭良樹. *Shang Yang chi-ch'i hsüeh-p'ai* 商鞅及其學派. Shanghai: Ku-chi, 1989.

———. *Han Fei chih chu-shu chi ssu-hsiang* 韓非之著述及思想. Chung-kuo che-hsüeh ts'ung-shu 35. Taipei: Hsüeh-sheng, 1993.

———. *Shang Yang p'ing-chuan* 商鞅評傳. Chung-kuo ssu-hsiang chia p'ing-chuan ts'ung-shu 5. Nan-ching: Nan-ching Ta-hsüeh, 1998.

Chi Yün 紀昀 (1724–1805) et al. *Ssu-k'u ch'üan-shu tsung-mu t'i-yao* 四庫全書總目提要. 4 vols. *Kuo-hsüeh chi-pen ts'ung-shu*.

Chiang Jung-ch'ang 蔣榮昌. "Chung-kuo wen-hua te kung-ssu kuan" 中國文化的公私觀. *Hsi-nan Min-tsu Hsüeh-yüan hsüeh-pao: Che-she pan* 西南民族學院學報：哲社版 1998.4: 1–17.

Ch'ien Chung-shu 錢鍾書. *Kuan-chui pien* 管錐編. 2d ed. 5 vols. Peking: Chung-hua, 1986.

Ch'ien Mu 錢穆. *Hsien-Ch'in chu-tzu hsi-nien* 先秦諸子繫年. 2d ed. Ts'ang-hai ts'ung-k'an. Hong Kong: Hong Kong University Press, 1956; repr., Taipei: Tung-ta, 1990.

———. *Ch'in Han shih* 秦漢史. Hong Kong: Hsin-hua, 1957.

Ch'ien Ta-hsin 錢大昕 (1728–1804). *Nieh-erh shih k'ao-i* 廿二史考異. *Shih-hsüeh ts'ung-shu* 史學叢書.

Chin Fa-ken 金發根. "Wang Fu sheng-tsu nien-sui te k'ao-cheng chi *Ch'ien-fu lun* hsieh-ting shih-chien te t'uei-lun" 王符生卒年歲的考證及潛夫論寫定時間的推論. *Kung-chu tsung-t'ung Chiang-kung pa-chih chin erh hua-tan Li-shih Yü-yen Yen-chiu-so ch'eng-li ssu-shih chou-nien chi-nien* 恭祝總統蔣公八秩晉二華誕歷史語言研究所成立四十周年紀念. *Bulletin of the Institute of History and Philology* 40 (1969): 781–799.

Ching, Julia. *Mysticism and Kingship in China: The Heart of Chinese Wisdom*. Cambridge Studies in Religious Traditions 11. Cambridge, 1997.

Ching, Julia, and R. W. L. Guisso, eds. *Sages and Filial Sons: Mythology and Archaeology in Ancient China*. Hong Kong: Chinese University Press, 1991.

Chou Chen-ho 周振鶴. "Ts'ung 'Chiu-chou i-su' tao 'Liu-ho t'ung-feng'— Liang-Han feng-su ch'ü-hua te pien-ch'ien" 從九州異俗到六合同風— 兩漢風俗區劃的變遷. *Chung-kuo wen-hua yen-chiu* 中國文化研究 1997.4: 60–68.

Chou Chien-chung 周建忠. *Ch'u-tz'u lun-kao* 楚辭論稿. Cheng-chou: Chung-chou ku-chi, 1994.

Chou Chien-kuo 周建國. "Shu-sun T'ung ting 'pang-chang' chih-i—chien hsi Chang-chia-shan Han-chien so-tsai lü p'ien-ming" 叔孫通定傍章質疑—兼析張家山漢簡所載律篇名. *Pei-ching Ta-hsüeh hsüeh-pao: Che-she pan* 北京大學學報：哲社版 1997.6: 44–53.

Chou, Eric. *The Dragon and the Phoenix: The Book of Chinese Love and Sex*. New York: Arbor House, 1971; repr., New York: Bantam, 1972.

Chou Fa-kao 周法高. *Chou Ch'in ming-tzu chieh-ku hui-shih* 周秦名字解詁彙釋. Chung-hua ts'ung-shu. Taipei, 1958.

Chou, Ying-hsiung. "The Linguistic and Mythical Structure of *Hsing* as a Combinational Model." In Deeney, 51–79.

Chow, Tse-tsung. "The Childbirth Myth and Ancient Chinese Medicine: A Study of Aspects of the *Wu* Tradition." In Roy and Tsien, 43–89.

———, ed. *Wen-lin: Studies in the Chinese Humanities*. 2 vols. Madison: University of Wisconsin Press, 1968–1989.

Chu Pi-lien 朱碧蓮. *Ch'u-tz'u lun-kao* 楚辭論稿. Shanghai: San-lien, 1993.

Ch'ü, T'ung-tsu. *Han Social Structure*. Ed. Jack L. Dull. Han Dynasty China 1. Seattle: University of Washington Press, 1972.

Ch'ü Wan-li. "Lun 'Kuo-feng' fei min-chien ko-yao te pen-lai mien-mu" 論國風非民間歌謠的本來面目. *Ku yüan-chang Hu Shih hsien-sheng chi-nien lun-wen chi* 故院長胡適先生紀念論文集. *Bulletin of the Institute of History and Philology* 34 (1963): 477–504.

Chūgoku chūshishi kenkyūkai 中國中世史研究會. *Chūgoku chūshishi kenkyū: Zokuhen* 中國中世史研究：續編. Kyoto: Kyōtō Daigaku gakujutsu, 1995.

Cohen, Alvin P. "Avenging Ghosts and Moral Judgement in Ancient China: Three Examples from the *Shih-chi*." In Allan and Cohen, 97–108.

Cook, Constance A., and John S. Major, eds. *Defining Chu: Image and Reality in Ancient China*. Honolulu: University of Hawai'i Press, 1999.

Couvreur, S., S.J., trans. *Li Ki ou Mémoires sur les bienséances et les cérémonies*. 2d ed. 2 vols. Ho Kien Fou: Mission Catholique, 1913.

Creel, Herrlee G. *The Origins of Statecraft in China*. Chicago: University of Chicago Press, 1970.

———. *What Is Taoism? and Other Studies in Chinese Cultural History*. Midway Reprint. Chicago: University of Chicago Press, 1970.

———. *Shen Pu-hai: A Chinese Political Philosopher of the Fourth Century B.C.* Chicago: University of Chicago Press, 1974.

Crump, J. I. *Intrigues: Studies of the* Chan-kuo Ts'e. Ann Arbor: University of Michigan Press, 1964.

———, trans. *Chan-kuo Ts'e*. Rev. ed. Michigan Monographs in Chinese Studies 77. Ann Arbor, 1996.

———, trans. *Legends of the Warring States: Persuasions, Romances, and Stories from* Chan-kuo Ts'e. Michigan Monographs in Chinese Studies 83. Ann Arbor, 1999.

Cutter, Robert Joe, and William Gordon Crowell, trans. *Empresses and Consorts: Selections from Chen Shou's* Records of the Three States *with Pei Songzhi's Commentary.* Honolulu: University of Hawai'i Press, 1999.

Davidson, Arnold I. "Closing up the corpses: diseases of sexuality and the emergence of the psychiatric style of reasoning." In Boolos, 295–325.

Davidson, James N. *Courtesans and Fishcakes: The Consuming Passions of Classical Athens.* New York: Harper Collins, 1997.

Dean-Jones, Lesley. "The Politics of Pleasure: Female Sexual Appetite in the Hippocratic Corpus." In Stanton, 48–77.

———. "The Cultural Construct of the Female Body in Classical Greek Science." In Pomeroy, 111–137.

Deeney, John J., ed. *Chinese-Western Comparative Literature Theory and Strategy.* Hong Kong: Chinese University Press, 1980.

Demiéville, Paul. *Choix d'études sinologiques (1921–1970).* Leiden: E. J. Brill, 1973.

———. *L'œuvre de Wang le zélateur (Wang Fan-tche) suivie des Instructions domestiques de l'Aïeul (T'ai-kong kia-kiao): Poèmes populaires des T'ang (VIIIe–Xe siècles).* Bibliothèque de l'Institut des Hautes Études Chinoises 26. Paris, 1982.

Despeux, Catherine. "L'ordination des femmes taoïstes sous les Tang." *Etudes Chinoises* 5 (1986): 53–100.

Dien, Albert E. "Introduction." In Dien, ed., 1–29.

———, ed. *State and Society in Early Medieval China.* Stanford, Calif.: Stanford University Press, 1990.

Diény, Jean-Pierre. *Portrait anecdotique d'un gentilhomme Chinois: Xie An (320–385) d'après le* Shishuo xinyu. Bibliothèque de l'Institut des Hautes Études Chinoises 28. Paris, 1993.

Dikötter, Frank. *Sex, Culture, and Modernity in China: Medical Science and the Construction of Sexual Identities in the Early Republican Period.* Honolulu: University of Hawai'i Press, 1995.

Dover, K. J. "Classical Greek Attitudes to Sexual Behavior." *Arethusa* 6 (1973): 59–70. Reprinted in Peradotto and Sullivan, 143–157.

———. *Greek Homosexuality.* Reprint, New York: MJF, 1989.

Duberman, Martin, et al., eds. *Hidden from History: Reclaiming the Gay and Lesbian Past.* New York: Meridian, 1989.

Dubs, Homer H., trans. (with the collaboration of Jen T'ai and P'an Lo-chi). *History of the Former Han Dynasty.* 3 vols. Baltimore: Waverly, 1938–1955.

Dull, Jack L. "Marriage and Divorce in Han China: A Glimpse at 'Pre-Confucian' Society." In Buxbaum, 23–74.

Durrant, Stephen W. "Smoothing Edges and Filling Gaps: *Tso chuan* and the 'General Reader.'" *Journal of the American Oriental Society* 112.1 (1992): 36–41.

———. *The Cloudy Mirror: Tension and Conflict in the Writings of Sima Qian.* SUNY Series in Chinese Philosophy and Culture. Albany, N.Y., 1995.

Eberhard, Wolfram. *Conquerors and Rulers: Social Forces in Medieval China.* 2d ed. Leiden: E. J. Brill, 1970.

Ebrey, Patricia Buckley. *The Aristocratic Families of Early Imperial China: A Case Study of the Po-ling Ts'ui Family.* Cambridge Studies in Chinese History, Literature and Institutions. Cambridge, 1978.

————. "The Economic and Social History of Later Han." In Twitchett and Loewe, 608–648.

————. *The Inner Quarters: Marriage and the Lives of Chinese Women in the Sung Period.* Berkeley and Los Angeles: University of California Press, 1993.

Eichhorn, Werner. "Bemerkungen zum Aufstand des Chang Chio und zum Staate des Chang Lu." *Mitteilungen des Instituts für Orientforschung* 3 (1955): 291–327.

————. "T'ai-p'ing und T'ai-p'ing Religion." *Mitteilungen des Instituts für Orientforschung* 5 (1957): 113–140.

Eliade, Mircea. *Le chamanisme et les techniques archaïques de l'extase.* 2d ed. Paris: Payot, 1974.

Englert, Siegfried. *Materialien zur Stellung der Frau und zur Sexualität im vormodernen und modernen China.* Heidelberger Schriften zur Ostasienkunde 1. Frankfurt: Haag und Herchen, 1980.

Englert, Siegfried, and Roderich Ptak. "Nan-tzu, or Why Heaven Did Not Crush Confucius." *Journal of the American Oriental Society* 106.4 (1986): 679–686.

Erkes, Eduard. "Some Remarks on Karlgren's 'Fecundity Symbols in Ancient China.'" *Bulletin of the Museum of Far Eastern Antiquities* 3 (1931): 63–68.

————. "Zur Sage von Shun." *T'oung Pao* 34.4 (1938–1939): 295–333.

Fantham, Elaine, et al. *Women in the Classical World: Image and Text.* New York: Oxford University Press, 1994.

Faure, Bernard. *The Red Thread: Buddhist Approaches to Sexuality.* Buddhisms: A Princeton University Press Series. Princeton, N.J., 1998.

Fei Xiaotong. *From the Soil: The Foundations of Chinese Society.* Trans. Gary G. Hamilton and Wang Zheng. Berkeley and Los Angeles: University of California Press, 1992.

Feng, H. Y., and J. K. Shyrock. "The Black Magic in China Known as *Ku*." *Journal of the American Oriental Society* 55 (1935): 1–30.

Fingarette, Herbert. "Following the 'One Thread' of the *Analects*." In Rosemont and Schwartz, 373–405.

Forke, Alfred. *Geschichte der mittelalterlichen chinesischen Philosophie.* Abhandlungen aus dem Gebiet der Auslandskunde 41. Repr., Hamburg: Cram, de Gruyter, and Co., 1964.

Foucault, Michel. *The History of Sexuality.* Trans. Robert Hurley. 3 vols. New York: Random House, Vintage Books, 1978–1986.

Frühstück, Sabine. "Managing the Truth of Sex in Imperial Japan." *Journal of Asian Studies* 59.2 (2000): 332–358.

Fukunaga Mitsuji 福永光司. "'Taijin fu' no shisōteki keifu: Jifu no bungaku to Rō-Sō no tetsugaku 大人賦の思想的系譜：楚辭の文學と老莊の哲學. *Tōhō gakuhō* 東方學報 41 (1970): 97–126.

Fung Yu-lan. *A History of Chinese Philosophy.* Trans. Derk Bodde. 2 vols. Princeton, N.J.: Princeton University Press, 1952–1953.

Furth, Charlotte. "Androgynous Males and Deficient Females: Biology and Gender Boundaries in Sixteenth- and Seventeenth-Century China." *Late Imperial China* 9.2 (1988): 1–31.

————. "Rethinking van Gulik: Sexuality and Reproduction in Traditional Chinese Medicine." In Gilmartin et al., 125–146.

Gernet, Jacques. *China and the Christian Impact: A Conflict of Cultures.* Trans. Janet Lloyd. Cambridge: Cambridge University Press, 1985.

Giles, Herbert A. *A History of Chinese Literature.* New York: Grove, 1923.

Gilmartin, Christina K., et al., eds. *Engendering China: Women, Culture, and the State.* Harvard Contemporary China Series 10. Cambridge, 1994.

Girardot, N. J. *Myth and Meaning in Early Taoism: The Theme of Chaos (hun-tun).* Hermeneutics: Studies in the History of Religions. Berkeley and Los Angeles: University of California Press, 1983.

Goldin, Paul Rakita. "Reading Po Chü-i." *T'ang Studies* 12 (1994): 57–96.

———. "Reflections on Irrationalism in Chinese Aesthetics." *Monumenta Serica* 44 (1996): 167–189.

———. "Insidious Syncretism in the Political Philosophy of *Huai-nan-tzu.*" *Asian Philosophy* 9.3 (1999): 165–191.

———. *Rituals of the Way: The Philosophy of Xunzi.* Chicago: Open Court, 1999.

———. "Personal Names in Early China—A Research Note." *Journal of the American Oriental Society* 120.1 (2000): 77–81.

———. "The View of Women in Early Confucianism." In Chenyang Li, 133–161.

———. "Some Commonplaces in the *Shiji* Biographies of Talented Men." In Puett.

Goldman, Alan. "Plain Sex." *Philosophy and Public Affairs* 6.3 (1977): 267–287.

Goodman, Howard, L., and Anthony Grafton. "Ricci, the Chinese, and the Toolkits of Textualists." *Asia Major,* 3d ser., 3.2 (1990): 95–148.

Graham, A. C. "The Final Particle *Fwu* 夫." *Bulletin of the School of Oriental and African Studies* 17.1 (1955): 120–132.

———. *Disputers of the Tao: Philosophical Argument in Ancient China.* La Salle, Ill.: Open Court, 1989.

Granet, Marcel. *Fêtes et chansons anciennes de la Chine.* Paris: Ernest Leroux, 1919.

———. "Remarques sur le Taoïsme Ancien." *Asia Major,* 1st ser., 2.1 (1925): 146–151.

———. *Danses et légendes de la Chine ancienne.* 2 vols. Bibliothèque de philosophie contemporaine; Travaux de l'Année sociologique. Paris: Félix Alcan, 1926.

———. *La pensée chinoise.* L'évolution de l'humanité: Synthèse collective 25b. Paris: Albin Michel, 1950.

———. *Études sociologiques sur la Chine.* Bibliothèque de sociologie contemporaine. Paris: Presses Universitaires de France, 1953.

de Groot, J. J. M. *The Religious System of China.* 6 vols. Leiden: E. J. Brill, 1892–1910; repr., Taipei: Southern Materials Center, 1989.

Guisso, Richard W. "Thunder over the Lake: The Five Classics and the Perception of Woman in Early China." In Guisso and Johannesen, 47–61.

Guisso, Richard W., and Stanley Johannesen, eds. *Women in China: Current Directions in Historical Scholarship.* Historical Reflections/Réflexions Historiques: Directions 3. Youngstown, N.Y.: Philo Press, 1981.

van Gulik, R. H. *Sexual Life in Ancient China: A Preliminary Survey of Chinese Sex and Society from ca. 1500 B.C. till 1644 A.D.* Leiden: E. J. Brill, 1961; repr., New York: Barnes and Noble, 1996.

Hall, David L., and Roger T. Ames. *Thinking from the Han: Self, Truth, and Transcendence in Chinese and Western Culture.* Albany: State University of New York Press, 1998.

Halperin, David M. "Why Is Diotima a Woman? Platonic *Erōs* and the Figuration of Gender." In Halperin et al., 257–308.

———. "Historicizing the Sexual Body: Sexual Preferences and Erotic Identities in the Pseudo-Lucianic *Erōtes*." In Stanton, 236–261.

———. "Is There a History of Sexuality?" In Baker et al., 413–431.

Halperin, David M., et al., eds. *Before Sexuality: The Construction of Erotic Experience in the Ancient Greek World.* Princeton, N.J.: Princeton University Press, 1990.

Handlin, Joanna F. "Lü K'un's New Audience: The Influence of Women's Literacy on Sixteenth-Century Thought." In Wolf and Witke, 13–38.

Hankel, Bernt. *Der Weg in den Sarg: Die ersten Tage des Bestattungsrituals in den konfuzianischen Ritenklassikern.* Münstersche Sinologische Mitteilungen: Beiträge zur Geschichte und Kultur des alten China 4. Bad Honnef: Bock und Herchen, 1995.

Hansen, Chad. *A Daoist Theory of Chinese Thought: A Philosophical Interpretation.* New York: Oxford University Press, 1992.

Harbsmeier, Christoph. "Eroticism in Early Chinese Poetry: Sundry Comparative Notes." In Schmidt-Glintzer, *Das andere China,* 323–380.

Harper, Donald. "A Chinese Demonography of the Third Century B.C." *Harvard Journal of Asiatic Studies* 45.2 (1985): 459–498.

———. "The Sexual Arts of Ancient China as Described in a Manuscript of the Second Century B.C." *Harvard Journal of Asiatic Studies* 47.2 (1987): 539–593.

———. "*Spellbinding.*" In Lopez, 241–250.

———. "Warring States, Qin, and Han Manuscripts Related to Natural Philosophy and the Occult." In Shaughnessy, *New Sources,* 223–252.

———. *Early Chinese Medical Literature: The Mawangdui Medical Manuscripts.* The Sir Henry Wellcome Asian Series. London: Kegan Paul International, 1998.

Hart, James A. "The Speech of Prince Chin: A Study of Early Chinese Cosmology." In Rosemont, *Explorations in Early Chinese Cosmology,* 35–65.

Hauser, Renate. "Krafft-Ebing's Psychological Understanding of Sexual Behaviour." In Porter and Teich, 210–227.

Hawkes, David. "The Quest of the Goddess." *Asia Major,* n.s., 13 (1967): 71–94.

———, trans. *The Songs of the South: An Ancient Chinese Anthology of Poems by Qu Yuan and Other Poets.* New York: Penguin, 1985.

Henricks, Robert G. *Philosophy and Argumentation in Third-Century China: The Essays of Hsi K'ang.* Princeton Library of Asian Translations. Princeton, N.J., 1983.

Henry, Eric. "The Social Significance of Nudity in Early China." *Fashion Theory* 3.4 (1999): 475–486.

Hershatter, Gail. *Dangerous Pleasures: Prostitution and Modernity in Twentieth-Century Shanghai.* Berkeley and Los Angeles: University of California Press, 1997.

Hightower, James Robert, trans. *Han Shih Wai Chuan: Han Ying's Illustrations of the Didactic Application of the Classic of Songs.* Harvard-Yenching Institute Monograph Series 11. Cambridge, 1952.

Hinsch, Bret. *Passions of the Cut Sleeve: The Male Homosexual Tradition in China.* Berkeley and Los Angeles: University of California Press, 1990.

———. "Women, Kinship, and Property as Seen in a Han Dynasty Will." *T'oung Pao* 84.1–3 (1998): 1–20.

Hirschfeld, Magnus, et al. *The Sexual History of the World War*. New York: Cadillac, 1946.

Ho Ch'i-min 何啟民. *Chu-lin ch'i-hsien yen-chiu* 竹林七賢研究. Taipei: Shang-wu, 1965.

Hobsbawm, Eric. *On History*. London: Little, Brown and Co., Abacus, 1998.

Holcombe, Charles. *In the Shadow of the Han: Literati Thought and Society at the Beginning of the Southern Dynasties*. Honolulu: University of Hawai'i Press, 1994.

Holzman, Donald. *La vie et la pensée de Hi K'ang (223–262 ap. J.-C.)*. Leiden: E. J. Brill, 1957.

————. *Poetry and Politics: The Life and Works of Juan Chi*, A.D. *210–263*. Cambridge: Cambridge University Press, 1976.

————. "Confucius and Ancient Chinese Literary Criticism." In Rickett, 21–41.

————. "The Place of Filial Piety in Ancient China." *Journal of the American Oriental Society* 118.2 (1998): 185–199.

Horiike Nobuo 堀池信夫. *Kan Gi shisōshi kenkyū* 漢魏思想史研究. Tokyo: Meiji, 1988.

Hoshikawa Kiyotaka 星川清孝. *Soji no kenkyū* 楚辭の研究. Tokyo: Yōtokusha, 1963.

Hsiao, Kung-chuan. *A History of Chinese Political Thought*. Vol. 1, *From the Beginnings to the Sixth Century* A.D. Trans. F. W. Mote. Princeton Library of Asian Translations. Princeton, N.J., 1979.

Hsiao Li 肖黎. *Ssu-ma Ch'ien p'ing-chuan* 司馬遷評傳. Chung-kuo li-shih jen-wu ts'ung-shih. N.p.: Chi-lin wen-shih, 1986.

Hsiao Ping 蕭兵. *Ch'u-tz'u te wen-hua p'o-i* 楚辭的文化破譯. Chung-kuo wen-hua te jen-lei-hsüeh p'o-i. Hu-pei: Hu-pei jen-min, 1991.

Hsieh Chin-ch'ing 謝晉青. *Shih-ching chih nü-hsing te yen-chiu* 詩經之女性的研究. 3d ed. Kuo-hsüeh hsiao ts'ung-shu. Shanghai: Shang-wu, 1934.

Hsieh Pao-fu 謝寶富. *Pei-ch'ao hun-sang li-su yen-chiu* 北朝婚喪禮俗研究. Peking: Shou-tu Shih-fan Ta-hsüeh, 1998.

Hsü Chih-hsiao 徐志嘯. *Ch'u-tz'u tsung-lun* 楚辭綜論. Ts'ang-hai ts'ung-k'an. Taipei: Tung-ta, 1994.

Hsü Cho-yün. "Comparisons of Idealized Societies in Chinese History: Confucian and Taoist Models." In Ching and Guisso, 43–63.

————. "The Roles of the Literati and of Regionalism in the Fall of the Han Dynasty." In Yoffee and Cowgill, 176–195.

————. "The Spring and Autumn Period." In Loewe and Shaughnessy, 545–586.

Hsü Fu-ch'ang 徐富昌. "Shui-hu-ti Ch'in-mu *Jih-shu* chung te kuei-shen hsin-yang" 睡虎地秦墓日書中的鬼神信仰. In *Chang I-jen hsien-sheng ch'i-chih shou-ch'ing lun-wen chi*, vol. 2, 873–926.

Hsü K'ang-sheng 許抗生. *Wei Chin ssu-hsiang shih* 魏晉思想史. Kuei-kuan ts'ung-k'an 28. Taipei, 1992.

Hsü Shih-ying 許世瑛. "*Shih-shuo hsin-yü* chung ti-erh shen ch'eng tai-tz'u yen-chiu" 世說新語中第二身稱代詞研究. *Chi-nien Tung Tso-pin Tung T'ung-ho liang hsien-sheng lun-wen chi* 紀念董作賓、董同龢兩先生論文集. *Bulletin of the Institute of History and Philology* 36 (1965): 185–235.

Hu Shih 胡適 (1891–1962). "Lun 'Yeh yu ssu chün' shu" 論野有死麕書. In Ku, ed. *Ku-shih pien*, vol. 3, 442–443.

————. "T'an-t'an *Shih-ching*" 談談詩經. In Ku, ed., *Ku-shih pien*, vol. 3, 576–587.

Huang Jen-erh 黃人二. "Kuo-tien Ch'u-chien 'Lu Mu-kung wen Tzu-ssu' k'ao-shih" 郭店楚簡魯穆公問子思考釋. In *Chang I-jen hsien-sheng ch'i-chih shou-ch'ing lun-wen chi*, vol. 1, 397–404.

Hucker, Charles O. *A Dictionary of Official Titles in Imperial China*. Stanford, Calif.: Stanford University Press, 1985.

Hulsewé, A. F. P. *Remnants of Han Law*. Vol. 1, *Introductory Studies and an Annotated Translation of Chapters 22 and 23 of the History of the Former Han Dynasty*. Sinica Leidensia 9. Leiden: E. J. Brill, 1955.

————. *Remnants of Ch'in Law: An Annotated Translation of the Ch'in Legal and Administrative Rules of the Third Century B.C. Discovered in Yün-meng Prefecture, Hu-pei Province, in 1975*. Sinica Leidensia 17. Leiden: E. J. Brill, 1985.

Hultkrantz, Åke. "A Definition of Shamanism." *Temenos* 9 (1973): 25–37.

Hung Chia-i 洪家義. *Lü Pu-wei p'ing-chuan* 呂不韋評傳. Chung-kuo ssu-hsiang chia p'ing-chuan ts'ung-shu 11. Nan-ching: Nan-ching Ta-hsüeh, 1995.

I Chung-t'ien 易中天. *Chung-kuo te nan-jen ho nü-jen* 中國的男人和女人. I Chung-t'ien suei-pi-t'i hsüeh-shu chu-tso, Chung-kuo wen-hua hsi-lieh 2. Shanghai: Wen-i, 2000.

Idema, W. L., and E. Zürcher, eds. *Thought and Law in Qin and Han China: Studies Dedicated to Anthony Hulsewé on the Occasion of His Eightieth Birthday*. Sinica Leidensia 24. Leiden: E. J. Brill, 1990.

Irani, K. D., and Morris Silver, eds. *Social Justice in the Ancient World*. Contributions in Political Science 354: Global Perspectives in History and Politics. Westport, Conn.: Greenwood, 1995.

Ivanhoe, Philip J. "Reweaving the 'One Thread' in the *Analects*." *Philosophy East and West* 40.1 (1990): 17–33.

Jay, Jennifer W. "Another Side of Chinese Eunuch History: Castration, Marriage, Adoption, and Burial." *Canadian Journal of History* 28.3 (1993): 459–478.

Johnson, David G. *The Medieval Chinese Oligarchy*. Westview Special Studies on China and East Asia. Boulder, Colo., 1977.

Kaizuka Shigeki 貝塚茂樹. *Kaizuka Shigeki chosaku shū* 著作集. Tokyo: Chūō Kōronsha, 1978.

Kaltenmark, Max. "*Ling-pao:* Note sur un terme du Taoïsme religieux." *Mélanges publiés par l'Institut des Hautes Études Chinoises* 2 (1960): 559–588.

————. *Lao Tzu and Taoism*. Trans. Roger Greaves. Stanford, Calif.: Stanford University Press, 1969.

Kanaya Osamu 金谷治. *Shin Kan shisōshi kenkyū* 秦漢思想史研究. Tokyo: Heirakuji, 1960.

Karlgren, Bernhard. *The Authenticity and Nature of the Tso Chuan*. Göteborg, Sweden: Elanders, 1926.

————. "Some Fecundity Symbols in Ancient China." *Bulletin of the Museum of Far Eastern Antiquities* 2 (1930): 1–66.

————. "Legends and Cults in Ancient China." *Bulletin of the Museum of Far Eastern Antiquities* 18 (1946): 199–366.

————. *Glosses on the Book of Odes*. Stockholm: Museum of Far Eastern Antiquities, 1964.

————, trans. *The Book of Odes*. Stockholm: Museum of Far Eastern Antiquities, 1950.

Keightley, David N. "Shamanism, Death, and the Ancestors: Religious Mediation in Neolithic and Shang China (ca. 5000–1000 B.C.)." *Asiatische Studien/Etudes Asiatiques* 52.3 (1998): 763–831.

Kierman, Frank A., Jr., and John K. Fairbank, eds. *Chinese Ways in Warfare*. Harvard East Asian Series 74. Cambridge, Mass., 1974.

Kinney, Anne Behnke. "Dyed Silk: Han Notions of the Moral Development of Children." In Kinney, *Chinese Views of Childhood*, 17–56.

————, ed. *Chinese Views of Childhood*. Honolulu: University of Hawai'i Press, 1995.

Kleeman, Terry F. "Licentious Cults and Bloody Victuals: Sacrifice, Reciprocity, and Violence in Traditional China." *Asia Major*, 3d ser., 7.1 (1994): 185–211.

Knapp, Bettina L. *Images of Chinese Women: A Westerner's View*. Troy, N.Y.: Whitston, 1992.

Knechtges, David R. "Riddles as Poetry: The '*Fu*-Chapter' of the *Hsün-tzu*." In Chow, vol. 2, 1–31.

Knoblock, John, trans. *Xunzi: A Translation and Study of the Complete Works*. 3 vols. Stanford, Calif.: Stanford University Press, 1988–1994.

Ko, Dorothy. *Teachers of the Inner Chambers: Women and Culture in Seventeenth-Century China*. Stanford, Calif.: Stanford University Press, 1994.

Kobayashi Masayoshi 小林正美. *Rikuchō Dōkyōshi kenkyū* 六朝道教史研究. Tōyōgaku sōsho 37. Tokyo: Sōbunsha, 1990.

Kohn, Livia. *Laughing at the Tao: Debates among Buddhists and Taoists in Medieval China*. Princeton, N.J.: Princeton University Press, 1995.

von Krafft-Ebing, Richard (1840–1902). *Psychopathia Sexualis, with Especial Reference to the Antipathic Sexual Instinct: A Medico-Forensic Study*. Trans. Franklin S. Klaf. New York: Stein and Day, 1965; repr., New York: Arcade, 1998.

Kralle, Jianfei, with Roderich Ptak and Dennis Schilling. "Böse Brut: Bao Si [褒姒] und das Ende von König You [幽王]." *Zeitschrift der deutschen morgenländischen Gesellschaft* 149.1 (1999): 145–172.

Kristeva, Julia. *About Chinese Women*. Trans. Anita Barrows. New York: Urizen, 1977.

Kroll, J. L. "Notes on Ch'in and Han Law." In Idema and Zürcher, 63–78.

Kroll, Paul W. "On 'Far Roaming.'" *Journal of the American Oriental Society* 116.4 (1996): 653–669.

Kryukov, Vassili. "Symbols of Power and Communication in Pre-Confucian China (on the Anthropology of *De*): Preliminary Assumptions." *Bulletin of the School of Oriental and African Studies* 58 (1995): 314–332.

Ku Chieh-kang 顧頡剛 (1893–1980). "*Shih-ching* tsai Ch'un-ch'iu Chan-kuo chien te ti-wei" 詩經在春秋戰國間的地位. In Ku, *Ku-shih pien*, vol. 3, 309–367.

————. "Yeh yu ssu chün" 野有死麕. In Ku, *Ku-shih pien*, vol. 3, 439–443.

Ku Chieh-kang, ed. *Ku-shih pien* 古史辨. 7 vols. Repr., Shanghai: Ku-chi, 1982.

Ku-tai Han-yü hsü-tz'u tz'u-tien 古代漢語虛詞詞典. Peking: Shang-wu, 2000.

Ku Tsu-yü 顧祖禹 (1631–1692). *Tu-shih fang-yü chi-yao* 讀史方輿紀要. Repr., Shanghai: Shanghai shu-tien, 1998.

Kuo Chen-hua 郭振華. *Chung-kuo ku-tai jen-sheng li-su wen-hua* 中國古代人生禮俗文化. Ch'uan-t'ung wen-hua yü hsien-tai wen-hua wen-ts'ung. Hsi-an: Shensi jen-min, 1998.

Kuo Hsing-wen 郭興文. *Chung-kuo ch'uan-t'ung hun-yin feng-su* 中國傳統婚姻風俗. Chung-kuo feng-su ts'ung-shu. Hsi-an: Shensi jen-min, 1994.

Kuo Mao-ch'ien 郭茂倩 (fl. 1084). *Yüeh-fu shih-chi* 樂府詩集. 4 vols. Peking: Chung-hua, 1979.

Kuo Mo-jo 郭沫若 (1892–1978). *Ch'ü Yüan yen-chiu* 屈原研究. 2d rev. ed. Shanghai: Hsin wen-i, 1952.

Kuo Shuang-ch'eng 郭雙成. *Shih-chi jen-wu chuan-chi lun kao* 史記人物傳記論稿. [Cheng-chou]: Chung-chou ku-chi, 1985.

Kuo Yin-t'ien 郭銀田. *T'ien-yüan shih-jen T'ao Ch'ien* 田園詩人陶潛. Repr., Taipei: San-jen, 1974.

Lai Han-p'ing 賴漢屏. *Shih-chi p'ing-shang* 史記評賞. San-min ts'ung-shu 159. Taipei, 1998.

Lao Kan. "The early use of the tally in China." In Roy and Tsien, 91–98.

Lau, D. C., trans. *Mencius.* New York: Penguin, 1970.

———. *Confucius: The Analects.* New York: Penguin, 1979.

Le Blanc, Charles, and Susan Blader, eds. *Chinese Ideas about Nature and Society: Studies in Honour of Derk Bodde.* Hong Kong: Hong Kong University Press, 1987.

Lee, Thomas H. C. "The Idea of Social Justice in Ancient China." In Irani and Silver, 125–146.

Legge, James, trans. *The Chinese Classics.* 5 vols. in 4. N.d.; repr., Taipei: SMC, 1991.

Levy, Howard S. "Yellow Turban Religion and Rebellion at the End of the Han." *Journal of the American Oriental Society* 76 (1956): 214–227.

———. *Chinese Sex Jokes in Traditional Times.* Asian Folklore and Social Life Monographs 58; Sino-Japanese Sexology Classics Series 5. Taipei, 1973.

Levy, Howard S., and Akira Ishihara. *The Tao of Sex: The Essence of Medical Prescriptions (Ishimpō).* 3d ed. Lower Lake, Calif.: Integral, 1989.

Lewis, I. M. *Ecstatic Religion: An Anthropological Study of Spirit Possession and Shamanism.* Pelican Anthropology. New York: Penguin, 1971.

Lewis, Mark Edward. *Sanctioned Violence in Early China.* SUNY Series in Chinese Philosophy and Culture. Albany, N.Y., 1990.

———. *Writing and Authority in Early China.* SUNY Series in Chinese Philosophy and Culture. Albany, N.Y., 1999.

Li, Chenyang. "The Confucian Concept of *Jen* and the Feminist Ethics of Care: A Comparative Study." *Hypatia* 9.1 (1994): 70–89. Reprinted in Chenyang Li, ed., 23–42.

Li, Chenyang, ed. *The Sage and the Second Sex: Confucianism, Ethics, and Gender.* Chicago: Open Court, 2000.

Li Chi. "The Changing Concept of the Recluse in Chinese Literature." *Harvard Journal of Asiatic Studies* 24 (1962–1963): 234–247.

Li Ling 李零. "The Formulaic Structure of Chu Divinatory Bamboo Slips." *Early China* 15 (1990): 71–86.

———. *Chung-kuo fang-shu k'ao* 中國方術考. Peking: Jen-min, 1993.

———. "An Archaeological Study of Taiyi (Grand One) Worship." Trans. Donald Harper. *Early Medieval China* 2 (1995–1996): 1–39.

———. "Tu Kuo-tien Ch'u-chien 'T'ai-i sheng shui'" 讀郭店楚簡太一生水. *Tao-chia wen-hua yen-chiu* 道家文化研究 17 (1999): 316–331.

Li Ling, and Keith McMahon. "The Contents and Terminology of the Mawang-dui Texts on the Arts of the Bedchamber." *Early China* 17 (1992): 145–185.

Li Meng-ts'un 李孟存, and Li Shang-shih 李尚師. *Chin-kuo shih* 晉國史. San-Chin wen-hua yen-chiu ts'ung-shu. T'ai-yüan: Shan-hsi ku-chi, 1999.

Li, Wai-yee. *Enchantment and Disenchantment: Love and Illusion in Chinese Literature.* Princeton, N.J.: Princeton University Press, 1993.

Li Yu-ning 李又寧, and Chang Yü-fa 張玉法, eds. *Chung-kuo fu-nü shih lun-wen chi* 中國婦女史論文集. Taipei: Shang-wu, 1981.

Liang Chang-chü 梁章鉅 (1775–1849). *T'ui-an sui-pi* 退庵隨筆. *Ssu-pu pei-yao.*

Liao, W. K., trans. *The Complete Works of Han Fei Tzu: A Classic of Chinese Legalism.* 2 vols. Probsthain's Oriental Series 25 and 26. London, 1939–1959.

Licht, Hans. *Sexual Life in Ancient Greece.* Trans. J. H. Freese. Ed. Lawrence H. Dawson. Repr., New York: Dorset, 1993.

Lin Chien-ming 林劍鳴. *Hsin-pien Ch'in Han shih* 新編秦漢史. 2 vols. Taipei: Wu-nan, 1992.

Lin Keng 林庚. *Shih-jen Ch'ü Yüan chi-ch'i tso-p'in yen-chiu* 詩人屈原及其作品研究. Chung-kuo ku-tai wen-hsüeh yen-chiu ts'ung-k'an. Shanghai, 1952.

Lin Yeh-lien 林葉連. *Chung-kuo li-tai Shih-ching hsüeh* 中國歷代詩經學. Chung-kuo wen-hsüeh yen-chiu ts'ung-k'an. Taipei: Hsüeh-sheng, 1993.

Liu Chen-tung 劉振東. *Chung-kuo Ju-hsüeh shih: Wei Chin Nan-pei-ch'ao chüan* 中國儒學史：魏晉南北朝卷. Kuang-chou: Kuang-tung chiao-yü, 1998.

Liu, James T. C. *Ou-yang Hsiu: An Eleventh-Century Neo-Confucianist.* Stanford, Calif.: Stanford University Press, 1967.

Liu Ta-lin 劉達臨. *Chung-kuo ku-tai hsing wen-hua* 中國古代性文化. 2 vols. Yin-ch'uan: Ning-hsia jen-min, 1993.

———. *Chung-kuo li-tai fang-nei k'ao* 中國歷代房內考. 3 vols. Peking: Chung-i ku-chi, 1998.

Liu Te-han 劉德漢. *Tung-Chou fu-nü sheng-huo* 東周婦女生活. Taipei: Hsüeh-sheng, 1976.

Liu Tseng-kuei 劉增貴. "Han-tai te hao-men hun-yin" 漢代的豪門婚姻. In Li Yu-ning and Chang Yü-fa, 20–49.

———. "Shih-lun Han-tai hun-yin kuan-hsi chung te li-fa kuan-nien" 試論漢代婚姻關係中的禮法觀念. In Pao Chia-lin, *Chung-kuo fu-nü shih lun-chi hsü-chi*, 1–36.

Liu Wen-ying 劉文英. *Wang Fu p'ing-chuan fu Ts'ui Shih Chung-ch'ang T'ung p'ing-chuan* 王符評傳附崔寔、仲長統評傳. Chung-kuo ssu-hsiang chia p'ing-chuan ts'ung-shu 27. Nan-ching: Nan-ching Ta-hsüeh, 1993.

Loewe, Michael. "The Campaigns of Han Wu-ti." In Kierman and Fairbank, 67–122.

———. *Crisis and Conflict in Han China: 104 B.C. to A.D. 9.* London: George Allen and Unwin, 1974.

———. "The Former Han Dynasty." In Twitchett and Loewe, 103–222.

———. "The Conduct of Government and the Issues at Stake (A.D. 57–167)." In Twitchett and Loewe, 291–316.

―――. *Divination, Mythology, and Monarchy in Han China*. University of Cambridge Oriental Publications 48. Cambridge, 1994.

―――, ed. *Early Chinese Texts: A Bibliographical Guide*. Early China Monograph Series 2. Berkeley, Calif., 1993.

Loewe, Michael, and Edward L. Shaughnessy, eds. *The Cambridge History of Ancient China: From the Origins of Civilization to 221 B.C.* Cambridge, 1999.

Lopez, Donald S., Jr., ed. *Religions of China in Practice*. Princeton Readings in Religions. Princeton, N.J., 1996.

Lu, Tonglin, ed. *Gender and Sexuality in Twentieth-Century Chinese Literature and Society*. SUNY Series in Feminist Criticism and Theory. Albany, N.Y., 1993.

Lü Ssu-mien 呂思勉. *Ch'in Han shih* 秦漢史. 2 vols. N.p.: K'ai-ming, 1947; repr., Hong Kong: T'ai-p'ing, 1962.

Ma Chih-su 馬之驌. "Wo-kuo ch'uan-t'ung chieh-hun te p'in-li" 我國傳統結婚的聘禮. In Li Yu-ning and Chang Yü-fa, 1–19.

Ma Tsung 馬總 (d. 823). *I-lin* 意林. *Ssu-pu pei-yao*.

Ma Tuan-lin 馬端臨 (1254–1325). *Wen-hsien t'ung-k'ao* 文獻通考. *Shih T'ung* 十通.

Ma, Yau-woon. "Confucius as a Literary Critic: A Comparison with the Early Greeks." In *Jao Tsung-i chiao-shou nan-yu tseng-pieh lun-wen chi* 饒宗頤教授南遊贈別論文集, 13–45. Hong Kong, 1970.

MacKinnon, Catherine A. "Does Sexuality Have a History?" In Stanton, 117–136.

Mair, Victor H. "Canine Conundrums: Dog Ancestor Myths of Origin in Ethnic Perspective." *Sino-Platonic Papers* 87 (1998).

―――, trans. *Tao Te Ching: The Classic Book of Integrity and the Way*. New York: Bantam, 1990.

―――, trans. *Wandering on the Way: Early Taoist Tales and Parables of Chuang Tzu*. New York: Bantam, 1994.

Major, John S. "Characteristics of Late Chu Religion." In Cook and Major, 121–143.

Makeham, John. "The Legalist Concept of *Hsing-ming*: An Example of the Contribution of Archeological Evidence to the Re-interpretation of Transmitted Texts." *Monumenta Serica* 39 (1990–1991): 87–114.

―――. "The Formation of *Lunyu* as a Book." *Monumenta Serica* 44 (1996): 1–24.

Malinowski, Bronislaw. *Sex and Repression in Savage Society*. Meridian Books M15, 1927; repr., Cleveland: World Publishing Co., 1955.

Manniche, Lise. *Sexual Life in Ancient Egypt*. London: Kegan Paul International, 1987.

Mansvelt Beck, B. J. "The Fall of Han." In Twitchett and Loewe, 317–376.

Maspero, Henri. *Mélanges posthumes sur les religions et l'histoire de la Chine*. Publications du Musée Guimet; Bibliothèque de diffusion 57–59. 3 vols. Paris: Civilisations du Sud, 1950.

―――. *Le Taoïme et les religions chinoises*. Bibliothèque des histoires. Paris: Gallimard, 1971.

―――. *China in Antiquity*. Trans. Frank A. Kierman, Jr. [Amherst]: University of Massachusetts Press, 1978.

Masubuchi Tatsuo 增淵龍夫. "Shunjū Sengoku jidai no shakai to kokka" 春秋戰國時代の社會と國家. In *Iwanami kōza sekai rekishi* 岩波講座世界歷史, IV, 139–179. Tokyo: Iwanami, 1970.

Mather, Richard B. "K'ou Ch'ien-chih and the Taoist Theocracy at the Northern Wei Court, 425–451." In Welch and Seidel, 103–122.

———. "Individualist Expressions of the Outsiders during the Six Dynasties." In Munro, 199–214.

———, trans. *Shih-shuo Hsin-yü: A New Account of Tales of the World.* Minneapolis: University of Minnesota Press, 1976.

McLeod, Katrina C. D., and Robin D. S. Yates. "Forms of Ch'in Law: An Annotated Translation of the *Feng-chen shih.*" *Harvard Journal of Asiatic Studies* 41.1 (1981): 111–163.

McMahon, Keith. *Misers, Shrews, and Polygamists: Sexuality and Male-Female Relations in Eighteenth-Century Chinese Fiction.* Durham, N.C.: Duke University Press, 1995.

Mead, Margaret. *Sex and Temperament in Three Primitive Societies.* New York: Morrow, 1935.

Meijer, M. J. *Marriage Law and Policy in the Chinese People's Republic.* Hong Kong: Hong Kong University Press, 1971.

———. "Homosexual Offenses in Ch'ing Law." *T'oung Pao* 71 (1985): 109–133.

———. *Murder and Adultery in Late Imperial China: A Study of Law and Morality.* Sinica Leidensia 25. Leiden: E. J. Brill, 1991.

Miao Wen-yüan 繆文遠. *Chan-kuo chih-tu t'ung-k'ao* 戰國制度通考. Ch'eng-tu: Pa-Shu, 1998.

Michaud, Paul. "The Yellow Turbans." *Monumenta Serica* 17 (1958): 47–127.

Moriya Mitsuo 守屋美都雄. *Chūgoku kodai no kazoku to kokka* 中國古代の家族と國家. Kyoto: Tōyōshi Kenkyūkai, 1968.

Morohashi Tetsuji 諸橋轍次. *Dai Kan-Wa jiten* 大漢和辭典. Rev. ed. 13 vols. Tokyo: Daishūkan, 1986.

Münke, Wolfgang. *Die klassische chinesische Mythologie.* Stuttgart: Ernst Klett, 1976.

Munro, Donald J., ed. *Individualism and Holism: Studies in Confucian and Taoist Values.* Michigan Monographs in Chinese Studies 52. Ann Arbor, 1985.

Murray, Dian. "The Practice of Homosexuality among the Pirates of Late Eighteenth and Early Nineteenth Century China." *International Journal of Maritime History* 4.1 (1992): 121–130.

Murray, Jacqueline, and Konrad Eisenbichler, eds. *Desire and Discipline: Sex and Sexuality in the Premodern West.* Toronto: University of Toronto Press, 1996.

Nakajima Chiaki 中島千秋. *Fu no seiritsu to tenkai* 賦の成立と展開. Matsuyama: Kan'yoshi, 1963.

Nakamura Keiji 中村圭爾. "'Kyōri' no ronri: Rikuchō kizoku shakai no ideorogii" 郷里の論理：六朝貴族社會のイデオロギー. *Tōyōshi kenkyū* 東洋史研究 41.1 (1982): 1–27.

———. "Rikuchōshi to 'chiiki shakai'" 六朝史と地域社會. In *Chūgoku chūshishi kenkyū kai*, 36–60.

Needham, Joseph. *Science and Civilisation in China.* 7 vols. projected. Cambridge: Cambridge University Press, 1956–.

Ng, Vivien. "Ideology and Sexuality: Rape Laws in Qing China." *Journal of Asian Studies* 46.1 (1987): 57–70.

———. "Homosexuality and the State in Late Imperial China." In Duberman et al., 76–89.

Nikkilä, Pertti. *Early Confucianism and Inherited Thought in the Light of Some Key Terms of the Confucian Analects.* Studia Orientalia 53 (1982) and 68 (1992).

Ning Chia 寧稼. *Wei Chin feng-tu—Chung-ku wen-jen sheng-huo hsing-wei te wen-hua i-yün* 魏晉風度—中古文人生活行為的文化意蘊. Ko-lun-pu hsüeh-shu wen-k'u. Peking: Tung-fang, 1996.

Nivison, David S. *The Ways of Confucianism: Investigations in Chinese Philosophy.* Ed. Bryan W. Van Norden. Chicago: Open Court, 1996.

Nylan, Michael. "Confucian Piety and Individualism in Han China." *Journal of the American Oriental Society* 116.1 (1996): 1–27.

———. "Golden Spindles and Axes: Elite Women in the Achaemenid and Han Empires." In Chenyang Li, 199–222.

Ōfuchi Ninji 大淵忍爾. *Shoki no Dōkyō* 初期の道教. Tōyōgaku sōsho 38. Tokyo: Sōbunsha, 1991.

O'Hara, Albert Richard. *The Position of Woman in Early China.* Catholic University of America Studies in Sociology 16. Washington, D.C., 1945.

Ou-yang Hsiu 歐陽修 (1007–1070). *Hsin Wu-tai shih* 新五代史. 3 vols. Peking: Chung-hua, 1974.

Overmyer, Daniel L. "Women in Chinese Religions: Submission, Struggle, Transcendence." In Shinohara and Schopen, 91–120.

Padel, R. "Women: Model for Possession by Greek Daemons." In Cameron and Kuhrt, 3–19.

Padgug, Robert. "Sexual Matters: On Conceptualizing Sexuality in History." In Baker et al., 432–448.

Pao Chia-lin 鮑家麟, ed. *Chung-kuo fu-nü shih lun-chi hsü-chi* 中國婦女史論集續集. Taipei: Tao-hsiang, 1991.

———. "Yin-yang hsüeh-shuo yü fu-nü ti-wei" 陰陽學説與婦女地位. In Pao Chia-lin, *Chung-kuo fu-nü shih lun-chi hsü-chi,* 37–54.

Paper, Jordan D. *The Fu-tzu: A Post-Han Confucian Text.* Monographies du T'oung Pao 13. Leiden: E. J. Brill, 1987.

Parker, Edward Harper. *Ancient China Simplified.* London: Chapman and Hall, 1908.

P'eng Ta-i 彭大翼 (fl. 1573–1595). *Shan-t'ang ssu-k'ao* 山堂肆考. *Ying-yin Wen-yüan ko Ssu-k'u ch'üan-shu* 影印文淵閣四庫全書.

Peradotto, John, and J. P. Sullivan, eds. *Women in the Ancient World: The Arethusa Papers.* SUNY Series in Classical Studies. Albany, N.Y., 1984.

Peterson, Willard J., et al., eds. *The Power of Culture: Studies in Chinese Cultural History.* Hong Kong: Chinese University Press, 1994.

Pines, Yuri. "Intellectual Change in the Chunqiu Period: The Reliability of the Speeches in the *Zuo Zhuan* as Sources of Chunqiu Intellectual History." *Early China* 22 (1997): 77–132.

Pomeroy, Sarah B., ed. *Women's History and Ancient History.* Chapel Hill: University of North Carolina Press, 1991.

Poo, Mu-chou. "The Completion of an Ideal World: The Human Ghost in Early-Medieval China." *Asia Major,* 3d ser., 10.1–2 (1997): 69–94.

———. *In Search of Personal Welfare: A View of Ancient Chinese Religion.* SUNY Series in Chinese Philosophy and Culture. Albany, N.Y., 1998.

Porter, Roy, and Mikuláš Teich, eds. *Sexual Knowledge, Sexual Science: The History of Attitudes to Sexuality.* Cambridge: Cambridge University Press, 1994.

Puett, Michael, ed. *Studies on the* Shiji: *A Volume of Essays on Sima Qian.* Forthcoming.

Pulleyblank, Edwin G. *Outline of Classical Chinese Grammar.* Vancouver: UBC Press, 1995.

Queen, Sarah A. *From Chronicle to Canon: The Hermeneutics of the* Spring and Autumn, *According to Tung Chung-shu.* Cambridge Studies in Chinese History, Literature, and Institutions. Cambridge, 1996.

Raphals, Lisa. *Sharing the Light: Representations of Women and Virtue in Early China.* SUNY Series in Chinese Philosophy and Culture. Albany, N.Y., 1998.

———. "Gendered Virtue Reconsidered: Notes from the Warring States and Han." In Chenyang Li, 223–247.

Richards, I. A. *Mencius on the Mind: Experiments in Multiple Definition.* London: Routledge and Kegan Paul, 1932.

Rickett, Adele Austin, ed. *Chinese Approaches to Literature from Confucius to Liang Ch'i-ch'ao.* Princeton, N.J.: Princeton University Press, 1978.

Ride, Lindsay. "Biographical Note." In Legge, vol. 1, 1–25.

Riegel, Jeffrey K. "Poetry and the Legend of Confucius's Exile." *Sinological Studies Dedicated to Edward H. Schafer.* Ed. Paul W. Kroll. *Journal of the American Oriental Society* 106.1 (1986): 13–22.

———. "*Li chi.*" In Loewe, *Early Chinese Texts,* 293–297.

———. "Eros, Introversion, and the Beginnings of *Shijing* Commentary." *Harvard Journal of Asiatic Studies* 57.1 (1997): 143–177.

Robinet, Isabelle. *Taoism: Growth of a Religion.* Trans. Phyllis Brooks. Stanford, Calif.: Stanford University Press, 1997.

Rosemont, Henry, Jr. *A Chinese Mirror: Moral Reflections on Political Economy and Society.* La Salle, Ill.: Open Court, 1991.

———. "Classical Confucian and Contemporary Feminist Perspectives on the Self: Some Parallels and Their Implications." In Allen, 63–82.

———, ed. *Explorations in Early Chinese Cosmology: Papers Presented at the Workshop on Classical Chinese Thought Held at Harvard University, August 1976. Journal of the American Academy of Religion Thematic Studies* 50.2. Chico, Calif.: Scholars Press, 1984.

Rosemont, Henry, Jr., and Benjamin I. Schwartz, eds. *Studies in Classical Chinese Thought. Journal of the American Academy of Religion* 47.3, Thematic Issue S (1979).

Roy, David T., and Tsuen-hsuin Tsien, eds. *Ancient China: Studies in Early Civilization.* Hong Kong: Chinese University Press, 1978.

Ruan, Fang-fu, and Yung-mei Tsai. "Male Homosexuality in the Traditional Chinese Literature." *Journal of Homosexuality* 14.3–4 (1987): 21–33.

Rubin, V. A. "Tzu-ch'an and the City-State of Ancient China." *T'oung Pao* 52 (1965): 8–34.

Said, Edward W. *Orientalism.* New York: Random House, Vintage Books, 1978.

Sailey, Jay. *The Master Who Embraces Simplicity: A Study of the Philosopher Ko Hung, A.D. 283–343.* Asian Library Series 9. San Francisco: Chinese Materials Center, 1978.

Sargent, Clyde Bailey. *Wang Mang: A Translation of the Official Account of His Rise to Power as Given in the* History of the Former Han Dynasty. Shanghai, 1947.

Saussy, Haun. *The Problem of a Chinese Aesthetic.* Meridian: Crossing Aesthetics. Stanford, Calif.: Stanford University Press, 1993.

———. "Repetition, Rhyme, and Exchange in the *Book of Odes.*" *Harvard Journal of Asiatic Studies* 57.2 (1997): 519–542.

Schaberg, David. "Remonstrance in Eastern Zhou Historiography." *Early China* 22 (1997): 133–179.

Schafer, Edward H. *Pacing the Void: T'ang Approaches to the Stars.* Berkeley and Los Angeles: University of California Press, 1977.

———. *The Divine Woman: Dragon Ladies and Rain Maidens in T'ang Literature.* San Francisco: North Point, 1980.

Schipper, Kristofer. "Science, magie, et mystique du corps: Notes sur le taoïsme et la sexualité." In Beurdeley, 11–42.

———. *The Taoist Body.* Trans. Karen C. Duval. Berkeley and Los Angeles: University of California Press, 1993.

Schmidt-Glintzer, Helwig. "Der Buddhismus im frühen Mittelalter und der Wandel der Lebensführung bei der Gentry im Süden." *Saeculum* 23 (1972): 269–294.

———, ed. *Das andere China: Festschrift für Wolfgang Bauer zum 65. Geburtstag.* Wolfenbütteler Forschungen 62. Wiesbaden: Harrassowitz, 1995.

Schneider, Laurence A. *A Madman of Ch'u: The Chinese Myth of Loyalty and Dissent.* Berkeley and Los Angeles: University of California Press, 1980.

Seidel, Anna. "Taoist Messianism." *Numen* 31.2 (1984): 161–174.

Serruys, Paul L-M. "Towards a Grammar of the Language of the Shang Bone Inscriptions." *Proceedings of the International Sinological Conference.* Taipei: Academia Sinica, 1982.

Shaughnessy, Edward L. *Sources of Western Zhou History: Inscribed Bronze Vessels.* Berkeley and Los Angeles: University of California Press, 1991.

———. *Before Confucius: Studies in the Creation of the Chinese Classics.* SUNY Series in Chinese Philosophy and Culture. Albany, N.Y., 1997.

———. "Western Zhou History." In Loewe and Shaughnessy, 292–351.

———, trans. *I Ching: The Classic of Changes.* Classics of Ancient China. New York: Ballantine, 1996.

———, ed. *New Sources of Early Chinese History: An Introduction to the Reading of Inscriptions and Manuscripts.* Early China Special Monograph Series 3. Berkeley, Calif., 1997.

Shaw, Miranda. *Passionate Enlightenment: Women in Tantric Buddhism.* Mythos. Princeton, N.J.: Princeton University Press, 1994.

Shen Chia-pen 沈家本. *Shen Chi-i hsien-sheng i-shu* 沈寄簃先生遺書. 2 vols. N.d.; repr., Taipei: Wen-hai, 1964.

Sheng I 盛義. *Chung-kuo hun-su wen-hua* 中國婚俗文化. Yü nei-wai min-su hsüeh ts'ung-k'an. Shanghai: Wen-i, 1994.

Shinohara, Koichi, and Gregory Schopen, eds. *From Benares to Beijing: Essays on Buddhism and Chinese Religion in Honour of Prof. Jan Yün-hua.* Oakville, Ont.: Mosaic, 1991.

Shirakawa Shizuka 白川静. *Shikyō* 詩經. Tokyo: Chūō Kōronsha, 1970.

Shun, Kwong-loi. *Mencius and Early Chinese Thought.* Stanford, Calif.: Stanford University Press, 1997.

Sivin, Nathan. "On the Word 'Taoist' as a Source of Perplexity: With Special Reference to the Relations of Science and Religion in Traditional China." *History of Religion* 17 (1978): 303–330.

Slote, Walter H., and George A. De Vos, eds. *Confucianism and the Family.* SUNY Series in Chinese Philosophy and Culture. Albany, 1998.

Smith, Kidder, Jr. "*Zhouyi* Divination from Accounts in the *Zuozhuan.*" *Harvard Journal of Asiatic Studies* 49.2 (1989): 421–463.

Sommer, Matthew H. *Sex, Law, and Society in Late Imperial China.* Law, Society, and Culture in China. Stanford, Calif.: Stanford University Press, 2000.

Spade, Beatrice. "The Education of Women in China during the Southern Dynasties." *Journal of Asian History* 13.1 (1979): 15–41.

Spence, Jonathan D. *The Memory Palace of Matteo Ricci.* New York: Penguin, Elisabeth Sifton Books, 1984.

van der Sprenkel, O. B. *Pan Piao, Pan Ku, and the Han History.* Centre for Oriental Studies Occasional Paper 3. Canberra: Australian National University, 1964.

Stanton, Domna C., ed. *Discourses of Sexuality: From Aristotle to AIDS.* Ratio: Institute for the Humanities. Ann Arbor: University of Michigan Press, 1992.

Steele, John, trans. *The I-li, or Book of Etiquette and Ceremonial.* 2 vols. Probsthain's Oriental Series 8–9. London, 1917.

Stein, Rolf A. "Remarques sur les mouvements du taoïsme politico-religieux au IIe siècle ap. J.-C." *T'oung Pao* 50.1–3 (1963): 1–78.

———. "Religious Taoism and Popular Religion from the Second to Seventh Centuries." In Welch and Seidel, 53–81.

Strickmann, Michel. "On the Alchemy of T'ao Hung-ching." In Welch and Seidel, 123–192.

Sukhu, Gopal. "Monkeys, Shamans, Emperors, and Poets: The *Chuci* and Images of Chu during the Han Dynasty." In Cook and Major, 145–165.

Sun Shu-ch'i 孫述圻. *Liu-ch'ao ssu-hsiang shih* 六朝思想史. Liu-ch'ao ts'ung-shu. Nan-ching: Nan-ching ch'u-pan-she, 1992.

Sun Xiaochun, and Jacob Kistemaker. *The Chinese Sky during the Han: Constellating Stars and Society.* Sinica Leidensia 38. Leiden: E. J. Brill, 1997.

Sung, Marina H. "The Chinese Lieh-nü Tradition." In Guisso and Johannesen, 63–74.

Swann, Nancy Lee. *Pan Chao: Foremost Woman Scholar of China.* New York: Century, 1932.

Tai Yen-hui. "Divorce in Traditional Chinese Law." In Buxbaum, 75–106.

Tamba Yasuyori 丹波康頼 (fl. A.D. 982–984). *Ishimpō* 醫心方. Peking: Jen-min wei-sheng, 1955.

Tanigawa Michio. *Medieval Chinese Society and the Local "Community".* Trans. Joshua A. Fogel. Berkeley and Los Angeles: University of California Press, 1985.

Tannahill, Reay. *Sex in History.* Rev. ed. N.p.: Scarborough House, 1992.

Tao Tien-yi. "Vassal Kings and Marquises of the Former Han Dynasty." *Bulletin of the Institute of History and Philology* 46.1 (1974): 155–172.

Taylor, Timothy. *The Prehistory of Sex: Four Million Years of Human Sexual Culture.* New York: Bantam, 1996.

Terrien de Lacouperie. *Western Origin of the Early Chinese Civilisation from 2,300*

B.C. to 200 A.D.; or, Chapters on the Elements Derived from the Old Civilisations of West Asia in the Formation of the Ancient Chinese Culture. London: Asher, 1894.

Thatcher, Melvin P. "Marriages of the Ruling Elite in the Spring and Autumn Period." In Watson and Ebrey, 25–57.

Thornton, Bruce S. Eros: The Myth of Ancient Greek Sexuality. Boulder, Colo.: Westview, 1997.

T'ien Ch'ang-wu 田昌五 and Tsang Chih-fei 臧知非. Chou Ch'in she-hui chieh-kou yen-chiu 周秦社會結構研究. Chou Ch'in Han T'ang yen-chiu shu-hsi. Hsi-an: Hsi-pei Ta-hsüeh, 1996.

Ting Tu 丁度 (990–1053) et al. Sung-k'o Chi-yün 宋刻集韻. 1037; repr., Peking: Chung-hua, 1989.

Tjan Tjoe Som. Po Hu T'ung: The Comprehensive Discussions in the White Tiger Hall. 2 vols. Sinica Leidensia 6. Leiden: E. J. Brill, 1949.

Tsai, Shih-shan Henry. The Eunuchs in the Ming Dynasty. SUNY Series in Chinese Local Studies. Albany, N.Y., 1996.

Tseng Ch'in-liang 曾勤良. Tso-chuan yin-Shih fu-Shih chih Shih-chiao yen-chiu 左傳引詩賦詩之詩教研究. Wen-shih-che ta-hsi 61. Taipei: Wen-chin, 1993.

Ts'ui Ming-te 崔明德. Li Ling 李陵. Li-shih cheng-i jen-wu hsi-lieh 2. Taipei: Wen-chin, 1994.

Tu Wei-ming. "Probing the 'Three Bonds' and 'Five Relationships' in Confucian Humanism." In Slote and De Vos, 121–136.

Tu Yung-ming 杜永明, et al. Hei Erh-shih-ssu shih 黑二十四史. 6 vols. Peking: Chung-kuo hua-ch'iao, 1998.

Tung Chia-tsun 董家遵. "Ts'ung Han tao Sung kua-fu tsai-chia hsi-su k'ao" 從漢到宋寡婦再嫁習俗考. Chung-shan Ta-hsüeh Wen-shih hsüeh Yen-chiu-so yüeh-k'an 中山大學文史學研究所月刊 3.1 (1934): 193–213.

T'ung Shu-yeh 童書業. Ch'un-ch'iu Tso-chuan yen-chiu 春秋左傳研究. Shanghai: Jen-min, 1980.

Twitchett, Denis, and Michael Loewe, eds. The Cambridge History of China. Vol. 1, The Ch'in and Han Empires, 221 B.C.–A.D. 220. Cambridge, 1986.

Uchiyama Toshihiko 內山俊彥. Chūgoku kotai shisōshi ni okeru shizen ninshiki 中國古代思想史における自然認識. Tōyōgaku sōsho 31. Tokyo: Sōbunsha, 1987.

Van Zoeren, Steven. Poetry and Personality: Reading, Exegesis, and Hermeneutics in Traditional China. Stanford, Calif.: Stanford University Press, 1991.

Vandermeersch, Léon. La formation du légisme: Recherche sur la constitution d'une philosophie politique caractéristique de la Chine ancienne. Publications de l'Ecole Française d'Extrême-Orient 56. Paris, 1965.

Vervoorn, Aat. Men of the Cliffs and Caves: The Development of the Chinese Eremitic Tradition to the End of the Han Dynasty. Hong Kong: Chinese University Press, 1990.

Wagner, Donald B. "The Language of the Ancient State of Wu." In Arendrup et al., 161–176.

Wagner, Rudolf G. "Lebensstil und Drogen im chinesischen Mittelalter." T'oung Pao 59 (1973): 79–178.

Wakatsuki Toshihide 若槻俊秀. "Chūgoku ni okeru injakan no hensen: Sanrin no inja kara shichō no inja e" 中國における隱者觀の變遷：山林の隱者から市朝の隱者へ. Bungei ronsō 文藝論叢 8 (1964): 13–20; and 9 (1964): 65–73.

Waley, Arthur. *Chiu Ko—The Nine Songs: A Study of Shamanism in Ancient China*. London: Allen and Unwin, 1955.

———, trans. *The Analects of Confucius*. New York: Random House, Vintage Books, 1938.

———, trans. *Chinese Poems*. Paperback ed. London: George Allen and Unwin, 1961.

———, trans. *The Book of Songs: The Ancient Chinese Classic of Poetry*. Ed. Joseph R. Allen. New York: Grove, 1996.

Wallacker, Benjamin E. "Liu An, Second King of Huai-nan (180?–122 B.C.)." *Journal of the American Oriental Society* 92 (1972): 36–51.

———. "*The Spring and Autumn Annals* as a Source of Law in Han China." *Journal of Chinese Studies* 2.1 (1985): 59–72.

Walsh, Roger. *The Spirit of Shamanism*. Los Angeles: Tarcher, 1990.

Wang, C. H. *The Bell and the Drum: Shih Ching as Formulaic Poetry in an Oral Tradition*. Berkeley and Los Angeles: University of California Press, 1974.

———. *From Ritual to Allegory: Seven Essays in Early Chinese Poetry*. Hong Kong: Chinese University Press, 1988.

Wang Chung-lo 王仲犖. *Wei Chin Nan-pei-ch'ao shih* 魏晉南北朝史. 2 vols. Shanghai: Jen-min, 1979–1980.

Wang Kuo-wei 王國維 (1877–1927). *Wang Kuan-t'ang hsien-sheng ch'üan-chi* 王觀堂先生全集. Taipei: Wen-hua, 1968.

Wang Lei-sheng 王雷生. "P'ing-wang tung-ch'ien yüan-yin hsin-lun—Chou P'ing-wang tung-ch'ien shou-pi yü Ch'in, Chin, Cheng chu-hou shuo" 平王東遷原因新論—周平王東遷受逼於秦、晉、鄭諸侯説. *Jen-wen tsa-chih* 人文雜誌 1998.1: 86–90.

Wang Mao 王楙 (1151–1213). *Yeh-k'o ts'ung-shu* 野客叢書. Ed. Wang Wen-chin 王文錦. Hsüeh-shu pi-chi ts'ung-k'an. Peking: Chung-hua, 1987.

Wang Shu-nu 王書奴. *Chung-kuo ch'ang-chi shih* 中國娼妓史. Chiu-chi hsin-k'an. Shanghai: Sheng-huo, 1934; repr., Ch'ang-sha: Yüeh-lu, 1998. [This book is bound together with that of Ch'en Ku-yüan.]

Waters, Geoffrey R. *Three Elegies of Ch'u: An Introduction to the Traditional Interpretation of the Ch'u Tz'u*. Madison: University of Wisconsin Press, 1985.

Watson, Burton. *Ssu-ma Ch'ien: Grand Historian of China*. New York: Columbia University Press, 1958.

———. *Early Chinese Literature*. New York: Columbia University Press, 1962.

———, trans. *Basic Writings of Mo Tzu, Hsün Tzu, and Han Fei Tzu*. Records of Civilization: Sources and Studies 74. New York: Columbia University Press, 1963.

———, trans. *The Columbia Book of Chinese Poetry: From Early Times to the Thirteenth Century*. New York: Columbia University Press, 1984.

———, trans. *The Tso chuan: Selections from China's Oldest Narrative History*. Translations from the Oriental Classics. New York: Columbia University Press, 1989.

———, trans. *Records of the Grand Historian: Han Dynasty*. Rev. ed. 2 vols. Records of Civilization: Sources and Studies 65. Hong Kong: Columbia University Press, 1993.

———, trans. *Records of the Grand Historian: Qin Dynasty*. Hong Kong: Columbia University Press, 1993.

Watson, Rubie S., and Patricia Buckley Ebrey, eds. *Marriage and Inequality in Chinese Society*. Studies on China 12. Berkeley and Los Angeles: University of California Press, 1991.

Wawrytko, Sandra A. "Prudery and Prurience: Historical Roots of the Confucian Conundrum concerning Women, Sexuality, and Power." In Chenyang Li, 163–197.

Weggel, Oskar. *Chinesische Rechtsgeschichte*. Handbuch der Orientalistik 4.6. Leiden: E. J. Brill, 1980.

Wei Chiung-jo 魏炯若. *Tu-Feng chih-hsin chi* 讀風知新記. Hsi-an: Shensi jen-min, 1987.

Welch, Holmes, and Anna Seidel, eds. *Facets of Taoism: Essays in Chinese Religion*. New Haven, Conn.: Yale University Press, 1979.

Wen I-to 文一多 (1899–1946). *Wen I-to ch'üan-chi* 全集. Peking: San-lien, 1982.

van de Wetering, Janwillem. *Robert van Gulik: Ein Leben mit Richter Di*. Trans. Klaus Schomburg. Zurich: Diogenes, 1990.

Whitman, Christina B. "Privacy in Early Confucian and Taoist Thought." In Munro, 85–100.

Wilbur, C. Martin. *Slavery in China during the Former Han Dynasty*. Anthropological Series, Field Museum of Natural History 34. Chicago, 1943.

Wile, Douglas. *Art of the Bedchamber: The Chinese Sexual Yoga Classics, Including Women's Solo Meditation Texts*. Albany: State University of New York Press, 1992.

Wilhelm, Hellmut. "Notes on Chou Fiction." In Buxbaum and Mote, 215–269.

Wilhelm, Richard, trans. *Li Gi: Das Buch der Riten, Sitten, und Bräuche*. 2d ed. Diederichs Gelbe Reihe 31. Munich, 1994.

Wolf, Margery, and Roxane Witke, eds. *Women in Chinese Society*. Studies in Chinese Society. Stanford, Calif.: Stanford University Press, 1975.

Wu Chou 武舟. *Chung-kuo chi-nü sheng-huo shih* 中國妓女生活史. Ch'ang-sha: Hunan wen-i, 1990.

Yang K'uan 楊寬. *Shang Yang pien-fa* 商鞅變法. Shanghai: Jen-min, 1955.

———. *Chan-kuo shih* 戰國史. 3d ed. Shanghai: Jen-min, 1998.

Yang Shu-ta 楊樹達. *Han-tai hun-sang li-su k'ao* 漢代婚喪禮俗考. Shanghai: Shang-wu, 1933.

Yang Ts'ai-hua 楊采華. *Ch'ü Yüan chi-ch'i tz'u-fu hsin-chieh* 屈原及其辭賦新解. Wu-han: Wu-han Ta-hsüeh, 1994.

Yates, Robin D. S., trans. *Five Lost Classics: Tao, Huang-Lao, and Yin-Yang in Han China*. Classics of Ancient China. New York: Ballantine, 1997.

Yeh Shan 葉珊 (=C. H. Wang). "*Shih-ching* 'Kuo-feng' te ts'ao-mu ho shih te piao-hsien chi-ch'iao" 詩經國風的草木和詩的表現技巧. In *Chung-kuo ku-tien wen-hsüeh yen-chiu ts'ung-k'an: Shih-ko chih pu* 中國古典文學研究叢刊：詩歌之部, vol. 1, 11–45. Ed. K'o Ch'ing-ming 柯慶明 and Lin Ming-te 林明德, Taipei: Chü-liu, 1977.

Yen K'o-chün 嚴可均 (1762–1843). *Ch'üan Shang-ku San-tai Ch'in Han San-kuo Liu-ch'ao wen* 全上古三代秦漢三國六朝文. 4 vols. 1893; repr., Peking: Chung-hua, 1958.

Yoffee, Norman, and George L. Cowgill, eds. *The Collapse of Ancient States and Civilizations*. Tucson: University of Arizona Press, 1988.

Yu Kuo-en. *Tu-Sao lun-wei ch'u-chi* 讀騷論微初集. Jen-jen wen-k'u 441–442. Taipei: Shang-wu, 1967.

Yu, Pauline. *The Reading of Imagery in the Chinese Poetic Tradition.* Princeton, N.J.: Princeton University Press, 1987.

Yü Tsung-fa 余宗發. *Hsien-Ch'in chu-tzu hsüeh-shuo tsai Ch'in-ti chih fa-chan* 先秦諸子學說在秦地之發展. Wen-shih-che ta-hsi 133. Taipei: Wen-chin, 1998.

Yü, Ying-shih. "Individualism and the Neo-Taoist Movement in Wei-Chin China." In Munro, 121–155.

Zau Sinmay. "Confucius on Poetry." *T'ien Hsia Monthly* 7.2 (1938): 137–150.

Zhang Longxi. "The Letter or the Spirit: The *Song of Songs*, Allegoresis, and the *Book of Poetry*." *Comparative Literature* 39.3 (1987): 193–217.

Zürcher, E. *The Buddhist Conquest of China.* 2 vols. Sinica Leidensia 11. Leiden: E. J. Brill, 1972.

Index

About the Author

PAUL RAKITA GOLDIN, who received his Ph.D. from Harvard University, teaches Chinese history and philosophy at the University of Pennsylvania. He is the author of *Rituals of the Way: The Philosophy of Xunzi* (1999) and numerous articles in scholarly journals. He is currently working on "A Reader of Traditional Chinese Culture," coedited with Victor H. Mair and Nancy S. Steinhardt, a volume of primary sources for the study of ancient Chinese culture.